Three Famous Impostors?

Three Famous Impostors?

An Inquiry About Judaism, Christianity and Islam

Adam Freeman

Copyright © 2016 by Adam Freeman.

Library of Congress Control Number:		2016903741
ISBN:	Hardcover	978-1-5144-7220-0
	Softcover	978-1-5144-7219-4
	eBook	978-1-5144-7218-7

All rights reserved. No part of this book may be reproduced or transmitted in any form or by any means, electronic or mechanical, including photocopying, recording, or by any information storage and retrieval system, without permission in writing from the copyright owner.

Any people depicted in stock imagery provided by Thinkstock are models, and such images are being used for illustrative purposes only. Certain stock imagery © Thinkstock.

Print information available on the last page.

Rev. date: 03/08/2016

To order additional copies of this book, contact:
Xlibris
1-888-795-4274
www.Xlibris.com
Orders@Xlibris.com
731750

Contents

Preface vii

1. Who wrote the Torah, Moses or a king? 1
2. Who is the source of the New Testament, Jesus or Paul? 24
3. Who wrote the Quran, the angel Gabriel or Muhammad's followers? 41
4. Who wrote the other sacred books of the Jewish Bible? 54
5. Is Oral tradition the answer to all the contradictions? 59
6. The three religions and their outside influences 74
7. God's chosen people? Cause of anti-Semitism 93
8. The sacrifices are over, thank God, the temple is destroyed ... 108
9. The creation in six days: a late addition 138
10. Life after death? Paradise or hell? Resurrection of Jesus? 149
11. The prophets and the prophecies 176
12. *Kashrut*, dietary laws, and the three religions 193
13. Circumcision and the three religions 206
14. Instead of liberty, religions impose death penalty on apostasy ... 219
15. Instead of equality, religions accept slavery and privileges 222
16. Instead of universal fraternity, the tribes 228
17. Instead of knowledge, religions demand submission 233
18. Instead of responsibility, destiny and Original Sin 243
19. The Ten Commandments. Which ones? For whom? 250

20 First Commandment: one God, totalitarian and immoral! 261

21 Second Commandment against idolatry, King Solomon, the Trinity, Kaaba 277

22 Third Commandment against blasphemy, Quran and the falsified Bible 295

23 Fourth Commandment: Shabbat, Jesus respected it, did not rise on Sunday 303

24 Fifth Commandment: honor your parents 312

25 Sixth Commandment: you shall not kill, Jesus not a pacific, jihad 315

26 Seventh Commandment: adultery, King David, Quran, and adultery 333

27 Eighth Commandment: you shall not steal from your brother, and the other? 349

28 Ninth Commandment: you shall not lie, Machiavellian lies, and Islam 353

29 Tenth Commandment: you shall not lust, Jerusalem, woman, Mohammed's wives 359

Your conclusions 379

Selected Bibliography 381

About the author 383

Preface

In a little library in the south of France, fifteen years ago, I read for the first time a tiny book entitled *Treatise of the Three Imposters*. These three imposters were Moses, Jesus, and Mohammed. No one knows much about this little book. Its author, the date and place where it was written remain a mystery. Already three centuries ago, the author feared. Religions were not accepting any criticism or doubt. Yet it was this little book that ignited a fire to study the texts of the three monotheistic religions. Thanks to the sacred freedom of faith, religious people have the right to preach that their religion is the truth. Newspapers, radio, and television have religious programs but very few dare to claim their skepticism, because tolerance is not a virtue of religions. And what about the freedom to doubt? Christianity have already accepted critics of their sacred texts. Only Islam is actively fighting against those who dare to question the Quran.

Religions should have been the source of love, brotherhood, solidarity, universality, and equality. They are, instead, the cause of division, hate, and genocides along the centuries. Religions divided humanity and pushed to crazy behaviors such as celibacy of preachers, whippings, terrorist explosions, or burning of nonbelievers. Religious wars are not belonging to the past but remain still a threat in our twenty-first century. Of course, religions are not the only source of war and hate. Nationalism, greed, colonialism, and dictatorship have also led to massacres.

Did the sacred texts come from God?

This book examines the religious texts to prove that they are manmade, not sent from God; not historical, but made up to serve a selfish purpose. The religious laws compete with the civil code, which one is better? The "moral values" of the three religions and the Ten Commandments will be compared to laic values.

The goals of this book are huge: it is to eradicate religious hate, genocides, pogroms, inquisitions by simply teaching skepticism. Because those who doubt will not be fanatics, hateful, or murderous toward others. Doubt erases extremism. This book doesn't attack God or rather the Creator. Its goal is to address the three monotheist religions. To attack religions does not mean denying the existence of God, the divinity, or the Creator, because God and religions are two completely different entities.

An important part of the book is dedicated to the Jewish Bible because the two other religions could not exist without it. Every criticism of the Jewish Bible is in fact a criticism of all three.

Some basics:

The Jewish Bible is composed of the five books of Moses or Torah, followed by the books of the prophets and the writings. The God of the Bible has a special name: YHWH or Jehovah, too easily translated to *God* or *Lord*.

For believers, the five books of Moses were dictated by God to Moses during the Exodus from Egypt. These five books are: Genesis, Exodus, Leviticus, Numbers, and Deuteronomy. The Jewish Bible has nearly 800 pages.

The Talmud is a heavy book of more than 6,000 pages and contains discussions between rabbis between 200 CE to 500 CE.

The Christian New Testament begins with four Gospels describing the life, death, and resurrection of Jesus, continues with the Acts of Apostles, and finishes with letters sent by the apostles to communities converted to the new religion. Matthew, Mark, Luke, and John are called the authors of the four Gospels. The three first ones, very similar, are called *the synoptic Gospels*. The Acts describe the life of the apostles after the death of Jesus.

The New Testament has nearly 250 pages. The Catechism contains a recapitulation of the Christian religion. Christians believe that Jesus was born on Christmas of the year 0 and died around + 35.

For Muslims, the Quran was transmitted by the angel Gabriel to the Prophet Muhammad in Mecca, a pagan city of Arabia. He was born in 570, received Revelation in 610, and died in 632.

The Quran has nearly 250 pages and 114 *suras* of different lengths.

The Hadiths are the sayings of Muhammad reported by his companions.

The first Temple of Jerusalem was built around 832 BC by King Solomon and destroyed around 586 BC by the Babylonians, then rebuilt by Ezra around 516 BC and destroyed by the Romans around +70. Jesus was buried in Jerusalem and resurrected there. After the death of Muhammad, the Muslims conquered Jerusalem and built the Mosque El-Aqsa.

1

Who wrote the Torah, Moses or a king?

For believers of the three religions, Moses wrote the Torah (the first five books of the Bible) and Deuteronomy (31.24) confirmed: *When Moses had finished writing the words of this law in a book* . . . Jews and Christians believe that the books of Moses were dictated to him by God during the forty years in the desert and were transmitted from generation to generation, without any change or error, not even one letter changed. The Quran mentions Moses dozens of times, calls him as a great prophet, and in (17.2) recognizes: *We (God) have given the Book to Moses to guide the sons of Israel.* So if the Torah is not divine, the New Testament and the Quran are wrong and would not be divine.

In this chapter, we will describe the doubts about the slavery and the Exodus of the Hebrews from Egypt. We will enumerate contradictions and errors found in the Torah and then give an explication: the author of the Torah is not Moses, but who?

Doubts about the slavery of the Hebrews in Egypt:

Jews consider the Passover as a *day of deliverance from slavery, the transition from slavery to freedom.* Several clues cast doubt on this period of slavery.

1. Why did God send the Hebrews to slavery? The Bible described Abraham arriving to the land promised by God, then because of a

famine, he left to go to Egypt and later returned to the Promised Land with flocks and cattle. But without any reason, God said to Abraham in Genesis (15.13) that *your offspring shall be alien in a land not their own . . . and they will be oppressed 400 years . . . And the fourth generation shall return . . .* What is the sin of Abraham? And why will his children and grandchildren be punished?

2. The Hebrew people developed too well in slavery. How did only seventy Hebrews and Jacob who went down to Egypt become, after only four generations, a nation of three million despite harsh slavery? Such a prolific form of slavery is unbelievable!

3. In Exodus (12.37), the number of Hebrews who left Egypt are over *600,000 foot soldiers*, and Numbers (1) lists the tribes totaling exactly 603,550 males over twenty years, not counting the tribe of the Levis, who totaled 22,000 males older than one month. This leads to a total population of about 3 million Hebrews who left Egypt. Yet according to Deuteronomy (7.7), "it is not because you are more numerous than other peoples, for you were the fewest of all." God has chosen this small nation just to prove His power. But a nation of 3 million people was not a small nation. According to archaeologists, at the time of Moses, the population of the powerful Egypt was less than 3 million. So maybe these verses were written in a different era during which the Jewish people were crushed, exiled, and diminished?

4. How did only two midwives, mentioned in Exodus (1.15), Shifra and Puah, manage to help tens of thousands of women give birth? After each birth, the Bible requests a sacrifice of doves. How did the women of the Exodus giving birth to hundreds of thousands of little babies find doves in the desert for sacrifice after every birth?

5. Regrets about the good life in Egypt: In Exodus (16.3), the Hebrews who had suffered the yoke of hard slavery regretted *"pots of meat and bread were satiating us . . ."* And in Numbers (11.5), these ex-slaves regretted the meat and fish *"they ate in Egypt for nothing, the cucumbers and melons, leeks, onions and garlic."* For slaves, their situation was not so bad! Some excavations in Egypt have shown that the builders of the pyramids were not slaves but workers who were well treated.

6. Gold, jewelry, and weapons brought out of Egypt: It is weird that the Hebrew people enslaved could leave Egypt with herds, jewels, and enough gold to build the golden calf and pay the fee of census, and had weapons to conquer the Promised Land. Where did these former slaves get the weapons to defeat powerful armies? Exodus (35) describes the Hebrews in the desert with *"loops, rings, necklaces, gold ornaments fabrics . . . azure, purple, scarlet, and fine linen . . ."* and Numbers (3, 49) count *"1365 silver shekels"* given to Aaron. For runaway slaves, this wealth is strange or maybe these details were added later for other reasons. Exodus (11.2) explains that the gold was given by the Egyptians. Hard to believe.

    In Exodus (9.6), as God's punishment, *"all the cattle of Egypt died,"* but later Exodus (12.12) says: *"I will pass through the land of Egypt, that same night, I will smite all the firstborn, both man and beast."* Has the writer forgotten that the livestock had already perished? If during forty years in the wilderness the Hebrews ate the manna, miraculously sent by God, what did their cattle eat?

7. In Exodus (12), the first day of the first month, so fourteen days before the D-Day of the Exodus, God warns Moses and asks him to prepare a lamb and *"on the tenth day of this month, they shall take a lamb for each father's house . . . Hold it in reserve until the fourteenth day of this month, then the whole community of Israel shall kill it in the evening."* Further, He explains that they should eat *"in a hurry . . . for seven days you shall eat unleavened bread . . ."* So the Hebrews knew in advance that they had to prepare and roast a lamb, what could be easier than preparing leavened bread for the D-Day?

8. How is it possible that Moses and the Hebrew people, who got free through divine intervention and escaped from Egypt, continued to practice slavery? Not only did they enslave foreign nations but also Hebrew people too. In fact, and strangely, in the middle of the desert, after running away from Egypt, Exodus (21), Lev (25.44), and other verses describe the status of the slaves: *"If you buy a Hebrew slave . . . If a man sells his daughter as a slave . . ."* But nowhere in the Jewish Bible is it mentioned that the patriarchs and prophets abolished or condemned slavery under Hebrew owners. This deficiency creates doubt on the historicity of the slavery of the Hebrew people under Pharaoh.

No archaeological evidence:

Egypt has documented every detail of its history but is totally silent about Moses. There is nothing about the ten plagues and the exodus of nearly 3 million slaves. The answer of some believers is that Pharaoh, humiliated, erased any episode about Moses from Egyptian writings. However, some believers use the discovery of a stele in El Arish in 1890 (preserved in the Museum of Ismailia in Egypt) to confirm the biblical narratives. This stele describes events that appear to be linked with the famous plagues of Egypt, the Exodus of the Hebrews, the big storm, the expulsion of the Hyksos, Pharaoh being snapped to the sky . . . But these arguments are not at all convincing and are not similar to the story of the Exodus. In addition, it is possible that the Bible writers have based their stories on ancient Egyptian legends to fabricate the story of the Exodus. The ten plagues are described in Exodus and then nothing, no other mention in the Bible about those miracles and the divine punishment, except in Psalms 78 and 105. However, Psalm 78 forgot to mention the three plagues (mosquitoes, ulcers, and darkness), and Psalm 105 forgot the two plagues (ulcers and the death of the cattle). These 3 million people wandering in the desert for forty years have left no archaeological remains. None! Is the discovery of chariot wheels at the bottom of the Red Sea proof of the sinking army of Pharaoh who were pursuing Moses and the Hebrew people? Not at all! Chariots have certainly tried to cross the Nile and its surroundings, and it is quite normal to find chariot wheels in the Red Sea. Why did we not find thousands of armor from soldiers buried in that sea?

The contradictions and errors in the Torah:

The Quran (4.82) states. *"If the Quran was not of God, they would find in it many inconsistencies."* This is valid for the three religions. Contradictions and mistakes will prove that they were written by humans and sometimes by liars. The three holy books are supposedly divinely inspired and therefore cannot include human errors or contradictions. This chapter describes a list of errors and contradictions voluntarily reduced. Other errors can be found on many websites.

1. In Genesis (2.17), God said to Adam that if he eats of the forbidden fruit, he would die the same day. Yet in Genesis (5.5), Adam eats the fruit and lives for 930 years. The rabbis have a bizarre explanation and say that man should have lived forever, but to God, one day is 1,000 years, so Adam died before becoming 1,000 years old. God has prohibited Adam from eating the fruit of the tree of knowledge, but the second tree, the tree of life, was not banned and therefore Adam could eat and become immortal. He did not eat from this tree.
2. In Genesis (6.3), God has decided to limit the life expectancy of men to 120 years, but many lived more than 120 years according to Genesis (11.11). To avoid any contradiction, the rabbis twist the meaning and explain that it was not referring to the age of men, but God gave 120 years to men to repent from their sins.
3. In Genesis (4.15), Cain killed Abel and God said to him: *"Whoever kills Cain shall be punished sevenfold."* And God marked him with a sign so that whoever met him would not kill him. Although this is a poor translation and the Hebrew text does not use the term *person*, this would be impossible because there was nobody living in the world at this time except Adam and Eve, and therefore nobody could have killed Cain. The rabbis have a ridiculous answer and say that the sign was to protect Cain from wild animals! How would wild animals recognize the sign stopping them from attacking Cain? Some Christian racists interpret it as the curse of the black skin and therefore slavery would be permitted by God.

    What was Cain's punishment? *"You will be a restless wanderer on the earth."* Yet a few lines later, in Genesis (4.17), Cain *"knew his wife, she conceived and bore Enoch. He built a city and named the city after his son Enoch."* What's more sedentary? For who would build this city when there weren't many humans? Cain's wife must be one of his sisters, so this is an incestuous relationship
4. Through the Flood, God destroyed the world because men were evil, and saved only Noah and his family. This destruction of mankind was unnecessary because after Noah humanity continued to be evil. Was the all-omniscient God wrong in His predictions? In Genesis (6.19) and (7.8), Noah went into the ark with a pair of pure breed animals, but in Genesis (7.2), he went with seven pairs.

5. For Genesis (11.25), Terah begat Abram when he was seventy, then he died at the age of 205 years, when Abraham was 205 - 70 = 135 years old. But a few lines later, (12.4), it is said that Abram was 75 years old when he left Haran after the death of his father. All these dates are not realistic.
6. Lot was the owner of a large herd. Why did he penetrate a village and what happened to his herd? Then in Genesis (19.8), the people of Sodom gathered around Lot because they wanted to *know* his envoys. Lot stopped them and said, *"I have two daughters who have not known man yet. I'll get them."* But a little further, a verse says: *"Lot went to talk to his sons-in-law, husbands of his daughters."* The existence of these in-laws contradicts the previous assertion of the virginity of his two daughters, unless Lot has other girls who are married. But we see later in the text that Lot only has two daughters. *"Arise; take your wife and two daughters . . . As well as his wife and two daughters . . ."* So either there is an error in the text or Lot lied. See chapter on adultery.
7. In Genesis (32.30), *"Jacob called the place Peniel: for he said, I have seen God face to face, and my life has been saved."* Exodus (33.11) confirms *"YHWH spoke to Moses face to face, as a man speaks to his friend."* But a few lines later, Exodus (33.20) says the contrary about seeing God: *"YHWH said, you cannot see my face, for man shall not see me and live."* But Deuteronomy (5.4) says that *"it is face to face that YHWH spoke to you on the mountain . . ."* Numbers (12.8) says: *"I talk to him face to face (or mouth to mouth), in clear sight, it is the image of God he contemplates."* The rabbis explain this contradiction by stating that Moses does not see the intrinsic reality of God. Not convincing!
8. In Genesis (1.31), God saw what He had done was good, but in Genesis (6.6), God regrets having created man.
9. In Genesis (26.33), Isaac names this place Beer Sheva. Does he not know that this place already had a name given by Abraham, his father? Genesis (21.31): *"He therefore called this place Beer Sheva because there, they swore to one another."*
10. In Genesis (32.28), God said to Jacob, *"Your name shall no longer be Jacob, but Israel."* Later, in (35.10), God repeats it and says, *"But now your name will no longer be Jacob, and gives him the name Israel."* Despite this repetition, he is called Jacob dozens of times

in the Bible stories, and God himself in Genesis (46.2) makes the mistake: *"God spoke to Israel in a vision at night, saying, Jacob! Jacob!"* For Abraham and Sarah, no similar error, and immediately after the name was changed they were always called by their new names.

11. In Genesis (33.14), Jacob promises to join his brother Esau in Seir; however, two verses later it says: *"Jacob went to Succoth."*
12. Genesis (36. 31) says, *"These are the kings that reigned in the land of Edom, before any king reigned over the children of Israel."* Did Moses know that the Hebrews would have a king several centuries later? Either Moses sees the future, or this text is written after the reign of kings.
13. In Genesis (37.10), Joseph had a dream and his father. Jacob was angry: *"I and your mother and your brothers, to bow down to the ground at your feet!"* Jacob and Joseph seem to forget that the mother, Rachel, was already dead and buried.
14. In Genesis (37.28), the Midianites sold Joseph to the Ishmaelite, yet further down, (37.36) says that the Midianites sold Joseph to Potiphar in Egypt.
15. In Genesis (48.8), Jacob considers two of Joseph's sons as his own, but strangely, a few lines later, he was surprised and asks: *"Who are they?"*
16. The stepfather of Moses was called Ruel in Exodus (2.18) but in (3.1) he is called Jethro!
17. In Exodus (6.3), God said to Moses, *"I appeared to Abraham, Isaac and Jacob as El Shaddai (supreme God) but with my name YHWH, I did not make myself known of them."* Yet when we look at a preceding text, Genesis (15.7), God told Abraham, *"I am YHWH who brought you out of Ur-Kasdim..."*
18. In Exodus (6.20), his father *"Amram chose his aunt Yocheved as his wife. She bore him two sons: Aaron and Moses."* But Leviticus (20.19) prohibits the bond between a man and his aunt: *"You shall not uncover the nakedness of thy mother's sister, nor of thy father's sister..."* Unless the ban came later, and at the time of the birth of Moses it was allowed. Also, why forget Miriam, Moses's elder sister?
19. In Exodus (9.5), God destroys all the cattle of the Egyptians. Yet, further, in (9.21), the servants of Pharaoh put their cattle in their houses, while others leave it in the fields. In Exodus (7.20), Moses and Aaron changed all the water into blood, so how did

Pharaoh's magicians do the same when there was no more water? Why are there two similar stories about the waters of Meriva, the one in Exodus (17.7), then the same revolt is mentioned in Numbers (20.13)?

20. Numbers (1) lists the tribes and totals them to 603,550 males over twenty years. Then in (3.45), there are 22,273 firstborn males older than one month among the eleven tribes. If there are only 22,273 firstborn males of more than a month to 603,550 males over twenty years, the Hebrews would have more than thirty children per family. Although this calculation is approximate, this number of 22,273 firstborn is incompatible with 603,550 males over twenty years.

21. In Numbers (12.1), *"Miriam and Aaron spoke evil about Moses because of the Ethiopian woman he had married..."* But Tsipora, the wife of Moses, was the daughter of Jethro, the priest of Midian. God becomes so angry because of their badmouthing that "Miriam found herself covered with leprosy, she became as white as snow." Miriam was sequestered out of the camp for seven days. So Miriam is punished but not Aaron. Why? If Aaron had been punished and covered with leprosy, he could not have served God, because in Leviticus (22), *"Everyone from the race of Aaron, with leprosy... shall not eat of the holy things."* Why this privilege and exemption from punishment, even temporarily, for Aaron?

22. In Numbers (25.1), *"the people indulged in debauchery with the daughters of Moab,"* or further in (25.6), it says that it is a Midianite girl who is put to death for having seduced a Hebrew! In Deuteronomy (2.19), God commands: *"the children of Ammon, do not attack them... I do not allow you any conquest on the land of the children of Ammon, because it is to the descendants of Lot I have given it for an inheritance."* Yet in Joshua (13.24), *"the children of Gad owned half the land of the Ammonites..."* Also, in Judges (11.32), Jephthah fought the Ammonites and God delivered them into his hands. And also in II Samuel (12.26), *"Joab attacked the capital of the Ammonites and captured Rabbah."* How did Joshua and Joab reject the divine order? Later, Jeremiah (49.2) predicts that *"Amon... will be reduced to a lamentable state of ruin..."* All this is confusing, unless the ban of Ammon was inserted much later after the time of Jeremiah.

23. Exodus (20.4) says that the sins of the fathers will be upon the children in the third and fourth generations. But Deuteronomy (24.16) says the contrary: *"sons shall not be put to death because of fathers."* And the prophet Ezekiel (18.20): *"a son shall not bear the iniquity of his father."*
24. Deuteronomy (17.16) prohibits the king from having many horses, yet King Solomon, God's beloved, violates this rule in 1 Kings (5.6): *"Solomon had 40,000 stalls for his chariots and 12,000 horsemen . . ."* While in II Chronicles (9.25), *"Solomon had 4,000 stalls for horses and chariots and 12,000 horsemen . . ."* I Kings (10.26) mentions other numbers: *". . . Solomon had 1,400 chariots and 12,000 horsemen."* The Talmud, Sanhedrin 21b, tries to explain it through illogical pirouettes.

The Anachronisms and chronological errors:

Abraham *followed the trail of enemies to Dan* in Genesis (14.14), but Dan is the region occupied centuries later by the tribe of the same name. How could Abraham have bought the cave to bury his wife Sarah and pay 1,000 silver coins when currency did not exist at that time? The phrase *to this day* is common in the Torah. Is it because it was written by later authors? Deuteronomy (34.10) says: *"he has not appeared in Israel a prophet like Moses, whom the Lord had communicated with face to face."* Whoever had written this not so modest little text must be someone who lived long after Moses. In addition, some experts have noted that the style of the text describing the death of Moses is identical to the preceding text and would therefore have the same author.

In Deuteronomy (4.41), Moses *"chooses three cities on the other side of the Jordan to the east; so that they might serve as a refuge to the murderer . . . They were Bezer, Ramot . . . And Golan . . ."* How could Moses choose these cities before they were populated with Hebrews? Genesis (36.31) gives a list of kings and states *"before any king reigned over the children of Israel."* The first king of Israel was Saul, who lived several generations after Moses! The answer given by believers is naive. They answer that Moses, being a prophet, knew the future.

In Exodus (16.34), Moses ordered *"as YHWH had commanded Moses, Aaron placed a full omer of manna before the ark of status."* But this ark will be built much later, in Exodus (25). Another misplaced addition!

In Exodus (17.14) and (24.4 and 7), *"YHWH said to Moses: set this as a memorial in the book... Moses wrote all the words of YHWH and all articles... Then he took the book of the Covenant, which was read to the people."* Which means that Moses wrote a book. Which book is it? Why has it never been mentioned? In what language was this book ever written? Not in Hebrew but in the Egyptian language, because Moses was an Egyptian prince! If this book did exist, there would be no need for oral tradition. But if this book was lost, why has it never been mentioned?

After this unique reference to the book, God gives further orders to Moses, but he never again writes them in his book. Why? According to Deuteronomy (2.12), *"In Seir, the Horites dwelled previously, but the children of Esau... settled in their place, as Israel did to the land of his inheritance, that YHWH gave him."* But Israel dwelled in the Promised Land long after the death of Moses. The believer's answer is that Moses is a prophet and knows the future. Should we doubt this answer?

Twelve tribes?

Jacob had twelve sons who became the heads of the twelve tribes of Israel. Yet, in Deuteronomy (33), Moses blessed the tribes but he forgot the tribe of Simeon. One explanation for this omission is that the tribe of Simeon already disappeared when the texts were written or reworked much later after Moses. The tribes of Simeon and Levi were cursed by Jacob. Moses and Aaron, being members of the Levi, it is hard to understand how this tribe cursed by Jacob becomes the holy tribe of the priests. Judges (1) recounts the conquest of Canaan by some tribes and omits others. In Judges (5), the prophetess Deborah mentions the names of some unknown tribes: Machir, Gilead, and Meroz.

Ten tribes, although blessed by God, have disappeared. How? The kingdom of Israel, including the ten tribes, was defeated. Jews were deported and replaced by imported pagans. This legend of the disappearance of the ten tribes of Israel should be rejected, because in reality only a small portion of the population of the kingdom of Israel was exiled as further details prove: According to Jeremiah, the Israelites form the north came to present offerings to the temple in Jerusalem after the exile. Assyrian records mention that only 27,280 prisoners were deported from Samaria, while other texts state the figure of 40,000, so only a minority of the population. The vast majority of Samaritan Jews remained in Samaria but they were pushed back by the Judeans returning from Babylonian exile. Instead of embracing their brothers, they rejected them because the Israelites who remained in the country refused to accept the monopoly of Jerusalem, the foreign rules imported from exile, and their new and emerging oral tradition.

Etymology of the name Moses:

"*... Pharaoh's daughter ... was the one who named him Moses (or Moshe in Hebrew) because, she said, 'I saved him from water.'*" How would Pharaoh's daughter know Hebrew grammar? Why would she give a Hebrew name to her adopted son whose origins must be hidden? Some claim that *ms* means *begotten*, as in Ramses, *Ra begat,* or Thothmosis, *born of Thoth*. If that is the case, why did God continue to call Moses by the Egyptian name Pharaoh's daughter gave him? The first four books mention Moses in the third person, while the fifth book, Deuteronomy, is written in the first person, so by Moses himself. In addition, the last chapter of Deuteronomy could not have been written by Moses because he could not have described his own death and burial. But if, as the rabbis agree, the last verses were written by Joshua, should we have doubts about the other verses as well?

The philosophers Voltaire and Spinoza: first skeptics against Moses!

From the beginning of the seventeenth century, Spinoza claimed that the Bible was written later, after the return of the Jews from Babylonian exile in the fifth century BCE by Ezra the scribe. Some even claimed that Moses is a character who never existed, copied on the Sumerian legends of King Sargon, who was rescued from the water and saved by a gardener. Sigmund Freud, in his work *Moses and Monotheism,* says that the inventor of monotheism is not Moses but the Pharaoh Ekhnaton who destroyed the statues of idols and established the worship of the sun as exclusive deity. Moses would be an Egyptian prince converted to monotheistic worship by the Pharaoh Ekhnaton ...

Voltaire, the famous philosopher of the eighteenth century, wrote several comments in his *Dictionary*, unfortunately almost unknown. Why the censorship? Because Voltaire attacks religions! Here are some excerpts:

> "... It is not likely that no Egyptian or Greek writer would have written these miracles to posterity... Indeed, it would not have been possible, if the Bible was known to all Jews, that the wise Solomon, inspired by God Himself and building a temple by his order, would adorn the temple of so many figures, against the express law of Moses...
>
> "All Jewish prophets who prophesied in the name of the Lord, from Moses until King Josiah, did not support in their preaching the laws of Moses. Would they not quote his own words a thousand times... No one recalled the text of Moses... The books attributed to Moses were written during the Babylonian captivity, or immediately after, by Ezra... The first known book was found at the time of King Josiah, and this unique specimen was brought to the king by the secretary Shaphan... This book found under Josiah was unknown until the return from Babylonian captivity; and it is said that Ezra was inspired by God, and he brought to light all the scriptures... If Moses said that God punishes the iniquity of the fathers to the fourth generation, would Ezekiel have dared to say otherwise? Is it true that Moses existed? If a man who commanded the whole land had existed among the Egyptians, such prodigious events, would they not be the main part of the history of Egypt? Sanchoniathon, Manetho, Megasthenes, and Herodotus, would they not have spoken? Josephus the historian... None of the authors has said a single word of the miracles of Moses. What! The Nile has been turned into blood, an angel will slay all the firstborn in Egypt, the sea is open, its waters have been suspended on the right and left, and no author has spoken about it! Nations have forgotten these wonders, but there will be a small people of barbaric slaves who have told us these stories hundreds of years after the event!"

The doubts about the slavery and the Exodus, the contradictions and errors, the lack of archeological and historical proof about Moses and the Exodus, all these can be explained by some verses of the Book of Kings, quite unknown to the believers. How is it that if Moses wrote the first five books of the Bible there are no references to these books for 800 years, not in the book of the Judges and not in the books of the Kings till the strange *discovery* made by King Josias and his accomplices?

An incredible discovery, a pious fraud, and initial evidence?

King Josiah of Judah reigned several generations after David and Solomon, between 640 and 609 BCE. In II Chronicles (34.14), this pious king cleans the country by destroying the idols and repairing the temple. Suddenly, in the eighteenth year of his reign, around 621, *"Hilkiayou the priest found the book of the law of YHWH given to Moses . . . brought the book to the king . . . when the king heard the words of law, he tore his clothes . . . the wrath of YHWH was poured out upon us, because our fathers have not kept the word of YHWH, to do according to all that is written in this book. Then the king sent and gathered all the elders of Judah and Jerusalem . . . to keep the YHWH's commandments."* And in II Kings 22 and 23, "The king gave all the people the following order: Celebrate Passover in honor of YHWH, as prescribed in the Book of the Covenant." In fact, the Passover had not yet been celebrated as such in the days of the judges or during the period of Israel's kings and Judah's kings. It was not until this year, the eighteenth of Josiah's reign, that the Passover was celebrated in honor of YHWH in Jerusalem.

This strange episode is too often ignored by believers, while some facts confirm the possibility of a sudden and mounted coup. The questions are numerous:

1. What was this book that was found?
Believers say it's the fifth book, Deuteronomy, written by Moses under divine inspiration. But because of contradictions (developed later), other believers gave another answer: they explain that the term *sefer Torah* simply means a book where the words of the Torah are written. Then why this emotion? Other rabbis explain that it was customary to open a book of Torah at random and read the first verse to find a prediction or a sign.

Unfortunately, the first verse that appeared was a curse, and this is why the king reacted as he did. But the rabbis' explanation is not convincing. Why is it written that this book was found? Can we rely on a page opened by chance to guide important decisions made by the king? This game of opening the book at random is reported nowhere else and never existed. And later, the prophetess Huldah received a visit from envoys of King Josiah (II Kings 22, 13 . . .) and predicted: *"YHWH says: I will bring evil upon this country and its people, all the things predicted in the book read by the king of Judah . . . He (King Josiah) will join his ancestors in peace in the tomb . . ."* But if this book is Deuteronomy, there is no mention of King Josiah's death. In addition, everything that the prophetess said is wrong because "things predicted in the book" are not misfortunes but the conquest of the Promised Land and the repetition of the law. In addition, King Josiah does not die of old age as promised by the prophetess, but by the spear of a soldier of Pharaoh Nekho. Almost unanimously, specialists consider this book of Deuteronomy, lost and found, not written by Moses, but by the priests, much later, to fight idolatry and to establish Jerusalem as the sole place for sacrifices. We do not accept this claim and believe that these specialists had not the courage to say that Josiah and his scribes wrote much more than this book from the traditions, memories, myths, and interests. For several reasons:

A. First of all, this book should be stone tablets. Where are the stones of the law engraved by the finger of God that would have been stored in the ark? According to Exodus (40.20) and later in Deuteronomy (31.26), Moses *"commanded the Levites . . . take this book of the Law and place it beside the ark of YHWH."* There should also be a book in addition to the tablets. Where are they now?
B. This roll was found *"while they were gathering the money given to the temple."* It is unlikely that unclean money would be kept in the temple next to the Torah.
C. Suppose it is Deuteronomy that was found. It would mean that for many generations Jews read the Torah without knowing how Moses died, where he was buried, and that he gave the power to Joshua.
D. In the desert, after fleeing from Egypt and still without a country, oddly, Deuteronomy (17.18) orders the kings *"for his use to write in a book, a copy of this doctrine in presence of the descendant's pontiffs*

of Levis. It will remain in his possession because he has to read it all his life..." So each king would have in his possession two books: one that serves as original and one that he writes himself. The Bible never mentions that this order was not followed and no king has been punished for its offense. If the kings had copied the book, it would not have been lost as reported in an episode of Josiah. The Talmud, Sanhedrin (21b) specifies that the king must write two copies of the book of the law, one that travels with him and another that remains in the temple. Where have all these books gone? The Talmud also states that Moses commanded the twelve tribes to each write a copy of the Torah. Where are all those copies? Ramban lists the 613 commandments and said that one of them is that every Jew should write a copy of the Bible. Where are all these copies and why have they all disappeared before King Josiah's time? Moreover, in Deuteronomy (31, 10), *"at the end of every seventh year at the festival of tents, you shall read this doctrine in the presence of all Israel..."* It is therefore impossible that the book is lost.

E. The Torah was strangely forgotten during a long period of eight centuries, from the Book of Judges till the middle of the Book of Kings. Nowhere is it written that the Book of the Torah was lost. But even if it was lost, kings had to write a book of the Torah themselves. Where are the copies, the one written by Moses and also the ones written by the kings? After this long period of nearly eight centuries, the Book of the Torah is discovered when cleaning the temple.

F. After the discovery of the book, *"the King instructed Hilkiayou the chief Priest... to remove from the Temple of YHWH all the tools that have been made for the Baal, the Asherah and for all the hosts of the heavens. He had them burned outside Jerusalem..."* It means that through centuries the Hebrews were worshipping other gods inside the temple. Where is the monotheism?

G. The decision to divide the books in five was a late decision, not contemporary of Moses's time. The Torah was not a small book but a scroll of about 70 cm that could not be lost in the small temple, which was only 30 meters by 10. In II Kings (22) and II Chronicles (34), *"Hilkiayou the high priest said... I have found the book of the Torah that YHWH passed to Moses."* The Torah includes five books and not only Deuteronomy. In Hebrew, the first words of each book are used to name each book of the Torah. For example, *Bereshit* (the beginning) is the Hebrew name of Genesis. *Ele Dvarim* is the Hebrew name of Deuteronomy. So if Hilkiayou had found only the book of Deuteronomy, he would have said, *"I found one of the books of the Torah or the Book Ele Dvarim,"* and not simply *"I have found the book of the Torah..."*

H. There is nothing original about Passover in Deuteronomy that is not mentioned in the other preceding books. The Passover rules are found in different books of the Torah and not only in Deuteronomy (the name means *repetition*).

The Book of Exodus (12.43) (13) (20) describes all the orders, sacrifices, and commandments necessary for the Passover. Exodus also describes the episode of the golden calf (32), the destruction of idolatrous altars (34). Leviticus describes the offerings and sacrifices, dietary laws, especially the Passover (33), the Feast of Tabernacles (33), Yom Kippur, the destruction of idolatrous enemies. Numbers (9) also describes the Passover. All this shows that there is nothing new in Deuteronomy and thus its discovery cannot lead to the compliance with the rules mentioned above.

I. Finally, according to II Chronicles (34.30), *"the king gave them all the words of the book of the covenant..."* The book of the covenant is the Torah, not only Deuteronomy. So the logic would be that the lost and found book would be the Torah, meaning all the five books of Moses.

2. And what about the tradition?

The rabbis say that oral tradition was transmitted from Moses to present day without interruption. In II Kings (23) and in II Chronicles (34), the written law was lost and then found and Josiah was surprised that the law announced in this book was not observed. But if the oral law had always existed without interruption, it should therefore be a reminder for the king to celebrate the Passover. There must have been a break in the popular oral tradition, which did not pass from generation to generation because *"such a Passover had not been celebrated in Israel since the prophet Samuel, and no king of Israel had done anything comparable to the Passover of Josiah..."* However, some kings before Hezekiah, according to II Chronicles (29), cleaned and purified the tiny temple (it was 30 meters by

10 meters in total) and nothing was found there, and in (30.21), celebrated Passover with great fanfare.

What other commandments were not observed? How can we be sure that this book found is the same as the original? Was it changed by the priests? Is it possible that Josiah, in connection with the high priest, invented this discovery in order to destroy all the idols? Some wise rabbis, including the Radak, recognized that *"during the 55 years of the King Menashe, the Torah was forgotten."* Is it possible that King Josiah (or Yoshi-yahoo in Hebrew) made up the character of Joshua (or Yesha-yahoo in Hebrew)? Because the bloody conquests of Joshua are contrary to the peaceful installation of the Hebrews in the Promised Land.

3. Why King Josiah and why at that time?

Because it is at the time of Josiah that writing and scribes, once virtually nonexistent, became popular and that the kingdom of Judea saw his population increase with the fleeing of Israelis from the north (occupied by the Babylonians). These Babylonians, once invulnerable, had a moment of weakness against Egypt, and gave to Josiah the hope he could expand his kingdom by expelling the idolaters. That's why the descriptions of genocide and the conquest of the Promised Land by Joshua came up, to create Hebrew nationalism, past and future. Descriptions of heroes like Moses, Joshua, David, and Samson galvanized national unity. Unfortunately, the strategy of Josiah was wrong because the Babylonian empire was still strong, and Josiah got killed by the Egyptians. It is a sad fate for this pious king who should have been cherished by God. How is it that the Torah ignored the names of three pharaohs who reigned at the arrival of Abraham in Egypt, at the arrival of Joseph, and at the time of the ten plagues, but knew the name of Pharaoh Nekho, who killed King Josias in II Kings (23)? Is it because it was written later?

4. Is the priest Hilkijaou a malignant who took advantage of the youth of the new king who reigned at the age of eight? Although it is stated that the discovery of the book occurs only eighteen years later, is it possible that the priest *"discovered"* a Bible more favorable to the priests? The high priest Hilkijaou took advantage of the youth of the new king to impose new laws: Jerusalem as unique center for sacrifices. The cast of the priests got huge profits, advantages, and higher status with the imposition of Jerusalem as a unique place for sacrifices.

5. The prophet Jeremiah is *"the son of Hilkijaou, one of the priests of Anathoth in the land of Benjamin, to whom the word of YHWH came in the days of Josiah the son of Amon king of Judah in the thirteenth year of his reign . . ."* The same Jeremiah (is he the son of the high priest Hilkijaou, who discovered the lost book of the law?) does not say a word in all his prophecies about this fundamental discovery. Yet it was exactly at the same time that he prophesied in Jerusalem. God spoke to Jeremiah dozens of times but never mentioned to the prophet the place where the book was. Jeremiah should have mentioned the story of the lost book now being found, but neither God nor Jeremiah and the other prophets did so. It is not understandable.

Another clue is found in the entire chapter of I Kings (13.2). It appears to have been added later and describes the arrival of a *"man of God who came from Judah to Bethel, according to the order of YHWH . . . And cried . . . Altar! Altar! So said YHWH, a son will be born to the family of David, Josiah is his name . . ."* So a few centuries before the fact, a prophet forecast the arrival of King Josiah. Is this anonymous prophet historical and real or did a writer just add this *"prophecy"* much later? This invented prophecy is more evidence that the Book of Kings was written at the time of Josiah by supporters of Josiah.

Jeremiah, author of the two books of Kings, is also the one who related this strange prophecy about the future arrival of Josiah. Is this a wonderful prophecy by an unknown prophet or was it Jeremiah who lived in the time of King Josiah who described a current situation? Gedalia, the grandson of Shaphan the scribe, was appointed governor of Judah by Nebuchadnezzar the Conqueror. Hilkijaou, Shaphan, Jeremiah, King Josiah, and Gedalia—are they innocent or are they all part of the conspiracy in the discovery of the book once lost but now *found*? Jeremiah (8.8) says: *"How can you say we are wise and we have the law of YHWH? Yes, but the lying pen of the scribes has made it a lie."* Was Jeremiah ashamed of the coup done by his father (the high priest who was an accomplice of the young King Josiah) and did not want to take part in it? But why, if he had such high morals, did he not denounce this? Unless he himself played a role in this discovery and even wrote some of the texts. Indeed, some sentences of Deuteronomy are similar to those of Jeremiah. For example: *"circumcision of the heart"* or *"Egypt, the iron furnace . . ."* Another prophet, Zephaniah, who prophesied at the same time under the reign of King Josiah, does not say a word about *"the discovery of the book."* Is it because of shame?

In conclusion, King Josiah and his helpers wrote and rewrote parts of the Jewish Bible in order to achieve two principal reforms: concentrate the worship of God only in the Temple of Jerusalem and eliminate idols and idolatry.

A second strange discovery after the return from exile

Nebuchadnezzar, king of Babylon, and his soldiers, *"burnt the house of God, broke down the walls of Jerusalem, put fire in all his palace . . . Nebuchadnezzar carried away captives into Babylon, those who had escaped from the sword, and they became subject to him . . . 70 years."* Later, in Ezra (1), *"YHWH stirred up the spirit of Cyrus . . . Thus says Cyrus, YHWH the God of heaven . . . ordered me to build him a house in Jerusalem . . ."*

Cyrus therefore sent to Jerusalem captive Jews to build the house of YHWH and speak with him, giving them all the spoils of the temple, such as the silver basins. Later, Ezra, the scribe chosen by Artaxerxes, a descendant of Cyrus, returns to Jerusalem with a royal pass and large amounts of silver and gold. Why did the Persian king choose Ezra? Was he the political and religious envoy of the Persian king? The Persian king should have known that *Jewish law* preaches nationalist opposition to foreign culture. Could it be that during the years of exile the laws were amended?

In Nehemiah (8.1 onward), *"all the people together . . . they found written in the Torah that YHWH had commanded by the hand of Moses, that the Israelites were to remain in huts during the festival since . . . the days of Joshua, son of Nun, until that day the children of Israel had not done so . . ."* This would mean that the Israelites did not celebrate the Feast of Tabernacles for a long time. But translators often take care to add, without any reason, *"with this solemnity,"* to say that there was no break but the tradition continued during the exile. Where is the truth?

Had King Josiah not celebrated Passover and the Feast of Tabernacles according to what is described in the Book of Kings? Did the Judeans observe the Feast of Tabernacles from the time of Joshua? Did they practice the law while in exile? Chapter 13 of Nehemiah seems to say they did not, and that the reading of the Torah was a discovery for the assembled people. Where did this book come from? Was it the same as that of King Josiah? Was it the same book read today? In the Talmud, Sanhedrin 21b, the Torah was originally given to Moses using Hebrew letters and Hebrew language. Later, in the time of Ezra, the Torah was written in the Ashuri (Babylonian) alphabet and in Aramaic language. Ultimately, the Hebrews kept the Ashuri alphabet and Hebrew language. So the Torah that we have today is a double translation from the original language. Has this double translation changed or falsified the writings?

Therefore, it would not be at the time of Moses but during the reign of King Josiah and the time of Ezra and Nehemiah that much of the Torah was probably written. Shortly before the capture of Jerusalem by Nebuchadnezzar and the deportation to Babylon around 620 BC, during the reign of King Josiah, a first draft of the Torah was written. Finally, during the exile and after the return to Jerusalem around 540 BC, the texts were completed. Memories of myths and oral traditions, as well as legends from exiles, were written down. Certainly, negotiations and compromises were necessary for the Torah to be accepted by the various editors, which explains all the contradictions and errors of the Torah.

The documentary hypothesis: four sources E, J, P, and D

During the nineteenth century, the many contradictions found in the Torah, the different styles, the double-sided stories, have led some experts to develop the *"documentary hypothesis."* The book *Who wrote the Bible?* is required reading for atheists and believers. The author Richard E. Friedman affirms, like his predecessors, that the five books of the Torah were not transmitted by Moses around 1400 or 1300 BC as the three religions claim but much later. This book is a must. This thesis not only belongs to Richard Friedman but is also known as the Graf-Wellhausen theory.

The Jewish Bible, as we know, would be the result of many compromises between different forces (today called political parties) and was written at different periods, with modifications, additions, and omissions. Based on the various names given to God, YHWH, or Elohim, and based on the language and interests, they distinguish several authors.

Around 900 BCE, the first author J used the name *Jehovah* or *YHWH* to refer to God. This author J was from the kingdom of Judah and lived during the reign of Solomon. He would have written chapters 2 and 3 of Genesis, plus other chapters based on oral legends.

A century later, a second author, named E, used the name *Elohim* for God. He would be a native of Israel and the northern tribes. His hero would be Moses, and would probably have been a Levite priest, descendant of Moses and not of Aaron.

A third author, J/E, after the destruction of the first temple, collected the texts, keeping the first two versions even when they did not appear identical or compatible.

The fifth book of the Torah, Deuteronomy, was written in 621 BC, at the time of King Josiah in Jerusalem, by a group of authors named D, as in *Deuteronomy*.

A fifth author, designated by the letter P, as in *priests*, representing the ritual sacrifices and interests of the priests at the time, wrote the first chapter of Genesis and other chapters during or after the Babylonian exile.

Finally, an editor named R, as in *redactor*, who lived during 400 BC or so (1,000 years after Moses), put together all the texts to form the Bible as we know it.

This theory, with variations among experts, is fundamental. And if confirmed, the Bible, basis of three religions, would therefore be a great fraud. Instead of being the voice of God, if the documentary theory is true, the Torah would have been written a thousand years after the death of Moses and would be a compromise of different religious views.

How else could you explain the following twists other than by conflict of interests and visions of the different times? The stepfather of Moses would be called Jethro during the Elohim period, but was called Ruel during the Jehovah period. Also, Moses received the tablets of the law on Mount Horev during the Elohim period but received it on Mount Sinai during the Jehovah period. Why does Joseph, while dying, give the first blessing to his grandson Ephraim even though Menashe is the elder brother? Because after the death of Solomon and the separation, the king of the north is Jeroboam, from the tribe of Ephraim.

Why does Exodus (20.23) forbid the *"gods of silver, gods of gold"* while Exodus (34.17) states: *"gods of molten metal"*? The first one comes from the Elohim source, while the detail of molten metal comes from the source Jehovah of Judah, who condemned King Jeroboam, who melted down two golden calves.

The accuracy of the source Jehovah allows the condemnation of Jeroboam, king of the north, but proves the innocence of Judah in the south, where the temple in Jerusalem was home to two gold-plated cherubs.

The episode of debauchery with the daughters of Moab, described in Numbers (1.5), is inconsistent and followed by the killing of a Midianite woman. Why? Because the beginning is from the Jehovah source and the end from the Priesthood source. How can we explain the resemblance between Moses who separated the sea in order to allow the dry passage of the Hebrews who were fleeing, and Joshua (in 3.16) who made it possible for the tribes to cross the Jordan River to the Promised Land?

The etiology, a writing system of sacred texts!

The etiology is the opposite of a prophecy and explains the present by inventing the past. Some experts, including James Kugel, author of the book *How to Read the Bible*, explain that the Bible was written in reverse, which is to say from the present to the past. Have you ever tried to explain to your children simple facts like why humans speak different languages? You will find it difficult, and in fact the biblical explanation is simple, even though it is false. According to the Bible, it is because they were punished for having built the Tower of Babel! Why does the snake crawl? The Bible says it's because he pushed Eve to sin! Why the rainbow? Because that is the sign of the covenant with God!

The best way to understand the anomalies of the stories is to ask two questions: what is the purpose of this Bible story? How does this situation fit in at the time it was written? To explain the state of desolation of Sodom and Gomorra, they used the story of Lot and the punishment of God, who brought fire to this region of the Dead Sea.

They also had to explain the name of the city of Beersheba twice. In Genesis (21.31), it was Abraham who named the place and said that it was because "they swore one to another." But in (26.33), it was Isaac who comes up with the name Beersheba because a well was found there. The verses of Genesis (23.2) and (35.27) specify: *"Kiryat Arba which is Hebron."* Indeed, Kiryat Arba took a new name, Hebron, but it means that it was written after receiving the new name.

What is the origin of the name of Israel? The name means *God' fight*. And so it was necessary to invent a struggle between Jacob and the angel of God. How does the Bible explain the name of Joseph? The Bible says that Leah finally had a child after so many years of sterility, and in Genesis

(30.23), says: *"God erased my shame."* She called him Joseph, saying, *"God will give me another son."* Another = *Yasaf* explains the name of Yosef = Joseph, but this reaction is illogical! The natural reaction is to thank God for giving her a child. Instead of that, she immediately asks for another child. In Deuteronomy (17.16), God would have ordered that if the Hebrew wanted to choose a king: *"he must not maintain many horses . . ."* To order such a thing in the middle of the desert, well before the entry into the Promised Land, is inconceivable! Unless it was written much later to condemn the attitude of King Solomon, who was described as an avid collector and dealer of thousands of horses!

Conclusions:

King Josiah and his accomplices wrote down some of the legends and traditions of the Hebrew people having in mind two main goals: to fight against the continual idolatry and the cult to other gods and to give to the priests of Jerusalem the monopoly of the sacrifices. After the second exile, Ezra had to preserve the Jewish people from assimilation and included several laws against mixed marriages.

2

Who is the source of the New Testament, Jesus or Paul?

Why so many contradictions and errors in the New Testament?

The New Testament does not mention the errors and contradictions of the Bible. Jesus says that the Bible is God's words, written by Moses and he makes no criticism against the writings but only complains against any additions made by the Pharisees. The New Testament would be an excellent exercise for police inspectors who must dissect testimonials to discover hundreds of faults and lies.

1. In Matthew (19.26), *"Everything is possible for God."* But in Judges (1.19), God cannot overcome the *"valley of the residents because they had chariots of iron."*
2. In John (2.11), Jesus turns water into wine at Cana, and it is *"the first miracle Jesus did"*. But a bit further, (2.23), *"in Jerusalem at the Passover feast, many believed in his name, seeing the miracles which he did."* But when Jesus healed the child of the officer, (4.54), this healing is called *"second miracle."*
3. In John (13.36), Peter asks Jesus, *"Lord, where are you going?"* A little further (14.5), Thomas asks: *"Lord, we do not know where*

you're going . . ." However, in (16.5), Jesus is surprised: *"None of you ask me: where are you going?"*

4. In II Cor. (5.10), *"we must all appear before the judgment of Christ, that each one may receive good or evil he has done,"* so Jesus is judge. Similarly, in John (5.22), *"The Father judges no one, but has given all judgment to the Son."* But later, John (12.47) transforms this Jewish concept of judgment into Jesus the Savior: *"For I came not to judge the world, but to save it."*
5. In Mark (1.6), *"John ate locusts and wild honey,"* but Matthew (11.18) says, *"John arrived, neither haven neither eaten nor drunken."*
6. Jesus had twelve disciples/apostles. Yet the comparison reveals differences: only Matthew and Mark mention Thaddeus, while only John mentions *"the beloved disciple"* and Nathanael of Cana but forgets Matthew. The book of the Apocalypse (7.4) forgets the tribe of Dan but mentions the tribes of Levi, Ephraim, and Menashe. The number of twelve tribes and apostles therefore was kept to preserve the symbol of twelve. Judas, after his death, is replaced by Matthias. But James, the brother of Jesus, and Paul, the founder of Christianity, are not counted so as not to spoil the symbolism.
7. Is the father of Joseph, the husband of Mary, called Jacob (as in Matthew 1.16) or Eli (as in Luc 3.23)? Genealogies differ according to each evangelist.
8. In Matthew (16.17), Peter had the revelation that Jesus is the Christ by *"my Father who is in heaven,"* while in John (1.41), his brother Andrew had revealed to him that Jesus is Christ.
9. In Matthew (9.18), the Jewish leader bows before Jesus and says, *"My daughter died there a moment ago,"* while in Mark (5.23) he says, *"My little daughter is at the end."*
10. In Mark (6.8), Jesus *"commanded his disciples to take nothing, except a stick,"* while in Matthew (10.9) and Luke (9.3), Jesus asks them not to take a stick.
11. In John (1.32), the Baptist did not know Jesus, but in Matthew (3.13) he knew him, and according to Luke, Jesus and John the Baptist were cousins.
12. In John (5.31), Jesus said: *"If I bear witness of myself, my testimony is not true,"* but further (8.14), he said: *"Although I bear testimony of myself, my testimony is true."* In John (10.30), Jesus said, *"I and the*

Father are one," but would disagree later. John (14.28) said: *"The Father is greater than me."*

13. In Matthew (5.16), Jesus asks that good deeds be visible, while in Matthew (6.1) he asks the opposite: *"beware of practicing your righteousness before men to be seen."*
14. In Acts (9.7), *"men who accompanied him ... heard a voice, but did not see him,"* while further, in (22.9), Paul said the opposite: *"Those who were with me saw the light, but heard not the voice of one speaking."*
15. In Matthew (10.34), Jesus the bellicose said, *"I came not to bring peace, but to bring a sword,"* but further, Jesus became peaceful and said: *"place thy sword into its place, for all those that take the sword shall perish by the sword."*
16. In Matthew (26.49), Judas kissed Jesus to point him out, while in John (18.3) there is no kiss.
17. In Acts (26.16), a voice gave orders to Paul on the spot, but in Acts (9.6 and 22.10) the voice said to Paul that he will receive further orders later in Damascus.
18. In Matthew (21.12), Jesus arrived in Jerusalem and drove the merchants out of the temple, but in Mark (11.11) Jesus enters Jerusalem and it was not until the next day, coming back from Bethany, that he enters again to chase the merchants.
19. In Mark (15.29), at the sixth hour, Jesus is on the cross for over three hours, while in John (19.14) he is still at the court of Pilate.
20. In Mark (15.27), two thieves were crucified with Jesus, but Luke (23.43) adds that one of them defended Jesus and talked to him.
21. In Acts (1.18), Judas bought a field with the money he received for betraying Jesus, while in Matthew (27.5) *"he cast down the pieces of silver in the temple, and departed, and went and hanged himself."*

We could add a long list of contradictions; for example, the signs on the cross, the last words of Jesus, or the trip to Egypt of the child Jesus . . .

The New Testament was edited several times

Paul writes in the letter to the Hebrews (1.1) that God *"has spoken several times to our fathers through the prophets, and in these last days spoke unto us through his Son."* Saul-Paul, not well known by the Christians, is the source of the New Testament. Without Paul, no Christianity. This mysterious Paul and the chronological order of the New Testament writings are the key to understanding the true Jesus. The New Testament begins with the four Gospels, continues with the Acts and the Epistles. However, this order is contrary to the chronological order, because the epistles of Paul were written around fifteen to thirty years after the death of Jesus but twenty to fifty years before the Gospels.

Paul did not know Jesus while he was alive and said nothing about the life and miracles of Jesus because he did not witness them, and probably the other apostles did not relate much to him. Is it then this Paul who is preaching the true (?) doctrine of Jesus whom he never knew? He claimed to have received this teaching from Jesus, who would have appeared to him a few years after his hanging. In the Epistle to the Galatians (1.1 to 16), Paul would have received directly from Jesus his teachings, not through the apostles: *"Not by man, but by Jesus Christ and God the father."* If we doubt the appearances of Jesus to Paul, the latter would have invented the teaching of Jesus, which would be only his doctrine. To believe or not in Paul's vision is actually the key to Christianity. Paul's epistles are the source of the Gospels, and Paul did not preach the Gospel of Jesus but his one. Indeed, in the Epistles we find teachings of Jesus repeated by the Gospels, and Christians say that of course the disciple accepted and reported the doctrine of their master. But this is not what Jesus said to Paul. Paul infiltrated the stories with his own doctrine and retroactively put it in the master's mouth to give it more weight. First example: Paul preaches about sexual abstinence. To "legitimize" the idea, Paul (or his followers) included, in the Gospel according to Matthew (19.11 to 12), the following: *"There are eunuchs who chose that life for themselves for the kingdom of heaven. May he that can understand, understand."* These words were supposedly spoken by Jesus, but they sound false and irrelevant. Second example: Paul, in his Epistle to the Romans (13.9), wrote: *". . . these are the commandments: Do not commit adultery, do not kill, do not steal, do not covet . . ."* And he summed up by saying: *"You shall love your neighbor as yourself."* These words from Paul will be put in the mouth of Jesus some twenty years later and reported with some variations in the synoptic Gospels. All will make the same deliberate mistake of forgetting the commandments of the Shabbat and of idolatry. Compare Matthew (10.18), Mark (10.19), and Luke (18.18). These cannot be the words of Jesus, who always respected the Shabbat. Paul's disciples simply put in

Jesus's mouth what their master Paul preached. Third example: One of the symbolic gestures of Jews returning from a pagan land was to shake the dust off their feet in order not to defile the Holy Land. Acts (13.51) says: *"Paul and Barnabas shook the dust off their feet and went to Icon."* But Matthew (10,14), some twenty years later, repeats Paul's words and distorts what Jesus said by writing: *"If they do not welcome you, if they do not listen to your words, leave that house or that city by shaking the dust off your feet ."* Fourth example: Paul, in his Epistle to the Corinthians (I, 11.23), wrote: *". . . Jesus took bread, and gave thanks, broke it and said, this is my body . . . after supper he took the cup and said, this cup is the new covenant of my blood."* Twenty years later, Luke, a faithful disciple of Paul, wrote in (22.19 to 20*), "took the bread, and gave thanks, broke it . . . saying, this is my body . . . he even took the cup after the supper . . . and said this cup is the new covenant of my blood . . ."* Exactly the same words! These are not the words of Jesus. Paul and Luke never knew Jesus. The words were invented by Paul and repeated by the Evangelist Luke!

Fifth example: The divorce. Again, Mark (10.11) repeats what Paul, his master, said in 1 Corinthians (7.11): *"Whoever divorces his wife and marries another commits adultery against her."* Sixth example: In his Epistle to the Romans, Paul writes: *"Bless those who persecute you; bless them and do not curse them!"* Luke repeated the same in (6.28): *"Bless those who curse you, pray for those who mistreat you."*

Seventh example: Matthew (24.31) repeats what Paul says in 1 Thessalonians (4.16*): "with the angels and trumpets."* Matthew (18.16) also repeats what Paul says in II Corinthians (13.1): *"with the need for 2 or 3 witnesses."* Matthew (24.43) repeats what Paul says in I Thessalonians (5.2): *"with the arrival of the Lord as a thief."*

Eighth example: In Matthew (6.5–9), Jesus shows them how to pray: *"This is how you should pray. Our Father who is in heaven . . . Give us this day our daily bread . . ."* But in Romans (8.26), Paul recognizes thirty years after *that "we do not know what to ask for when we pray."* The explanation of this contradiction is that the Evangelist, noticing the lack mentioned by Paul, found the solution by putting the words in Jesus's mouth and added instructions on how to pray. Also, in Acts (20.35) Paul repeats: *"the words of the Lord . . . It is better to give than to receive."* There is no proof anywhere in the Gospels that Jesus ever said these words. Did Paul make this up? Luke and Mark, the two disciples of Paul and the two presumed authors of the Gospels, were less docile than he wanted. In 1 Timothy (1.3),

Paul urges his disciples not to be *"tied down by endless genealogies."* Luke, his faithful and sometimes stubborn disciple, enumerates many false genealogies. Paul could not change all the facts because of the vigilance of the Notsrim-Nazarenes, whose goal was to protect the original teaching of Jesus. This confrontation explains the contradictions found in the New Testament.

Paul's followers wrote false Epistles:

Of the fourteen Epistles of Paul, only the following are authentic: the first Epistle to the Thessalonians, the two Epistles to the Corinthians, Philippians, Philemon, Galatians, and finally the one to the Romans. According to the Protestant minister Gerd Theissen and other specialists, the Epistle to the Ephesians, the second letter to the Thessalonians, to the Colossians, the two letters to Timothy and Titus were not written by Paul but were drafted by the school of Paul long after his death.

In II Thessalonians, the ETB (ecumenical translation of the Bible) admits that Paul is not the real author and that *"a Christian writer, imbued with the teaching of Paul, thought it was necessary to correct . . . false and dangerous interpretation of the expectation of Christ . . ."* Although this writer signs this letter with the name of Paul, it is not designated as a forgery but explains that *"Christian and Jewish literature have frequently used this process"; that is, to write fakes.*

Similarly, the Epistle to the Hebrews has not been written by Paul. On the question of who is the real author of this Epistle, probably written around 135, Origen replied: *"Truthfully, only God knows."* According to Luther, this letter was not written by Paul or any other apostle. Hebrews, the last bastion of Nazarenes, was retrograded in 1914 by the Church as having only *"indirect authenticity" (?)*. The ETB suggests as possible authors: Luke, Clement of Rome, Apollos, or Barnabas. The Epistle of Paul to the Hebrews, the one of James, Jude, the second and third Epistle of John, and the Apocalypse are all rejected by Protestants. A letter of Paul to the Corinthians and a letter from the Corinthians to Paul mentioned in 1 Corinthians (5.9) and (7.1) have disappeared and no one knows their content. Philippians (3.1) mentions other letters. What was their content? Did the Church publish all the letters in its possession or only a selection?

Did Paul write while he was in Rome "in chains" in his luxury prison?

Did the censorship of his Roman guards influence his texts and convince Paul to write that it is better to preach about pacifism, to accept payment of taxes, and submission to authority rather than to adopt the rebellious Jewish Messianic views? The Church gives no details on all of the Christian texts. Did the Church collect these Epistles from the hands of the recipients scattered in the four corners of the Roman Empire, Galatia, Ephesus, and Rome? Did Paul, Timothy, Sylvain, Peter, Jacques, and others have an extra copy of their letters in their possession or did they rewrite them from memory, and of course, after adapting them to their view?

Is Paul the source of the New Testament?

It is generally accepted that Mark and an enigmatic man named Q would be the two sources of the Gospels. Paul is never mentioned as playing a role in the development of the Gospels. For some, the words of Jesus recorded by disciples served as source to write the Gospels a few decades later. The discovery of some manuscripts in Egypt in 1945 seems to prove them right, because the newly discovered Gospel of Thomas contains these loggias. However, since these texts ignore the resurrection of Jesus and contradict the canonical Gospels, they were rejected. Yet, there is another and better explanation: Paul is the inspiration and also the master censor of Christianity and demands in Titus (3.9): *"Avoid foolish questions, genealogies, and contentions . . . Get away, after a first and second warning, from the one who causes divisions . . ."* He says in 1Thessalonians (5.21): *"Examine all things; hold what is good."* The slim epic of Jesus has been transformed by Paul and his followers, then reported by the Evangelists.

After the disappearance of Jesus, his teachings have been remodeled in a doctrine quite different. Paul himself asked to remind of his gospel in II Timothy (2.8): *"Remember Jesus Christ . . . of the seed of David raised from the dead according to my gospel."* Paul in Galatians (1.6) reprimands the new converts who seem to adhere to *"another gospel."* But no detail is given about the content of this other gospel. Paul would be the major source of the New Testament, and through the writings of his faithful followers, put in the mouth of Jesus his own gospel.

Therefore, it is recommended to read first the Epistles of Paul, then Acts, and finally the Gospels, in this order.

Paul acknowledges that he is clever and misleading

In 1Corinthians (9.20) and 2 Corinthians (12.16), Paul explains his tactics: *"I became as a Jew to be accepted by the Jews . . . I am myself under the Law, in order to win those under the law"*; *"as an astute man, I have convinced you . . ."* Again in Romans (3.7), *"and if through my lie, the truth of God is revealed . . ."* So for him, the goal can explain lies. In Acts (21, 23), Paul takes a misleading vow to avoid the wrath of the Jews, who suspected him of betraying their faith. Paul is servile when he says in (Acts 26.2): *"I think myself honored, King Agrippa, having to justify myself to you,"* without remembering the crimes of the king's ancestors. Paul asked the slaves to serve their masters and not to anger the rich and summed up his strategy in I Corinthians (10:33): *"I strive in all things to please all, not seeking my own advantage, but that of many, that they may be saved."* Paul is often accused of lying and repeats too often that he does not lie: *"In what I write, here before God, I lie not,"* Galatians (1.20). *"Let no man think me a fool,"* in 2 Corinthians (11.16). *"I'm not lying,"* in Romans (9.1). Should we believe Paul or should we doubt him?

The authors of the canonical Gospels are numerous and unknown:

The three Synoptic Gospels and John are declared *"sacred"* by the Church even though no one knows the identity of their authors and critics agree that they are not the writings of just one author but of successive authors.

The Evangelist Matthew Levi cannot testify of the life of Jesus because, according to his own testimony, he himself was recruited only when Jesus was already thirty years old. So his accounts of the miraculous birth of Jesus and the three wise men at his birth were only rumors, not firsthand accounts. Matthew is the most Jewish and closest to the historical Jesus, if we extirpate Christian additions.

It is generally accepted that Mark was the first of the Evangelists and influenced Matthew and Luke. This classification conceals the importance of Matthew and it is absurd that Matthew was inspired by Mark, because Matthew was a contemporary of Jesus, so a direct source, while Mark is a disciple of Paul and Peter, so a later source. This Matthew's last name was Levi and he was the son of Alpheus and had a seat at the house of customs (according to Mark 2.14). However, in other texts, it is written that the son of Alpheus was called James. *"The Gospel According to Levi"* would have softened hatred if the name had not been changed!

Mark, servant of two masters: His original name was John-Yohanan in Acts (12.12), and at age forty-five, he left Jerusalem to accompany and serve Paul and Barnabas, his uncle, to Antioch (Acts 12.25). It is said that later he abandoned Paul and returned to Jerusalem, which deeply upset Paul (Acts 15.37): *"Barnabas was determined to take with them John, also called Mark. But Paul did not agree to take as a companion a man who had left them before . . . Their disagreement worsened . . . Barnabas took Mark . . ."*

Mark is called *"my son"* in the First Epistle of Peter (5.13). Was Peter so familiar to the home of Mark that the servant recognized his voice (Acts 12.14)? Mark, this servant of two masters, was he truly a loyal servant or did he give his own version of the facts? Papias, the bishop of Hierapolis who lived in Turkey in 125, wrote in *The Judgments of the Lord* that a certain John (another one) reported that *"Mark was the interpreter of Peter and wrote exactly about everything he (Peter) did, but in no particular order, he would remember what was said and done by the Lord."* But the Gospel of Mark is written in an orderly way, proving that the texts were rewritten more than a few times. Mark does not boast about being a witness of Jesus, yet he is one of the first evangelists.

The Evangelist Luke is not a pagan doctor who converted: He is said to be a pagan native of Antioch but he alone reported about the circumcision of Jesus, the Jewish redemption rite of newborns, the Jewish rite of purification of Mary, and Jesus's visit to the Temple at the age of twelve. Luke (2.22) is mistaken when he talks about "their purification," because only the mother who gave birth must be purified, not the father, and the redemption of the newborn requires the payment of 5 shekels without bringing the baby to the temple.

Luke, with or without Mark, was the travelling companion and helper of Paul.

Irenaeus of Lyons, around 185, said that the Gospel of Luke is the one that Paul preached. But in the Epistles and Acts, Paul ignores Mary's virginity while this is a major element in the Gospel of Luke. It is therefore likely that the virginity of Mary was added well after Luke and Paul's writings. Marcion, preacher himself and the one who published the letters of Paul, stated that the only authentic Gospel of Luke was the one that he himself had corrected. Marcion had a disciple named Lucanus or Luke. Could he be the true author of this Gospel?

John: Some say that John was the brother of James and the son of Zebedee. He was a fisherman and one of the first disciples of Jesus. But this hypothesis is hard to accept because this Gospel is too mystical and well written to be the work of an illiterate fisherman. It is also hard to believe that he survived up to the year 100 (period during which they say this Gospel would have been written). Yet the Gospel of John never mentions a word about Paul or the virginity of Mary.

The Acts of the Apostles: It is a common belief that Luke wrote a book that included two parts, his Gospel and the Acts, and that in the second century the church separated the two parts. However, the Acts contradict his Gospel so much that one doubts that the same person could have written both stories.

The other Epistles: The Epistle of James was not written by James, the brother of Zebedee, who died around the year 44, nor by James, the brother of the Lord, who died circa years 62. It would have been written by an unknown late in the first century, in an elaborate Greek language unknown to both Jameses. But not a word about the resurrection of Jesus, nothing about Jesus appearing to James, or about the virginity of their mother! Who is the author of this letter and where was it written? We don't know, but we can assume he was Notsri-Nazarene and not Christian.

The Epistles of Peter were absolutely not written by Peter, known to be illiterate. Were they written instead by Sylvain with Mark *"his son"* by his side? Why is Jesus not mentioned? It is known that the Second Epistle of Peter dates from about 125 and could therefore not have been written by Peter himself! The forger is revealed by his mistakes: he mentions that the first generation disappeared (3. 4) and there is a collection of letters and scriptures from Paul written, therefore, after the death of Peter. This epistle would have only one purpose: to show the friendship that existed between Paul and Peter: *"Our beloved brother Paul... wisdom given to him."*

According to some Christian scholars, John wasn't the author of his first epistle. According to others, the Epistles of John were not written by John the disciple, but instead by another John, the elder, who was a Presbyter. But why does he not mention Paul?

Faced with all these counterfeiters, what does the Church say? Absolutely nothing!

The Gospels are full of add-ons and contradictions:

The "Jesus seminar," created in 1985, found that 85 percent of the words supposedly spoken by Jesus are inauthentic. Another group of German researchers concluded that it was 50 percent. The *Encyclopedia Britannica* lists thousands of versions of the Gospels. It's hard to know which version is right.

In 1Thessalonians (2.16), the Jews opposed to the conversion were punished, *"the wrath has come upon them."* Yet the destruction of the temple took place in 70, after the death of Paul, who therefore could not have been a witness.

Luke assures that his gospel comes from eyewitness accounts but adds the story of the demon tempting Jesus. No witness was there. Also, in Luke (22.40 to 45), none of the disciples who were sleeping could have seen Jesus *"be in agony."*

The NIV said about the story of the adulterous woman, John (8.1 to 11): *"... This is an unknown story inserted later."* Therefore, Jesus drawing on the floor before judging this woman and later forgiving her is an invention. Verses 43 to 46 of chapter 4 of the Gospel of John seem to have been tampered with. Their construction appears artificial, and the sentences seem to have been put in the wrong place. It says that Jesus returns to Jerusalem from the feast, which is described later in chapter 5. These sentences should be moved to the beginning of chapter 6.

André Frossard, a pious Christian, writes in his notes on the Gospels, published by Desclée Brouwer: *"After the epilogue of chapter 20 of the Gospel of John, chapter 21 was most likely added by one of John's disciples who more than likely used the notes left by the Evangelist."* This bold assertion would mean that the resurrection of Jesus in the Sea of Galilee was made up by a disciple of John. But who is this man John and who is the disciple of John and what are the notes that would have been used to write the story? And finally, how did André Frossard know that these notes existed?

In the book entitled *Urbi and Orbi - 2000 Years of Papacy* published by Gallimard (1995), two priests, Francesco Chiovaro and Gerard Bessiere, wrote that in the second century: *"The Jewish traditions, the taste at the time for the esoteric, fueled people's curiosity with fanciful speculations about God and his Christ. False Gospels, false Acts, false Apocalypses and false letters of the Apostles swarmed everywhere . . ."*

But no exegete asks the important questions: if so many verses were included to serve the purpose of forgers, how can we be sure that the other verses were not invented by other more skilled forgers as well? We cannot help mentioning Matthew (22.44): *"The Lord said to my Lord."* That is a bad translation of Psalm 110. It was made by a forger who didn't speak Hebrew. Since Jesus spoke Hebrew, he would never have made the mistake of using the expressions *master*, *lord*, and *god* interchangeably. Reread the Bible, Psalm 110!

The erased events

It is said that Jesus began his ministry at the age of thirty years. We know nothing about his life prior to age thirty, only a brief and very problematic mention of his visit to the temple at the age of twelve as transmitted by Luke. Did Jesus work as a carpenter with his father? Did he take refuge in the desert with the sect of Qumran? Did he learn the rudiments of medicine or magic? Nothing, no information whatsoever is given! Or maybe that age was used only as a plagiarism of II Samuel (5.4): *"David was 30 years old when he became king."* In Mark (10.46): *"They came to Jericho, then Jesus left the city . . ."* What happened in Jericho that it had to be erased? Jesus's violence against the fig tree as written in Matthew (21.19) is hard to understand because the explanation has been erased.

The resurrection of Lazarus is told only by John, who wrote much later. Why is this miraculous resurrection ignored by the other Evangelists? Or is this event a made-up addition by John?

Paul was the first critic of the epics of Jesus, and asked his companions to do the same. Paul himself was censored in Acts (18.19 to 23). He left Ephesus, stating that it was imperative to go to Jerusalem to celebrate what was, obviously, a Jewish feast. He therefore went to Caesarea and then to Jerusalem, but for what? We are never told. It is simply written, *"He praised the Church"* and then left immediately to go to Antioch, which is many thousands of kilometers away. Did he do all this traveling for nothing? Was there some event that has been erased? If yes, which one?

Jesus contradicted himself in Matthew (18, 22). Jesus teaches that we must forgive 77 times but forgets that a few lines earlier he taught that forgiveness has to be given 3 times. In the same paragraph, Jesus mentions the Church, which did not exist at the time, and cursed those who do not forgive, *"Let him be to you as a Gentile or a tax collector."* This contradicts the opening statement of Jesus to the Gentiles and tax collectors. Matthew himself was a publican-tax collector.

The Gospel of Matthew (previously named Levi, the tax collector) was written in the Holy Land but with geographic errors. In Matthew (19.1) it is written: *"Jesus left Galilee for the territory of Judea by passing through Jordan."* There is no need to cross the Jordan River to go from Galilee to Judea. Therefore, either Matthew is not the real author of this passage or the translator did a terrible job at relaying the message, or the village of Jesus is not located in Galilee but rather on the other side of the lake.

In Mark (5.1), Mark described Gerasa to be at the edge of Lake Galilee, but this village was located tens of kilometers south of the lake. Was Mark ignoring the geography of Israel, where he was living? In Mark (7.31) he writes: *"Jesus left the region of Tyre and traveled through Sidon, passing through the Sea of Galilee and finally crossing the borders of Decapolis."* How is that possible? Sidon is at the opposite direction and there was no road between Sidon and Galilee at the time, only through Tyre.

Also in Mark (10, 12), it is written that Jesus said: *"If a woman leaves her husband and marries another, she commits adultery."* That would be impossible, because during Jesus's time, Jewish women were not allowed to divorce. This proves to be an addition written to suit the Romans, whose women were allowed to divorce.

Finally, in Mark (8.4), there is an unnecessary multiplication of bread. Why did the disciples ask: *"How can a man satisfy them here in the wilderness?"* Were they unaware that earlier, in (6.35), Jesus had multiplied the loaves of bread?

In Luke, Jesus's movements are described by someone who does not know the country but knows the Jewish rites of circumcision, the redemption of newborns, and the purification of women. In Mark, Jesus would have gone only once to Jerusalem, while according to John he went there several times. The length of Jesus's public appearance varies from one year in the Synoptic to three years in the writings of John. Why don't the Acts describe Paul's death? They instead end with Paul continuing to preach in Rome!

Some say all these contradictions and improbabilities prove the honesty of the Church, which presented the case of "Jesus" as it is, even with few historical facts. The reality is totally different. The Church has tried many times to correct many inconsistencies but could not undo all the contradictions. Too many versions were already widespread and it was impossible to recover all the versions to correct them.

The New Testament was rewritten with successive changes

John Robinson, who wrote *Re-dating the New Testament*, admits that there are very few benchmarks that allow dating precisely the texts of the New Testament. Thousands of experts have tried, unsuccessfully, to find out when and who wrote each verse of the New Testament. A benchmark for dating the New Testament is the fall of Jerusalem in 70. Since no one believes in prophetic power, we can conclude that when the fall is predicted, the text must have been written after 70. Therefore, the Gospel of Mark was written before 70, and then other texts would have been added after 70, including the *prophecy* of the destruction of Jerusalem.

The first version of Mark was written before 70. Its second release came out after the Gospel of Matthew. The Gospel of Luke's first release came after 70. The second version was written after 90. The first version of John was written before 70. The second version after 100. Scholars still do not agree and everyone is bringing up reasonable arguments. A different view would resolve all the contradictions.

The delay and the goals

The miracles done by Jesus, his crucifixion, and his resurrection are followed by an incomprehensible long silence of several decades. The arrival of the Messiah, the incarnation of God, and the miracles he performed and his healings are very important events. Why didn't the disciples immediately write about these events and instead waited for a period of twenty to seventy years? These texts were not presented in Jerusalem, not even in the Holy Land, but far away. If the story was invented, it was better to put some distance in time and space between this epic (virtual or real) and its description in the Gospels. The odyssey of Jesus was therefore published far from Jerusalem, long after the death of Pilate and Caiaphas, and only after being sure that the actors and witnesses were no longer alive to contradict the stories.

The partisans of Christianity advance the dates of writing the Gospels to give them more historical veracity. An example: excavations carried out in High Egypt allowed the discovery of small pieces of papyruses now preserved at the University of Oxford. In the book *Witness of Jesus* (1996), the authors Carsteen Peter Thiede and Matthew D'Ancona take a closer look into these three tiny fragments of papyrus, the largest one measuring 4.1 cm and the other 1.3 cm.

They conclude too quickly that these pieces of papyrus would go back to approximately + 50; that is to say, less than one generation after the crucifixion. They conclude from those facts that the Gospel would have been dictated by the apostle Mathew-Levi himself, an eyewitness to Jesus's life.

Opponents to Christianity refute that the Gospels were written during the second century and therefore are pure imagination. We also refute this date because we believe that after the destruction of the temple in 70 no Christian theologian would have used Judaism to build the new religion and convert the pagans. The fact that the Gospels were openly inspired by Jewish writings, and in every detail, is proof that their roots predate 70. After the year 135, the date of the destruction of Jerusalem, the Judaism of Jesus would have been an inconvenient fact to erase. Even though they tried later to erase some facts, it was too late because the first writings were already known. Moreover, it is hard to explain the passages that talk about the glorious return of the son of man, the time frame ends prior to the generation of the disciples, according to Mark (13.26 to 30): *"Then they will see the Son of man coming in the clouds . . . He will gather his elect from the end of the earth to the uttermost part of heaven . . . This generation shall not pass till all these are not fulfilled."* Was this scripture another contradiction of the Gospel that has not been corrected? Similarly, Luke announces, *"this child will reign over the house of Jacob, the Lord will give him the throne of David, He will be the light to lighten the Gentiles and for glory to your people Israel."* If the Gospel was written after 70, we already knew that Jesus, at that time, had been rejected by Israel, so he never reigned over the house of Jacob. So why all do all these false prophecies? The reason is that the Gospels were written in different stages and periods.

The Gospels of Luke and John were fixed after the fall of Jerusalem in 70 +. All the scholars, believers or not, agree on this point. So why isn't it made clearer? Why isn't the fall of Jerusalem described when this event is so important for Jews and the birth of Christianity? Did they want to hide something?

Up to 170, the four Gospels existed but not in their final form. The Church then put some order but took away some sixty *Apocrypha* cited by the Church itself in the second century. Saint Justin, who wrote the *Life of Christ* around +160, ignored the four Gospels and mentioned only the *Loggias* or words of Jesus. This would mean that the four Gospels were not yet finalized in +160.

Eusebius of Caesarea (265–340), secretary to Emperor Constantine, was a forger who fabricated the list of the first alleged popes. He would have developed the official history of the beginnings of Christianity. St. Jerome in the fourth century complained about falsification in the Scriptures, and so the pope put him in charge of *harmonizing* and writing a coherent version in Latin.

It was not until the Council of Carthage in 397 that the New Testament will be fixed permanently in its current form, but without the mention of the Apocalypse. We are far from the following dates: 65–70 Mark, Luke 65–80, 75–90 Matthew. Most likely, some bits of the Gospels were written around and on those dates.

In the book *Against Celse*, Origen writes about the attacks of Celse: *"... some faithful have reworked the original text of the Gospel 3 or 4 times or even more ... in order to prevent criticism of the texts."* Today, just like Celse, most Christian specialists recognize that the writings have undergone many editorial changes and have been continuously modified by the first missionaries, who had to convince skeptics asking too many questions. Each corrected passage was included in the writings, and each problematic one was removed or altered. The four main goals were to push back heresies, convert the pagans, blame the Jews, and to lay the foundation of the liturgy. But everything is relative and there is reason to doubt the veracity of stories reported two centuries after the fact.

Conclusions:

James, Jesus's brother, remained faithful to the sect after the death of Jesus. Twenty years later, Paul, a smart outsider, penetrated the sect but was obliged to leave. This Paul, who needed to be accepted by Rome and the pagans, built a fake epic of Jesus with the help of his disciples to achieve his goals.

3

Who wrote the Quran, the angel Gabriel or Muhammad's followers?

According to Islam, around 610, the Prophet Muhammad received the revelation in a cave near Mecca, the angel Gabriel ordered him to *"read, recite, declaim Iqra,"* which is the origin of the word *Quran*. So the word of God was dictated to Muhammad to relay it to the Arabs. This revelation is not original but copied on Ezekiel (2.9): "A hand held out to me and in this hand there was a book roll. He unrolled it before me, and the roll was written on the front and the back and contained lamentations, complaints and groans. And he said to me, Son of man . . . eat this roll, and go speak to the house of Israel. I opened my mouth and He made me eat this roll . . ." Muhammad probably knew about Ezekiel and also about this passage from the Gospel of John (16.13): "When the Comforter comes . . . He will speak only what he hears, and he will tell you things to come."

Is the Quran really dictated by a divine angel or written by men? According to (41.41), the Quran is a divine book and *"no error is found in it anywhere."* The slightest mistake would therefore prove that it is book fabricated by man.

Contradictions and errors of the Quran

The Quran, like the New Testament, never mentions the errors and contradictions of the Jewish Bible. On the contrary, the Quran (2.4) accepts as truth *"what was revealed before you."* But we will note two types of errors, those related in the Bible and those within the Quran. Muslims justify the first category of differences by saying that the Bible has been falsified (discussed in the chapter about the Third Commandment). And so what is the second type of errors?

1. Creation: In Quran (3.59), man was created from dust, while in (15.26) he was made from clay. In (11.61), of mud or earth. Yet in (16.4), God created man from a drop of sperm, and in (96.2) from a blood clot. But that's not all, because in (21.30), (24.45), and (25.54), it is written: *"we created every living thing from water."* A hadith of Quran (4.546) states that *"the child will look like his mother if she ejaculates before the father and vice versa."*

In Quran (22.65), God *"holds the sky from falling on earth without its permission."* This is another primitive vision or a total ignorance of astronomy. In (2.29), *"He created for you all things on earth, and then He turned to the sky and shaped the seven heavens."* It contradicts the verse (79.27), which says: *"He shaped the vault . . . then He has made the earth."* The verse (51.49) states that God *"created all things in pairs"* and ignores asexual reproduction.

2. Abraham: In Quran (21.55), Abraham destroyed all the idols of his ancestors except the largest, but in (19.41) there is no destruction of the idols but under the threat of his father Abraham pulled away from him. Who was the first Muslim? The word *Muslim* means "submit to the one God," and so all the patriarchs were Muslims, including Abraham and Moses and Jesus.

In (6.14) (6.163) and (39.12), Muhammad is the first Muslim: *"Say I received the order to be the first Muslim . . . I am the first subject."* Yet in (2.132), (28.52), and (3.52), Abraham and Jesus had come before him. And in (7.143), it would be Moses. Muhammad contradicts himself.

In (2.125), *"Abraham and Ishmael established the foundations of the Kaaba temple"* when they visited Mecca, yet the verses (32.3), (34.44), and (36.2) say Muhammad was sent to a people *"that we have sent no one before you to warn them," "a people whose fathers were not warned."* So it contradicts the affirmation that Abraham and Ishmael came to Arabia to build the Kaaba. And Abraham and Ishmael were just recuperated by Muhammad to sanctify the Kaaba, a former pagan temple.

3. Noah and Lot

In (66.10), Lot's and Noah's wives betrayed their husband, but in the Bible there are no mentions of betrayal by Noah's wife, and Lot's wife only turned her face. In (11.42*)*, *"the waves came up, and the son of Noah was swallowed by the waves,"* while in (21.76) and (37.77), *"we saved Noah and his family from a cataclysm . . . we saved his offspring."* In (7.82) and (27.56), to the imprecations of Lot, the people of Sodom *"in reply, said drive them out of the city these people who purify themselves."* Verse (29.29) reports the same story but gives another answer: "show us the punishment of God if you speak the truth." Which answer is correct?

4. Moses

In (28.9), it was the wife of Pharaoh who adopted Moses, but in the Bible it is the daughter of Pharaoh. The Quran (28.29) reported the arrival of Moses in Midian with several errors: *"the priest of Midian had seven daughters"* in Exodus (2.16), not two. Moses did not have to work eight years for Tsipora his wife, the daughter of the priest, as mentioned in the Quran. Muhammad mixed the stories of Jacob and Moses for no reason except for lack of a good memory. In (20.71) and (26.49), Muhammad says that Pharaoh crucified his enemies, and in (7,120), Pharaoh threatens to crucify magicians, a punishment unknown at this time. Another historical error is found in (20. 86 . . .): *"the Samaritan has misled the people . . . the Samaritan also threw them."* But the Samaritans appear a thousand years after Moses's time. In (5.20*)*, *"Moses said to his people: Remember the blessing of God when he chose among you prophets, he made you kings."* But the Hebrews had no king before Moses, only after.

5. Was Miriam Jesus's mother or the sister of Moses?

Miriam in Hebrew or Mary in English is the sister of Moses and Aaron and the daughter of Amram. There is another Miriam or Mary who is the mother of Jesus in the Gospels. These two Maries lived in very different times and yet the Quran confuses them. In (3.33), Amram was the grandfather of Jesus, while in the Bible he is the father of Moses,

Miriam, and Aaron. In (19.28), Mary the mother of Jesus *"came back to her with the child. They said: Mary, your act is monstrous. O sister of Aaron, your father was not unworthy . . ."* This Mary is not the sister of Aaron! And finally, (66.12), *"And Mary, daughter of Amram, who was a virgin . . ."* Muhammad and editors of the Quran confused both Mary the sister of Moses and the mother of Jesus. Muhammad therefore believed that Jesus was the nephew of Moses by his sister Miriam. How can the Muslims believe in this monumental error for centuries? They cite a hadith stating that this contradiction was reported to Muhammad, who answered that there was no error. He explained that in his day many Jews named their children after holy men and women.

Another explanation given for this error is that indeed, Mary had a half-brother named Aaron, unknown to all Christian texts. Moreover, in (66.12), *"Mary, daughter of Amram, who was a virgin and to whom we breathed our spirit."* Defenders of the Muslim faith are forced to say that yes, the father of Mary was named Amram, although according to the Gospels his name was Eli.

Muhammad is wrong a second time regarding Mary, mother of Jesus, when in (19.23) he tells the episode of the date tree. This popular legend comes from the apocryphal gospel in Arabia at the time of Muhammad. Muhammad is wrong again when he mentions in (5,110*) "the ripe age of Jesus"* when in fact Jesus died at the age of thirty-three. The same verse is wrong again when he tells about the story of Jesus who built a clay bird and breathed life into it.

6. The golden calf and Aaron, brother of Moses

In (20.85), a Samaritan made the golden calf in the desert *and ". . . the Samaritan replied . . ."* Not only it does not correspond to the writings of the Bible, but also the city of Shomron did not exist at the time of Moses. In addition, (20.92) confirms the guilt of Aaron, *"You therefore have disobeyed me."* In (4.48), *"God does not forgive that adds the gods."* Yet (4.153) says the opposite: *"They adopted the calf after having evidence. We have erased their sins."*

7. Haman, minister of the Persian king or of Pharaoh?

Several verses tell the legend of Moses but they wrongly introduce the character of Haman, who belongs to another legend, that of Esther, which takes place a thousand years later, not during the exile in Egypt but during the exile of Babel. In (28.38), Pharaoh says, *"You, Haman, bake bricks and build me a tower..."* And in (40.36): *"Pharaoh said, Haman, build me a tower. I reached for the ropes to ascend to heaven the God of Moses...."* Haman would be for the Quran a minister of Pharaoh, when in fact he was minister of the Persian king Xerxes, mentioned in the book of Esther in the Jewish Bible. This King Xerxes reigned around 486 BC (Book of Esther), when the Pharaoh of Egypt lived around 1490 BCE. And finally, the tower comes from the legend of the Tower of Babel and has nothing to do with Pharaoh and Haman.

8. Jonas:

The Quran claims to be clear, though in (37.145) Jonas says, *"We were rejected sick on the bare earth,"* while in (68.49), *"without a blessing from your Lord, he would have been rejected infamous on the bare ground."* In (14.4) and (30.47), *"the apostles we sent ... every people in its own language ... we sent apostles each to his people."* But Jonas was sent to another people, to Nineveh. In addition, for the Quran, Jesus, Moses, and Muhammad were not sent only for their people but for all humanity.

9. King Saul in the Quran (2,249*): "And Saul said when he went with his troops ... to the river. Whoever drinks it is not mine. Will be mine who did not taste at least once in the palm of his hand..."* Muhammad or one of the editors of the Quran has tangled with the episode of Judges (7.5*): "God said to Gideon ... Those who laps the water with his tongue as a dog laps, you shall set apart ... Those who drank in their hand...."*

10. The Quran (18.83) tells of an erroneous story of *Dhul Quarnim*, who is in fact Alexander the Great. He was certainly not a Muslim and did not live in the era of Gog and Magog but in the fourth century BCE. He built altars to the gods of Olympus.

11. Confusing Ishmael with Jesus:

In (19.23), Mary, in pain, gave birth, under a palm tree to Jesus, who, though a newborn, speaks to her: *"Do not grieve, your Lord put a stream at your feet ... fresh dates ..."* Muhammad has mixed the story of Hagar and Ishmael with that of Miriam and Jesus. Genesis (21.17) said that the unhappy Hagar, abandoned in the desert and thirsty, discovered a source and gave water to her son.

12. Johanan, the Baptist:

The Quran (19.7) affirms that God announces the birth of John, or Yohanan in Hebrew, which means *God forgive*. *"O Zacharie, we announce you a son. His name is John, a name we have not yet given anybody..."* The god of the Quran and its editor are wrong because the name John/Yohanan existed long before the Baptist and the prophet Jeremiah mentions it several times, such as in (42.1): *"All troop leaders as John/Yohanan son of Kaareah..."*

13. Jesus and the Trinity:

In (5.116), God asks Jesus, *"Did you say to men: take me and my mother as gods besides God?"* But Christians do not believe in a Trinity of Father, Mother, and Son, they believe in the Father, Son, and Holy Spirit. Muhammad did not know that he was influenced by a dissident Christian sect of Arabia.

14. Will Christians be cast into hell?

In (2.62) and (5.69), Christians will go to heaven, while in (5.72) and (3.85) *"whoever seeks a religion other than Islam will not be accepted"* in paradise and *"Whoever adds the gods, God forbid him the garden."*

15. The divinity of Jesus:

In (3.45) and (4.158*)*, *"Jesus will be shown in this life and in the other, close to the Lord,"* *"God raised Him."* Yet in (21.98), *"you and your gods other than God... will result in Gehenna (hell)."* So Jesus will go to heaven or hell?

16. Verse (2.256) says *"no compulsion in religion,"* while (4.56) says the contrary: *"those who do not believe our verses, we will push them into the fire"* and (9.5): *"Kill the unbelievers... If they repent and make prayer and... then let them free."*

17. The Quran (113.2) asked for God's protection *"against the evil that He created, against the evil of darkness... the evil of those who blow on knots, against the evil of the envious when he is jealous."* These are childish fears against the darkness, witches, and the evil eye, not God's message.

18. God told Muhammad (34.50): *"If I digress, I digress... at my expense."* But he forgets that he has responsibilities, and if Muhammad is mistaken, he deceives more than one billion Muslims.

19. It is forbidden for Muslims to marry Christians who remain Christian according to (2.221), while (5.5) allows marriage without mentioning the obligation for them to convert to Islam.

20. Food in hell?
In (88.6), *"they did eat that Dari,"* yet in (37.66), they eat the fruit of the tree of Zaqqum, which are like heads of Satan, and drink a boiling mixture. And finally in (69.36), *"No other food than filth."* A triple contradiction!

21. An elementary exercise:
If a young married man dies before having children, his parents will receive 1/3 of his property in (4.11), his widow will receive 1/4 in (4.12), and two sisters will receive 2/3 in (4.176). The total exceeds 3/3. Another exercise: If a married father of two daughters died, his parents will receive 1/3 of his assets in (4.11), his wife will receive 1/8 in (4.12), and his daughters receive 2/3 in (4.11), more than 3/3.

22. *"Everything goes back to him in a day that lasts 1,000 of your years,"* in (32.5), while *"the angels and the spirit ascend to God in a day of 50,000 years,"* in (70.7).

23. In (56.7), on the day of judgment, there would be three different groups, those of the right, those on the left and those in front, while in (90.18), there would only be 2 groups, those of the left and those on the right. This separation of right and left is copied from the Gospel of Matthew (25.41).

24. A single day is enough for Allah to destroy the people of Ad, in (54.16) but it takes *"inauspicious days"* in (41.16) and *"8 days and 7 nights'* in (69.7).

25. In (25.20), before Muhammad, Allah sent only *"apostles who ate and went to the market,"* while in (22.75), *"God chooses messengers from angels and from men."*

26. In (53.13), Muhammad had seen God, *"he saw Him again near the jujube tree...,"* and in (81.23), *"your companion is not evil, he saw Him in the bright horizon..."* While in (6.103) it says: *"no human eye can reach Him,"* and in (42.51), *"it has been given to no mortal that God speaks to him except by revelation or from behind a veil or a messenger...."*

27. On Judgment Day, in (23.101), *"they will ask no more,"* while in (37.26), *"they will turn toward each other to ask,"* and (52.25), *"their interrogators will turn towards each other..."*

28. *"Every animal and every angel... fear God and do what they are ordered"* in (16.49). Yet the famous Iblis is disobedient, (2.34): *"When we said to the angels to prostrate to Adam, they prostrated except Iblis who refused with pride..."*

29. Judgment Day, in (69.25), *"he who is given his book in his left hand"* go to hell, but in (83.11), *"he who is given his book behind his back... fall into fire."*

30. *"Nobody changes the words of God"* in (6.34) and *"nothing can change the decrees of Allah"* in (6.115), and *"God's words does not change"* in (10.34). Yet when Muhammad needed to, he changed them. In (2.106), *"Whether we abrogate a verse or deface it, we bring in a similar or better one,"* and in (16.101): *"Sometimes we substitute one revelation for another, for God knows what He reveals."*

All these contradictions prove that the sacred texts are invented by men.

Other points about the language of the Quran

Muslims say that the Quran is not only inspired by God, but also dictated by God. Yet certain verses cannot have been written by God: the first Sura, which is a thanksgiving and a prayer to God, and the last two in which Muhammad says that he *"takes refuge in God."* Verse (17.1) is not written by God either because it thanks God for his nocturnal journey to *"the far away mosque."*

The verses (19.64), (27.91), (37.161), (75.2), (81.15), (90.2), and probably many others have not been sent by God. The word *says* would be a simple addition to Muhammad's sermons to make them appear more divine... It would be bizarre for God to swear on Himself, as in (75.1), (17.1), and in (19.64), it is the angels who speak and not God.

Muhammad, alone in a nearby cave in Mecca, received revelations dictated by the angel Gabriel. Why always without anyone around to witness it? This angel made several appearances to Muhammad yet not one witness saw him. Muhammad had difficulty convincing the skeptics when just one public appearance of Gabriel would have convinced all unbelievers. Do we have to accept it with a blind and irrational faith? How can we be so sure that these are the exact words of Gabriel that Muhammad reported?

The Quran is written in Arabic, and so the angel Gabriel, who spoke Hebrew with the Jews, also spoke Arabic with Muhammad. The verse (16.103) says that the Quran is written in pure Arabic language, yet many terms are of Hebrew and Aramaic origins as well as other languages. For example, the Hebrew words in the Torah *shehina*, paradise, hell, or the Greek word *Injil* used for *Gospel*. Why not simply use the Arabic word *Bisharah* for that purpose? To that question, Muslims answer that the verse (16.103) shouldn't be translated by *pure Arabic* but rather by *clear Arabic*. In addition, some specialists of the Arab language dared to point out grammatical errors and styles in the Quran.

Was Muhammad illiterate?

Islam proclaims that its prophet was illiterate and therefore, it is a proof that the Quran was whispered by an angel, because an illiterate could not have produced such *pure* text. It also gave more authority to his revelations, and countered the accusations that Muhammad plagiarized ancient texts and was suspected of using a Christian or Jewish imposter to develop his verses. They use the verse (7.157): *"also for those who follow the messenger, the unlettered prophet...."* But the real words are *al nabi al'ommi*, used also in other verses, like (2.78) and (3.20), and designate the people who have not yet received the sacred book.

Several hadiths describe Muhammad as somebody who can read and write. Hadith of Bukhari (3.65 and 114) says: *"Once again, when the Prophet wrote a letter or had planned to write a letter..."* When Muhammad's health worsened, it *"prevented him to write this statement..."* In Bukhari (7, 62, 88), it is said that *"the Prophet wrote (a marriage contract) with Aisha when she was 6 years old."* Muhammad was also able to erase some words in the treaty of Hudaibiya. All of that proved that Muhammad knew how to read and write.

Muhammad, like the great majority of his people, was uneducated but not illiterate. He was a sharp business man, and Kadijah, his first wife, would not have chosen an illiterate man to run her businesses. She needed a person who knew how to maintain accounts with names of customers and suppliers. Why then did the angel Gabriel order Muhammad to read if he could not read? Some Muslims answer that the word *iqra* does not mean *read* but *recite*.

Some verses lead us to think that Muhammad himself wrote the Quran. For example, the verse (29.48): *"You were not able to read (or to recite) any book before this one, you did not write any..."* This would mean that Muhammad did not write any book until the arrival of the Quran. Yet in (25.5), the unbelievers said: *"These are old stories he has written down..."*

Muhammad never read biblical texts himself, not because he was illiterate but because they were not yet translated into Arabic. He received oral narratives from his Jewish and Christian friends that he memorized. This is why the stories in the Quran are scrambled, incomplete, and mix biblical writings, fables, and post-biblical traditions. The Quran cites the Torah and the Gospels dozens of times but with no details, from memory. It never specifies what part of the Bible the passage is from, and it is as if Muhammad didn't know that the New Testament was divided into several Gospels and Epistles. Paul's name is not mentioned in the Quran, which is surprising since he is at the origin of Christianity.

The official version of the written Quran and the questions it brings up:

Jews affirm that the Bible was immediately set in writing by Moses, and Christians claim that the Gospels are Jesus's words written right after his death by witnesses living at the time. The Muslims also affirm that while Muhammad was still alive his followers wrote his words on animal skin, stones, pieces of ceramic, and wood. They did so in order not to forget them. How can we be sure that these are really the same words without any selection or modification?

After the death of Muhammad, when a great number of his disciples start dying in combat, there was the danger of Muhammad's teachings and words being lost forever. So the caliph Abu Bakr asked Zayd, who was an educated man, to collect all the verses. At first, Zayd refused and argued that while Muhammad was alive he never asked anyone to write the Quran. Later, Zayd gathered all of Muhammad's sayings and a council decided which ones to keep and which ones to get rid of. However, around 650, the Caliph Uthman decided to write a version of the Quran as well. Why did he decide to do that if there was already an accepted compilation of Muhammad's words? Uthman asked Zayd again to rewrite another version of the Quran based on his first edition, but this time with the assistance of Uthman's companions. Why did he ask Zayd to do such a thing? What did he want to modify?

That new version of the Quran, the one we know today, was adopted.

This Caliph Uthman said he changed the text *"for spelling and punctuation reasons,"* and sent copies of these rectified texts to new Muslim communities with orders to burn the ancient texts. Why? Did he fear the comparison of ancient texts with the new official Quran? How was he allowed to burn the divine texts? Uthman was assassinated. Why? Ali, who replaced Uthman, was also assassinated. Why? Is the Quran we have today the same as the one of Muhammad? If Uthman, the caliph, needed to cancel the different versions of the Quran to keep only one, how can we be sure that this version is authentic? Why aren't there any existing fragments of the original Quran or of any of the copies written by the first caliphs, not even copies distributed by Muslims conquerors throughout the empire?

Many brave Western scholars come to the conclusion that the Quran, as we know it today was gradually rewritten over a period of a century after Muhammad's death. Yet a Hadith of Bukhari in (52.233) states that the Quran was already written while Muhammad was still alive: *"Allah's Apostle forbade travel to hostile countries with a copy of the Quran."* If there was a written version of the Quran during Muhammad's life, what became of it? A manuscript, the one in Tashkent, dates from the time of Caliph Uthman, who left a sample of his blood inside. If that is the case, it would be so easy to do a DNA test in order to authenticate the story.

Some skeptics accused Muhammad in (16.103) of simply repeating what someone had whispered in a barbaric language to him: *"He who instructs him is only a man."* But Muhammad refutes this by saying that what he preaches is in a *"pure Arabic language,"* according to (26.195). In fact, the first biography of Muhammad was written by Ibn Ishaq more than a century after the Prophet's death. Other versions, such as the one by Tabari, were written two centuries after his death. Why such a long delay?

Abrogating verses and abrogated verses:

What was the first verse whispered by the angel Gabriel and recited by Muhammad? What was the last one? The Quran, like the New Testament, has a problem with its chronology. The revelations took place over a period of twenty-three years in Mecca and in Medina. Why did the authors of the Quran classify the verses according to their length and not in chronological order, not according to the different locations, not even in any logical order? The chronological order of the verses would have shown the temporality of the verses, written to meet the needs of the moment and not according to the revelation of an eternal God.

Logically, the Quran had to be divided in two parts, the suras said in Mecca and those later said in Medina. Those of Mecca, the first ones, before the Hegira, eighty-six in number, are shorter and ask for morality and charity, because in the early years Muhammad and his group were weaker than the infidels of Mecca, and preached tolerance and coexistence. The verses of Medina, twenty-eight in number, are said after 622, when Muhammad, stronger, goes on the offensive, has political ambitions, became intolerant and aggressive toward non-Muslims.

To understand the thinking of Muhammad, it is essential to find the chronological order of the verses and their contradictions. For example, the verse (2.256) *"no compulsion in religion"* chronologically precedes intolerant verses (8, 39), (9.5). And certain later verses abrogate some earlier ones. This is proof that these verses are not divine. In (2.106) and (16.101): *"We abrogate a verse, we bring a similar or better," "We may substitute one revelation by another, because God knows what He reveals."* And so we can find in the Quran a sentence and the opposite. Muslims explain this principle with an analogy: a doctor changes his treatment according to the patient's condition. But then why mix the verses in the Quran rather than classify them according to their chronology and the health of the sick? And how to know what is the last verse, the good one?

The Quran (5.15) says about Jews and Christians: *"Our apostle came to you to expose a large part of the book that you are hiding and to erase an important part of it."* Can Muhammad erase what God said to Jews and Christians prior? The Quran itself—(7.203), (8.31), (11.35), (29.50), (30.59)—reported the skepticism of the disbelievers who accused Muhammad of being an impostor: *"When you come with a verse, they say, did you not invent that?" "All these are nothing but old stories that He invented . . ."* "*What signs of his God does he show!" "You are only an impostor...* Yet, in (6.34) Muhammad said that *"no one changes the words of Allah."* Also in (6.115): *"nothing can change his decrees,"* and also in (10.64): *"the words of Allah do not change."* This makes sense because God sets his laws without making mistakes. If God inspired Muhammad, why is he hesitant? Muhammad corrects himself according to the situation. Those skeptics Muhammad tried to convert accused him and in (32.3) complained by saying: *"If only the Quran were revealed to him in one piece."* Each time Muhammad paid them a visit, his verses were different and sometimes contradicting. The Quran (13, 39) recognizes the temporality of the sacred texts and writes: *"Every age has its book. Allah clears and confirms what He wants."* How many verses have been changed or canceled? We can find a tolerant verse written during the beginnings of the Quran in Mecca and another fanatical verse written later in Medina, during the time of the conquest.

4

Who wrote the other sacred books of the Jewish Bible?

Believers and religions experts are not unanimous about the authors of the prophecies and other writings. Joshua would have written the last eight verses of Deuteronomy and also the book of Joshua, except the story of his own death, which would have been written by Eliezer, the son of Aaron, or by the prophet Samuel. Samuel would have written the Book of Judges, but some believe that Solomon is the author. The remark of Judges (19.1), *"at that time, Israel had no king,"* seems to indicate that Israel had a king at the present time and some believe that the chapters after chapter 24 were completed by Gad and the prophet Nathan.

Samuel also wrote most of the chapters of I Samuel (see I Sam 10. 25). The prophet Isaiah wrote the rest of I Samuel and II Samuel and I and II Kings. Samuel and Isaiah would have compiled the old stories of the prophets living in the time when these events took place.

Hezekiaou the king and his assistants would have written the Book of Isaiah, the proverbs of Solomon and Ecclesiastes. According to Jewish tradition, the elders at the time of Ezra would have written the books of Ezekiel, the Minor Prophets, and Daniel and Esther. The book of Isaiah was written by Isaiah, who lived around 742 BC. Experts say that this book should be divided into two parts, with two authors. The second part, from chapter 40, was written by another scribe after the return from exile, 200 years after Isaiah. According to the elders of the Talmud, King Hezekiah wrote the book of Isaiah, Proverbs, and Ecclesiastes. So the prophet Isaiah is not the author of his prophecies.

The Psalms were written by David, though some argue that parts were written by Moses or Solomon or other scribes after the exile of Babylon.

For the rabbis, the men of the great assembly would have written the texts of Ezekiel, the twelve minor prophets, Daniel, and Esther. Ezra would have written not only the book that bears his name, but also the Book of Nehemiah and Chronicles. For the Talmud, Baba Batra 15a, the book of Jeremiah was written by Jeremiah, who also wrote the books of Kings and Lamentations. Jeremiah would witnessed the destruction of Jerusalem, but why does he use the third person after chapter 25? It would be because his book was destroyed by king Jehoiakim and he was obliged to rewrite another. But how did Jeremiah remember exactly the first book if it was destroyed? Is the second version identical to the first, or has it been modified?

The book of Job is an enigma, and if some claim that Moses wrote it, others claim it was written centuries later, during the time of the judges. A minor rabbi of the Talmud even says that Job never existed. In fact, we know nothing about Job.

The book of Ezekiel describes little except that its author was the son of Buzi the priest, and that he suffered deportation. But some rabbis say that this book was written by the wise men of the great assembly, who also wrote Daniel and the book of Esther.

The Talmud (Baba Batra 14.72) says that Ezra wrote Chronicles. But Abrabanel, in the introduction of the Book of Samuel, wrote that it is not Samuel who wrote the Book of Samuel, and Ezra did not write the Chronicles but only harvested earlier traditions.

This short chapter has highlighted doubts about the authors of these sacred texts because in fact, we do not know who wrote these texts, if there is only one author, and if these texts were revised several times.

Exodus (20.4) says that the sins of the fathers will be upon the children in the third and fourth generations. But Deuteronomy (24.16) says the contrary:" *sons shall not be put to death because of fathers.*" And the prophet Ezekiel (18.20): *"a son shall not bear the iniquity of his father."*

Repetitions inside the texts are inexplicable. Just fold the pages of your Bible. For example, Isaiah (36.4) repeats exactly what is said in 2

Kings (18, 19) or Jeremiah (52) repeats what is said in 2 Kings (24.18), or 2 Samuel (22) repeats Psalm (18). Jeremiah, inspired by God, repeats himself because (6.12) is similar to (8, 10); (10, 11) copy (51.14); (16.14) copies (23.7); and (30.10) copies (46.27). Of course, the believers say that the texts were written from two contemporary witnesses describing the same episode. But using exactly the same words is highly suspicious!

Deuteronomy (17.16) prohibits the king from having many horses, yet King Solomon, God's beloved, violates this rule in 1 Kings (5.6): *"Solomon had 40,000 stalls for his chariots and 12,000 horsemen . . .,"* while in II Chronicles (9.25), *"Solomon had 4,000 stalls for horses and chariots and 12,000 horsemen . . ."* I Kings (10.26) mentions other numbers: *". . . Solomon had 1,400 chariots and 12,000 horsemen."* The Talmud, Sanhedrin 21b, tries to explain it through illogical pirouettes.

In II Samuel (24.13), *"So Gad came to David, saying . . . Would you like seven years of famine in your land, or . . ."* But in I Chronicles (21.11): *"Gad went to David . . . Accept either three years of famine, or . . . ."* A Jewish wise man, the Radak, explained that the country was already having three years of famine; plus three years, this adds up to six, and to have seven we need to add a year without harvest. Okay, but where do you start counting?

In II Samuel (6.23), *"Michal, the daughter of Saul had no child till the day of her death."* But in II Samuel (21.8): *"The king took . . . and the five sons that Michal, daughter of Saul, bore to Adriel of Meholah, son of Barzillai."* To have Michal as wife, David brings the philistine 100 foreskins for II Samuel (3.14) but only 200 for 1 Samuel (18.25).

In 1 Kings (9.23), *"The chief leaders, placed by Solomon to oversee the workers, numbered 550 . . ."* While according to II Chronicles (8.10): *"The chief leaders placed by King Solomon numbered 250 . . ."* Rashi explains that this difference comes from the fact that there were 300 foreign leaders. Where does he draw this information? In another discrepancy between (I Kings 5.29), *"3300 men were responsible for policing the workers,"* but II Chronicles (2.17) says: *"3600 leaders were responsible for the people at work."* Rashi explains this distortion of 300 foreign chief leaders by saying that they were assistant chiefs included in Chronicles but excluded in the book of Kings. It would explain these two discrepancies. But this is not convincing because there is an attempt to make all these workers, including the assistant chiefs, out to be foreigners and admit that Solomon used his own subjects as slaves. So why did they say "to oblige our people to work" if these workers are foreigners? It seems strange that impure foreigners had built the first temple, including the Holy of Holies.

The book II Chronicles (13) says that during a battle between the kingdoms of Judah and Israel *"and there fell of Israel on this day 500 thousand chosen men."* Of course this number is impossible! In I King (16.6): *"Baasha, having slept with his fathers, was buried in Tirzah; he was succeeded by his son Ela . . . In the 26th year of the rule of King Asa of Judah, Elah son of Baasha became king Israel."* But in II Chronicles (16.1): *"the 36th year of the reign of Asa, Baasha, king of Israel, came up against Judah . . ."* If Baasha died in the twenty-sixth year of the reign of Asa, how can he go up against Judah ten years later? The rabbis explain that the thirty-sixth year should not be counted from the reign of Asa but from the beginning of the kingdom of Israel. The count should start after the division of the kingdom of Solomon into two kingdoms. They want us to believe the contrary to what is clearly written.

In II Kings (8.26), Ahaz became king at the age of twenty-two, while in II Chronicles (22.2) Ahaz became king at age forty-two. How do the rabbis explain this difference? Again, through a round of twists and turns, they explain that King Jorum, the father of Ahaz, lost his authority and was only king in name.

In II Kings (24.8), Jehoiachin became king at the age of eighteen, while in II Chronicles (36.9) he was much younger, only eight years old. Here again, they say that the father of Jehoiachin had his son enthroned at the age of eight years but he remained active as king for ten more years.

In I Samuel (9, 17), Saul is anointed king by Samuel, who received a divine revelation. Yet further in I Samuel (10, 21), it was by a draw that Saul was chosen as king. The third version, in I Samuel (11), says Saul became King after unifying the people and winning the battle against the Ammonites. But I Samuel (11.7) said: *"He sent messengers throughout the territory of Israel . . . The children of Israel were 300,000 and there were 30,000 of Judah."* Chapter 11 was probably written after the division of the kingdom of Solomon into two territories. Israel and Judah were never known as two entities before the separation. And the census in the desert gave more than 600,000 adult males. What happened to the more than 270,000 missing Hebrews?

In II Chronicles (28.19), *"the Eternal humiliated Judah because of Ahaz king of Israel."* Huge mistake, because Ahaz was king of Judah! And in II Chronicles (3.4), the height of the porch was 120 cubits or about 60 meters, a great porch unless it was a mistake, because I Kings (6.2) states that the entire building was only 30 cubits high. In II Samuel (23.8), *"the head guard... killed 800 men with his spear,"* but in I Chronicles (11.11), *"he raised his spear, making 300 corpses."* In 1 Kings (7.23), the diameter of the basin was 10, the circumference was only 30. Where they unaware of Pi = 3.14?

The three religions contradict each other. If one religion is right and holds the truth, it means that the other two are wrong. A perfect example could be regarding the Messiah, who had not yet appeared for Jews while Jesus was the Messiah for the Christians.

5

Is Oral tradition the answer to all the contradictions?

Was there a second Torah that was oral and not written? The rabbis say that along with the written Torah known by everyone another Torah was transmitted orally from generation to generation from the time of Moses. These orally transmitted laws, they say, preceded the written Bible and were given to the Hebrew people by God in Sinai. Certain Jewish sects like the Karaits and the Samaritans, as well as most Christians, refute these oral laws and consider them to be of human source, not from God. Which version is the real one?

Do we need an oral version of the Torah?

Abraham, according to Genesis (26.5), was blessed and received *"my commandments, my statutes and my doctrines."* The word *commandments* is a translation of the plural of "Torah." The plural would mean that there are two Torah, one written and one oral. But the Torah was not yet transmitted at the time of Abraham. Often, the rabbis state that long ago nothing was written down and that oral tradition was frequent because most men did not know how to read or write. This argument was used over and over again by the three religions. However, when you read Exodus (17.14) and

(24.4 and 7) you might think differently, because it says: *"YHWH said to Moses, write this as a memorial in the book . . . Moses wrote all the words of YHWH and all the statutes . . . and he took the book of the Covenant, which he read to the people,"* which means that Moses did write a book. But where is this book that is never again mentioned? In what language was this book written? Not in Hebrew but in Egyptian, because that was the language of Moses, the Egyptian prince! The whole book of Genesis takes place centuries before Moses. Who transmitted the legends of Creation to Moses? Is it God? If not, the story of Creation should be rejected!

In Deuteronomy (29.28), it is written: *"The secret things belong to YHWH, our God, but the revealed things are for us and our children till the end of time so that we may do all the words of this Torah."* This verse makes it clear that the commandments must be respected as written and not be extrapolated or changed! Thus, the written laws would not need to be explained, and there would be no need for any explanation or oral tradition from the rabbis.

The concept of an oral Torah appears nowhere in any of the writings, and God never ordered anyone to follow the oral traditions of the Torah. If the oral version of the Torah coexisted with the written Torah, why did the rabbis add new rules as the centuries went on? Why didn't they just reveal everything at one time? If it is true that God wanted an oral tradition of the Torah, why then did the rabbis disobey him by writing it in the Talmud? If this divine oral law was passed down from generation to generation, there should be no discussion among the wise men about its meaning, but just one clear command.

Each page of the Talmud contains different opinions of rabbis on all subjects. In the Talmud, Baba Batra 15a and b, some rabbis affirm that the character of Job is a parable and he never existed. Those who do say he existed don't agree on the time he lived. Some say he was a contemporary of Moses, while others say he lived during the days of Ahasuerus. The opinion of the majority was kept; the opinion of the minority was noted but rejected. How can this minority opinion be divine and yet rejected by rabbis? These discussions are proof that there is no divine oral law, only the views of human rabbis.

Another example, the Talmud, Sanhedrin (99 a) describes several opinions about the arrival of the Messiah. If there had been only one oral law, there would be only one version. Would the Messiah arrive *"when darkness will cover the world"* or *"the days of the Messiah will last 40 years"* according to rabbi Eliezer or *"70 years"* according to rabbi Ben Azariah or *"the Messiah has already arrived in the days of Hezekiah"* according to Hillel. The different views of the rabbis therefore prove that there was no preexisting oral law, but only the fixation on the doctrines during this period.

The oral laws were created to give power to the Rabbis

The oral laws should explain only obscure points of the written Torah and not create new laws. For example, what should a person do or no do on Shabbat? The Bible does not enumerate any bans, yet the rabbis gave thirty-nine of them. The sentence *"You shall not boil a calf in its mother's milk"* should be understood simply as it is written and not as claimed by the rabbis, who forbid eating any meat, including chicken, with any dairy product.

To impose their power, the priests included in the Bible the famous verse from Deuteronomy (17.8) that recommends: *"If a matter of judgment is hidden from you... you shall come to the Kohanim, the Levites or the judge who will sit at that time... You will act according to their statement and get care to comply with any instructions... And whoever does not obey the decision of the pontiff... This man must die..."* This verse reinforces the monopoly of the tribe of Levites and appears in Deuteronomy, written and added later. Let us remind the rabbis that this power is also for the judges.

According to the rabbis, to deny the oral law is equivalent to denying the written law. Flavius Josephus related in his book *Jewish Antiquities* that the Pharisees asked people to respect a certain oral tradition, while the Sadducees require people to only respect the written laws. Therefore, if the Sadducees sect had survived, oral tradition would not have existed. The rabbis defend the Pharisees, so often criticized for their oral tradition, and say that they have managed to keep the Jewish people united. Many ancient peoples have disappeared; the Sadducees, Karaites, and other Jewish sects who rejected the oral tradition are all gone and only the rabbinic Judaism practicing the oral tradition remains today despite hatred and genocide. This is true, but the Jewish religion has only 15 or 16 million believers, while Christianity and Islam each have over a billion believers. Funny success! Furthermore, is the preservation of a people the ultimate goal? The rabbis also say that those who doubt the oral law will eventually leave Judaism.

This is not a good argument, because if the spoken commandments are false, we must not adopt it. Rabbis, priests, and imams have answers to all the questions and are able to describe heaven, hell, and reincarnation. But when they have no answer to a subject like the birth of a baby born crippled or blind, they recognize that *"God's ways are inscrutable."* God did not give them all the answers!

At the beginning of our era, before and after the exile, rabbis put the oral laws in writing and composed the Mishnah. During the fifth century, other rabbis wrote the Guemara, which is a collection of works from the Mishnah. The Talmud includes the Mishnah and the Guemara. But there are two Talmud, the one written in Jerusalem in 370, which differs in some respects from the more important one written in Babylon in 650. In Judaism today, the Talmud and the lessons of the rabbis are taught more than the Torah. The *yeshivot* or religious schools dedicate 85 percent of the study time to teaching the Talmud and only 15 percent of the time to teaching the written Bible. They say that *"The written law is like water while the oral law or Mishnah, is like wine."* They also said the study of the oral law is more useful than the Torah.

The Talmud, Hagiga 27a says that the fire of hell has no power over the wise because he is well above humans. For Gittin 57a, *"one that mocks the words of the wise will be boiled in excrement."* Eruvim 21b says to *"be more attentive to the words of the wise than to the words of the Torah as . . . for he who transgresses the orders of the wise deserves the death penalty . . ."* The rabbis add that even if we think that a rabbi made a mistake in the transmission of the oral law, we have to execute what the rabbi says anyway because God told us to listen to the rabbis. Baba Batra 12a says that a rabbi is greater than a prophet. This is exactly the fight of Jesus against the Pharisees on. In Mark (7, 23), Jesus says: *"Stay away from me, you who act like men and despise the commandment."* Or in Mark (7, 8): *"You give up the command of God and follow the tradition of men."*

The oral law "twists" the writings to explain the contradictions

The oral law is not just a *manual* of the written law, it has other purposes that the rabbis avoid mentioning. Aware of the problems of certain texts, they had to *invent* answers to solve contradictions and errors and reconcile the different versions, even if the answer distorts the written law.

A first example: Adam and Eve did not have any daughters and had only two sons, Cain and Abel. Therefore, there were no women to procreate. The oral tradition came up with a strange explanation. In the Hebrew Bible, it is written that Eve gave birth to *"and Cain,"* while for Abel it is written *"and ahiv and Abel (and his brother and Abel),"* and so, they concluded, with Cain, Eve also bore one twin sister, and with Abel she bore two twin sisters. Absolutely illogical!

A second example: In Genesis (6, 3), God punished men and reduced their lifespan to 120 years. However, after this punition, men lived more than 120 years. The commentator Rashi explained that God gave men 120 years on earth to repent or He would cause the flood. Nothing close to the text.

Also in Genesis (21.9): *"Sarah saw the son of Hagar laugh . . ."* and asks Abraham to expel Hagar and Ishmael his son. This reason seems insufficient and Rashi decided that Ishmael was an idolater, committed incest, and was a murderer. Where does he get all this? It is nowhere mentioned in the Bible. As a matter of fact, dozens of Hebrews gave to their children the name of Ishmael until the beginning of Islam in 632. We have a rabbi named Ishmael ben Elisha, active in the Talmud, grandson of Ishmael ben Elisha, high priest of the Second Temple. Ishmael Ben Yose also was a wise man in the Talmud. If, as Rashi said, the name Ishmael designated a murderer and a sinner, Jews would not have given that name to their children. No, the change took place only after the arrival of Islam, which hijacked the name Ishmael! Rashi found an answer to this new contradiction in Genesis (25.9 and 17), *"Abraham was buried by Isaac and Ishmael . . . Ishmael died and joined his ancestors."* So Rashi explained that Ishmael repented and became a righteous man toward the end of his life, and therefore the Jews could give their children the name of Ishmael. Another clue is in the comparison of two texts. In II Samuel (17.25), *"Amasa was the son of a man named Ythra the Israelite who Abigail . . ."* while in I Chronicles (2.17), *"Abigail bore Amasa, Amasa's father was Yether the Ishmaelite."* This confusion shows that for biblical history Ishmael was not an outcast and neither were his descendants.

Hagar took Ishmael on her shoulders when they were sent away by Abraham, but Ishmael was already sixteen years old. A rabbi explains that we must not take the words at face value. The words are very important, yet alterable at will of the rabbis. Esau, whose firstborn rights were stolen by Jacob, would receive our sympathy, but the oral tradition explains the inexplicable by inventing what is not written. They said that Esau was an impious man that practiced idolatry, murder, and adultery. Rashi said that after the death of Sarah, Abraham married his former slave Hagar, whose name was changed to Keturah. Where is that written? Nowhere! So what right does he have to say that?

The name of Avraham was Avram, which is the blending of Av-Aram, which means *father of the country of Aram*. Then when God chose him to be the patriarch of Israel, he became Avraham, blending the words: *Av Amon Goyim*, which means *father of many nations*. Now the letter R should disappear. Rashi explained this error by saying that the letter R is part of his former name and could not be removed out of respect.

Moses had received the Torah at Mount Sinai according to some verses and Mount Horev according to others. The Talmud, in the Shabbat Treaty, says that originally it was called Mount Horev but it was changed into *Sinai* because hatred (*sina* in Hebrew) descended on the people on the same day the Torah was given. Did they forget that hatred already existed in Pharaoh's time? But above all, did they forget the correct spelling for Mount Sinai, written with *sameh* = s while the word *sina*, which means hatred, is written with a *chin* = ch?

Yet another example: King David committed adultery with Bathsheba, the wife of Uriah. But this king symbolizes unity, the greatness of the Jewish people and also he is the ancestor of the Messiah to come. So the rabbis have to change the texts, but the texts were unfortunately already written. The solution they found is explained in the chapter on adultery.

How is it possible that Solomon, the beloved king of God, had 1,000 concubines, most of them foreigners and idol worshippers? The answer is that Solomon didn't have sex with these women! So why all these women? Why keep thousands of virgins until their death? Solomon's immorality is even more inexplicable! Joseph married Osnath, the Egyptian priest's daughter. The Targum Yonatan explains that in fact Osnath was the daughter of Dina, who was born after the rape of Shechem. This explanation is totally contrary to the biblical writings.

Can the oral tradition and the rabbis change the written law?

God's biblical law condemns adulterers and homosexuals to death; however, this rule is no longer applied. Why? Because God and Moses asked to respect the wise men of every generation and they took the decision to cancel these laws. So the rabbis can change other laws of the Torah (as they canceled the death penalty for adulterers). They could also, if they wish, cancel the *kashrut*, Shabbat, and circumcision.

Jewish by the father or the mother?

The oral law said that it is by the mother, but the Bible repeats dozens of times *"Abraham's semen . . . David's semen . . .,"* which means that the transmission of Jewishness is through the father. Moses had children with Tsipora the Medianite, Joseph with Potiphar the Egyptian priest's daughter, and Solomon had hundreds of foreign wives and concubines. From these relationships were born thousands of children that would be considered as bastards according to the rabbis. In I Kings (14.21), King Rehoboam was the son of Solomon and Naamah the Ammonite. Yet not a word about any of these children, are they Jewish? Yes, because these children of a Jewish father were considered Jewish according to the law without having to convert.

The Pharisees altered the paternity rule, and from the second century onward the child of a Jewish father and a non-Jewish mother was not considered Jewish. Only a child born of a Jewish mother is considered Jewish. Why this change?

Some rabbis explain that the 613 orders become mandatory only after the giving of the Torah to Moses at Sinai, and so Jewishness came from the father before the Torah and from the mother after the giving of the Torah. Yet, according to Numbers (31), so after the giving of the Torah, Moses ordered the conquest of the Promised Land, killed all the men of Midian, and captured women and children. Moses became angry and ordered: *"Kill all male children and all women . . . Those who have not lived with a man, let them live for you."* These virgins of Midian would later give birth to bastards according to the rabbis, but nothing is said about their conversion. How could Moses order taking in the virgins of Midian and at the same time prohibit mixed marriages? Similarly, in Deuteronomy (21.11), when the Hebrews took possession of the Promised Land, *"a woman's beautiful figure, and you like her and you want to marry her, she shall shave . . . head and cut the nails . . . and she will become your wife."* No mention of conversion of these non-Hebrew women who give birth to

Jewish children. In the New Testament, there is further evidence that Judaism is transmitted through the father. Indeed, the first Nazarenes, before becoming Christians, retained circumcision and the dietary laws for all, converted Jew or Gentile. In Acts (16.1), Paul was forced to circumcise his disciple Timothy: *"Timothy . . . Paul wanted to take him with him . . . He circumcised him, for all knew that his father was a Greek."* His father was Greek but not his mother!

The Messiah in Judaism and also in Christianity is a descendant of the lineage of the father, David and Joseph, not of the mother. The genealogical lists given by Matthew and Luke show a patriarchal system. The rabbis use two verses to prove that they are faithful to the biblical writings: Deuteronomy (7.3) cites *"your daughter do not give her to his son, and his daughter do not take her as the wife of your son . . . Or else it would detach him from Me . . ."* This verse condemns intermarriage. At the time of Judges, Ruth, the Moabite wife of Naomi's son, follows her stepmother to the Promised Land to Bethlehem after her husband dies. There, she married her second husband, Boaz. No religious conversion was ever imposed on Ruth. Their child would be the descendant of King David and Jesus. This story also contradicts the divine order in Deuteronomy (23.4): "An Ammonite or Moabite will not be admitted into the assembly of Yahweh even after the tenth generation." The rabbis explain that this rule applies only to men and not to women. This argument must be rejected because the Bible does not mention women separately. To the contrary, (23.9) says that the son of Egyptians *"may be admitted into the congregation of YHWH in the third generation"* with no mention of conversion.

The rabbis also use Ezra (10.3) to explain why Jewish roots are only gained through the mother. A certain Chehania writes: *". . . God make it our commitment to turn away all these foreign women and their children . . ."* This proves that the children of these non-Jewish wives were themselves gentiles. Yet, further down, Ezra (10,11 et 19) mentions that only the foreign women and not their children are sent away.

If Jewishness come from the women, Ishmael is not Jewish because he is the son of Hagar. In that case, why are Jews, especially rabbis, called Ishmael? Note also that the title of *Cohen* is transmitted through the father, not the mother! So Jewishness, which was from the father, became Jewishness from the mother. Why this change? The reason is mostly historical and not theological. It is easy to prove Jewish origins through the woman's lineage but it is very hard to determine paternal origins. During times of war, the Roman soldiers killed their male enemies and raped the women. Therefore, it would have been very inconvenient to have all these bastard and non-Jewish children running around.

Another example, the Prozbul or how to change the written law:

In Deuteronomy (15.1), *"every 7 years, you will practice the remission of law . . . Every creditor shall remit his debt."* This divine law, beautiful and socially progressive, was difficult to enforce because creditors did not want to lend in the years preceding the cancellation of debts. This law was also hurting borrowers who couldn't find any more lenders. Hillel, at the time of Jesus, dared to cancel the law set out by God with the famous *Prozbul*! Can a rabbi change God's law? If so, it would also be possible to adapt other archaic laws that are impossible to apply. Yet, in Jeremiah (31, 36) God said that His laws are not to be changed.

The fallow should take place every seven years:

In Exodus (23.10), *"For six years you shall sow your land and gather in the fruit, but on the seventh day you shall give it rest and abandon the fruits . . ."* This beautiful rule is inapplicable, and the Torah does not give enough details on its implementation. What should the people eat during the total fallow year? This could have been a great law if it had clarified that each plot, in its turn, should be unplanted every seven years. The rabbis cannot admit that they are powerless to cancel this incomplete law. They instead used a *trick* and allow a fake sale of the land to non-Jews for a period of one year. And so through this farce Jews can continue to cultivate a land that does not belong to them. At the end of the year, the sale is automatically revoked.

Lending with interest is prohibited:

In Exodus (22, 24): *"If thou lend money to any of my people . . . Require not from him any interest . . ."* Pay attention that the interdiction concerns only lending to Jews by Jews but allows taking interest from Gentiles. To get around the loan to Jew by Jew, the rabbis have found a solution by using a scaffold. For example, when a borrower needs money, he sells his camel to the lender against 100 shekels of silver. The lender pays him 100 shekels against this camel and sells back this camel immediately for 120 shekels, which will be paid by the borrower only after twelve months. Thus, the borrower receives 100 shekels but will pay back 120 shekels a year later. This scaffold system makes the loan with interest possible through Jews. The Quran also prohibits interest loans, and Muslims themselves are also using the same system or another fictitious system of *leasing*.

The *kippah* or the Jewish cap:

The Bible does not say much on this subject except the mention of the tiara for the high priest. The *kippah* became a distinguishing sign for the Jews. Why? The Talmud Kiddoushim (31a) says that a certain rabbi *"did not walk four cubits bareheaded."* This attitude became a tradition among the Jews who wanted to imitate this rabbi, then an obligation under the Shoulhan Aruch, saying that the *kippah* reminds a believer that God is above his head. It is in fact another law imposed by the rabbis to prevent the assimilation of Jews.

Paul, in his Epistle to the Corinthians (I, 11.4), writes: *"Every man who prays or prophesies with his head covered dishonors his chief. But every woman who prays or prophesies with her head uncovered dishonors her chief."* How? Why do the pope and the bishops wear a cap? Why are Catholics to take off their hats when entering a church while the priest always wears a head covering? Why does a Jew cover his head as a mark of respect to God, when for a Christian it is considered a lack of respect? What about the imams, why do they cover their heads?

The Hebrew New Year and the three festivals (see chapter on influences)

Breaks in the oral transmission:

The first break would be the breach of a command found in Deuteronomy (17, 18), which requires from the kings: *"When he holds the royal seat, he will write for himself two copies of this Torah in a book . . . It will remain in front of him because he has to read it all his life . . . so that he respects and executes the entire contents of this doctrine and the present status."* But this commandment seems to have never been observed and is never repeated in the Bible.

The second break happened when the book of the Torah had been lost and found again during the time of King Josiah (see the chapter on this strange find). If the oral tradition existed at that time, the righteous ones who were continuing to practice the commandments should have intervened to assert that they were still practicing the law even in the absence of the book.

The third break took place during the Babylonian exodus. The exiled people certainly did not keep the traditions, and upon returning to the Promised Land they cry with emotion during the public reading of the Torah by Ezra and Nehemiah. In Nehemiah (8.14), *"they found written in the Torah . . . they discover the Feast of Tabernacles, build huts and remained seven days . . . since the days of Joshua the son of Nun, until this day, the children of Israel have not done that . . ."* Which therefore clearly confirm that there was a break in the Feast of Tabernacles. To hide this break that occurred in the written and oral tradition, the rabbis add as a side note *"with such solemnity,"* to say that the Feast of Tabernacles has always been celebrated since the time of Moses. In complete opposition to what is written!

Why did we need the explanation of Rashi in the eleventh century? Rashi wanted to give the simplest explanation for the most obscure verses of the Bible by selecting from among the huge range of opinions. But if there are different opinions, it means that there was no divine oral transmission but the various human explanations for obscure or contradictory verses.

Muhammad misinterprets Jewish oral tradition

Muhammad could not read the Bible, not only because he was illiterate but also because the Bible had not yet been translated into Arabic. The Jews of Arabia orally transmitted to him the legends of the Bible and the opinions of the Talmud, which took a prominent place among the Jews. The Quran makes no difference between the biblical writings and oral tradition, and so is an amalgam of the Bible, Talmud, and fables. For example, the story of Joseph described in the Quran (12) sounds like a legend told in the evening by a fire pit, with errors, such as the currency used at the time, the dirham. Or the story of the crucifixion of Joseph's friend. Crucifixion was used by Persians long after Joseph's time, not by Pharaoh. In the Bible, Joseph's master threw him in prison for trying to seduce his wife, while in the Quran the master believed in the innocence of Joseph. Why was Joseph thrown in jail if the husband believed in his innocence?

Another invention about Abraham reported in the Quran (2,260): Abraham asked God: *"Show me how You give life to the dead . . . He said, take four birds, cut them . . . then put a piece of each on every mountain, and call them back to you. They will come back to you swiftly . . ."* This episode is never mentioned in the Jewish Bible, which tells a totally different story involving a heifer, a goat, and a ram that are cut in half but do not come back to life.

Another example: King David is mentioned in six passages of the Quran but nothing is said about his adultery or his collaboration with the enemies of Israel. Nothing is ever mentioned about Abraham giving his wife to Pharaoh and lying by saying that she is his sister. Two things might be the cause: either Muhammad deliberately erased the depravity of the patriarchs and kings, or he knew only positive fables about the patriarchs that were orally transmitted to him.

Faced with the many contradictions between the words of Muhammad and the Hebrew texts, Muslims assert that Jews had falsified the Bible and that Islam is based on the original text and therefore the truth. However, Muhammad knew just one Bible, the same that existed after the return from the Babylonian exile and the same Bible that Jesus knew. See chapter on the third commandment on blasphemy.

Christianity and its oral tradition!

Luke the Evangelist said that he is transmitting what the *"eyewitnesses have transmitted to us . . ."* Matthew describes the miraculous birth and childhood of Jesus, yet he has never witnessed it because he met Jesus only when he was thirty. Mark accompanied Peter and Paul some twenty years after the death of Jesus. John wrote his gospel some seventy years after Jesus's disappearance. Finally, there is Paul, who acknowledged that he never met Jesus during his lifetime. In the New Testament, the texts are presented in a nonchronological order. Paul's texts are placed after the Gospels, and this is certainly to hide the important influence of Paul, who was the true founder of Christianity (explained more in detail in the chapter "Who Wrote the Sacred Texts?").

Facing issues with the early believers, opponents, and skeptics, evangelists were forced to invent answers and included them in their texts. These additions are in fact a disaster for Christianity because the comparison of texts with their additions shows that these texts are neither divine nor do they describe actual facts. In Mark (7.1), Jesus opposed the Pharisees, who added to the written law: *"You give up the command of God for the tradition of men."* Jesus was actually the first Karaite, a Jewish sect that flourished in the eighth century, and like Jesus and the Sadducees, rejected the oral laws adopted by rabbis and retained only the written texts. Karaism accepts interpretations of the text when it is not clear, but these interpretations could be challenged and could evolve while respecting the written text. After its golden age during the tenth century, Karaism declined and only counted a few thousand followers.

Yet on the other hand, for Christianity, like Judaism, God's revelation could not be confined solely in written texts. In John (21.25), *"Jesus did many other things . . . I do not think the world itself could not contain the many books that would be written."* Paul, in II Thessalonians (2.15) and I Corinthians 11, 2 tells his disciples: *"Therefore, brothers . . . hold the traditions which you were taught by us, either orally or in writing." "I congratulate you on that in everything you remember me, and hold the traditions as I have sent them."* Traditions, only several years imposed by Paul, Jesus was made divine, because only God could change the law He gave, and to impress the pagans.....?. But if Jesus is divine, there would not only be one God, but two. Why the Trinity? After the death of Jesus, his disciples changed many of the laws of God, such as the *kashrut*, circumcision, Shabbat, or the holidays. If these followers are only human, they have no authority to change the laws of God. In addition, they cannot themselves be divine as this would lead to the pagan polytheism. What is the answer given? It is said that they are acting under the influence of the Holy Spirit. Just like the famous Jewish oral tradition changed the laws, it granted the disciples, and later the papacy, a great and necessary infallibility. The Holy Spirit is a necessity that gives the disciples the dimension they do not have. In Matthew (10, 20), Jesus gives confidence to his disciples who were not educated or talented. He said: *"It is not you who speak, but the Spirit of your Father speaking through you."* Therefore, if it is the Spirit of the Father, one must observe the words of the disciples like they were those of God.

Through this, the Church later established its sprawling power without argument from anyone because it had received its infallibility through the Holy Spirit.

In John (20, 22), hours after his resurrection, Jesus *"breathed on his disciples and said to them, Receive the Holy Spirit. Those whose sins you forgive are forgiven; whose sins you retain, will be retained."* But if the disciples had already received the Holy Spirit, why did Jesus send it again? Acts (1.8) says: *"You will receive power when the Holy Spirit has come upon you. You will be my witlessness . . ."* And in Acts (2.2 to 4): *"Then there appeared to them as tongues of fire . . . They were all filled with the Holy Spirit."*

Paul preferred to use the appearances of Jesus, more convincing than the Holy Spirit, on the road to Damascus, to Corinth (Acts 18.9), and to Jerusalem (Acts 23.11). Peter used the Holy Spirit when he needed to give power to his words. In Acts (10.47): *"While Peter was speaking, the Holy Ghost fell on all of them who were listening to him."* The Holy Spirit seems to appear when you need it, and when Peter was caught eating unclean food, he used the Holy Spirit in Acts (11.1 to 10) to cancel the Jewish rules and ate the forbidden reptiles. It's an easy process, and anyone could use it to explain any improper action. In Acts (8.17) and (19.2) it says: *"And the apostles laid on them their hands, and they received the Holy Spirit."* And *"Paul laid hands on them and the Holy Spirit came on them, and they spoke in tongues and prophesied."* The apostles are now able to transmit the Holy Spirit.

This transmission of the Holy Spirit allowed generations of popes to gain great power and influence. Yet that type of infallibility is contrary to what is written in Romans (3, 10 and 23): *"There is none righteous, not even one . . . for all have sinned and come short of the glory of God."* Acknowledging its mistakes, the Church would admit that the Holy Spirit has not been fully transmitted. Since its beginning, Christianity has lost contact with Jesus, who was a very orthodox Jew. He opposed the conquest of Judaism by the Pharisees who had a preference for oral traditions over written texts. For him, as for the Karaite sect, written texts had to prevail. His refusal of oral traditions is the main reason why the rabbis boycotted Jesus. Christianity adopted the Jewish Bible and calls it the Old Testament, but rejected the later texts such as the Talmud. Thus, it cannot, unlike Judaism, use the Jewish oral tradition and their arguments, even if they are misleading. So how do they explain the adultery of David, supposed to be the ancestor of the Messiah?

The oral tradition and the Hadiths of Islam

The Hadiths are words attributed to Muhammad or to contemporary observers who reported on his doctrine and on his public and private life. These Hadiths range from a total of 7,000 to some 50,000 depending on who you ask. They were put in writing some 200 years after Muhammad's death by Bukhari, Muslim, Dawud, and Malik, and classified according to their degree of reliability. Bukhari collected around 300,000 Hadiths but authenticated only 7,000. Tens of thousands of Hadiths are therefore incorrect. How can we be sure that the selected Hadiths are authentic and not fake ones? How can we find the true words of Muhammad transmitted seven generations later? According to Muslim believers, these Hadiths are authentic because they were collected after checking their transmission chain. And if there was a doubt or a break in the chain, the Hadith is classified as not being genuine.

Yet compilers like Bukhari lived 200 years after Muhammad, and so some skeptics doubt the authenticity of their work. Muslim scholars from all periods relate their doubts about the authenticity of thousands of Hadiths. Others suspect that Islamic law or Sharia law preceded the Hadiths and received a noble and divine origin by claiming they came from the Prophet Muhammad. Muslims claim that their texts were sufficient to regulate the life of their believers. Yet the five daily prayers, a pillar of Islam, are not mentioned in the Quran but were added by a Hadith. Despite the falsifications and improvements of the Islamic texts, Muhammad is described as violent, sensual, sexual, a robber, murderer.

6

The three religions and their outside influences

The three religions have been influenced by beliefs that preceded them, but of course they say they have received their orders from God. If they admitted outside influence, their faith would be pure plagiarism. How can we explain the similarities between the biblical texts and the legends of Sumer and Egypt? Gary Greenberg's book *101 Myths of the Bible* is a must to understand the influence of exiles.

Judaism and the influence of the two Egyptian exiles

Abraham and Sarah, after having lived in Egypt, returned with their flock. Then, the first exile starts with Joseph, who married Asnath, the daughter of an Egyptian priest. They had two sons, Ephraim and Menashe, who became two tribes of Israel. Did Joseph and his two Egyptian sons introduce some elements of Egyptian culture into Judaism? Joseph's children shouldn't even have been considered Jewish, because of the Pharisee law that you could not be considered Jewish if you were born from a non-Jewish mother. What do the rabbis say about that? They answer that Joseph would have converted his wife and circumcised his children. This is mentioned nowhere in the Torah! Such an important fact should have been. Jacob and Joseph died in Egypt and were embalmed like Egyptians and not buried as Jews.

In Genesis (15.13): *"Your seed should sojourn in a land, where it will be enslaved and oppressed for 400 years."* However, if one counts the years of slavery in Egypt, it has only been 210 years. To that, a rabbi replied that the counting of the 400 years would have begun from the birth of Isaac (why?) and would also include the forty years in the desert with Moses. But how can we include these forty years of exodus in the desert with the so-called period of slavery?

Moses was raised in Egypt by an Egyptian princess at the court of Pharaoh. Therefore, he must have been influenced by traditions and beliefs of ancient Egypt. Egypt worshipped a multitude of deities, but in the middle of the fourteenth century BC, 100 years before Moses, the Pharaoh Akhenaten rejected all gods except the sun god Ra, represented in the form of a disc. This Pharaoh died very young and his successors restored the old beliefs. Scholars argue that he invented the worship of the one god. Is the name Aten (Sun = supreme god) connected to Adon or Adonai, which in Hebrew means Lord God? Did Akhenaten influence Moses?

A book called *The Book of the Dead* found in the Egyptian tombs of the pharaohs proves that a universal monotheism existed. *"You're the One and only God, the God of the earliest beginnings of time . . . You created Earth and made man."* Life in ancient Egypt was regulated by an omnipotent cast of priests who, like the Hebrew priests, were the only ones allowed to enter inside the temple, called also the house of God, while the simple believers were only allowed to stand outside. Before entering, the priests had first to be purified, cut their nails, and shave their entire body. They were circumcised, and celibacy was not imposed. According to the story of Joseph, Genesis (47.22), *"the priests received a fixed portion from Pharaoh and they ate the portion allocated by Pharaoh."* These priests of Egypt did not have a full-time job but received their food from Pharaoh. Is the Hebrew sect of priests a product of the Egyptian exile?

Deuteronomy (22.11) forbids Hebrews from wearing clothes of mixed material, such as wool and linen. Why? No explanation is ever given. Maybe the explanation comes from Egypt? Indeed, according to Herodotus, the famous historian of the fifth century BC who traveled through Egypt, *"The Egyptian clothes were made of linen, with fringes around the legs . . . They wrapped themselves in a white wool coat. But they do not wear the wool coat inside the temple, and we do not bury them with this dress. The laws of religion forbid it."*

Also for Herodotus, the fringes on the Egyptian clothes served only as ornament but they were necessary because they prevented the clothes from fraying. Similar to Deuteronomy (22.12), which orders: *"You shall make fringes with the cords around the garment with which you cover yourself."* In Numbers (19), God commands: *"to choose you a red cow, intact that has no fault . . . We shall kill it . . . The pontiff Eliezer will scoop the animal's blood with his finger . . . seven sprinklings . . . we will then burn the cow . . ."* This command has no meaning and is not understood till today. Did the Hebrews borrow the sacrifice of the red cow from the Egyptians? This sacrifice existed in Egypt and would have replaced the previous sacrifice of human redheads in honor of the god Osiris. The sun god Ra had many names, including a secret name, and the Egyptian gods destroyed mankind by a flood. Herodotus reported that circumcision was practiced in Egypt for reasons of cleanliness. Baby Moses was already circumcised when he was found by the Egyptian princess. If it was not noticed by the Egyptians, it means that the Egyptians too were circumcised. So was circumcision a product of the Egyptian exile? See chapter on Circumcision.

Also, *"The Greeks wrote . . . starting their hand from left to right, the Egyptian from right to left."* Just like the Hebrews! Sacrifices were practiced in Egypt: *"The animal is led to the marked altar where he should be slain, the fire is lit, then the wine is poured on the altar and near the victim, the animal is then slaughtered after invoking God . . . in order to chase away misfortunes."* The Egyptians see the pig as an unclean animal. No Egyptian will use the same knife or a pot than a Greek. Similar to Judaism.

The snake that pushes Eve to eat the forbidden fruit would come from Egyptian mythology, which deified the snake. The snake is also found in Moses, Prince of Egypt, whose stick turns into a snake, and then later in Numbers (14.9) God commands Moses to make a bronze snake to heal the Hebrews who were bitten by the poisonous snake. Solomon himself was also married to one of Pharaoh's daughters, for whom he built a temple. The New Testament confirms in Acts (7.22) that Egyptian influence existed: *"Moses was wise in all of the wisdom of the Egyptians."*

The second exile in Egypt

Nebuchadnezzar destroyed Jerusalem and exiled the Judean elite to Babylon. The Judeans who stayed in Jerusalem murdered king Gedalia, who was deposed by the conquerors and *"soon all the people, great and small, and the leaders feared the Chaldeans"* according to II Kings (25.26) and Jeremiah (43.6). Probably some of them returned to Judea as Jeremiah prophesied (44, 28): *"Only a few who escaped the sword shall return out of the land of Egypt to the land of Judah."* What did they bring back from this second Egyptian exile?

The influences of the two Babylonian exiles:

The first exile: Ten of the twelve tribes inhabited the northern kingdom of Israel, destroyed around 722 by the Assyrians. These ten tribes were exiled to Assyria and then lost. In reality, only a portion of the ten tribes was exiled and most remained in Israel and lived with *"the people from Babylon, from Couta, and from Hamat"* brought to Samaria to replace the exiled population, according to II Kings (17, 35). About 20 percent of the population of the northern kingdom was deported to Assyria and a similar number took refuge in the southern kingdom of Judah and the remaining population, almost 60 percent continued to practice the Jewish law, with or without Assyrian influence. Among them the Samaritans, who preserved the ancient Paleo-Hebrew writing while the Judeans adopted the Aramaic square script during the time of exile. This type of writing is still used today.

The second exile: After the destruction of the northern kingdom of Israel by the Assyrians, the southern kingdom of Judah was destroyed by the Babylonians in 586, followed by the deportation of the elite of Judah. But the texts do not seem to agree. In 2 Kings (24), 7,000 to 10,000 people were in the first deportation, and suggests that all the people of Judah were exiled. Jeremiah (52) speaks of three successive deportations of 3,023 and then 832 and 745 people. The numbers listed in the book of Jeremiah seem more plausible. Around 5 to 25 percent of the Jews in Judah were deported. Judah was not emptied of its population during the Babylonian era and so the description of an empty country is a myth made up by the exiled Judean elite to prove that they are the *"true Israel."*

Zoroastrianism is one of the first monotheistic religions with one God: Ahura Mazda. Is it possible that the Jews who went into exile in Babylon drew the concepts of monotheism, Satan, angels, and the Last Judgment from there? King Cyrus was a Mazdean and is described very positively in the Bible as a liberator whom God asked to reconstruct the temple. Deprived of the temple, the Jewish people gave up the sacrifices and established prayer in the synagogues. Fifty years later, around 539, the Persian Cyrus conquered Babylon and then allowed the Judeans to return to Jerusalem to rebuild their temple. Babylon was the most advanced civilization at the time; therefore, to preserve some of the prestige they have lost, it is possible that the exiled Judeans made up Babylonian origins for Abraham by saying he was born in Ur during the time of the Chaldeans, but that area was nonexistent at the time.

The Creation and the Tower of Babel are described in Genesis, which is the first book of the Bible, and then silence. Not a prophet or even a scribe mentions these two extremely important stories. Is it because they were added after the Babylonian exile? Adam and Eve received a great punishment for their sin and no forgiveness was possible. However, Judaism allows repentance and remission of sins. Is this contradiction a product of the mixture of foreign Babylonian myths with Judaism?

The Kaddish was instituted by the sages. It is praise of God said at the time of death to help the soul of the deceased. Why in Aramaic? Because, according to the rabbis, *"the forces of evil speak Aramaic but do not understand Hebrew"* or *"evil forces are terrorized when they hear the Kaddish in Aramaic."* Do not laugh! It would have been more honest to say that this prayer flourished in Babylonia where the Aramaic language was used, and continued after that the Judeans left Babylonia.

Other examples of Babylonian influence can be found in the laws about the birthright and the status of the concubine and her children. And so Ishmael, the eldest of Abraham, had no rights and was driven out with his mother Hagar, according to the code of Hammurabi but contrary to the Law of Moses. Similarly, Abraham's concubine Keturah, who was mentioned in I Chronicles (1.32), disappears from the biblical landscape and her children inherit nothing. The oil poured on the head of the anointed king was a common custom in the Middle East since the fourteenth century BC. The prophet Ezekiel was deported to Babylon in a village named Tel Aviv. This name will be used to designate the economic capital of Israel (3.15). Some claim that the legend of baby Moses, who was found in a floating basket, was copied from that of the Mesopotamian king Sargon. Believers argue the contrary, saying it's the other way around.

In fact, there is a millennium of mingling of neighboring civilizations' traditions and myths. The Code of Hammurabi, discovered in 1902 in the ancient city of Susa, was probably set by a king of Babylon and dated from 1700 and 2000 BC, or 300 to 500 years before Moses. It includes laws engraved on stone that have points in common with the Jewish laws but also differences. They are the emanation of king while the Jewish laws come from God and they worship the images of their gods, while this is forbidden by the Bible.

The Babylonian exile had a decisive importance on the Bible, which would have been written or edited during and after the exile and not by Moses. In the early period of their history, the Hebrews had their own God who led them to victory. It was the period of monolatry. Then a second period with destruction and exile that forced them to recognize that their god was lower than the one of their conquerors, or that their god is punishing them because of their sins, or finally that God is universal and deals with all people. Modern Judaism combines these last two concepts: the universal creator god would have a chosen people, but the Jews are sinners and deserve all the misfortunes that befall them, including the Nazi genocide, and would continue to be punished until the arrival of the Messiah. This half century of exile in the Persian Empire added the story of Moses, a universal monotheism, and turned to the god of the Hebrews who was made god of the universe.

The destruction of the Temple, the exile and the spiritualization of Judaism:

After the destruction of the Jerusalem Temple by the Romans in 70, a small group of Judeans led by Johanan ben Zakkai fled to Yavneh and established an alternative religious center without a temple. A new rebellion in 135, led by Bar Kokhba, was put down by the Emperor Hadrian, which completely destroyed Jerusalem, renamed it Aelia Capitolina. Without a temple, Judaism lost much of its rationale and almost half of the 613 orders of the Bible were no longer applicable. To avoid assimilation, the rabbis pushed to the extreme dietary rules to prevent any Jew from eating at the same table with a Gentile, and gave a list of thirty-nine prohibitions for the Shabbat.

Noah's Ark and the Flood

Because the *"sons of Elohim took wives and Nefilim mingled with human women, YHWH saw that the wickedness of man was great in the earth. YHWH said, I will blot out man whom I have created from the face of the earth, from man to animals, from the insect to the bird in the sky."* Who was guilty, the human or these fallen angels? The Almighty God could have simply waved his hand to make them good! Yet in Genesis (1.31), after creating man, *"God saw all that He had made, and it was very good."* Didn't God know that the man He had created would sin? Why destroy the children and animals, what have they done wrong? On the other hand, why aren't fish and marine mammals (whales and dolphins) destroyed like other animals? After this destruction, humanity did not become better, and God, once again, was mistaken.

In Genesis (6.15), the ark was *"300 cubits long, 50 wide and 30 tall,"* 150 meters long by 25 meters wide and 15 meters high. How can several million pairs of animals enter the ark? A wooden boat of this size without metal reinforcement would break and sink. The flood lasted almost 365 days or more and Noah would have stored in the ark enough food needed for one year. Even a boat the size of the *Queen Mary* cannot contain this number of animals and their food. What did they eat during this long year? At that time, preserves were not yet invented and Noah's family could not eat vegetables and fruits preserved over 365 days. The rabbis answered that Noah's family could have eaten fishes. And the carnivores? Did they devour a cow, sheep, or goat? How did the Australian kangaroo and the salamander of the Galapagos arrive in the ark? How long did it take him? All animals *"that day even entered the ark."* How did millions of species enter into the ark in one day? How did these animals return to their continents? How did the white bear and the elephant survive at the same temperature? A rabbi of the Middle Ages named Nachmanides recognized that it is an inexplicable miracle.

In Genesis (6.18): *"Fifteen cubits above, the waters were high and the mountains were submerged."* According to some, the height of the rain would be 15 cubits or 7.5 meters, which would not cover the highest mountains. According to others it would be 7.5 meters above the mountains, so thousands of meters water. Impossible! Where are those billions of cubic water? In Genesis (8.11*), "the dove returned in the evening, holding in its beak a fresh olive leaf."* This is illogical because the olive trees do not grow at the top of the highest mountain. Indeed, when the waters recede, what appears first is the high land. Generations of archaeologists have searched without success the remains of the ark on the famous Mount Ararat. Yet the highest mountain on earth is not Mount Ararat.

In Genesis (6.19), God commands Noah: *"bring into the ark two of every species, male and female."* But a little later, in Genesis (7.2), God said to Noah: *"You shall take with you seven pairs of every clean animal, a male and its female; a pair of the animals that are not clean . . ."* So is it one or seven pairs of clean animals? Why this contradiction? In Genesis (8.20), Noah used clean animals for sacrifices, which would lead to the disappearance of the pure species if he had taken with him only one couple. It would have been to avoid their disappearance that he took seven couples. But the *kashrut* rules were introduced much later by Moses! Also, how can Noah make a sacrifice, in Genesis (8.20), to appease God if these rules were introduced much later? If there was only one pair of clean animals, the sacrifice made by Noah would have eliminated a pure animal species.

Nothing is said about Noah, *"the just and irreproachable."* But after the flood, in Genesis (9.21), *"he drank his wine, and was drunk, and he began to stand naked in the middle of his tent."* Did he deserve to be saved? Noah, his wife, and three sons would be the only survivors of the flood, so with which woman did his sons have children? By incest?

In Genesis (9.2), God said to Noah: *"Anything that moves, everything that lives, will be your food . . ."* Yet a little later, God established a covenant with Noah and also with *"every living creature that is with you, birds, livestock . . ."* What is this alliance of God with the animals? Another contradiction: in Genesis (6.4), there would be *"Nefilim"* or giants or fallen angels who came to earth before the flood. But in Genesis (7.21), all creatures on land and in the air perished except those located on the ark. So how, in Numbers (13.33), could the spies sent by Moses to explore the Promised Land report: *"We even saw the Nefilim, the children of Anak, descendants of the Nefilim"*?

These incongruities can be explained by bad plagiarism of a double legend. According to Gary Greenberg, author of *101 Bible Myths*, this legend would originate in the Egyptian city of Hermopolis, a legend that the Jewish people would have known during the Egyptian exile. A flood is described on the stele of Nippur in Egypt, which dates from about 3000 years BC. Another origin is Gilgamesh, the hero of a Sumerian legend written almost eighteen centuries BC. Some fragments found date from the seventh century BCE, during the exile of the Judean elite in Persia.

The story of a deluge is too similar to that of the Bible. According to Raymond Tournay in *The Story Begins in Sumer*, the eleventh tablet says: *"... Gilgamesh, do climb inside the boat an offspring of any living being ... domestic and wild animals ... For six days and seven nights, the wind persisted, the torrential storm rattled the earth ... It's Mount Nicir the boat docked ... When came the seventh day, I made out the dove and let her go: the dove went, rushed, but no perch not appearing to it, turned around ... I made out the raven and let him go; Raven went and ... did not turn around. Having everything out to the four winds, I went to sacrifice, I poured an offering to the top of the mountain ... The gods smelt the aroma."*

The mixture of these two influences explain some contradictions of the flood story, which is, in fact, not one but two stories with two different authors. This legend, captured at two exiles, would have been assimilated in the Bible long after Moses. According to the Talmud, Sanhedrin (108b): *"Three copulated in the ark, and were all punished: the dog, the raven and Ham. The dog was ordered to be attached, the raven spits and Ham was punished in his skin."* With whom did Ham copulate?

The Quran described, but in the disorder, the legend of Noah. Sura (23.27): *"Build an ark ... Make enter the ark two of every kind ..."* A pair, not seven pairs of animals. The Quran does not know the refinements of the problem of the sacrifices. The Quran (11.44) adds unknown details of the Jewish Bible and tells of a son of Noah: *"the son was engulfed ... the ark anchored at Mount Judi."* But the Quran contradicts itself since in (21.76): *"And Noah ... We saved the catastrophic cataclysm and his family with him."* According to the Quran, the son of Noah died and the ark rested on Mount Judi, while for the Bible Noah's son is also saved and the ark landed on Mount Ararat. The Quran does not mention that the flood was universal but was a partial destruction, that of guilty people. Finally, Muhammad ignored that Noah *"... planted a vineyard. He drank wine and became drunk, and he began naked in his tent."* Muhammad never mentions the misconduct of the patriarchs and prophets.

The Tower of Babel

According to Genesis 11, *"The whole earth was of one language ... build us a city and a tower, whose top may reach unto heaven ... confound their language ... That's why we named it Babel, because there YHWH confused their language, that they should not understand each other."* The Bible played on words that make sense only in Hebrew: *"This is why it was called Babel, because the Lord balal (confounded) the language of all men..."* But confused = *bilbel* or *balal* in Hebrew, is close but different from *Babel*. The name Babel would have a logical origin: door of god = bab El, and not what is written in the Bible. If we read Genesis (10–5, 20 and 31), which precedes the story of the Tower of Babel: *"Each according to his tongue, his tribe, his people... Nimrod... the beginning of his rule was Babel... These are the children of Ham, by their families and their languages..."* This chapter on genealogy therefore says that people spoke different languages. Note that the episode of the Tower of Babel appears between two genealogies as if it had been inserted later, after the Babylonian exile. It appears in Genesis and then is never mentioned again. No prophet mentions and forecasts the return to a universal language on the coming of the Messiah. Isaiah (13) and Jeremiah (50) mention Babylon but never talk about this tower and the multiplication of languages. This legend about a language being common to all mankind already existed in the Sumerian epic of Enmerkar. The Judeans in exile in Babylon would have been impressed by the high temples of the god Marduk, probably square and not circular. These "skyscrapers" measured over 10 meters.

The Jewish calendar and the influences of the Babylonian Exile

The Torah gives different names to the months of the year. They are numbered 1 to 12, in Numbers (28.16), *"the first month, the 14th day of the month is the eternal Passover,"* and further, (29.1), *"the seventh month, first day..."* Later, after the arrival in the Promised Land, only four months are identified by their names: the first month was Aviv, the month of the departure from Egypt; the second was Ziv; the seventh was Etanim; and the eighth was Bul. In I Kings (6.1): *"... Solomon built the house of YHWH in the fourth year of his reign over Israel, in the month Ziv, which is the second month."* And further, I Kings (6.37), *"the fourth year in the month of Ziv, the foundations of the house of YHWH were laid, and the eleventh year, in the month Bul, which is the eighth month, The house was finished..."* And yet as I Kings (8.2), *"all the men of Israel assembled themselves to King Solomon, in the month of Etanim, which is the 7th month, in the feast."*

But after the second return from exile in Babylon, the calendar changed and took other names that are still used today, including in Israel.

Ezra used numbers to designate the months, but Nehemiah mentions months sometimes by numbers and sometimes by names borrowed from the Babylonian exile: Kislev, Nissan, and Elul, names without any meaning in Hebrew. For example, the month of Nissan or Nissanu in Babylonian is the month of the Passover sacrifice; Heshvan, which means eight in Babylonian, is, however, the second month of the Jewish calendar after the exile; and Adar or Adaru corresponds to the earth work month. But the summit of this calendar is the adoption of the month Tammuz, the name of the Sumerian god of fertility. Ezekiel (8.14) mentions: *"He brought me to the entrance of the house of YHWH Lord ... women sat weeping on Tammuz ... you will see even more great abominations than this one."* And it is after this abomination that the Judeans returning from the Babylonian exile named their month! How many Jews know this? Very ancient texts called *the Babylonian chronicles* and kept in the museum of London describe the capture of Jerusalem by Nebuchadnezzar and use the names of the month of Tevet, Tishri, Kislev Adar, and Nissan. These texts definitively prove that the names of these months are not Hebrew but Babylonian, and that they were assimilated during exile in the fourth century BC.

For Exodus (12.1), the Jewish year begins during the month of Aviv, the month of Passover: *"This month is for you the beginning of the year, it will be for you the beginning of months of the year."* But the Judeans, after the second Jewish exile, changed the calendar and till today celebrate Rosh Hashana or the New Year in September-October and Yom Kippur ten days later. Leviticus (23.24) mentions: *"In the 7th month, on the first day of the month, there will be a solemn rest for you ... But in the tenth day of this month, which is the Day of Atonement..."* No mention that this is the first month of the New Year. Leviticus (23.27) recognizes that Yom Kippur is celebrated on *"the tenth day of this 7th month which is the Day of Atonement."* The seventh month and not first month! In addition, Yom Kippur should have been the last day of the year since we ask forgiveness for the sins of the past year and not be on the tenth day of the seventh month. How could Judaism disobey God and change the date of the New Year? Why are Jews not returning to the original Jewish calendar? Why do they refuse to celebrate January 1, which is the Christian New Year, but they celebrate a new year that is a Babylonian product? The rabbis, as usual, found the answer: they say that Adam and Eve were created in the month of Tishrei, and thus it is when the New Year is celebrated. From where did they know? Where is it written? How is it possible to contradict God who states that the first month is Aviv, in the spring, and not Tishrei, in autumn? The Karaites, Jews who follow only the written law, celebrate the New Year on Aviv 1, in the spring, not in the month of Tishrei, which is around September.

Are Jewish holidays ordered by God or are they agricultural festivals?

In Exodus (23.14), God ordered the celebration of three holidays, *"the feast of unleavened bread . . . the harvest festival. . . the feast of the ingathering (Assif in Hebrew)."* Passover, the feast of matzoth or of sprouting?

The lamb's blood on the door allowed God to recognize the Hebrew people *"and pass over"* without killing them. The lamb was prepared on the tenth day of the month of Aviv, so four days before the escape from Egypt. So why didn't the Hebrews have time to prepare leavened bread? Why did this escape take place on the fourteenth day of the month when there is a full moon? These contradictions and other clues can be explained. Originally, a ritual sacrifice of a lamb was practiced in the spring in order to increase the herd's fertility. Unleavened bread or *matzoth* came from the original sprouting festival held in the spring, during the month of Aviv, as reported in Exodus (23.15).

Shavuot, the gift of the Torah or the harvest festival?

The first fruits of the harvest were probably celebrated without any precise date because the ripening of the wheat varied. That is why we find in the texts two reasons that have no logical link between them. Exodus (23.16) and Numbers (28.26) ordered this feast without setting a date, but Deuteronomy (16.9) sets the date after the seven days of Passover: *"You shall count seven weeks, we will immediately start cutting the harvest."* Thus, just like Christians have set the date of Jesus' birth on the same day as the Sol Invectus, the Roman festival of the sun, the Hebrews fixed the date of the gift of the Torah to the same period as the harvest.

Sukkoth, the festival of tents or the Ingathering festival?

Jews celebrate *Sukkoth* by building a tent to remind them of their wandering in the desert. Lev (23.42), *". . . You will remain in tents for seven days . . . so that your generations will know that the children of Israel dwelled in tents . . ."* However, that date is also mentioned in Exodus (23.16) and

(34.22) as *"the feast of the ingathering..."* Numbers (29.12) mentions that date, but only describing the necessary sacrifices without any mention of tents. King Jeroboam of Israel, wanting to distinguish himself from the traditions of Judah, pushes this festival to the fifteenth of the eighth month, so a month later. Nehemiah (8.14) seems to describe the discovery of the Feast of Tents by the Judeans who returned from exile. This holiday, like Easter, takes place on the fifteenth; that is to say, during the full moon. The Hebrews stayed in the desert for forty years, and there was no historical reason to fix this festival of tents on 15 Tishrei except for agricultural reason. Besides, how can God order in Lev (23.40): *"To take on the first day the fruit of a citron tree, the branches of a palm tree, twigs of a plaited tree, and willows..."* In the middle of the Sinai desert? No, only an agricultural people could have carried these fruits and plants. Is it possible that this tents festival (or ingathering festival) later turned into a religious holiday? These tents were constructed by peasants in the vineyards and fields to be closer at the time of ingathering.

The unleavened feast is linked from the beginning to the Exodus from Egypt. The two other agricultural festivals, the harvest festival and feast of ingathering, are not. They will become the feast of weeks (or the giving of the Torah) and the huts (or *Sukkot*). King Josiah replaced these two agricultural feasts with two religious holidays, requesting the people to assemble in the Temple of Jerusalem. And in Deuteronomy (16.16) he changed their names to *"the feast of the unleavened bread, the feast of the weeks, and the feast of the tents."* This verse mentions Passover as the first feast of the year—further evidence that the year begins with the spring and not with the fall. The three main Jewish holidays were agricultural festivals that preexisted, and instead of fighting against these pagan festivals, religious leaders included them in the sacred texts.

The Book of Esther, Purim and its Babylonian origins

Esther, a beautiful Jewish woman, was chosen by a Babylonian king, Ahasuerus, and with the help of her uncle Mordechai saved the Jewish people from a massacre ordered by the wicked Hamman. This book, included in the Jewish and Christian Bible, is the occasion of the feast of Purim. Yet this story has nothing to do with the Jewish people and contains historical mistakes. The Persian history ignored a Jewish queen named

Esther. The Book of Esther said that the king send his order to exterminate the Jewish peoples in 128 countries. Yet this decree was discovered nowhere during any archaeological excavations. This explains why the book of Esther and Purim are not among the manuscripts of the Dead Sea. Ancient Persia was tolerant and would not issue an order to kill all the Jews. Ahasuerus reigned between 486 and 465 BC. And it is written in (2.6) that Esther came to Suze with her uncle Mordechai during the deportation in exile, which took place in 587 BCE. The beautiful Esther would have been more than 100 years old during the reign of Ahasuerus. How could Esther hide her Jewishness when everybody knew that her uncle was Jewish?

God is never mentioned in this book. Why? Mordechai and Esther's names are too similar to those of the Babylonian gods Marduk, the guardian of heaven, and Ishtar, the goddess of fertility. And finally, the name of this festival, *Purim*, means *dice*, which is weird and inappropriate. The Torah prohibits any innovation, commandments, or festivals. So how is it that the festival of Purim has been added?

The Quran speaks about Haman, (28.8 and 38) and (29.39), but strangely this Haman is the right hand of Pharaoh. How can Pharaoh ask Haman in (40.36): "Build me a tower that I reach the ropes to ascend to heaven the God of Moses." Pharaoh lived centuries before Haman and a thousand kilometers away from him. Muhammad mixed the episodes of Pharaoh, Esther, and the Tower of Babel!

Christianity and its Jewish and pagan influences

Jesus's epic described by the Gospels is a construction built *a posteriori* on previous Jewish prophecies that have nothing to do with Jesus. Christians do not understand that in fact Jesus was a Jew and remained fully respectful of Jewish law. He is circumcised, and after his birth his mother purifies herself at the temple according to Jewish law. Jesus always ate kosher food and never entered the impure house of a non-Jew. Jesus respected the Shabbat and never violated it. He respected the sacrifices in the temple and did not oppose it. Jesus had no intention of changing Jewish law and instead opposed the Pharisees who added new rules. Even his death is that of a Jew. His body is buried the same day in a shroud. Some twenty years after the death of Jesus, Paul appears, who wants to open Judaism to the Gentiles, and removes circumcision and *kashrut* to facilitate their entry.

Christianity is in fact not the religion of Jesus but of Paul. Suppose that the Roman Emperor Constantine did not choose Christianity but Mithraism, which was a fashionable religion in his time, what would have happened? There would be no Christianity, only a small sect called the Nazarene-Notsri within the Judaism.

The resurrection of Jesus is a plagiarism of pagan cults: many religions mention a *"suffering God"* like Tammuz, Adonis, Osiris, Attis, who die and are resurrected. The early Christians knew about those pagan mythologies and this is mentioned in the Gospels. Christian writings are inspired by these myths. Buddha, born of a virgin, would teach at the age of twelve, fed 500 people with a small basket of cakes, walked on water, and presented the other cheek. The Hindu texts mention the metaphor of the mustard seed before the Gospels. Krishna was born of a virgin, purified in a river, named *Good Shepherd*, and was the cause of a massacre of thousands of newborns. Dionysus transformed water into wine. Mithra, sun god of Persia, was neglected for centuries and reappeared around the fourth century BC and became popular in Asia Minor, where Saul-Paul, the founder of Christianity, was born. Alexander the Great conquered territories that practiced the cult of Mithra, a cult already well known in Greece.

The Roman Emperor Commodus was initiated into the cult of Mithra, but it was only after the conversion of Constantine, who converted to Christianity in 312, that the decline of Mithra began. Finally, after a burst under the time of Julian the Apostate (331–363), it disappears forever. The common points with Christianity are as follows: Christians have chosen December 25 as Jesus's birthday, inspired by the winter solstice of Mithraism. Mithra had twelve companions and traveled a lot like Jesus. He was single, but if Mithraism was closed to women, Christianity invited them to join, because Christianity could not give up this public. The women were easy to convert, unlike requiring circumcision for Gentile males.

He was a great sage called the good shepherd, the truth, the way, the light, the savior, and redeemer. He loved people and served as a mediator with the gods. His sacred day was Sunday, called the Lord's Day. He performed miracles. Mithraism includes a *"memorial meal."* *"He who shall not eat my body and drink my blood will not . . . have salvation"* is a sentence of Mithraism that strangely resembles the Christian Last Supper in that the cult of Mithra shares meat and drinks blood. Later, and for simplicity, this is symbolized by the bread, the flesh, and wine, the blood. Like Jesus, he is considered the *"son of the right of brilliant father,"* and like him, he dies and rises. Mithraism also includes *"an initiation baptism."* The shepherds witnessing the birth of Jesus, described by Luke (2.8), have not been randomly selected among other possible witnesses as farmers or winemakers. These same shepherds remind those who helped at the birth of the god Mithra. According to Matthew (23.9), Jesus asked: *"Do not call anyone on earth your father, for one is your Father."* But the head of the Catholic Church calls himself pope = dad, copied from the name of the great Mithras priest who was *Pater Patrum*.

Islam and its many Pagan, Christian, and Jewish influences

Some pagan practices of the time *"of ignorance"* (pre-Islamic) are maintained by Muhammad. The name of Muhammad's father was Abed Allah, or God's servant, and this shows that the God Allah existed among some Arabs. The verse of the Quran (2.184) "You who believe, fasting is prescribed for you as your predecessors" proves that the fast of Ramadan was practiced before Muhammad. Similarly, the Kaaba existed before Muhammad and was worshiped by Arab pagans, who kissed the black stone. A Hadith of Bukhari (3.128) reports that Muhammad replied to his beloved wife Aisha: *"If the people had not been so close to the pre-Islamic period of ignorance, I would have dismantled the Kaaba and opened two doors, one to enter and the other to exit"*—further evidence that the Kaaba is a residue of the pagan period and has nothing to do with Abraham and Ishmael.

Circumcision was also practiced by the Arabs before the coming of Muhammad. The five daily prayers, the ablutions, and the Ramadan would be the product of the Sabaean influence, a sect mentioned in the Quran (2.62), (5.69), and (22.17) to which belonged four members of Muhammad's family. There would also be a plagiarism of Persian and Indian ideas like the description of paradise with its wide-eyed *houris*, called *paaris* in the Persian tradition, and also the night journey of Muhammad on his wonderful Burqa donkey.

Christian influences

The first wife of Mohammed, Kadijah, had a cousin named Warraka who converted to Christianity and could read Hebrew. One verse (16.103) confirmed that some opponents accused Muhammad of receiving his teachings from a Christian blacksmith of Mecca and his answer was: *"We know what they say: the one who teaches him is only a man. But the one they think is of barbaric language while this is of clear Arabic language."*

This argument is weak because Christians of Mecca, as well as Jews, spoke perfect Arabic. Muhammad has learned from this Warraka some expressions from the New Testament: (7.40), *"Those who deny our signs... not come to the garden than a camel in the hole of a needle."* Muhammad knew not the official New Testament, but stories about Jesus reported by disdainful Jews or heretic Christians. The bizarre story of the sleepers in the cave described in the Quran (18.8) is a legend reported by Gregory of Tours a few decades before Muhammad. These seven Christians distribute their goods to the poor and took refuge in a cave and fall asleep for two centuries... The Quran refers to this legend with some variations. The child Jesus giving life to a clay bird, (3.49), is inspired by the apocryphal Gospel of Thomas. Similarly, in (19.22) the baby Jesus sitting under a palm tree and Mary eating the dates come from the apocryphal Gospel of Jesus's childhood. The affirmation of Muhammad (3,157), Jesus, *"They have neither killed nor crucified him, but someone similar was in front of them"* comes from heretical Christians who could not accept that God could be killed.

Jewish influences by biblical and Talmudic stories

Some say that the first translation of the Hebrew Bible in Arabic was that of Saadia Gaon two centuries after Muhammad, and the translation of the New Testament a millennium after Muhammad. Others assert, without evidence, that the Jews living in Arabia at the time of Muhammad would probably have translated their Bible into Arabic. This is unlikely because the Arabic language was not yet established. Anyway, even if there was an Arabic translation of the Bible, the Quran never mentions a written version of the Jewish or Christian Bible, because only verbally transmitted legends and superstitions were known to Muhammad. He was inspired by biblical stories transmitted orally, often erroneously, but also by the Talmud and other Jewish traditions.

Rabbis who dared to read the Quran have discovered the influences of the Talmud and other Jewish texts. Here are some examples. In the episode of Cain and Abel in the Quran (5.31), a crow scratches the earth to bury Abel. This description is a plagiarism of the Targum Jonathan ben Uzziah. The next verse, (5.32), cannot be the logical continuation of the previous verse: *"that is why we have prescribed to the children of Israel that whoever kills . . . it is as if he killed all mankind . . ."* It is inspired by the Mishna, Sanhedrin (4). The name of Abraham's father is *Terah* in the Bible, Genesis (11.26), but *Azar* in the Quran (6.74). Muhammad confused Eli-Azar, the adoptive slave-son of Abraham in Genesis (15.2) with the father of Abraham. The legend related in (21.62), where Abraham broke the idols and accused the greatest idol because it does not speak, comes from a collection of Jewish tales called *Midrash Raba*.

The Bible describes Aaron as the one who built the golden calf, yet despite this sin Aaron became the high priest who alone could enter the Holy of Holies and his family inherited this role forever. Through ignorance or to avoid this imperfection of Aaron, Muhammad gave a different version and accused another, (20.85): *"the Samaritan has led them astray . . . the adornment of the Egyptians . . . the Samaritan also threw them."* But the Samaritans did not exist at the time of Moses! Is it possible that Muhammad had mixed the golden calf with the two golden calves of Jeroboam in Samaria? The verse of Ose (8.5), *"Your calf, O Samaria . . . The calf of Samaria will be cut into small pieces"* has been misunderstood by Muhammad. Muhammad talks about the plagues of Egypt but mistakes them for five instead of ten in verse (7,132) and only nine in verses (17.101) and (27.12).

The Talmud and Jewish legends, more than the Bible, served Muhammad. But the Talmud has not yet been translated into Arabic and it would be his Jewish friends living in Medina that would orally transmit passages from the Talmud and Jewish legends without mentioning that they did not come from the written Torah. Here are some examples. The Quran (21.105) probably cites Psalm (37.11) when it writes: *"After the warning, we have written in the Psalms: our righteous slaves will inherit the earth."* According to (55.19), an impenetrable barrier prevents the sea and the river from mixing. This idea is inspired by Psalm (104.9). The Quran (2,187) says: *"Eat and drink until dawn, not to distinguish the white thread from the black thread."* This verse is copied from the Talmud (Brachot 9B), except that it originally says white and blue thread. Another example is the verse (9.30), which says: *"the Jews say Ozair (Ezra) is the son of God . . ."* This is foreign to the Jewish faith. Where does it come from? Is it a mistake or the beliefs of a Jewish sect?

The Quran (27.18) describes the armies of Solomon *"came to the valley of ants, one ant said..."* and Solomon understands the language of ants. This episode is unknown to the Bible but found in a Jewish text, Otsar Hamidrashim, written some centuries before Muhammad. Muslims pray by bending until their forehead touches the ground, and a practicing Muslim can be recognized from the spot on his forehead. Nehemiah (8.6) reports that Jews *"bowed their heads and worshipped God with their faces to the ground."* So is it possible that this ritual is originally from Judaism and was abandoned by the Jews, only to be used by the Muslims later?

On one hand, Muhammad was influenced by post-biblical Judaism, yet on another, as he grew more and more frustrated by the opposition of the Jews, he tried to move away from this religion. One example is the Muslim calendar. While the Jewish calendar has twelve lunar months and an intercalary month, Muhammad prohibits the intercalary month and complicates the Muslim calendar; and so the holidays are never held in the same season. The word Ramadan means *burning,* but is sometimes celebrated in the winter. Fasting during Ramadan requires a big effort during the long summer days and becomes easier during the short winter days. Muhammad only mentions childish stories written about the prophets of the Bible and completely ignores Isaiah, Jeremiah, and Ezekiel. Muhammad drew his verses from Jewish legends transmitted to him orally, and therefore the mistakes are unintentional or voluntarily committed to suit his needs.

On one hand, the Quran is proud of its biblical sources repeated dozens of times; on the other hand, Muslims cannot accept the claim that the two other religions are older than Islam and say that Islam is the oldest religion, existing since Creation. Muhammad would not be the founder but the last of the messengers after Abraham and Moses, who were also Muslim—that is to say, submitted to the one God. The Quran, (2.53, 3.4, and others) says that God gave the book to Moses, *"God revealed the Torah and the Gospel a long time ago to guide men."* So if the Torah or the New Testament is false, is the Quran itself also false? According to the Quran (60.54), *"We (God) have given the guide to Moses and the book (the Bible) as inheritance to the sons of Israel..."* Muhammad had at least thirteen wives, among them were at least one Jew and one Christian. Did they teach him what they knew about their respective religions?

7

God's chosen people? Cause of anti-Semitism

Is planet Earth chosen by God or is it just another among billions?

The Earth is one among millions of planets and galaxies, and yet God had focused on planet Earth, so insignificant. Yet life on our planet is a miracle that requires several conditions. If the angle of inclination of the Earth was different, if gravity was different, if the distance of the sun to Earth was different, or if the ocean currents were different, life on Earth would be impossible. All the conditions for life are met on the small planet Earth. Is it a coincidence or divine intervention? And what if we discovered life elsewhere?

Was the human species chosen by God?

Religions proclaim that the human species was chosen by God and the Quran (17.70) says: *"The son of Adam . . . We have placed them well above many of our creatures."* God created man, and not the animal, in His image. If that is true, God showed lack of imagination, because man has so much in common with the animals: two eyes, two ears, a nose, the same DNA (close to 90 percent), the same reproductive, digestive, and respiratory systems as mammals. None of the three religions advocate vegetarianism and instead order man to eat animal meat. God Himself too easily destroyed animals by bringing the flood and the ten plagues of Egypt: *"fish of the river died ... the frogs died ... and all the cattle of Egypt died ... And YHWH turned the wind, which took away the locusts and ... drowned in the Red Sea ... YHWH ... slew all the firstborn of the animals."* Some believers hate dogs, explained by Deuteronomy (23.18): *"You shall not bring into the house of YHWH the money of a prostitute or the price of a dog for the fulfillment of any vow, because both are an abomination to YHWH."* Why the dog? Perhaps since the Egyptians worshiped dogs, Judaism wanted to push away this idolized animal. Some Jews believe that by saying the verse Exodus (11.7), *"As for the children of Israel, not a single dog will bark at them,"* a dog stops barking. We bet that this verse does not calm the dogs! For Christians too, humans have no moral obligation toward animals, and Matthew (7.6) says that we must not give what is holy to dogs. And Islam compares the dog to something unclean. Despite this cruelty to animals, Deuteronomy (22.6) says: *"if you come across a bird's nest ... You are required to let the mother fly away before you take the chicks or the eggs..."* Deuteronomy (21.10), *"Do not plow with an ox and an ass together"* because the donkey will suffer on the flat surface and the ox will have a hard time on the steep terrain. But these concerns are, in fact, intended for the benefit of man and not that of the animal.

Individuals chosen by God

There are many stories in the Jewish Bible where a patriarch has two sons and one of them is chosen while the other is disqualified or even cursed without a valid reason. This is the case with Cain versus Abel. Cain gave offerings of vegetables and fruits to God, who refused them but accepted the fatty parts of the firstborn of Abel's cattle. Is God a carnivore who prefers meat offerings? Later, Abraham had a first son, Ishmael, sent away with his mother when the second son Isaac was born. How can a father chase away his son under the pressure of one of his wives? This same Isaac also had two sons, the eldest was Esau and the youngest was Jacob. Esau cooked for his father, who enjoyed eating meat just like God. Jacob managed to steal the birthright and a greater share of the inheritance from his brother by receiving the blessing of his dying and blind father. However, Deuteronomy (21.15) prohibits the transmission of the birthright based solely on preference. This dishonest Jacob will become the father of the twelve tribes of Israel.

We should have more sympathy for the excluded than for the chosen ones. Moses, Jesus, and Muhammad are the privileged chosen ones to whom God speaks daily. What do they have that is so special to have been chosen by God? Nothing and even the contrary! The characters of Moses, Jesus, and Muhammad will be discussed in later chapters. King David will be studied in the chapter on adultery. Dozens of pretenders claimed to be God's chosen Messiah, expected by the Jewish people. Here is a very partial list: Judas of Galilee, a zealot who led the revolt against the Roman census; Simon Atronges, Theudas, and Jesus, who all lived during Jesus's time. Then came Bar-Kokhba, Alroy, Molch, and the famous Shabbat Tzvi, and finally the famous rabbi Lubavitz, who died in 1994. None of them has brought peace to the world.

Are the Jewish people chosen by God?

Long before the Jews, the Egyptians considered themselves chosen by the god Ra, the Greeks by Zeus, the Romans by Jupiter, and the Vikings by the god Odin. Why did God choose the Jewish people? The oral tradition, without any evidence, says that the Torah was given by God to many people who refused it. Abraham was the only one who accepted it, and so God chose him. Yet the Torah was given to Moses a few generations later, not to Abraham. In Deuteronomy (7.7) it is written *"it is not because you are more numerous than other people, for you were the fewest of all."* This statement, however, contradicts the Torah, in which more than 3 million Hebrews came out of Egypt, not a minor people at this time.

Deuteronomy (7.6) says: *"You are a people for God... He has chosen you... to be his special people among all peoples... You have been chosen by the Lord, He loves you..."* In Deuteronomy (26.19), it is written: *"You will be his people... He gives you dominion over all the nations..."* Also, Exodus (4.22) says: *"Israel is my firstborn son."* Jeremiah (10.16) confirms: *"He is the creator of the universe, and Israel is his tribe."* *"It is a people that dwells alone and is not counted among the nations,"* says Numbers (23.9). Their laws, particularly dietary laws, will keep them separated: *"It is I, YAHWEH, your God, who has separated you from the people, and so you will separate the clean animal from the unclean . . ."* Such a comment would incite hatred from those not included! Even during the exile, Jeremiah (31.35) claimed that God kept the Jews as His preferred people. In Deuteronomy (14.21), God commands the Hebrews, *"You shall not eat of any dead animal, give it to the outsider to eat or sell it to outsiders because you are a people holy to YHWH, your God."* Does it mean that God is concerned about the health of the Hebrews but not of others? In their prayers every Friday night, Jews thank God for having chosen them among all the other people. Some rabbis say that Jews have different souls from others without any evidence and without explaining how or when they received that soul. Does a new convert to Judaism also receive a different soul? Yes, they say. And when does he get it? God could have easily proven that the Jewish people are the chosen ones by creating them different from the rest of humanity, with three eyes for example. But no, the Jew is similar to other humans.

During the Exodus, in Numbers (1. 2), the Hebrews were 603,550 adult males and 22,000 Levite males, a total of over 3 million Hebrews. The world's population at that time was about 100 million. So the Hebrews counted for nearly 3 percent. The percentage today is less than a tenth of what it was during the time of Moses. Some historians argue that 2,000 years ago Jews accounted for 8 percent of the world population and therefore they should be today more than 500 million, but they are only 15 to 17 million. Their percentage declined because the Bible exaggerated their number and because of massacres and assimilation. If they were God's chosen, then why has the number declined so dramatically? If growing numbers are a proof for being the chosen people, then Muslims or Christians should be the chosen ones! If the Hebrew people were chosen by God, why did God allow the destruction of the two Hebrew kingdoms? Why the exile? Why the pogroms and massacres of the Crusades? Why the expulsion from Spain? Why the Holocaust and Hitler?

If not in quantity, maybe in quality? In a world population of more than 7 billion, Jews represent only 15 to 17 million people, or less than 0.3 percent of the world's population. However, out of a total of 740 Nobel Prize awardees, the number of Jewish Nobel Prize winners add up to more than 164 or 22 percent. As for Muslims, with a population of about 1.2 billion people, they only have seven Nobel Prize awardees. The Jews received almost 55 percent of the Nobel Prize awards in economics, 38 percent of the Nobel Prize awards in physics, 29 percent of the Nobel Prize awards in Medicine, and 28 percent in chemistry.

Karl Marx; Trotsky; Spinoza; Bergson; Sigmund Freud; Einstein; Blum; the Italian Giuseppe Mazzini; the filmmakers Goldwyn, Mayer, and Spielberg; the painters Pissarro, Modigliani, Soutine, and Chagall; the writers Franz Kafka and Marcel Proust. These names are only a small number from the long list of famous Jews. How can one explain this phenomenon? Is it because the Jewish people are chosen by God? Not necessarily! These Jewish geniuses are mostly nonbelievers who have separated themselves from Jewish traditions and see the world in a totally different way. Most of them weren't religious at all and were mostly Jewish opponents of Judaism, such as Spinoza, Marx, and Einstein. Their opposition has probably led to develop their genius. Spinoza was declared anathema in 1656 and was excommunicated from his community and his synagogue for expressing doubts. There was also Primo Levi, who no longer expected to see God during the Holocaust. Einstein claimed that he was convinced that most of the stories of the Bible were not true, and refused to believe in a God who punished or rewarded humans according to their actions. He also refused to believe that prayers had any effects. Is the genius in the genes of the Jews, whether or not they are religious or atheist? Or is it due to the historical situation of the two last century in which Jews were more educated than non-Jews?

The choosing of the Jew is the main cause of anti-Semitism

Nothing stirs up hatred for Jews like the claim of being the chosen people of God! Jewish racism created racism towards the Jews. What should be the reaction of other people towards the chosen one? The reaction is hatred and the desire to prove that the Jewish people are not chosen by God. First Christianity and then Islam, declaring themselves the new and true religions, had to deny or cancel the election of the Jewish people. They did so by eliminating or forcing the Jews to convert, or by genocide or by granting them the status of second-class citizens to prove their inferiority.

The Jews answer that, on the contrary, the notion of being chosen does not show arrogance but humility before God. The notion of being chosen is not racist, and as a matter of fact, they say that the coming Messiah will come from the descendants of Ruth the Moabite, who converted to Judaism. Moreover, it does not give rights but duties. The Gentiles can convert to Judaism by accepting the 613 orders and become themselves the chosen of God. These arguments are not convincing, and the difficulties in converting to Judaism prove that it is a closed hereditary clan. Reading the Jewish Bible is forbidden to non-Jews by the Talmud, so how can a non-Jew convert to Judaism and become part of the chosen people?

Some rabbis say that the Jews will go to a better paradise than non-Jews because the reward for observing the 613 commandments of Jewish law is much larger than for the observation of the seven laws of Noah. Similarly, hell for the Jews would be more severe than for the Gentiles. Ezra (4.1) reports that during the construction of the Second Temple the people of Judah, who were nicknamed *adversaries,* offered to help with the construction but were pushed away by the Jews returning from exile. These people of Judah were not all opponents but Judeans remaining in Judea and continuing to live their life until the return of exiles. This elite group of people, the ones sent to exile, considered themselves as having the exclusive right of building the temple and refused their offer to help. Nehemiah (4 and 6) says that when the Judeans returned from exile they rebuilt the walls of Jerusalem, but the former residents, Ammonites and Arabs, *"conspired together to attack . . ." and offered to "confer,"* but Nehemiah refused to meet them for fear of falling into a trap. What if the suspicions of Nehemiah were unfounded and their intentions were good? And what if they honestly wanted to cooperate in the rebuilding of Jerusalem? What if they had been included into the work? Wouldn't they have become Jewish? In fact, they did not attack the exiles who were coming back to Jerusalem! Regarding these attacks, the rabbis responded that every nation has a different mission in an area where it excels. For Africans it is music, for the Japanese it is martial arts, and for the Jewish people it is to excel in the truth that God has transmitted to them through the Torah. This statement is elitist. Some rabbis add that God himself would have created anti-Semitism in order to preserves Jews from assimilation. Without this hatred, they would be assimilated into other cultures and Judaism would have disappeared.

"The Jewish chosen people" is the cause of the two other religions

At the time of Jesus, the pagans, rejected by Judaism, were easy prey for Paul and the early Christian missionaries. Paul, the real founder of

Christianity (not Jesus the Jew, who remained a Jew), wanted to convert the pagans but faced obstacles imposed by the Pharisees. One of them was circumcision. And so he gave up and created the new Christian religion. In Matthew (23.13), Jesus, or rather Paul, accuses the rabbis: *"Woe to you, teachers of the law and Pharisees, hypocrites! You close the door of the kingdom of heaven before men . . . You do not let those who wish to enter . . . You travel all over land and sea to win a single convert, and when you have won, you make him worthy of hell twice more than you."* In I Thessalonians (2.15), Paul went further: *"Forbidding us to speak to the Gentiles that they may be saved . . ."* Christianity would not have existed if the Jews had not stubbornly made circumcision mandatory. Paul understood that pagans will not accept circumcision, and to achieve his goal he was forced to remove the circumcision requirement.

The Quran (3.187) writes *"God's covenant with those who had the book was: show it to men, do not hide it. But they threw it behind their backs . . ."* Muhammad complains in (5.18) that *"the Jews and the Christians say: we are the sons and loved ones of God."* And in (5.64), *"The Jews say: the hand of God is closed . . . His two hands are open."* And again in (5.82): *". . . the most hostile to the believers are the Jews and the liars (idolaters) . . . the closest ones to love the believers are certain Christians."* And again (62.6): *"Jews, do you claim to be the only ones close to God?"*

Two verses show the change of Muhammad towards the Jews: (5.7): *"the food of those who have the book (Jews) are permitted to eat and yours is permitted to them. You are allowed to marry the women of the believers and of those who had the book before you."* This friendly attitude became hate when the Jews rejected Muhammad, and later he took his revenge on them, (5.56): *"You, who believe, do not be friends with those who mock and make fun of your religion. . ."* History would have been different if Judaism more easily accepted the conversion of the Gentiles, Christianity and Islam would not have existed. These two religions are born from the Jews' refusal to expand its circle and accept other people. The Jews wanted to live apart to preserve themselves from any assimilation despite persecution. But at what price? Spinoza said: *"They separated themselves from all other nations, to the point that they have turned towards them the hatred of all other peoples, not only because of their external customs, customs contrary to other nations', but also because of the practice of circumcision."*

Much later, Nazis invented the myth of the superior Aryan race, and with that came the need to annihilate the Jews. Himmler stated: *"There are two elected people. One of the two is too many. They must be exterminated."* This led to genocide. Unfortunately, God didn't intervene in favor of his chosen people.

Can Judaism survive the curse of being God's chosen people? The idea of the chosen people is a consequence of the national monolatry and should disappear with the installation of universal monotheism. However, the Jewish people never accepted monotheism. If they had, that would have destroyed the concept of being the chosen ones. Both beliefs persist among the Jews today. Now it seems that it is too late to cancel this notion, because if they do it would contradict the entire Torah, the New Testament, and the Quran. Only atheists or confident Israelis who do not feel threatened could repel this notion of being God's chosen people.

The Talmud and Jewish racism

Many quotes from the Talmud have been used to explain that Jews are racists who believed themselves to be superior to others. Very often, the quotes are false or poorly translated and relate to minor ideas. However, in all honesty, yes, there are some verses in the Talmud saying that the Jewish people are the chosen ones and that the Gentiles are second-class humans. For example, Sanhedrin 57a says a Jew can keep what was stolen from a Gentile. According to Sanhedrin 58b, Rabbi Hanina said that *"if a gentiles hits a Jew, he deserves to die . . . because it's like attacking God . . ."* This is based on the reaction of Moses, who slew an Egyptian for beating a Hebrew slave. According to Sanhedrin 58b, a non-Jew who practices the Sabbath is punishable by death. According to Sanhedrin 59a, Rabbi Yohanan said: *"a Gentile who studies the Torah deserves death, for it is written that Moses gave us the Commandments as our heritage, not theirs."* With that said, how can a Gentile ever convert?

According to the Talmud, Avoda Zara 22a, Gentiles are suspected of having sex with livestock, and one should not be left alone with the Gentiles because they are capable of killing you. A little further, Avoda Zara 22b writes that a Jewish sage reported having seen at the market a Gentile having an indecent relationship with a goose and then strangle it, cook it, and eat it. Another said he saw an Arab doing the same with a piece of meat that had a hole in it. According to Avoda Zara 26a, a Jewish woman should not help a Gentile woman give birth for fear that she will help in the delivery of an idolater. Similarly, a Jewish woman must not be helped by a Gentile woman for fear that she might kill her during childbirth. Other wise rabbis allow it only if the delivery is done in the presence of others. Still, according to Avoda Zara 26b, some wise men ask that a Gentile not circumcise a Jewish baby lest his knife sterilize the baby.

According to Baba Metzia 24a, if someone finds a lost object, if the majority of the people are Jewish, the found object has to be announced. But if the majority of the people are Gentile, this is not required. According to Baba Kama 113a, in a dispute that arises between a Jew and a Gentile, the Jew can defend himself by using Gentile or Jewish laws if those laws are favorable to him. He is also allowed to simply use subterfuge. According to Yebamoth 61a, Jews are considered men while the non-Jews are not.

This type of racism comes directly from the Bible. For example, Deuteronomy (15.2) asks the forgiveness of the debt every seven years for a Jewish brother, but *"the stranger, you can force him to pay, but what your brother has of yours, your hand abandons it."* Or according to Deuteronomy (23.20), *"your brother is not required to pay any interest . . . to the stranger, you can lend with interest . . ."* Isaiah (61.5) promises that at the arrival of the Messiah, *"foreigners will take care of your flocks, the sons of foreigners will work in your fields and will tend to your vines."* The great Jewish philosopher of the twelfth century, Rambam, in his famous book *Yad Hazaka*, allows the killing of the one who says that the Torah is not from God. According to Shoulhan Aruch, which sets the daily conduct of the Jews, one must return a lost item to a pious Jew but not to a Gentile or to an atheist Jew. The former chief rabbi of Israel Ovadia Yosef continues the statements of the Talmud and reportedly said in 2010: *"the Gentiles are born to serve the Jews, and if they don't, they have no place in this world."*

Jews, the chosen ones for Jesus; pagans, the chosen ones for Paul! The concept of *chosen people* is an important but confusing element in Christianity. Jesus has nothing to do with it. He was Jewish and was concerned only with the Jews until his death. Paul, twenty years after the death of Jesus, wanted to convert the pagans to a more acceptable Judaism, but the Jews opposed this to preserve their status as the chosen people and rendered his task very difficult. This is precisely what Jesus reproached the Jews for in Matthew (23.13). Paul did not persuade the Jews, so they chased him away and he turned his message toward his new pagan public.

In chapters 9 and 11 of his letter to the Romans, Paul is trying to find a solution and describes an olive tree whose root is Jewish but its branches pagan. He described the Jews who rejected him, saying, *"they are enemies for your sake, but regarding the chosen, they are beloved for the sake of their fathers."* Paul, chronologically the first to write, imposed his views and we can find his bipolar reasoning in the Gospels.

On one hand, Jesus confirms that the Jewish people are chosen of God. Matthew (2.6) describes the birth of Jesus, where God says, *"For thee shall come a Governor that shall rule Israel, my people."* Later, in Matthew (15.24), Jesus himself says: *"I have been sent only to the lost sheep of the house of Israel"* and not for the pagans. *"The little dogs eat the crumbs that fall from their masters' table."* What could be more powerful than this sentence, which proves that Jesus is a Jew who came only for the Jews? However, this fact was then suddenly turned into something else by Paul, the creator of Christianity. On the other hand, because of their opposition, the Jewish people would lose the exclusivity of being the chosen people. According to Matthew (21.43), Jesus prophesied *"the kingdom of God will be taken away and given to a nation, bringing forth the fruits thereof."* Then comes the change that transforms Christians into the chosen people (24. 30): *". . . All the tribes of the earth will mourn . . . He will gather his elect from the four corners . . ."* And (28.19) says: *"Go and teach all nations, baptizing them in the name of the Father, the Son and the Holy Spirit."* We found the same course in Luke (1.68 . . .) at the birth of Jesus says, *"Blessed be the Lord God of Israel, for he has visited and redeemed his people . . . you go before the face of the Lord to his people."* Further in (7.16): *"God has visited his people."* Then comes the change with the Good Samaritan, not a Levite, who is said to have given the first aid.

After having been separated from the Jews, Christians try to capture the title of the chosen people. This is according to the epistle of Peter (I, 2.9), not written by the apostle Peter but long after his death, which gives the title of the chosen people to new converts: *"You, on the contrary, you are a chosen people . . . Who once were not a people but are now the people of God . . ."* For Christians, the destruction of the Second Temple by the Romans in 70 was a punishment from God, who had changed who he wanted as his chosen people. How do Christians explain the destruction of the First Temple? How do Christians explain their early and difficult centuries?

Of course, these verses were written by Paul, who was pushed back by the Nazarenes-notsrim and driven away by the Jews. He found a solution by granting the title of chosen people to the pagans. After centuries of persecution, the Church finally recognizes the Jews as being the *elder brother*. As a matter of fact, who are Christians? Aren't they pagans who converted to Judaism without suffering the constraints (such as circumcision and keeping kosher)?

Muhammad's veneration for the Jews transformed into hatred

The passages in the Quran about the chosen people contain obvious contradictions and are divided into three distinct chronological but deliberately mixed categories.

1. In the beginning, Muhammad acknowledged that the Jewish people are the chosen ones of God and considered the Bible as the word of God. He had sympathy from the Jews of Arabia and recognized, in (6.155), that Moses received *"the book that explains everything, a guide and a grace..."* Muhammad thought that he was going to receive help from the Jews and for that reason flattered them by giving them the title of God's chosen people. In (44.32) and (2.47), he wrote: *"The sons of Israel... We have consciously placed them on top of the world."* Or in (5.20): *"... when God chose among you prophets, he made you kings, he gave you what he had not given to anyone. My people enter the holy land that God destined for you."* Or in (17.104), a hyper-Zionist declaration from Muhammad: *"... We said to the sons of Israel, live in the land, and when the promise of the next life is fulfilled, we will let you come in crowds."* And finally, (55.16) recognizes that the Jewish people are the chosen people, or more precisely, were the chosen people, *"Yes, the son of Israel, we gave them the book, illumination and the prophecy... we have put them above the worlds... But they quarreled..."* Muhammad reportedly said all this around 630 AD, and it means that until then the Jewish people remained for him the chosen people despite all their sins. And so, therefore, there was no new reason for disqualifying the Jews after that date except maybe the refusal of the Jewish people to accept Islam!
2. The big change, its true and false cause:
   The vast majority of Jews and Christians did not accept the message of Muhammad and probably laughed at his ignorance and ridiculed him. One reason for this refusal was that Muhammad

did not belong to the chosen people and therefore couldn't claim to be a prophet. From (5.18): *"Jews and Christians say: we are the beloved of God. Tell them, why is he punishing you for your sins? You are only mortals that He created."* Many other verses, (5.61), (6.109), and also (2,111 and 121): *"They say, will enter into the garden only Jews and Christians... Jews and Christians will only be pleased with you if you follow their religion."*

Muhammad asked his disciples to fight the Jews who were mocking him, and came up with new theological but illogical arguments. He, who used to pray facing Jerusalem, out of spite, decided without any explanation to pray facing Mecca. This change occurred in 624, and all throughout the Quran there is not a single mention of Jerusalem, the city of the ancient Jewish temples.

According to (4.155), also repeated in (5.13 and 78): *"We cursed them because they broke our pact... they wrongfully killed the prophets."* So it appears that God has broken his pact with the Jewish people because of their sins and also because they had refused to accept the prophets.

3. Muhammad spread hatred against the Jewish people who have not accepted him and attacked the Jews, killing some of them, converting some by force and others by threatening them with hateful condemning verses: (2. 61): *"They have suffered the wrath of God because they did not believe the signs of God and slew the prophets wrongfully..."*

(5.13 and 78*):* *"Because they have broken the covenant, we have cursed them... The sons of Israel who were unfaithful were cursed..."*

(7.166): *"We have told them: you will be monkeys who we reject... He will send them someone to torment them until the day of resurrection."*

Jews are not only called monkeys but also pigs in (5.60): *"those whom God has cursed... He made monkeys and pigs."*

Finally, strengthened by his successes, Muhammad suggests that Muslims are the new chosen people: (3.110), *"You are the best nation among men..."* He finally detached himself from Judaism, taking as a starting point not Moses but Abraham.

In fact, who are the Muslims? They are the pagans in a hurry to abandon idolatry and convert to a monotheism similar to Judaism, but repelled by the two peoples of the Book, decided to create their own religion and spread revenge. The Islamic world has very few illustrious men it can be proud of, and very few Nobel Prize winners, very few inventors, very few artists, very little of everything. Why? Is Islam the cause? And this, in spite of the manna of oil. The reasons for the delay can be the lack of freedom of speech and the banning of any innovation by Sharia law, obscurantism, superstitions, belief in witchcraft, and tribalism. Their major contribution was the invention of the Arabic numerals, which in contrast to Roman numerals allow all calculations. But this invention preexisted the arrival of Islam and may have originated in India. Their biggest success is the meteoric rise of Islam and the rapid conquests of the 3 continents, including southern Europe.

Ishmael, ancestor of the Arabs? Jews and Arabs related through Abraham?

The short answer is no and no! Yet the Arabs and also, oddly, the Jews have for centuries spread these two errors. We can understand why the Arabs would hold such a lie. This genealogy gave them a certain dignity. But the acceptance of this lie by the Jews is incomprehensible. Muhammad first took Moses as an example, but rejected by the Jews, he decided to find a better ancestor, Abraham. Probably, if the Jews had accepted Muhammad he would have kept Moses and Ishmael would have been forgotten just as Esau had been forgotten. Then, strengthened by his victories, Muhammad declared that Abraham *"was neither Jew nor Christian"* but the first Muslim. Which is true, because the word *Muslim* means *"submitted to God."*

According to Islam, Abraham transmitted his monotheism to his eldest son Ishmael, who became the ancestor of the Arabs. With this recovery, Islam hits two birds with one stone: it grants the Arabs a certain nobility by giving them a famous ancestor, and retrieves the pagan temple of the Kaaba by stating that it was built by Abraham and Ishmael. This Ishmael, who is almost never mentioned in the whole Quran, became the ancestor of all Muslims. This theory does not hold water because of the following reasons:

1. Ishmael is essential to the foundations of Islam. Indeed, Islam claims to be the continuation predicted by the sacred texts of

the Jews and Christians. In Deuteronomy (18.17), God promises Moses, *"I will raise among them a prophet from their brethren, like you, and I will put my words in his mouth, and he will tell them everything I commend him."* Muhammad wanted to be that prophet foretold by the Bible. The Quran (73.15) says: *"Yes, we sent an apostle who will testify to you, just like we have sent an apostle to Pharaoh."* Muhammad claims to be related to Ishmael without giving any evidence. If Ishmael did give the Divine Law to Muhammad, it is mentioned nowhere in the Quran. The transmission was done through the lineage of Abraham, Isaac, and Jacob, while Ishmael is not known to have transmitted anything to anyone. Muslims claim that the Jewish patriarchs Abraham, Isaac, Jacob, and Moses are true prophets, yet they are not the ancestors of Muslims, but of Jews.

2. Abraham passed his legacy to Isaac, not to Ishmael, according to Genesis (17. 20): *"for my Alliance, I will confirm it on Isaac . . ."* The Quran (29.27) says: *"We gave to Abraham, Isaac and Jacob and established in his descendants prophethood and the Book."* Therefore, the prophecy was given to Isaac and not to Ishmael! Another verse, (2.136), mentions Ishmael with the patriarchs, but not as a prophet. In addition, Muhammad contradicts himself and is mistaken when he says in (19.54) that Ishmael *"was an apostle and prophet."* Nowhere does the Bible state Ishmael is a prophet.

3. According to all three religions, Ishmael was the firstborn son of Abraham with his servant Hagar. Ishmael means *"God hears"* in Hebrew but has no meaning in Arabic. To be meaningful, this name should have been *Isma-Allah*. There is no mention of the name Ishmael in any Arabic texts before Islam. No Arab baby was named Ishmael since the time of Abraham to Muhammad, while many Hebrews continued to be called Ishmael. In fact, the name Ishmael was *Arabized* and monopolized by Muhammad and was abandoned by the Jews after the introduction of Islam.

4. How did the rabbis explain the cruel abandon of Ishmael? In Genesis (21.9): *"Sarah saw the son of Hagar laugh . . ."* and asks Abraham to expel Hagar and Ishmael his son. This reason seems insufficient but the Rabbi Rashi decided that Ishmael was an idolater, committed incest, was a murderer, and therefore deserved to be abandoned. Where did he get all this? It is

nowhere mentioned in the Bible. Rashi found an answer to this new contradiction in Genesis (25.9 and 17), *"Abraham was buried by Isaac and Ishmael . . . Ishmael died and joined his ancestors."* So Rashi deducted that Ishmael repented and became a righteous man toward the end of his life, and therefore the Jews could give their children the name of Ishmael. This theoretical construction is used to explain more than a millennium after the writing of the Torah, why Ishmael was abandoned and then reintegrated. It explains why the Jews had continued to name their children Ishmael. But after the advent of Islam, the name Ishmael was monopolized by the Arabs and no Jews received this name. We have a rabbi named Ishmael ben Elisha, active in the Talmud, grandson of Ishmael ben Elisha, high priest of the Second Temple. Ishmael Ben Yose also was a wise man in the Talmud. If, as Rashi said, the name Ishmael designated a murderer and a sinner, Jews would not have given that name to their children. No, the change took place only after the arrival of Islam, which hijacked the name Ishmael!

Another clue is in the comparison of two texts. In II Samuel (17.25), *"Amasa was the son of a man named Ythra the Israelite who Abigail . . ."* While in I Chronicles (2.17), *"Abigail bore Amasa, Amasa's father was Yether the Ishmaelite."* This confusion shows that for biblical history, Ishmael was not an outcast and neither were his descendants.

Another error: in Genesis (17,25), Ishmael was thirteen years old when he was circumcised by Abraham, but later, when chased away with his mother Hagar, (21.14), the big thirteen- to sixteen-year-old boy sits on the shoulders of Hagar as if he was a toddler. A rabbi explains that we must not take the words at face value. The words are very important, yet alterable at will by the rabbis. Rashi said that after the death of Sarah Abraham married his former slave Hagar, whose name was changed to Keturah. Where is that written? Nowhere! So what right does he have to say that?

8

The sacrifices are over, thank God, the temple is destroyed

This title is deliberately provocative because religions try to forget the sacrifices mentioned in the Bible. The sacrifices represent almost 343 commands, among 613 of the Jewish Bible, but believers speak very little about them, as if to hide the dark side of the holy writings. Does God need to be satisfied by the sacrifices? If God needs them, that would mean he has a gap to fill and would be imperfect.

For chronology, at the beginning, humans were sacrificed to the gods. Then, instead of humans, animals were sacrificed. An individual with sin, meaning someone who has violated a divine order, provided animal sacrifice as a replacement of his own person. The animal was used instead of the humans because it was said that the human lost his human soul and became now like an animal. The replacement should be rejected and each should pay for his sins. Also, why sacrifice an edible animal and not an insect, for example? And why is part of the sacrifice eaten by the priests?

Around 950 BC, Solomon built the first temple in Jerusalem. In 587 BC, this temple was destroyed by King Nebuchadnezzar, who exiled some of the people to Babylonia. Later, Persians, having taken over Babylonia, allowed exiles to return to Jerusalem to rebuild their temple, the second, which was completed around 515. Herod the Great, the half-Jewish king appointed by Rome, enlarged the second temple in 20 AD. After the Jewish revolt in 70 AD, the Roman armies of Titus destroyed the second temple which was never again rebuilt. Jews mourn the destruction of the two temples and commemorate this day on the ninth of the month of Av by fasting. The temple was not a place of gathering for the faithful, but, according to Exodus (25.8), was the house where God resided. God asked: *"Build me a sanctuary that I may stay among them."* This is a residue of monolatry because the infinite God would not need a house to live in.

Was the story of Abraham and Isaac invented to cancel human sacrifice?

In the Mayan religion, prisoners, and especially children, orphaned or illegitimate, purchased or imprisoned, were sacrificed to attract the favor of the gods. In general, the ritual sacrifice was performed by decapitation and by taking the heart of the sacrificed. See the Mel Gibson movie *Apocalypto*. The pagan world believed that the firstborn was the child born from the union of God and a female goddess and thus had to be sacrificed. Judaism is progressive compared to religions that preceded it. Paradoxically, there is the weird order from God to Abraham to sacrifice his son.

Sarah, Abraham's wife, had no children and pushed her husband to sleep with her slave Agar. They had a son, Ishmael. Later, when Sarah finally had a son, Isaac, Abraham sent away both Agar and Ishmael to the desert with just a jug of water and some bread. Where is the love? Later God asks Abraham to sacrifice Isaac, *"Your only son, the one you love . . . And offer him as sacrifice . . . Abraham took the knife to cut his son's throat."* At the last moment, God stopped him, satisfied with Abraham's total submission and rewarded him, *"I would bless you and your children's children."* What a great example of fanaticism for today's modern jihadists. Religious people answer that God wasn't cruel because He knew that Abraham would obey him, and He simply wanted Abraham to be an example to all the believers. What about the suffering of Isaac?

Assume for a moment that a terrorist says that in a dream, God asked him to blow himself up in a crowd. We would call him a dangerous lunatic and prevent him from achieving his purpose. Yet this is somewhat the case for Abraham, the patriarch of three religions. His blind faith leads him to commit murder. He is a fine example for all fanatics and terrorists! Yet, this fanatic Abraham, ready to sacrifice Isaac, tried to convince God to postpone the destruction of Sodom. Why these contradictory attitudes?

This interrupted sacrifice is barbaric, cruel, and absurd, and Abraham acts like a religious fanatic. Isn't this order contrary to what God ordered him previously when He told him to leave the pagan rites? Is it not God who promised him a seed? Why then does He ask him to destroy that posterity? Abraham shows the summit of fundamentalism by accepting to perform the wildest of all terrorist acts. He should have objected to the cruel and incomprehensible order of God. If God prohibits murder, how can He order the murder-sacrifice of this young boy? This interrupted sacrifice not only demonstrates the blind submission of Abraham, but also God's sadism. Why does God need to test Abraham's faith? God knows everything beforehand, and therefore knew that Abraham would execute His request, so why this unnecessary test? Wouldn't Isaac be traumatized all his life by this interrupted sacrifice? Instead, Abraham is rewarded for his blind obedience and becomes the father of three religions, when he should have been condemned as a fanatic.

Clues and contradictions in the story lead us to other conclusions: This sacrifice, be it Isaac or Ishmael (as the Muslims want), is contradicted by biblical texts. How can God promise (Gen. 16.12 and 17.20) at the birth of Ishmael that he *". . . And over all his brothers shall he dwell . . . He will be a great nation,"* then ask him to be sacrificed? And what about Isaac (Genesis 21.12), how can God promise him that *"the posterity of Isaac will bear your name,"* then ask him to be sacrificed? Isn't Abraham surprised by the illogical behavior of God, who promises him a numerous posterity and then tells him to kill his son? The Bible refers to Isaac as *"the only son, whom you love,"* but he is not the only son of Abraham! A rabbi replied that he was the only son of Sarah, yes, but here it is a question of Abraham! Is Ishmael, the eldest son, not loved by Abraham? See the following chapter on "Isaac or Ishmael sacrificed?"

Abraham deceives his son by answering, *"God will choose the holocaust, my son."* Some try to exonerate Abraham of this lie by stating that the old Hebrew had no punctuation and Abraham, in fact, said to Isaac, *"God will choose, The Holocaust (is) my son."* It makes no sense. It is said that by stopping Abraham, God cancelled all human sacrifices, and in Deuteronomy (18.10), God forbids them completely, *"Let not find anyone among you who sacrifices by fire, son or girl, who practices enchantments . . ."*

And Leviticus (18.21) and (20.2) and Deuteronomy (12.31) says: *"Whoever among the Israelites or foreigners staying in Israel, someone would deliver his seed Moloch must be put to death."* Yet throughout the Bible, stories of human sacrifices continue and Jeremiah (32.35) confirms this: *"They have passed through fire their son and daughters in honor of Moloch, abominable act..."* But while God forbade and punished human sacrifices to other gods, especially Moloch, He demanded human sacrifices in his favor. In Numbers (31.25), He ordered Moses to divide the spoils between the warriors who took part in the expedition: *"... As tribute for the Lord ... a head for 500 human individuals, oxen, donkeys ... and give it to Eleazar the priest as an offering to YHWH."* As the total of prisoners was 16,000, the number of virgins sacrificed to the Lord would be thirty-two.

Leviticus 27 is not clear about sacrifices: *"If someone made a vow to offer a person to the Lord..."* is sometimes translated as *"If someone promises by a vow value estimate of a person to the Lord..."* The first translation is correct, the second tries to hide the human sacrifices.

In Judges (11,29), *"Animated by the spirit of YHWH ... Jephthah made a vow to YHWH, if you'll deliver the children of Ammon in my power, the first person to come out of my house ... I will sacrifice to You."* Jephthah won the battle and returned home, *"Here comes his daughter to meet him with tambourines ... He fulfills the vow he had made."* He sacrificed his daughter to God, who animated the spirit of Jephthah and therefore wanted this human sacrifice and did not stop him at the last minute like Abraham. This episode disturbed the rabbis, who claimed that, in fact, Jephthah did not sacrifice his daughter but stopped his gesture. But the writings are clear: *"He fulfills the vow he had made. She had never known a man ... From year to year the daughters of Israel mourn the memory of the daughter of Jephthah."* How the wise men have the audacity to change the sacred texts when they are clear! This vow could have been released by a judge as reminded by Jeremiah (8.22). Then why is it that Jephthah did not go to Pinhas, the judge? Inexplicable also that the omniscient God allowed this vow. God saved Isaac at the last moment. Why did He not save the poor girl?

And again, 1 Kings (13.2): a man of God came from Judah *"and it is the human bones that will burn on the altar."* II Kings (16.3), King Ahaz *"followed the example of the kings of Israel, he even passed his son through the fire..."* In II Kings (17. 17), during the reign of King Hosea, *"they had passed their son and daughters in the fire..."* And according to II Kings (21.6), King *Manasse "made his son pass through the fire."* Even in the days of

Ezekiel (20.26), six centuries BC, the Judeans continued human sacrifice: *"I have been defiled by their own gifts in that they caused to pass through the fire firstborn . . ."*

Oddly, the biblical story that tells of the long life of Isaac never mentions any further reference to his interrupted but traumatic sacrifice. If God himself had canceled the human sacrifice, the texts after Abraham are contradictory, because in Exodus (13.1), *"YHWH spoke to Moses and said: Sanctify to Me all the firstborn among the children of Israel, both man and beast, it is mine."* But in Exodus (22.28), *"Your first born son, you give to Me."* The simple understanding is that the firstborn should be sacrificed to God. In Numbers (3.11) and (8.17), God says to Moses: *"Every firstborn belongs to me, children of Israel, man or beast. The day that I smote all the firstborn in the land of Egypt, I consecrated them to me. And I have taken the Levites in exchange for all the firstborn of the children of Israel and I have given you as assistant . . ."* This means that all the firstborn Jewish babies should have died, just like the firstborn babies of the Egyptians died from the plague, but they have been saved by God and therefore belong to him. This thinking is absurd, because everything already belongs to God, from the firstborn to the youngest.

Numbers (18.15) allows the redemption of the firstborn: *"Every first fruit of the womb of any creature, which must be offered to YHWH, man or beast, is mine. Only you will have to release the firstborn of man and the firstborn of unclean animals, as you will be free too. As for redemption, you will grant the . . . at the rate of five pieces of silver . . . But the firstborn of cow, sheep, goat, you cannot release them: they are holy."* It means that the firstborn of clean animals will be sacrificed to God and then eaten by the priests. But this rule is abandoned even in modern Israel, and the firstborn of cattle and sheep is eaten by ordinary Jews. By using dishonest subterfuge, the breeders pierce the ears of cattle and sheep, rendering the firstborn unclean to be sacrificed and permitted to be eaten. What is this need that God has for the firstborn? It means also that the tradition of sacrificing the firstborn was replaced by a payment to the priest. This tradition is still practiced in *pidion ha ben*, or buying back the oldest son, as practiced to this day by the Jewish people. The priests win twice. They cancelled the useless human sacrifice and replaced it with a payment to the temple but continued the sacrifice of the purebred animals that priests can eat. It is important to note that the human sacrifice didn't benefit anyone in particular.

In conclusion, these quotes prove that human sacrifices continued after the time of Abraham and after the prohibitions of God. There are two possible explanations: either the people continued to sacrifice humans despite the divine prohibitions and the interrupted sacrifice of Abraham, or the bans were added by later editors who wanted to expunge the tradition of human sacrifice, which was still practiced. By this story, the later Bible writers wanted to permanently cancel the sacrifice of the firstborn by order of God, who is the only one able to cancel traditions. And so the sacrifice of Isaac never occurred and was invented to prohibit human sacrifices, which was still being practiced up to the time of kings and beyond. Was this episode inserted by King Josiah or by Ezra and Nehemiah?

Was it the sacrifice of Isaac or of Ishmael?

For Jews and Christians, it is the sacrifice of Isaac, while for Muslims it is that of Ishmael. Although the Bible clearly states that the interrupted sacrifice concerns Isaac, the choice of words is odd because in Genesis (22.2) it is written: *"God replied, take your son, your only son, whom you love, Isaac..."* even though Isaac was not the only son of Abraham. Ishmael was the eldest and was the only son for thirteen years.

Muslims say that the Bible was counterfeit and the name of Ishmael was replaced by the one of Isaac. The Jewish rabbis gave a bad explanation. They say that Isaac is the only son of Sarah, but here we're referring to Abraham, not Sarah. Also, is it possible to love a son and not another? The Quran does not mention that it is God who orders Abraham to sacrifice his son, but it says that Abraham was told in a dream to sacrifice his son. The Quran (37.100) seems to assume that the sacrifice refers to Isaac and not to Ishmael. There is a description of the interrupted sacrifice, then *"we told him of the birth of Isaac..."* Even if Muhammad said that the written texts of the Torah had been falsified, he should have been a bit more insistent and louder. Instead, the verse (11.71) says: *"and his wife stood laughing when we announced Isaac, and after Isaac, Jacob."* Isaac could not have any descendants if he was the one to be sacrificed, and so it would be Ishmael to be sacrificed. Islam could have used this verse to confirm that according to Muhammad the person intended to be sacrificed was none other than Ishmael, yet no Hadith confirms that Muhammad named Ishmael as the one God intended for the sacrifice. On the contrary, some companions of

Muhammad, including Abbas al Muttalib, mentioned that according to Muhammad Isaac is the one sacrificed.

The two religions, Judaism and Islam, are competing to grab the sacrifice: is it Isaac or is it Ishmael? But there is one thing they're forgetting, that this human sacrifice interrupted, whether of Isaac or Ishmael, was a late addition which sole purpose was to prohibit human sacrifice by God's divine order. In fact, these sacrifices never occurred. Incorrect terms like *"only son, whom you love"* were included well after the time of Abraham by Judean scribes who had forgotten about Ishmael, Abraham's eldest son. The Sunnis, mostly Arab Muslims, want the sacrificed son to be Ishmael while non-Arab Muslims, the Shiites, do not claim that halo, which would have promoted Arabs.

Kippur, the most important day in Judaism and the cleansing of the Temple:

This holiday, observed by the great majority of Jews, including those who don't practice the faith, is celebrated through fasting for twenty-five hours and prayers asking forgiveness for sins. Where does this come from? Leviticus (16.29) describes cleaning the altar and suddenly: *"This will be for you an eternal law in the seventh month, on the tenth day, you shall afflict your souls, and do no work . . ."* It is repeated in Numbers (29.7) and Leviticus (23.27): *"the tenth day of this seventh month, which is Yom hakippourim. . ."* However, the word *lekapper* appears first in Exodus (30, 10) and likely means to *"purify"*: *"Aaron shall purify the horns once a year . . . we purify it in your generations . . ."* These quotes prove that the present Jewish calendar is no longer the same one as the one of the Torah, because in modern times Yom *hakippourim* is celebrated ten days after the Jewish New Year, not the seventh month as mentioned in the Torah. Also, is it possible that the word *lekapper* originally meant annual cleaning or purification of the altar, only to be later transformed to mean sin, mortification, and fasting? Because, logically, if on Yom Kippur the Jews ask for forgiveness for their sins of the past year, this day should have occurred on the last day of the year and not the tenth day of the seventh month. When some rabbis were asked about this, they gave no convincing answer, only more complicated answers. They said that the year ended at the time of Kippur *"from the standpoint of judgment"* (?). Having Yom Kippur on the tenth day of the seventh month actually has no meaning.

After the Torah of Moses, Kippur disappears and this solemn day is no longer mentioned in the books of kings and by the prophets. There are no remarks about the Jewish people who infringe or respect Yom Kippur. The prophet Ezekiel describes a certain cleansing of the sanctuary, but it occurs on a different date, and there was no fast. Nehemiah (8 and 9) describe the meeting of the people returning from exile and assembled in the square, (8.2), on the *"the first day of the seventh month."* Without mentioning that this day is the New Year. Then in (8.13) it says *"the second day"* of that month, then in (9.1) it is written *"the twenty-fourth day of this month the children of Israel were assembled for a fast . .,"* after the feast of Tabernacles. All this occurred through the month without any mention of the tenth day of the month, Yom *hakippourim*, the most solemn of days in Judaism, as if Yom *hakippourim* did not exist! These contradictory texts lead to the following questions: what connection is there between cleaning the gold horns of the altar and the blood of a sacrificed animal and mortification and fasting of Jews today? Is it possible that Yom Kippur is an added feast inserted after Nehemiah?

Ashura, or the copy of Yom ha Kippurim by Islam

According to some Hadiths, Muhammad wanted to know the meaning of Yom Kippur and so he asked the Jews who were fasting what it meant. He then decided to adopt it and declared that the goal of this fast was to help fade away the sins of the past year. *Ashura* means *tenth day*, just like the Jewish Yom Kippur.

After attempting to be accepted by the Jews and not succeeding, Muhammad decided to differentiate himself from them. Not only did Muhammad change the direction of prayer from Jerusalem to Mecca, he also extended this fast to the ninth and tenth day. Finally after the introduction of the fast of Ramadan, the fast of Ashura became optional or simply changed significance for some Muslims, like the Shiites who flagellate themselves on that day.

Animal sacrifices before the time of Moses

Cain was the first man in the Jewish Bible to offer a sacrifice to God. *"Cain presented the product of the earth as an offering to YHWH . . . And*

Abel offered the firstborn of his cattle, the fat portions. YHWH showed favor to Abel and his offering." It seems that God preferred the offering of meat more than the vegetable offering. And so sacrifices and offerings existed before Moses's time! Jewish commentators had to justify God's preference; otherwise, it would seem that God himself, who by preferring one sacrifice over another without any reason, encouraged murder. One explanation of the rabbis is that the offering of Cain must have been of lower quality than the one of Abel. But it is written nowhere in the texts. Another explanation, bizarre and unfounded, says that Eve conceived Cain with the devil and that is why God refused his offering. So would that mean that we are all descendants of the devil? Moreover, how can God say to Cain, *"If you improve yourself, you will be forgiven."* How could the son of the devil improve himself? A more acceptable explanation is that the name *Cain* represents the neighboring people of Israel, the dangerous Kenites. The legend of Cain and Abel is in reality about the cruelty of the Kenites.

According to the Ten Commandments, Cain's punishment was death. But God gives him another punishment: *"You'll be a fugitive and a wanderer in the world."* But God was wrong, because some verses later, in Genesis: *". . . Cain knew his wife . . . and built a city . . ."* Before the flood, Noah *"built an altar to God and took two of every four legged animal, and every clean bird, and offered the burnt offering on the altar. The Lord inhaled the delicious smell . . ."* and promised not to curse the earth. Again, it seems that God loves that barbeque smell!

Genesis (46.1) says: *"Jacob-Israel . . . and came to Beersheva, where he sacrificed victims to the God of his father Isaac."* According to which ritual? Before the Law of Moses?

Then in Exodus (3.18), God commands Moses to: *"Go with the elders of Israel, to the king of Egypt and say to him . . . and now we would like to go to three days' journey into the wilderness to sacrifice to YHWH our God."* So sacrifices existed before the Law of Moses! You can find similar examples in Exodus (5.8), (5.17), and (8, 8 . . .).

Later, (18.1) says: *"Jethro, the priest of Median, Moses's father-in-law . . . offered a burnt offering and sacrifices to God. And Aaron and all the elders of Israel came to share the meal with the stepfather of Moses."* But Jethro is not Hebrew, he is the priest of Median, and so his sacrifice cannot be accepted because *"for whoever sacrifices to other gods will be destroyed"*! And was that meat kosher? In Exodus (12.5), the Passover sacrifice is done with a lamb or a goat less than a year old, and it must be *"roasted in the fire."* Yet in

Deuteronomy (16.2 and 7), this sacrifice can be done with a cow, cooked and not roasted. Why the change? Is there a reason for the change or is it merely a scribal error?

Aaron's tribe: the Levites, first cursed, then later made powerful

We often forget that if Aaron belongs to the tribe of Levi so does his brother Moses! Levi was one of the twelve sons of Jacob, but not the favorite. To avenge the rape of their sister, *"Simeon and Levi, Dinah's brothers, each took their sword and slew all the males"* from the family of Shechem; and because of this violence, according to Genesis (49.1), when Jacob blessed his sons he said: *"Simon and Levi are brothers; their swords are weapons of violence... That my mind is united to their assembly! For in their anger they slew a man; and in their wickedness... Cursed be their anger, for it was fierce, and their wrath for it was cruel! I will divide them in Jacob and scatter them in Israel."* So how does this tribe of Levi, who was cursed by Jacob, become the tribe of priests? Why did God choose them to be the priests? Why didn't Levi and Simon receive the same fate?

Another example: Aaron was appointed by God to be high priest, but in Exodus (32) he was the one responsible for making the golden calf: *"Moses delayed to come down from the mountain... Aaron answered them, peel off the gold which are in the ears of your wives, your son and daughters, and bring them to me... Having received the gold from their hand, he threw them into the mold and made a metal calf, and he said: Here are your gods, O Israel, who brought you out of Egypt."* Three thousand died, punished by God because they worshiped the golden calf, but Aaron, who built the golden calf, will become the high priest, one of the few to enter the Holy of Holies, and his sons would dominate the priesthood forever. That is incomprehensible! Is it possible that a scribe opposing the power of the Aaronite priests inserted the story of the golden calf?

The cursed tribe of Levi becomes the privileged clan of priests and would receive a *"tithe for the service they do, the tabernacle service."* Levis do not own land and are to receive compensation or gifts of sacrifices from other tribes who own land to cultivate. In Numbers (18:20): *"The Lord said to Aaron: You shall have no inheritance in their land, and there will be no part for you in their midst..."* Yet further, in Numbers (35.1), the Levites have possessions: *"Give the Levites... cities to dwell. You shall give to the Levites* land around these towns ... for their goods and for their pets ... 48 cities, with their land." Joshua (21) describes in detail the forty-eight cities owned by the Levis.

Genesis (12) tells the story of Miriam and Moses. *"Miriam and Aaron talked bad about Moses because of the Ethiopian woman whom he had married, because he had married an Ethiopian."* God became so angry that *"Miriam was made leprous, she became white as snow."* Miriam was forced to live far outside the camp and was reinstated after seven days. So it seems that Miriam was punished but not Aaron. Why this privilege? Why punish one and not the other? Not even a temporary punishment for Aaron? Maybe because if Aaron had been punished and covered with leprosy, he could not have served God, because according to Lev (22), *"any individual of the race of Aaron with leprosy shall not eat of the holy things lest he become impure."*

In Deuteronomy (17.12): *"... He who does not obey the priest, established to serve your God ... This man must die ..."* This verse thus gives the priest and the tribe of Levites absolute power. So Levi, cursed by his father and by God, will become the tribe of priests, the guards of the temple and servants of God? What did they do to be chosen by God? This tribe is dedicated, from father to son, forever, to the service of the tabernacle and to the service of the Temple of Jerusalem. Among the Levites, we distinguish the *Cohen* or priests who are in charge of the sacrifices made to the temple in Jerusalem.

The Jewish Bible describes many ways that God has punished the Hebrew people as a whole because of their disobedience, but it's always because of their idolatry that they are punished. It's not because of the violation of other laws, such as the Shabbat or kosher laws. Why is that? The reason is simple, it is because idolatry undermines the unilateral power of the priests, and violations of Shabbat or kosher laws only affect them slightly.

The struggle between Moses and Aaron erased

In Exodus (3.1), Moses married Tsipora, the daughter of a priest named Jethro who was from Median. But in Numbers (10.29), this priest is called Raouel. The sons of Moses and Tsipora are Gershom and Eliezer. They are only mentioned once in Exodus (18.3), but they do not matter and are soon forgotten. The rabbis of the Talmud explain that Moses converted his wife and father-in-law, but there are no references of it in any writing. Unlike the sons of Moses, Aaron's sons are often mentioned and play an active role. The term *"Aaron and his sons"* is mentioned dozens of times. Numbers (26.58) gives the genealogy of the Levites without mentioning the sons of Moses. Eleazar, the son of Aaron, succeeds his father, according to Numbers (20.26). Then it will be the turn of Phinehas, grandson of Aaron. And finally, as written in Chronicles (23.13), the family of Aaron establishes power forever, *"Aaron and his sons had the eternal responsibility of holding the holy functions, and they formed a class apart."*

And the sons of Moses? Nothing is ever mentioned! It is Joshua and not the sons of Moses who bring the Hebrews into the Promised Land. They inherit nothing and completely disappear from the history and memory of the Hebrew people. Why are the sons of Aaron the ones who succeed while the sons of Moses are barely mentioned and are so quickly forgotten? One rabbi answers that political power is not hereditary, while the religious power of the family of Aaron is! What are the qualities that allowed Aaron and his descendants to gain eternity in the priesthood? However, modern civilization rejects hereditary power. The Talmud, Bava Batra 110a, gives another reason: Jonathan, son of Gershom, son of Menashe/Moshe, is the idolatrous priest talked about in Judges (18.30). If you take away the *N* in the name *Menashe*, it becomes Moshe. And that's why Menashe was written with the N on top, out of respect for Moses and also to compare Moshe the son of Jonathan to King Menashe, who also practiced idolatry. This argument from the Talmud doesn't hold water for three reasons: first, the name of Moses is very often mentioned without any change in its spelling. Second, the book of Judges could not mention Menashe the king who ruled several generations after the writing of this book. If they did, they would have had to acknowledge that the books of the Bible were written well after the fact. And that would have been impossible because the son of Gershom, son of Moses, did not live during that time. Thirdly, what about the other son of Moses? It would have been simpler to accept what was written: a certain Jonathan, son of Gershom, who was from the tribe of Menashe. But this would bring up another problem: what about the existence of priests who are not from the tribes of the Levites?

The prophets seem to be part of Moses's camp and the priests appear to support Aaron. The prophets are the ones who minimize the role of the sacrifices, and here are some examples: in Isaiah (1.11), *"What matter the multitude of your sacrifices? I am saturated with your burnt offerings of rams...*

Your incense is an abomination to me." Jeremiah (7.21) calls out the imposed sacrifices as lies: *"I have not commanded your ancestors the day I brought them out of Egypt . . . about burnt offerings and sacrifices."* So, for Jeremiah, if not God, who invented the rules of sacrifices? Did the Torah contain other false rules? Micah (6.6) also opposed the sacrifices. Finally, Hosea (6.6) and (8.13) concluded: *"I desire mercy and not sacrifice . . . The victims they offer to me, they immolate them to eat the flesh, the Lord takes no pleasure from that . . ."*

Exiled in Babylon, the prophet Ezekiel (40 to 48) describes his divine vision of the future temple, totally different from the first temple and different from the second temple rebuilt after the return from exile.

Sacrifices, a form of taxation to profit only a certain cast

A person who sins should be put to death according to the law. Leviticus (17.11) explains that *"the vital principle of the flesh is in the blood . . . for it is the blood that makes atonement for the soul."* So blood is necessary. The goal of the sacrifice was to transfer the punishment to an animal, and put it to death instead of the sinner. But this transfer is neither logical nor moral!

Some want to idealize sacrifices. Richard Friedman, author of the famous book *Who wrote the Bible?* is mistaken when he says: *"The function of sacrifice is misunderstood . . . when men want to eat meat, they take the life of an animal . . . This is a sacred act that must be performed by a priest."* He is wrong. What about the donation of flour, fruits, cakes, etc.? These sacrifices don't take away the life of any animal. And why are sacrificed animals eaten anyway?

Exodus (30.12) orders that a census of the Hebrews in the desert be done and asks that *"everyone will pay to the Lord in order to redeem himself . . . so that there be no mortality among them because of this operation."* Why should one pay to be counted? It is also written: *"half will be reserved for the offering to the Lord."* To whom does the other half go? How does making a payment save an individual's life? What about the slaves in the desert who have no money? This whole chapter makes no sense and is anachronistic!

In Genesis (8.21) and Exodus (29.18), God appreciates the smell of the animal sacrifice made by Noah after the flood and the one that Aaron made to him as well, *"Thou shall burn the whole ram on the altar . . . It will be a pleasant smell like sacrifice to the Lord."* The same thing is written in Leviticus (1 and 2), where God requires a good quality sacrifice accompanied by a nice smell, *"the son of Aaron the priest will put the limbs, head and fat on the wood placed on the fire which is on altar . . . Then the priest shall burn all on the altar, burning a sweet savor unto the Lord."* Does this mean that God appreciates the smells of grilled meat?

God commands that a specific list of sacrifices be done, most of which will be eaten by the priests. Regarding oblations it says: *"the offering shall be of flour in cakes unleavened mixed with oil . . . The remainder of the offering will be for Aaron and his son."* Further, God says that the offering, *"you will season them with salt . . . sign of the covenant with your God."* What do we have here? Delicious grilled meat, bread, and salt—is it God who needs all of this or the son of Aaron? Besides, Deuteronomy (18.1) confirms: *"It is given to the pontiffs descendants of Levi, the tribe of Levi in general, no part nor inheritance like the rest of Israel, it is from sacrifices to the Lord and its heritage that they survive."* Part of the sacrifices serves as a daily diet for the priests.

Some sacrifices listed in Leviticus and in Numbers:

> *"If a person sins inadvertently . . . he will bring to offering a female goat that is without blemish."*

> *"If someone touches any unclean object . . . It will offer a female sheep or goat as a repentance of the sin . . . or two turtledoves . . . or flour."*

> *"The breast shall be given to Aaron and his sons and you will give the right thigh to the pontiff . . ."*

> *"When a woman gives birth . . . she will bring a lamb of a year old as a burnt offering and a young pigeon for repentance of sin . . ."*

> *"The leper, when he becomes pure again . . . will give two live birds . . . on the eighth day he will give two lambs without blemish, and one ewe without blemish, plus three tenths of flour."*

> *"When a woman will be done with her period (menstrual period) after seven days, after which she shall be clean; on the eighth day, she will bring two doves."*

"On the fourth year, all the fruit of the new trees will be devoted to the festivities in honor of the Lord."

"Whoever kills a beast whole or kills the flock, will give to the priests the shoulder, the jaws and the stomach."

Numbers (5.8) says: *"If there is no one to claim restitution of an ill-gotten object, that object is given back to the Lord, and to the priest . . . every offering of all the holy things from the children Israel will be given unto the priest that they are presented to . . ."*

Numbers (15.27) says: *"If it is a person who has sinned unintentionally, he should bring a she goat of a year as a sacrifice . . . Each day, they will give two lambs of one year without blemish as a continual burnt offering . . . a tenth of fine flour mixed with the fourth of crushed olive oil."*

Numbers (28,11) says once a month at each new moon, *"you shall offer a burnt offering to YHWH, two young bulls, one ram, seven lambs of a year old and without blemish."*

Why all these sacrifices? Why does God need these animal sacrifices, the flour, and the fruits? A woman who gives birth must also bring for sacrifice, a lamb and a dove or two doves, according to Leviticus (12.6). Where can they find these thousands of animals and birds for sacrifice? But what is even more unbelievable is that these laws were made during the time in the desert.

Finally, the sacrifices mentioned in the Bible could not be performed because Aaron and his two sons would never have had enough time to make the thousands of daily sacrifices for the births, the circumcisions, and the purifications. They would have had to do it for 3 million Hebrews in the desert. Moreover, the meager herds of these runaway slaves would never have been enough. At that time, women were deprived of rights, were treated as irresponsible minors and not as adults. And they should be forced to bring sacrifices? Was it only for the big appetite of all the priests?

King Josiah destroyed all the altars of sacrifices to other gods in II Kings (23.9), and canceled the sacrifice made to the *"pontiffs of high places."*

That is to say, in other cities besides Judah in order to centralize all the sacrifices in one place. However, if in Deuteronomy (12,11) God orders the centralization of sacrifices only in *"the place chosen by the Lord...,"* a few lines later God gives a totally opposite order: *"kill the animals and eat the flesh, in every city..."* This order is understandable, because it would have been impossible that whenever a Hebrew wanted to eat meat he would have to go make the sacrifice and kill the beast in Jerusalem. Also, doesn't this contradict the order that says: *"Whoever kills a beast or a flock will give to the priests the shoulder, the jaws and the stomach"?*

Ezekiel (40.46) reports: *"the priests in charge of the sacrifice of the altar are the sons of Zaddok, who among the descendants of Levites come close to the Lord to serve him."* This struggle for power between groups within the Levites is further evidence that these sacrifices are only for the priests' selfish gains. If there is factional fighting, that can only mean that these laws were made by the priests themselves and not by God.

The prophecy of Jeremiah (31.14) is quite significant: *"In those days... I will satisfy the priests with offerings of fat..."* Is this abundance of grilled meats the best reward for the priests? Yet Jeremiah (7.22) contradicts the entire Torah and makes God say, *"I said nothing, commanded nothing to your ancestors, the day I brought them out of Egypt, about burnt offerings, nor sacrifices."* This bold statement means that the sacrifices were invented much later and therefore that the biblical writings were falsified. This contradiction is further evidence that there were several Jeremiah who wrote his prophecies.

After the destruction of the Second Temple by the Romans and the exile of the Jewish population, it became clear that the sacrifices were not to continue. The texts do not talk about any prayer done at the temple during the time of sacrifices; it is only after the destruction that the sacrifices were replaced by prayers. The rabbis then came up with the solution, which was already implemented during the preceding Babylonian exile. They replaced the sacrifice by prayers, and the temple by the synagogue. The end of the sacrifices of thousands of animals and the cruelty of these practices should be a great progress. Prayer is better than bloody sacrifice!

If Titus had spared the temple, thousands of cattle, sheep, or pigeons would continue to be sacrificed and their blood would still be spilling, smelly on the steps of the court of the temple. The Jews themselves would have been shamed. The destruction of the temple saved them from this bloody obscurantism. Ramban was the first one who understood how these sacrifices were primitive and useless.

Why aren't sacrifices practiced in Jerusalem today?

Fortunately, there are no sacrifices practiced in Jerusalem today. Why is that? Was it because the temple was destroyed?

The Second Temple was destroyed by the Romans around 70 AD and since then the sacrifices were no longer practiced. On the ruins of the Jewish temple, the Muslims built the Al Aqsa Mosque. Deuteronomy (12.5) requests that the sacrifices be centralized in one place, *"only to the place which YHWH your God has adopted..."* But after arriving in the Promised Land, Samuel and Saul, David and Solomon ignored this centralization and made sacrifices in different places, which would confirm that this centralization was ordered by the priesthood of Jerusalem in the time of King Josiah, a few centuries after Moses. The sacrifices are not dependent on the existence of the temple since they were made in the desert, in Shiloh, and in Beit El before the construction of the first temple, and in Bethlehem and elsewhere as mentioned in 1 Samuel. Also, for nearly two centuries the northern kingdom continued to practice sacrifices outside the temple of Jerusalem. The Judean people, first scattered then gathered again in the Promised Land, waited for the messianic days of reconstruction as if the temple was essential for the resumption of sacrifices. Malachi (3.4) affirms and believes that at the arrival of the Messiah the temple (the second) would be rebuilt and sacrifices would resume and *"YHWH will take pleasure in the offerings of Judah and Jerusalem as it was in ancient days."*

In fact, this second temple was not built by the Messiah but by Ezra and Nehemiah and was expanded by Herod. Upon their return to Jerusalem, in Ezra (3.6), *"they began to offer burnt offerings to YHWH before they had laid the foundation of the Lord's Temple."* So the rebuilding of the temple is not a condition for the resumption of sacrifices. Yet since the destruction of the second temple the Jews prayed: *"God of our ancestors . . . rebuild your house identically . . . Reintegrate priests, restore choirs and concerts of the Levites, Return Israel to its land . . . we bow down to the three pilgrimage festivals: Passover, Pentecost and Cabanes . . . We offer the required sacrifices, the daily offerings and the added donations . . ."*

So is it the existence of the ark that is needed to start the sacrifices?

What is important is not the physical place but the presence of the Ark of the Covenant, which had disappeared. Yet sacrifices were made before the construction of the ark, in Exodus (24.5) where Moses *"charged the young men of Israel to offer burnt offerings and to sacrifice as victims, bulls to YHWH . . ."*

In the desert, the Hebrews had only a mobile temple: the tabernacle described in Exodus (25): *"a sanctuary that I live among them . . . a wooden ark, you . . . lay them in the ark the Statute that I give thee . . . And thou shall make two cherubim of gold . . . their extended wings . . . This is where I will visit you."* The Ark of the Covenant or testimony is therefore a safe, considered to be the earthly throne of God, and containing the tablets of the law given to Moses, and the sacrifices were made in its presence. This mobile tabernacle moved according to the movement of the troops. In Judges (20.26), *"all the people went to Bethel . . . and offered sacrifices to the Lord . . . For the ark was there at that time."* Again, in I Samuel (11.15), *"all the people made sacrifices before YHWH and Saul"* at Gilgal, *"because the ark of YHWH that day was with the children of Israel."* Yet this is not always the case. In Judges (6.26), Gideon built in Ofra an altar and made sacrifices under the command of the Lord. Moreover, it is impossible to conceive that all the sacrifices were made where the tabernacle is, because it would mean that all the Hebrews had to make numerous travels from their place of residence to the tabernacle for many occasions: birth of a child, a woman's menstrual period, for healing, and for impurity.

This ark containing the tablets of the law written by the hand of God is so holy that according to II Samuel (6,7) a man named Uzzah was struck down because he had touched it (to prevent it from falling). The ark was placed in the first temple by King Solomon, who said in 1 Kings (8.13) that God resides in the temple for eternity. He was mistaken! This ark is never mentioned in the Bible, not even during the destruction of the first temple, not even during the construction of the second temple and its destruction. The sacrifices continued despite the destruction of the first temple and the disappearance of the Ark of the Covenant. In Ezra (3, 3), after their return from exile, the Judeans built an altar without the Ark of the Covenant to offer sacrifices. After the construction of the second temple, was the ark found again and was it placed back in the new temple? Was the ark hidden away by the priests? During the five centuries of the second temple, were sacrifices renewed without the ark?

In addition, according to the testimony of the Roman general Pompey, when the second temple was destroyed, the Holy of Holies was empty and he did not find the ark inside. If Pompey told the truth and the ark was lost before the destruction of the second temple, the priests were conducting sacrifices without the presence of the ark! Finally, let's assume that the original ark was destroyed or had disappeared, could they not build a new ark by simply following the details described in Exodus (25)? If the first destroyed temple could be rebuilt, why would it not be possible to make a new ark? A rabbi confirms that religious Jews do not seek the Ark of the Covenant, because when the Messiah comes, he will designate the location and place it in the rebuilt temple. Yet according to the Book of Maccabaeus, the Judeans, under the leadership of Judas the Maccabean, built a new altar similar to the first one after taking Jerusalem from the hands of Antiochus and will rebuild with new tools and *"present a sacrifice according to the Torah on the new altar . . . Make sacrifices of peace and gratitude."* And so they would make sacrifices after building a new altar themselves. Since sacrifices were made before the building of the ark, or after its destruction, it would prove that the lack of the ark does not explain the cessation of sacrifices.

The *tekhelet* color and the clothes of the high priest

A rabbi added that to make sacrifices other conditions must be met: one must know exactly the definition of the *tekhelet* color. So the priests cannot perform their service without clothes colored in *tekhelet*, which is the color blue or indigo. We know almost nothing about its manufacturing process. Why is it that Judaism, which boasts of its oral tradition and the sacred right of the rabbis to judge in matters of religion, cannot have more information on the color *tekhelet?* Exodus chapter 28 is devoted to the description of the garments of the high priest. But why would a Hebrew living in the desert at the time have such a concern unless it was a detail added much later?

So when did the garments of the high priest disappear? And is this disappearance a good enough reason to stop the sacrifices imposed by the Torah? In Exodus (24.5), Moses himself ordered a sacrifice to be done, and this long before any description of the priest's clothes, mentioned (Exode28). Moreover, Numbers (15.38) requires that the *tallit* garment or fringe be of the color *tekhelet*. No one knows how to reconstruct this *tekhelet* color, so by this same logic we should have canceled the wearing of this fringed drawstring attire. But the Jews continue to wear these *tallits* or fringe by finding an alternative of this unknown *tekhelet* color.

One last hurdle: the doubt about the descendants of the Kohanim priest

Some of the sacrifices, the mandatory ones, must be done only by the Kohanim. In Ezra (2.62) it is written: *"the descendants of the priests researched . . . their genealogy, but nothing could be found, so they were stripped of their priesthood."* The above quote shows that the sacrifices were made in the absence of any Kohanim being identified. Since sacrifices continue until the destruction of the second temple, which means that even if the Levitical genealogy was lost the sacrifices continued. And finally, if their genealogy is hard to establish, why do the Jewish laws prevent, till today, a Cohen from marrying a divorced woman (in Lev.21.7)?

Another excuse that is sometimes given in order not to rebuild the temple is that Jews are waiting for the arrival of the Messiah in order to rebuild the temple. But this claim is wrong and the first and second temples weren't built by the Messiah but by humans and was even ordered by non-Jews, like Emperor Cyrus.

The sacrifices should therefore have continued with or without the temple, with or without an ark, and should have continued till today in independent Israel. But they have stopped, and all the obstacles mentioned above are false excuses.

During the Middle Ages, the famous rationalist Maimonides, in his book *Guide for the Perplexed*, compared the ritualistic sacrifices of the pagans *"at the time, the custom was to serve God by performing sacrifices; God allowed these cults to exist, but instead of letting the sacrifices be directed towards . . . created objects that have no reality, He ordered man to make the sacrifices towards His Name and to Him."*

It means that for the Hebrews accustomed to perform sacrifices to gods and idols, it would have been too drastic to cancel them and it was better to channel those sacrifices in order to satisfy the true God. So God deceived the Hebrew people, considered immature. It would be like a father saying to his baby that if he does not eat, the evil witch will come and get him . . . Is it possible that by this same logic other biblical rules were invented to suit the religion?

An example of a strange sacrifice is described in Leviticus (14.52). It says that to combat rampant leprosy in a house, it is necessary to spray the blood of a bird in order to purify it. How can the blood of a bird purify a house and stop the spread of leprosy? That sounds like some primitive belief!

Unlike Maimonides, who gives no values to the sacrifices and says that they are just an extension of paganism, another rabbi named Nachmanides explains that sacrifices existed before idolatry, even in the days of Cain and Abel, and are an unexplained secret. According to Nachmanides, if it is written in the Torah that God accepts the sacrifices of Abel and Noah and enjoyed their pleasant aroma, then it means that sacrifices have a positive value in themselves. Another rabbi says that the love of God needs to be expressed through prayer and also through a physical act, which is the act of sacrifice. Other rabbis explain that a sacrifice is a kind of penalty that a Jew who breaks the law of Moses has to pay. Just like today, when a driver violates traffic laws he has to pay a ticket. But how is the birth of a baby an offense punishable by a fine?

These divergent explanations are unconvincing. The simplest explanation is that these sacrifices were imposed by the powerful tribe of priests for their benefit. In 66, the procurator Florus stole the gold of the temple. That was the spark that led to the Jewish revolt, followed by the destruction of the temple in 70. Only the western wall still exists. A group of Pharisees led by Yohanan Ben Zakkai left Jerusalem to establish a rabbinical school in the small coastal town of Yavneh. It is at that time, after 70, that the ritualism, the sacrifices, and the merchants of the temple were no longer practiced and were replaced by a less bloody Judaism.

If the Temple had not been destroyed by the Romans, the sacrifices would have continued and Aaron's descendants would have continued to benefit from the meat and flour and other foods given as sacrifice by the Hebrews to the temple. Thousands of cattle and pigeons would have been slaughtered in the temple. Today, this barbaric ritual sacrifice would neither be possible nor acceptable, even if all the right conditions were met. The destruction of the second temple gives an excuse to avoid the shame of the rituals forever.

In fact, Jewish life is more spiritual without the temple and its bloody and barbaric sacrifices. Some Jews would just prefer to build the temple without any of the bloody sacrifices too offensive to the sensibility of our modern times. But how can they cancel the practice of sacrifices if it has been ordained by God? The end of the practice of sacrifices forced rabbis to enhance or exaggerate other rules in order to prevent assimilation, and so dietary laws and the Sabbath became the two pillars of Judaism.

Judaism and its evolution in three phases

The first phase would be the monolatry phase; that is to say, a particular god among other gods, who protects his chosen people, the Jewish people, who pay the god through sacrifices in order to obtain his favors. Some within the Jewish community accept other second-class deities whom they serve from time to time, like the gods Baal and Ashtar. This phase gave birth to the texts of the Exodus, the ten plagues of Egypt, the conquest of the Promised Land, and a long list of sacrifices made to the particular God of the Hebrews, and especially to the priests.

The second phase takes place after the defeats of the Hebrew people and during their exile in Babel. This defeat and this miserable situation led to the belief that there is one universal God. To suit this new belief, new legends are added to the Bible, but the idea of the Jews being the chosen people and the Alliance is never erased. The liberal government of Babel allowed its subjects to continue to practice their religion. This phase takes place without any sacrifices being done because the temple had been destroyed. However, the hope of renewing the sacrifice is always latent. Hope became reality after the construction of the second temple.

The third phase appears after the destruction of the second temple and the new dispersion. The sacrifices have become impossible and the Jewish are struggling to prevent assimilation. The rabbis use alternative methods: prayers replace the sacrifices and the rules of the *kashrut* and the Shabbat are becoming increasingly minute. The *kippah* and the need for *minian* (ten Jews present for prayer) are imposed. These rules are not written in the Bible, but they were developed by rabbis to preserve the Jewish people from assimilating with others. It is the time of the Talmud that has lasted until today. The Jews who are trying to spiritualize their religion certainly do not want to rebuild the temple, because that would bring back the sacrifices and would therefore make their religion appear primitive.

The sacrifices replaced by the prayer— is that allowed by the Bible?

Nowhere does the Jewish Bible order the recitation of prayers. Although the Bible describes individual or public prayers, they are supposed to be spontaneous and not ordered. After the destruction of the temple, the rabbis found it was necessary to replace the sacrifices with prayers. They searched through the Scriptures to justify their innovation and they found in the verse of the prophet Hosea (14.3) the following, *"Take with you words, and turn to God! Tell him: Whoever has sinned accepts repair, the bulls will be paid by our lips."* In fact, this verse is difficult to translate. But assuming that the translation indicates the replacement of sacrifices by prayer, who can change the divine laws of sacrifices? Only God.

By manipulating mere words the rabbis can change the meaning of the verses. This might be the case here, and they would have added the letter M to the word *pri*, which became *parim*. Where the original word, as reported by the Septuagint, was *pri* and further *msfatinou*, which means *"fruit of our lips."* The meaning of the verse from Hosea would therefore not have asked to replace the sacrifices with prayer.

Even today, the believers, Jewish, Christians, and Muslims alike pray for rain, good harvests, or a good marriage as if their God was an agronomist, a doctor, or a marriage counselor. In 1999, Taliban leaders organized a gathering of thousands of Afghans in the desert to pray for rain.

Jesus accepted sacrifices and did not drive merchants out of the temple

The New Testament describes Jesus chasing the traders out of the second Temple as if he opposed the sacrifices. However, Jesus accepted the sacrifices. In Luke (2.24), Jesus's parents come to the temple in Jerusalem *"to offer in sacrifice two turtledoves or two young pigeons, as it is written in the law of the Lord."* In Matthew (8.4), Mark (1.44), and Luke (5.14), Jesus orders the leper he just healed to *"go show yourself to the priest and offer the gift that Moses commanded . . ."* as ordered in Leviticus (14). So it seems that Jesus recognizes the need for sacrifices. In Matthew (5.23), Jesus reprimands an angry brother: *"First go and reconcile with your brother and then come and offer your offering . . ."* (of course, at the temple). Jesus did not cancel the sacrifice.

You cannot attack the merchants of the temple as described in the Gospels and also, like Jesus, practice offerings and sacrifices as suggested by the written law. Merchants at the temple were essential for the sacrifices imposed by Jewish law. Without them no sacrifices would have been made. Those merchants are the ones who brought pigeons and lambs and exchanged currencies.

Jesus, though he himself, according to the Gospels, did not ever present any sacrifice in the temple, was not against any written rules of the temple but against all the additional sacrifices invented by the priests for their own personal gain. It sounds more like the priests, wanting to protect their privileges, had to get rid of this nuisance who was Jesus. It therefore seems that the scene of Jesus in the temple is a made-up addition. Jesus has no problem with offerings and sacrifices. Luke (19.45) describes the scene of Jesus in the temple after his triumphal entry into Jerusalem on a colt. Mark (11.15), however, separates the two events with his return to Bethany. John (2.15) dates the scene at the beginning of Jesus's ministry, two years before his death, and makes no connection between the scandal and his death. Matthew (21,23) describes Jesus, who is hailed at the temple, on his donkey, driving the merchants away and returning the next day despite the scandal as if it nothing had never occurred, *"and while teaching . . ."* the priests ask him a question without attacking or excluding him. And during his trial, Jesus was never accused of ransacking the temple and his accusers seemed to have forgotten this event that probably never took place. Matthew (23.18) is critical of the priests: *"If someone, you say, swears by the altar, it is nothing. But whoever swears by the offering that is upon it, he has committed . . ."* but is not opposed to the sacrifices. In Matthew(24), Jesus asked that when you are offering your gift at the altar, if you remember that your brother has something against you, leave your offering there before the altar and first be reconciled with your brother, then come and offer your offering.

In Matthew (24.1–2) Jesus comes out from the temple and says, *". . . There will not be left here one stone unturned."* The beginning of chapter 24 has no connection with the following text because it was added seventy years later. If Jesus had preached against the temple and had predicted its destruction, how is it possible that his disciples returned to Jerusalem and to the temple to pray? If Jesus preached for a spiritual temple, without sacrifice and without merchants, why is it that after his death his followers, and even Paul, went there to present their offerings? Jesus strangely reappears, according to Acts (22.18), to Paul while he is praying in this impure temple. The disciples continued to patronize the temple without any opposition of the priests.

According to Acts (2.46): *"And they were all frequenting the temple regularly and daily . . ."* And further in (3.1) it says: *"Peter and John were going up to the temple at the hour of prayer, which was the ninth."* They miraculously escaped from prison, and in Acts (5. 21 and 42): *"They came early in the day, in the temple and taught . . ."*. And more than fifteen years after the death of Jesus, Paul will still *"make offerings . . . some Jews from Asia found me purified in the temple . . ."*

The scene of Jesus against the temple has been added by Paul or by his followers for several reasons. Entrance to the temple was prohibited to pagans Paul wanted to convert. And in Acts (21. 28), Paul was accused by the Jews: *"This is the man who teaches . . . against the people, against the law and against this place, the temple. He even brought Greeks into the temple and has defiled this place!"* In addition, the Jewish Diaspora, because of the distance, could not apply the rules of the sacrifices at the Temple of Jerusalem because of the distance and therefore could not be purified during the time of birth or at their death. This temple and its sacrifices was an obstacle for the Jews of the Diaspora and also to the Gentiles who converted to the new sect. It was therefore necessary to make the temple appear less important. Paul found an additional argument: Jesus, by sacrificing himself, canceled once and for ever the need for any other sacrifices. The political and economic opposition of the priests against Jesus was transformed into a religious opposition. Jesus opposed the corrupt priests and collaborators, and without this scandal, the opposition of the Sadducees priests against Jesus would have appeared to be inexplicable. Paul wanted to export his new religion, and therefore he had to erase its connection from the Temple in Jerusalem. Paul had to invent a new faith transportable to Rome. John (4.21) also invented a scene where Jesus said to the Samaritan woman: *"It is neither on this mountain nor in Jerusalem that you will worship the Father."*

In conclusion: Jesus was not opposed to animal sacrifices or to the offerings at the temple (as written in the Jewish law), but he was opposed to the additional sacrifices that the priests made for their own interests. It was not Jesus but Paul and his followers who allegedly invented this scandal at the temple in order to relocate the new religion and to legitimize its destruction by the Romans and to allow the new worship center to be far from Jerusalem.

Jesus's death turned into the ultimate sacrifice!

The essence of Christianity is that God sacrificed his one and only son to save us from our sins. According to Romans (5.9): *"We are justified by his blood."* To achieve this goal, Christian writings strive to transform Jesus into a lamb that was sacrificed on the day and time of Easter. Because Jews sacrificed a lamb on Easter, Jesus rightly was hanged on that day, against all logic, since according to Mark (14.2) Jewish priests said: *"Let it not be during the feast so that there will be no uproar among the people."* However, to make him look like the Passover lamb, Jesus was exhibited in public and exposed in the streets of Jerusalem on Easter Friday, the day during which thousands of pilgrims flock to the temple. The Gospels mention the time and death of Jesus, between the sixth and the ninth hour, between 12:00 hours and 15:00 hours. This time is symbolic, because noon was usually the time when the lambs were killed in the temple, and therefore Jesus had to be sacrificed like the lamb for Easter. His sacrifice permanently cancels the need for other sacrifices required by Jewish law.

In I Corinthians (5.7) is a comparison to the Lamb, *"Christ our Passover is sacrificed for us"* and in Hebrews (7.27), (9.12 and 26), and (10.10): *"Jesus does not need as those high priests, to offer up sacrifice . . . He did once for all when he offered himself . . . he entered into the holy place, not with the blood of goats and calves, but by his own blood, having obtained eternal redemption . . . Now, at the end of time, Christ appeared once to put away sin by the sacrifice . . . We are sanctified through the offering of the body of Christ once and for all."* So Jesus dying on Friday at the sixth hour negates the sacrifices to come and the need to go to the temple to purify oneself. If that were true, why would Paul and the disciples continue to go to the temple to purify themselves after the death of Jesus? It seems that the death of Jesus at Easter is a late invention that completes the symbol of the sacrificial lamb. But human sacrifice was prohibited from the time of Abraham, and this prohibition is repeated several times in the Bible. Some Christians respond that Jesus is God's son but he is also human and therefore this sacrifice should be forbidden by God himself. This contradiction proves that this notion of Jesus as a lamb sacrificed is a late addition and is totally disconnected from the Judaism that Jesus practiced.

Jewish sacrifices were cruel and unnecessary, but how does their replacement with the bloody sacrifice of God the Son solve the problem? The Catholic Catechism says in sections 385–421, which we summarize as follows: *". . . By his sin and disobedience to God's command, Adam lost his holiness . . . for him and for all human . . . The victory over sin won by Christ gave us a better possession than us that sin was removed . . . Christ, through the cross and redemption, broke the power of the evil one . . . ."* The Church does not explain how Christ broke the power of the evil one! Are there no other evil ones since the time of Jesus? Has the devil been neutralized, and do we already live in heaven because of Jesus's sacrifice? If that is so, how do we explain the horrors and the sins of this world since the time of Jesus to this day?

The sacrifice of God the Son is totally illogical. Adam and Eve, who were guilty of original sin, should have been put to death (but survived). To delete this sin, God the Father would hang his Son. Judas the traitor and the cruel Pilate therefore allow, through the killing of Jesus, the redemption of mankind. They should be blessed! Furthermore, if Jesus was sacrificed to erase the original sin, why is the punishment continued till today? Why does man continue to only eat his bread by the sweat of his brow, and woman continue to suffer during childbirth?

In Exodus (12.5), the lamb must be pure; however, Jesus's body was bloody and wounded by the whips and was unclean during the time of his hanging. Moreover, Jesus was not sinless, because in Mark (1.9) it says "... *Jesus was baptized by John in the Jordan."* This baptism was one of repentance preached by the Baptist. If Jesus was opposed to animal sacrifices in the temple, how can he accept human sacrifice? If Jesus wanted to sacrifice himself, why is he surprised that God has abandoned him? Why does God allow him to die, and why doesn't he answer the prayers of His Son? Jesus would have gone to his death or committed suicide; which itself is a sin forbidden by Jewish law. Jesus, being of divine nature, could have avoided the agony and the pain of a hanging. He says himself, in Matthew (26.53): *"Do you think I can pray to my Father, and he would not send me at once more than twelve legions of angels?"* But Jesus did not pray to his father and does everything written in the Scriptures, including drinking vinegar. Doesn't God, the Father Almighty, have no other way to redeem the sins of men than sending His Son to live a miserable life and eventually end up a hung man? Christianity says that man is reconciled to God by the murder of His Son and God forgives the sins of man because they killed His Son. This is completely illogical!

Furthermore, if Jesus, God the Son, has so often forgiven sins without requiring a sacrifice, as in Luke (5.20), why couldn't God the Father do the same? It is not written anywhere in the Bible that the death of a person can get his sins forgiven. On the contrary, everyone is responsible for his conduct and should be punished for his sins. In Exodus (32.33), the one who sins must die and not another person, and nowhere is it mentioned that the blood of a sacrificed Jew saves sins. Jesus therefore, could not die for our sins. By his sacrifice, Jesus takes away the sins of the world. This substitution of responsibility is immoral, and God sending his son to earth so that he may be sacrificed is immoral too.

Proverbs (21.3) says that God prefers justice and equity to sacrifice. Moreover, according to Isaiah (43.25 and 44.22) and Ezekiel (18. 27), God knows how to *"erase transgressions"* and forgets the sins of men, and if the man *"turns away from all his transgressions that he has committed, he shall live and not die."* Jesus's sacrifice is unnecessary because with the Yom Kippur, all sins against God are forgiven, and that is the time when the Jewish ask for forgiveness of sins they have committed against their neighbor. So if the sins are forgiven, Jesus's sacrifice is useless!

Jewish law demands the sacrifice of animals but not the blood of a man hanged by pagans. Moreover, human sacrifice was canceled after the aborted sacrifice of Isaac according to Deuteronomy (12.30). How then is it possible that Jesus, who did not change even an iota of the laws, offers himself as a sacrifice? In addition, when Jesus' brother, James, mentions Isaac's aborted sacrifice, he does not mention the sacrifice of Jesus, because he and his brother Jude remained Notsrim/Nazarenes, so for that reason, they ignored this concept of Jesus being sacrificed. Jesus did not sacrifice himself; he was simply seized by the Roman forces, convicted, and hanged!

In Luke (2.23), it says that Joseph and Mary practiced the Jewish rite of *Pidion ha ben*, which goal is precisely to avoid being sacrificed to God. So why then would Jesus be later sacrificed for the sins of men? And finally, in Luke (2.38), by mimicking Isaiah, Anna the prophetess *"spoke of him to all them that looked for redemption in Jerusalem."* She foresaw in Jesus the liberator of Jerusalem. This prophetess was mistaken! If sins had already been forgiven by the sacrifice of Jesus, his new appearances and Parousia are unnecessary. God sacrificed His only Son to save us from our sins. What is this sacrifice since Jesus rises thirty-six hours later and goes to heaven!

For Christianity, animal sacrifices were canceled because Jesus is the ultimate sacrifice, *"the Lamb of God who takes away the sin of the world,"* as written in John (1.29). And in the Epistle of the Hebrews (7.27), Paul, or rather the forger who writes under the name of Paul, says that animal sacrifice is now useless since Jesus is the last sacrificial lamb. This is wrong because Paul continues to make sacrifices more than twenty years after the death of Jesus. Acts (21.26 and 24.16) describe *"Then Paul took the men, purified himself and went the next day with them into the temple, declaring the days of purification would be fulfilled and the offering presented for each of them . . . I came to bring alms to my nation and to present offerings."* Paul says in Hebrews (10.3), *"but the memory of sins every year by these sacrifices, for it is impossible that the blood of bulls and goats take away sins."* Yes, the sacrifices do not remove sin forever, and if the sinner sins again he will have to renew his sacrifice.

The moral scandal of "indulgences"

For the Catholic Church, these indulgences were the partial or total forgiveness of sins through prayer, mortification, pilgrimage, and especially by the payment of a certain sum of money. The amount was negotiated between the sinner and the priest. These treasures amassed served to pay for the construction of new churches like the famous St. Peter's Basilica in Rome. Martin Luther denounced the excesses, the commissions paid to intermediaries, and the corruption of the Church, who took advantage of the fear of hell that Christians had during the Middle Ages. This was the beginning of the schism between Catholics and Protestants. In his dictionary, the French philosopher Voltaire wrote, *". . . What was the reason the north of Germany, Denmark, three quarters of Switzerland, Holland, England detached themselves from the Roman communion? Poverty! The indulgences, deliverance from purgatory of souls, were sold too expensively and these souls from these countries had too little money. The prelates and monks engulfed the entire income of a province. We then took a religion that was a better bargain."*

The Quran does not object to the sacrifices

And its position is ambiguous. Indeed, the Qur'an came several centuries after the destruction of the Jewish temple and thus after the cessation of Jewish sacrifices, and does not seem to decide if God wants sacrifices or not. Verse (22.36) says: *". . . The beasts of offerings from the sacraments of God. It's good for you. Invoke upon them the name of God when they are dressed for the sacrifice, and when they are lying on their sides, eat it and give to the poor . . . Neither their meat nor their blood reach only God, but your loyalty will touch him."* Verse (6.14) says *"God feeds and does not need to be fed."* During the pilgrimage, thousands of sheep are sacrificed. Why? On what beliefs do they base these sacrifices?

The Quran does not understand the refinements of the Jewish Bible and mentions in (23.28) that Noah brought into the ark *"two of every kind."* The Jewish Bible gives two versions, one in accordance with the Quran and the other adapted to different sacrifices. Verse (7.2) writes *"of every pure quadruped, you will take seven couples."* It is said that Noah offered sacrifices to God. If that were the case, that would have caused the disappearance of some species since there was only one couple of each kind in the ark. The Quran says nothing against the pseudo-sacrifice of Isaac-Ishmael, but gives to Abraham the medal of *"first Muslim"* because he submitted to the cruel order from God.

In Islam, Aaron is a prophet, but unlike in the Bible, he is not involved in the preparation of the golden calf and had even tried to dissuade the people from building the golden calf. According to the verse (20, 89), *"Aaron told them: my people, you are only tempted by this calf. Your Lord has mercy on you, follow me and obey me."* Why this change? Why is Islam trying to improve the image of this Hebrew priest? Verses (5.27) and (37.107) mention the sacrifices of Cain and Abel, of Isaac and of Ishmael. But if the God of Muhammad does not require sacrifices, why does he accept these stories and why does he accept some and reject others?

9

The creation in six days: a late addition

The three monotheistic religions are unanimous: God created the world in six days. This statement is very weak and only based on Moses receiving the word of God. Therefore, doubts about Moses receiving divine revelation inevitably led to doubt about the Creation in six days. Without Moses and his divine revelations, Judaism, Christianity, and Islam cannot explain the Creation of the world in six days.

On the first day, *"In the beginning, God created the heavens and the earth... He makes a distinction between light and darkness. God called the light Day, and the darkness He called Night."* This first day is impossible because in the Bible the sun and stars were created on the fourth day. This, not only contradicts the science that says the Earth, the sun and stars, and the galaxy were created together, but is also impossible because there is no light or darkness on Earth if the sun had not yet been created! In addition, when it is day on one side of the Earth, it is night on the other. This, the Bible writers did not know. How can be morning without sun?

On the second day, God created the atmosphere between the sea and the clouds. The rabbis say that on that day God also created hell. How do they know? They answer that at the end of each day it is written that God is satisfied, except on the second day, where the phrase *"it's good"* is omitted. Thin argument! But if God created hell the second day, before the creation of man, so God already knew that man would sin. God, and not man, would be guilty of creating sin!

On the third day, *"God said, let the earth bring forth vegetation . . ."* God created plants and trees on day three, so before the creation of the sun? But without sun and photosynthesis, plants cannot create chlorophyll and cannot live. How do they explain this failure? Jewish believers said that the historical truth is not so important, what is important is the harmony between the Creation of the first three days and the last three days.

On the fourth day, God *"made the greater light to the kingdom of the day, the lesser light to the kingdom of the night."* But God had already created light and darkness on the first day. What was the source of light on the first day before the sun is created? According to the rabbis, the light became visible on the fourth day. It's weird that God created an invisible light on the first day! What about the millions of stars? In Qur'an (67.3), *"God created seven skies, one above another."* No, there are not seven skies and this description is primitive. Verse (41.12) says: *"And the nearest sky, we have decorated with lights that protect it."* But it is wrong to believe that the stars were created after the earth and it is also wrong to believe that they are close, since they are very distant stars.

On the fifth day, *"God blessed them by saying: fill the waters, inhabitants of the seas, birds, multiply on the earth . . . fifth day."* God would have created the fish and birds on the fifth day, before the humans and the animals. And the whales, which are mammals?

On the sixth day, *"God created . . . grazing animals according to their kinds, and all those who crawl on the ground according to their kinds. . . . And wild animals, all the birds of the air . . . I assign any green plant for food . . . It was the sixth day."* Were all animals first herbivores, including carnivores and raptors? When did carnivores stop eating grass?

On the seventh day, *"God shabbat"* is almost always mistranslated as *God rested*. The Hebrew word *shabbat* does not mean *rest* but to stop or cease, and so God stopped his work this seventh day. The Quran (50) confirms that Creation occurred in six days and just says: *"We created the heavens and earth . . . in six days without fatigue overtaking us."* Muslims say they understand the divinity of God better than anyone else and that God cannot get tired. They forget to mention that they take this information from Isaiah (40.28): *"the Creator of the utmost limits of the world never feels fatigue or weariness."* Throughout the six days of Creation, and especially after the sixth day, *"God looked at everything he had made, and it was very good . . ."* Yet Adam, Eve, and humans are so bad that God punished them by destroying the earth by flood. God is a poor prophet and He wasn't able to control what He created!

Why doesn't God want man to eat the fruit of *"the tree of good and evil"*? God should want man to eat a lot of this fruit in order to distinguish right from wrong! Is there really such a fruit or is this a superstition? God threatens *"the day you eat of it you shall die."* Yet Adam and Eve eat but do not die and live for several centuries. Some believers respond that if they had not eaten the fruit of good and evil they would have been immortal. But why was the tree called the *tree of immortality* if they were already immortal?

Gary Greenberg, in his wonderful book *101 Myths of the Bible*, explains that most of the contradictions come from the mixture of two different influences, one from Egypt and one from Babylon.

The three religions and their ignorance of astronomy!

The three religions believed that the Earth was a disk in the center of the universe and that the sun revolves around it. Psalm 104 says: *"You have founded the earth on its support columns that cannot be moved."* Similarly, I Samuel (2.8) says that *"the pillars of the earth are YHWH."* Job (9.6) has the same belief that God *"made the earth tremble to its foundations and undermine the pillars that support it."* According to Matthew (2.9) of the New Testament, *"...There's the star they had seen in the East before them, till it came to being above the place where the child was, she stopped."* A star that twinkles then stops is incompatible with astronomy. It is a remnant of pagan beliefs.

Some rabbis say that they have irrefutable proof that the Bible knew that the Earth was round long before the discoveries of Copernicus, Magellan, and Christopher Columbus. Isaiah (40.22) states that *"It is He who sits above the circle of the earth."* Job (26.7) and Proverbs (8.27) say: *"when He drew a circle on the surface of the abyss."* The best proof would be in the Zohar: *"The earth rotates around like a ball . . . This is why, when it is day for some it is night for others. And there is a place where there is a long day and where night is extremely short."* This astronomical description is amazing, but the Zohar was written in the thirteenth century (and not by Rabbi Shimon Bar Yochai in the first century AD, as some rabbis like to say). This is not too surprising considering that we know that some Greek scholars, such as Ptolemy, Parmenides, Pythagoras, Euclid, and Aristotle, argued that the earth was round and turned on itself before the first century. Many scholars—Greek, Egyptian, Persian, and Indian—knew that the Earth was round well before Jesus and Christianity.

Some Jews were familiar with these theories from the time of the Babylonian and Greco-Roman occupations. Aristarchus of Samos, a Greek astronomer living in the third century BC, already made calculations on the distance between the Earth, Moon, and Sun and knew that the Earth revolved around itself and around the Sun: *"The stars and the sun are immobile. As for the Earth, it moves around the sun on the circumference of a circle having its center in the Sun."* The first traces of heliocentric (the Earth revolves around the sun) theory dates back to five centuries before our era. At this time, there were not yet proven facts, only intuitions. This heliocentric theory failed because it was condemned by the Church, which imposed geo-centrism (the sun revolves around the Earth). Even the Holy Roman Empire in the fourth century and the bishops of the early Christian centuries knew it. Charlemagne, the first emperor of the Carolingian Empire (742–814), was represented in a statue of the ninth century holding a globe representing the world, proof that the world was considered spherical. All this knowledge was refuted by Christianity, which stopped the progress of astronomy.

In Poland, Copernicus asserted, again unsuccessfully, that the planets revolve around the sun. In the sixteenth century, Kepler and Tycho Brahe, with more precise observations, showed that the planets revolved in ellipses rather than circles. Galileo then took over but was forced to deny his words because for centuries the Church had accepted only one possibility: the Earth as the center of the universe and the sun and stars revolving around it. Christianity accepted later that the Earth revolves around the sun.

The Quran (41.12) says: *"He has established seven heavens . . . and the nearest heaven, we decorated with lights that guard."* Then in (37.6), *"We decorated with a star ornament the nearest heaven."* This assertion is wrong and the stars are in the entire universe. The Quran repeats false beliefs that the sun revolves around the Earth. Verse (2.258) falsely says to Abraham, *"it is God who brought the rising sun . . ."* The Quran (13.2), (31.29), and (35.13) also state that *"God has subjected the sun and the moon sail to their appointed term."* No, the sun is stationary while the Earth revolves around the sun, and the moon revolves around the Earth! Verse (14. 33): *"He has given you the sun and the moon in their gravitation."* Verse (36.38): *"And the sun runs its haven according to the judgment of the Almighty who knows."*

How does Islam respond to these errors? It claims that the sun, according to recent astronomical discoveries, is not still, but has a trajectory due to the expansion of the universe. And so the divine Quran precedes astronomy? This argument is unacceptable because the Quran mentions only the sun and moon as moving stars but forgets to mention the Earth, which they consider immobile. The Quran (13.2) states that *"God has placed the high heavens without any visible pillars,"* which means that the sky is supported by invisible pillars. Another remnant of primitive beliefs! Verse (25.61) says: *"Blessed is he who put in the sky . . . a moon shines."* Muhammad did not know that the light of the moon came from the sun.

How old is the universe, 5,800 or millions of years old?

In October 1996, Pope John Paul II stated that evolution is not incompatible with the catholic faith, and that God wanted the evolutionary process. Yet the concept of evolution contradicts the first chapter of Genesis. Why would God Almighty not reach the end of the evolutionary process? Why would He create dinosaurs and mammoths only to destroy them? Some modern believers want to reconcile biblical beliefs with science by rereading Genesis (1.1), which says *"In the beginning God created the heavens and the earth."* They come to the conclusion that the planet Earth existed before the six days of creation and therefore there is no contradiction between the geological age of the universe, which could be billions of years old, and the biblical age. This argument does not hold because even with this differentiation between the creation of the universe and the six days of biblical creation, man and animals would only have been in existence for 6,000 years, which is in total contradiction with science.

To resolve these contradictions, a rabbi named Zamir Cohen has explained the following: if archaeologists found old bones that are millions of years old, they're simply remnants of previous worlds destroyed by God who decided that there would be seven worlds. Each world would exist for 7,000 years. Our world, the fourth, will soon be destroyed. Others say that every world only lasts 6,000 years and is then destroyed gradually in a span of 1,000 years. Still others say that God created twenty-six worlds that were all destroyed. Other believers argue that the first five days of creation are in *"a referential time different from ours,"* and that we are unable to understand the plan of God, who can speed up the time and the different phases of evolution

To reconcile Genesis with science, some creationists assert that a day to God in the Bible is not a twenty-four-hour period but a period that can last up to millions of years. They take as evidence Psalm (90.4), *"a thousand years in thy sight are as yesterday."* In the New Testament, II Peter (3.8) adds, *"With the Lord one day is as a thousand years and a thousand years is as one day."* In the Quran, the Creation took take place in six days and the Sura (7.54) confirms: *"Your Lord is God who created the heavens and the earth in six days, and then he sat on the throne."* Yet the Sura (32.5) states that *"From heaven, God orders everything on the earth and everything goes back to Him in a day that lasts 1000 years."* Further, (70.4) says *"the angels and the spirit ascend to God in a day of 50,000 years."* So does the day have twenty-four hours, 1,000 years, or 50,000 years?

A Muslim website quantifies each day period and says that the first day period lasted 8 billion years, the second day period lasted 4 billion years, and the third 2 billion years, and so and so on. But *"There was evening and there was morning, and it was a day,"* is repeated six times in Genesis and it applies only to the day we know, a day of twenty-four hours. Some religious people claim that the Bible stories are metaphors and not to be taken literally, so that changes everything. How many years is man supposed to live? According to Genesis, God warned Adam that if he eats from the Tree of Good and Evil he would die. However, after eating from the tree, not only did Adam not die but lived up to 900 years old. How do they explain this contradiction? The rabbis explain that if Adam had not eaten the forbidden fruit he would have lived forever, and so by becoming mortal Adam confirms God's punishment. This response is unacceptable. Wasn't there another tree in the Garden of Eden, the Tree of Eternal Life? Was Adam supposed to live forever before committing his sin? According to Genesis (6.3), *"the Lord said . . . the man is flesh: yet his days shall be 120 years."* But Noah lived to be 950, Terah 250, Abraham 175, Sarah 127, and Ishmael 137.

Who appeared first, man or animals? In Genesis 1, it says, *"Elohim God made the beast of the earth after his kind, and cattle after their kind, and every creeping thing of the earth after his kind. God saw that it was good. And God said, let us make man in our image, after our likeness and let them have* *dominion . . ."* While in Genesis 2, it's written: *"YHWH-God said, it is not good that the man should be alone; I will make him a help meet. The Lord God made every beast of the earth, every beast of the field and every bird of the air, and brought them to Adam to see what he would call them. And whatever the man called every living creature, that was its name."* These two stories are contradictory. In the first, the animals were created before man; in the second, the animals were created after man.

Also in another verse, Adam and Eve, noting their nakedness after they had sinned, God punishes them and *"made for man and woman garments of skins, and clothed them."* Why is it so important to replace clothing made from leaves with animal skin? Why is God giving the bad example that animals should be killed for their fur? Why did God create animals directly, both male and female, while Eve needed a rib from Adam?

Another contradiction is whether plants were created before or after humans. In Genesis (1.11), *"God said, let the earth . . . plant fruit trees . . . The earth brought forth grass . . . third day."* Yet Genesis (2) says that after the creation of man *"no product of the field had yet appeared on the earth, and every herb of the field before it grew . . ."* The contradiction is obvious because there are two different creation stories.

Was woman created before or after animals?

Here also, there are two different stories. The first one is according to Genesis, where God is called Elhoim, and *"God created man in his own image . . . male and female he created them . . ."* This explanation is not very clear and the wise rabbis, in their oral tradition, explain that male and female were created jointly like Siamese twins but were later separated. What about the stallion and the mare, where they made jointly as well? Verse (51.49) says, *"We have created everything in pairs."* But some species only have one gender. In this first story, Adam and Eve were created on day six, after the plants, trees, fish, birds, and animals.

In Genesis 2, God is called YHWH-Elohim. There, first Adam is created, then the plants and trees, the animals and birds, and finally Eve (who was created from one of the ribs of the courageous Adam). The creation of fish is not mentioned in Genesis 2. In Genesis (2.18), after creating Adam, God recognizes *"it is not good that man should be alone;*

I will make a helper at his side. God formed of earth material all the wild animals and all the birds of heaven and brought them to Adam to give them a name." This paragraph is funny and deserves further reading, because God, after stating that He will make a companion for Adam, created animals, not the woman! God created animals after creating Adam unlike what Genesis (1) describes and He created the animals before Eve! Did a copyist transcribe the paragraph wrongly? What about the fish, why do they remain nameless?

If God creates woman from the rib of Adam, in all logic, Adam should have one less rib. The rabbis explain that *rib* and *side* are the same word in Hebrew, and side is not about rib but has a metaphysical meaning. In the Talmud, Yebamoth 63a, Rabbi Eleazar explains the sentence found in Genesis: *"this is bone of my bones and flesh of my flesh."* The Talmud explains that Adam had sexual intercourse with all the animals but was not satisfied until he cohabited with Eve. This wise man is considered to be inspired by God! In Genesis 2, God brings the animals to Adam, who names them one by one. But bringing all the animals in the Garden of Eden would have killed a large number of them. They would have been unsuitable for this climate.

The sexual reproductive organs of animals and humans are similar. This is strange! Did God imagine the sexual system even before Adam and Eve were created? Was Adam asexual or was he already established male with male sexual organs? They say God created male and female animals, so did they have both the sexual organs? Did God copy the sexual organs of animals when He later created Adam and Eve's sexual organs? To these questions, a rabbi responds by saying that Adam did have a physical body but one made of light, and that it was only after the original sin that God *"made him clothes made of skin."* This answer creates even more confusion. Did Eve also have a body made of light before the original sin? This body of light, was it female? Did Adam and Eve have navels? If their body was made of light, why did they cover up with fig leaves? And again, why is it said to *"dust you will return"*? And if they have a body made of light why do they need to eat? The famous *"body made of light"* argument is also used to answer the question about the age of Adam and Eve. When were they created? Were they created without bodies and ageless? Did they transform into their material bodies after the original sin? If they had a *"body made of light,"* why does God, in Genesis (2.7), create them using dust from the ground?

What would have happened if Eve had obeyed God and rejected the snake and the forbidden fruit? Adam and Eve would have lived forever in paradise, and hell would have been useless. This simple decision that Eve made would have changed God's divine projects.

Was man made in the image of God or of the monkey?

In Genesis (1.26), *"God said, let Us make man in our image, in our likeness..."* This statement leads to several questions: did man look like God from the beginning and still look like him today? Is Eve also made in the image of God? Was Adam created as a baby who grew into an adult? If he was born a baby, how did he learn to walk and talk? If Adam was created in the image of God and man has sexual needs, instincts, a desire for food, and aggressive behaviors, does that mean that God does too? The religious say that *B'Tselem = in the image* means in the image of God intellectually and not physically. This explanation is not acceptable, because as we can see in (5.3), *"Adam ... bore a being in his image = B'Tselem, and called the son Seth,"* which means that *B'Tselem* is physical. Man is similar to animals, especially other mammals. So if man was created in the image of God, so are animals! Just like birds, fish, insects, and others animals, man has two eyes, a mouth with teeth, a brain, and sexual needs just like cats, pigs, rats, and others mammals. Man has legs and arms, a heart, a digestive system similar to that of many other animals. We should ask ourselves the question: did God lack imagination when He created man and animals? Do humans and all other creatures come from a common ancestor as evolutionists claim? Some Jewish wise men explain that at the time of Enoch, the grandson of Adam, God had transformed the humans who were behaving badly into half monkeys. That would explain the archaeological discoveries of bones of Lucy and other human ancestors. This belief was echoed by the Quran in (2.65) and (7.166): *"those who violated the Sabbath, you know that we have told them: you are as monkey rejects."*

The Evangelist John (5.37) says: *"You have never heard his voice"* speaking of God. That verse contradicts what Adam says in Genesis (3.9) *"I heard your voice in the garden and I was afraid."* In Islam, Sura (15.26) argues that *"man, We created him from a malleable clay mud,"* but also in Sura (2.30): *"When thy Lord said to the angels: I am going to place on earth an heir, they said: Are you to appoint a sewer of disorder that sheds blood while we praise and cry out your holiness . . . He instructed Adam of all the names, then presented them to the angels . . . He says: Adam, reveal their names . . . When We said, bow before Adam, they bowed except Iblis, who refused with pride and was one of those who believed not"* The Quran repeats several times the story of creation and always Iblis replied, *"I'm better than this creature. You created me from fire and you created him from clay."* What is the significance of these verses? Did God want Adam to be superior to the angels? Did he want him as heir? Did Iblis, the rebel angel, right to expect that man would spread evil while God ignored it? Was he correct in refusing to bow to Adam?

The story of Creation is parachuted into the Jewish Bible!

There are two different stories (both erroneous) about Creation. A tale, probably inserted after the Babylonian exile, called God *Elohim*. This God created the animals, and lastly Adam as both male and female. Another story written before the exile says God, who was called *YHWH Elohim*, created Adam, the animals, and finally Eve from one of Adam's ribs. This double tale was inserted very late, as evidenced by the following clues:

1. In stories that occur centuries later, the Creation is *"monolatry,"* meaning a national god fighting for his protégés against other national gods. But the story of the Creation, purely monotheistic and universal, is a product of the Babylonian exile.
2. Genesis (2.24) tells us that God made only one woman for Adam: *"Therefore a man shall leave his father and mother and shall cleave to his wife and they must become one flesh."* Abraham and all the patriarchs were polygamous, and could not *"become one flesh"* with their wives, which of the five or six? Adam's strict monogamy is contrary to the polygamy of the patriarchs, their descendants, and of the kings described in the Bible. All of them had many wives and concubines. Monogamy in Genesis is further evidence that the story of Creation was written much later than the other books, and certainly after the exile.
3. All the texts of the Bible ignore the story of Adam and Eve and make no reference of it anywhere. No prophet predicted that with the arrival of the Messiah, man will be freed from the constraints

of work by the sweat of his brow and women will be free from the pain of childbirth. There is no reference to these two punishments.

4. The story of the original sin is contrary to the Jewish vision. While throughout the Bible the sinner can be forgiven if he repents from his mistakes and makes sacrifices to God, the original sin is final and no forgiveness is possible. Even the innocent animals are punished and must give birth in pain. Yet Job (10.9) seems to know the Creation of Genesis: *"Remember that you molded me like clay, and you will make me return to the dust."* But the text of Job is dated between the seventh and second century BCE and thus confirms that the Creation comes from the period of the exile.

5. The story of the original sin states that the sin of Adam and Eve will fall on all of mankind forever. But in Exodus (20.5), it says God *"continues the crime of fathers upon the children unto the third and fourth generation."* As we can see, it's only in a few generations. Then the prophet Ezekiel in (18.20) ignores this divine order and writes the opposite: *"the son shall not bear the sin of the father."* Did he not know that the descendants of Adam had to earn their bread by the sweat of their brow forever? These five indicators show that the Creation story was inserted into the Bible after the Babylonian exile. Also, whoever does not believe that God spoke to Moses cannot accept the story of Creation, because for Jews, Christians, and Muslims the sole source of the story of Creation is found in Genesis, where God spoke to Moses.

10

Life after death? Paradise or hell? Resurrection of Jesus?

After death, the body rots and decays. Believer and nonbeliever cannot accept that this may be their final time on earth. The three religions, and others, offer the hope of life after death. Biblical Judaism is almost silent on these issues, but the resurrection of Jesus is a pillar in Christian belief and paradise is a pillar of Islam.

Jesus's resurrection did not happen

Like the Pharisees, Jesus and Paul believe in the resurrection of the dead, while the Sadducees did not. Many times, Jesus told his disciples that he would rise again after three days, and as promised, he appeared in front of them. But in Matthew (28.17), *"They saw him and worshiped, and yet some doubted."* In Mark (16.11), Mary Magdalene, the first witness, told them that Jesus was alive: *"but they did not believe."* Luke (24.37 to 41) says: *"they felt fear, they saw a spirit . . . yet they believed not and remained astonished."* So despite the prophecies, despite his appearances after his death, despite signs on his hands and feet, and despite their faith, his own disciples did not believe in his resurrection and required tangible evidence.

Paul understood that this resurrection is central to his success, and convincing the people would be most difficult. The unbelieving crowd mocks Paul preaching in Athens. Acts (17.32) says: *"when they heard of a resurrection of the dead, some mocked him, saying, we will hear you again."* Paul says in I Corinthians (15.16): *"For if the dead are not raised, not even Christ has not been raised."* Has anyone seen the dead rise? For the Catechism, *"The resurrection of Jesus is a highest truth of our faith... established by the documents of the New Testament..."*

This resurrection of Jesus achieved four objectives: a) to deify Jesus, whose body does not decay like other human bodies; b) to continue the story, because without this resurrection his epic ends miserably; c) to convert the pagans by promising them life after death; and d) to transform Paul into an apostle even if he never met Jesus during his lifetime. Without this resurrection, Paul would have remained a second-class disciple, arriving too late, and would never have been able to preach the Gospel of Jesus.

Christianity tries to prove the resurrection by using a strange argument: they say if there were no resurrection, Jesus, by announcing his resurrection in the Gospels, would have been either a liar or a fool. So his resurrection should be true. But they are forgetting a third possibility: Jesus is neither a liar nor a fool, but his disciples are, they are the ones who invented his resurrection and other legends.

The Quran (4.157) refutes the Christian faith, *"Jesus, son of Mary, the messenger of God, was neither killed nor crucified, but they saw someone who looked like him... God has raised Him."* This means that the Quran not only refuses Jesus's death, but also his resurrection. Who is telling the truth? If the Quran can be critical of the New Testament, why do Muslims reject any criticism to their faith?

The resurrection of Jesus and Paul's visions

Paul says in Acts that while he was on his way to Damascus he had a vision that transformed his life and made him a fervent disciple of Jesus. This apparition of Jesus on the road to Damascus is a pure invention of this newcomer Paul. Not being one of the first disciples of Jesus, Paul must invent this appearance to compete with the other Apostles, James and Peter, whom he will exceed soon thanks to his intellectual level. Paul needs this vision. In I Corinthians (9.1): *"Am I not an apostle? Have I not seen the*

Lord?" To invent this vision, he plagiarized what he knew best, the Jewish Bible. Paul's vision in (Acts 9.7) is inspired by two texts of the Bible from Deuteronomy (4.12), *"you hear the sound . . . but perceive no picture, nothing but a voice,"* and Daniel (10.7), *"I, Daniel, alone saw the vision, and the men who were with me did not see it . . ."* These two contradictory and plagiarized texts led to the contradictory texts of Acts (9.1 and 7): *"The men with him . . . Hearing a voice, but seeing no one."* But further in (22.9), the opposite is stated: *"Those who were with me saw the light, but they heard not the voice of the speaker."* Why did the copyists repeat this mistake? Is it because two different copyists wanted to include two images from the Jewish Bible?

Why did Jesus appear to Paul, his former enemy, a few years after his death? Why would Jesus need to take another emissary when he already had twelve? Why did Jesus not predict the mission of this newcomer in the Gospels? Paul never said to the other apostles nor to the Council of Jerusalem that Jesus appeared to him on the road to Damascus, or that he received Jesus's orders. Galatians (2) and Acts (15 and 21.21 to 26) describe Paul facing the Council of Jerusalem, but nothing is said about the appearances of Jesus. Paul should have said to James and to the Nazarenes that he was acting on behalf of Jesus's commands, but he did not do that because he knew it would have been rejected as heresy by James, who remained Nazarene-Notsri. The only time Paul confirmed to the Jews that Jesus appeared to him is in Acts (22): Paul pulled this joker card in order to save his skin, just before being expelled from the sect and from Jerusalem. In II Corinthians (12.1 to 9), Paul did not say that Jesus appeared to him but hesitated. Was it real? Was he really *"taken up to heaven in the body or out of the body"*?

Paul said to the Galatians (1.1) that he has not been appointed apostle by Jesus the human, whom he never knew, or even elected as substitute apostle like Matthias, but by the risen Jesus and God the Father. But Paul did not mention this appearance on the road to Damascus either. It would have been decisive if he had, and made him equal to the other apostles. However, suspected of lying, through a process that will last for three to fourteen years, Paul understood that he cannot say any longer that Jesus appeared to him alone. He developed the idea of resurrection, which was in the imagination of the sensitive Mary Magdalene.

As a sharp strategist, he shared the apparitions and turned his opponents into accomplices. I Corinthians (15.4 to 8): *"Christ . . . rose again the third day, and he appeared to Cephas, then to the twelve, then, at once, to more than 500 brothers . . . Then he appeared to James, then to all the apostles, and last of all, he appeared to me too, Paul . . ."* Paul, genius, did not monopolize this resurrection. By sharing the glory, he canceled the opposition of those who rejected him by making them accomplices of the lie. Note that Paul mentions disdainfully that Jesus appeared to James, the heir of Jesus, after having appeared to 500 brothers. The women, the Virgin Mary and Mary Magdalene, are not mentioned. That is contrary to the version of the four evangelists but corresponds to Paul's mentality. Not only is this assertion contrary to the Gospels, but it is also illogical, because apart from Peter-Cephas, there would be eleven apostles left, or rather ten, since Judas was already dead.

The inconsistencies regarding the resurrection of Jesus

For Christians, the resurrection of Jesus was announced in the biblical texts in Jonah, Psalm 16, and in Isaiah, but these texts have nothing to do with Jesus. Jesus's own statements, which repeatedly state that he will rise again, obviously cannot be used as evidence. Luke and Matthew (12.38) argue that the sign will be the resurrection after three days. But in Mark (8.12), Jesus say: *"Truly . . . there will not be given a sign to this generation."* Mark was not aware of the resurrection story that will be added in his Gospel. According to the NIV (which cannot be suspected of heresy) and dozens of Christian experts, the Gospel of Mark ends after the disappearance of Jesus's body but before the resurrection: *"These final verses are not confirmed by a number of witnesses. Some copyists even stated that verse 8 marked the end of the Gospel."* So Mark, the first evangelist and former collaborator of Paul, ignored the resurrection of Jesus. Is this the reason for his dispute with Paul, who needed this resurrection? The numerous testimonies described by the four evangelists must be rejected because they are reported by interested people, and because they contain contradictions.

Paul makes no mention of the resurrection of Jesus, and that would prove that these details are added much later. The evangelist A mentions a detail that would prove the reality of the resurrection, but the same detail is lacking in the evangelist B. The apocryphal Gospel of Peter, written around 150 CE, did not mention that Jesus appeared in front of the apostles, and we understand why this Gospel was rejected.

The details of the Resurrection invented to convince the nonbelievers

The first Christian missionaries made up unrealistic details:

1. Jesus carrying his cross: Some skeptics said that Simon of Cyrene, the one who carried the cross of Jesus, was crucified in his place. To counter this doubt, John (19. 17) gave the emphasis: *"Jesus carrying his own cross..."*
2. Jesus is indeed dead: Some argued that Jesus did not clinically die but only fainted, and the cold of the grave would have woken him up and he could have run away. Again, John (19.33) was the only one to refute this possibility with two details: *"The soldiers came... and seeing him dead already, did not break his legs, but one of the soldiers pierced his side with a spike and immediately came out blood and water."* How were the Roman soldiers sure he was dead? Why did the soldiers pierce the side of Jesus if he was already dead? Because it was important to prove that the heart had stopped beating after being pierced by the spear, thus this mixture of blood and water. The soldiers break the legs of the other two who were also hung to accelerate their death. Why did they only pierce the side of Jesus and not break his legs like they did for the other two? For two reasons, the first would be to fit four prophecies in Psalms (22.18), Exodus (12.46), and Numbers (9.12): *"You will not break a bone,"* which refers to Passover and the Exodus from Egypt. And also to fit to the prophecy of Zechariah: *"They turn their eyes upon me whom they have pierced,"* which had no relation with Jesus's story. The second reason would be to prove that Jesus was indeed dead.

We will notice false details in John's narrative (19.18 and 32): If Jesus was crucified with two other criminals, *"one on each side and Jesus in the middle,"* it would be illogical that the *"soldiers broke the legs of the first and of the other who were crucified with him"* and only dealt with Jesus last, even when he is in the middle. A detail of course, but very significant, and shows that the story is not convincing. Matthew does not mention the story of the spike and Jesus's pierced flank. Mark reports only that Pilate asked the centurion if Jesus is indeed dead. Luke makes no mention of the spike that pierced the side of Jesus when he describes Jesus showing his injured body to the disciples.

3. Nicodemus's request in the four Gospels: Nicodemus and Joseph of Arimathea, two notable Jews, asked Pilate if they could bury Jesus in their family vault. However, it is unlikely that a Jew would enter the house of Pilate, the impure pagan, especially on the day of Passover. Had the three Synoptic Gospels forgotten this religious prohibition, which they themselves evoked several times in their own stories? To answer this late objection, John (18.28) adds that Pilate came out of his place to meet Jews who refused to enter.

4. Location of the grave: This detail was included to answer the suspicion that Joseph of Arimathea, owner of the tomb, moved the body to bury it elsewhere, in a secret tomb, and the disciples would have gone to the wrong tomb. However, only three Synoptic Gospels report that the women had seen the location of the grave. But in Mark, this sounds quite made up because it is added at the end of the chapter. And also, it seems that John didn't know that the women had seen the place of the tomb. According to the advocates of the Resurrection, the accusation of fraud would have been easy to demonstrate by opening the tomb to exhibit the decayed body of Jesus. For this to happen, it would be necessary that Jesus and his crucifixion be historically accurate and that we know where he was really buried. However, apart from the Gospels, there is no historical evidence of the existence of this Jesus or the place of his burial or the year of his death. In addition, the accounts of the Resurrection would have been published fifteen to sixty-five years after the fact, and so no one could verify the location of the grave or if there was a guard or if any burial garments were left.

Finally, the disciples seem to not have proclaimed loudly and immediately the resurrection of their master, because nowhere the New Testament mentions the reactions of the Roman and Jewish authorities to this miracle, a miracle that would have threatened their power. Nowhere is the search for the missing body mentioned. Acts (26.24) is the proof: the governor Festus had not heard of the resurrection of Jesus and never tried to search for the missing body, as he said to Paul, *"You are a fool, your great knowledge is driving you insane."*

5. Spices and balms: In Mark (16.1), the women went to the tomb with spices on Sunday after the burial of Jesus. So that's three days after his death, and the spices were useless. Also, for Luke it was after the crucifixion but before the Sabbath (which was respected) that the women prepared the spices and on Sunday, the day of the Resurrection, they brought the spices, which remained useless. So according to the Synoptic Gospels, Jesus is buried without spices. John, however, gives a different version. He says that Mary of Magdala, six days before Passover, pours a pound of perfume on the feet (not the head) of Jesus. And Nicodemus wraps, on Friday, his body with strips and herbs.

    Despite these differences, the four Gospels agree that the perfume was used for burial, and this requires explanation. If Jesus is divine and has resurrected, his body does not need this unnecessary balm, used to prevent unpleasant odors from the putrefaction of the corpse. And if his body is human, the fact that the balms were unused (according to Luke) would result in the putrefaction of his body. But the body of Jesus reappeared without any putrefaction.

6. Strips: The three Synoptic Gospels describe the shroud but ignore the strips. Only John mentioned them. Nicodemus envelops the body with the strips, then on Sunday the tomb is empty. *"Simon saw the linen cloths lying there and the cloth that had been placed on Jesus's head, not on the ground, but rolled up in a place by itself."* This detail would serve to prove that the disciples did not steal the body and did not bother to remove the strip and fold the cloth. But if the strips were left in the vault, a naked Jesus would have woken up from his Resurrection.

7. Guards: They're mentioned only in Matthew (27.63 to 64 and 28.12) where the priests asked Pilate: *"Command therefore that the tomb be guarded until the third day, lest the disciples come steal his body and say to the people: he is raised from the dead. . . The high priests met with the elders, and after deliberation, gave a large sum to the soldiers, saying: Say that his disciples came at night, and they have removed him while you were asleep . . . So they took the money and did as they were told. And this belief is widespread and still persists today among the Jews."* The disciples were therefore suspected of stealing the body, but Matthew eliminated this suspicion by inventing the

story of the guards, keeping an eye out at the tomb. Mark, Luke, and John were not aware of these guards. Moreover, it is impossible that the priests went to see Pilate *"the next day, which followed the preparation,"* because that day was the Passover and Shabbat, and priests are forbidden to enter the house of Pilate the impure. Even if we accept Matthew's account of the guards around the grave, it is hard to accept their fainting.

8. Rolled rock: The four Gospels unanimously mention this heavy rock but the descriptions differ. For Matthew (28.5), both Maries saw an angel who rolled back the stone and spoke to them. For Mark (16.4), Salome was the third visitor. The stone was already rolled back and a young man in white talked to them. For Luke (24.4), two men in dazzling apparel had already rolled back the rock and were talking to the women, and the third visitor was Jeanne. For John (20.1), Mary Magdalene alone discovered the already empty tomb and two angels in white appeared to her, but long after Peter and the other disciples had returned home. The only common thing to the four Gospels is the white clothes of the angels or men.

   In John (20.26), after his resurrection, *"Jesus came, the doors being shut."* But if Jesus is a virtual body that can walk through closed doors, it would be useless to open the tomb and roll back the rock from the tomb! But if Jesus is a real body who eats fish after his resurrection, who helped him to move the cover of his tomb and push the round stone from the tomb? Moreover, does God the Son need help and is he unable to move the stone vault by himself, he who performed so many miracles?

9. Discovery of the tomb: The four accounts of the discovery are made up and contradictory. For Matthew (28.2), after the Sabbath, both Maries *"went to the tomb . . . An angel of God descended from heaven, rolled the stone and sat on it . . . and said, I know that you seek Jesus who was crucified. He is not here, for he is risen."* This story is unrealistic because if Jesus had already risen and come out, why would he need the angel to roll away the stone and open or close the tomb? Jesus appears later to the two women, who touched his feet.

   For Mark, the stone was already rolled away by a man dressed in white when the women (who were three this time) arrived at the tomb. They received an explanation from the angel and fled without seeing Jesus. Mark verse (16.9) is an addition: Jesus appeared in front of Mary Magdalene. How if she had run away? For Luke, the stone is already rolled and the two men in white announce to the women (at least five and not the same ones as before) that Jesus rose, but he does not appear to them. Although they have not seen the resurrected Jesus, they transmit to the disciples the miracle.

For John, Mary Magdalene alone went to the tomb, discovered that the stone was already rolled back, and seeing neither Jesus nor angels, she returned to call Peter and the beloved disciple, who came and found that the body had disappeared and they returned home. It is only after they left that the two angels and Jesus appeared to Mary Magdalene who stayed there and cried. So Jesus would not show himself to Peter, the future pillar of the Church, or to his beloved disciple but hid for a few minutes to catch Mary Magdalene by surprise. And this too is unlikely and annoying for the apostle Peter. Why was Jesus hiding? Peter and the beloved disciple did not see the two angels who had finished their work. Did the angels also hide from Peter and the disciple? Mary Magdalene knew Jesus well, but is it possible that she confused him with a gardener according to John (20.15)? Why is this gardener called Lord? Simply because this text was written without any relation to reality. Its sole goal was to invent a faith.

In Matthew (28.7), the angel asks the women to tell the disciples that Jesus is risen and will come to Galilee. Yet an angel does not need to be in a physical form to send a message. It could have appeared to the disciples anywhere. In addition, women, as the shepherds, did not have the right to testify.

For the apocryphal Gospel of Peter, written around 150 CE, the resurrection and ascension of Jesus are one event, without the appearance of Jesus to the apostles. This Gospel said that Jesus came out of the tomb carrying the cross. It is impossible that the cross was buried with him in the grave!

In the Acts, there is no mention of any women, while in Matthew, Mark, and John, Jesus appears first to women, including to Mary Magdalene. For Luke, the women do not see the risen Jesus but still announce his resurrection at the sight of the empty tomb because *"angels appeared to them and announced that he was alive."* This version would be the real one: women had a vision but it was not enough to convince nonbelievers. Luke, and he alone, would have invented the story of the two disciples of Emmaus.

10. Appearance of Jesus on the road to Emmaus as narrated by Luke (24.13 to 34): Two of the disciples, who did not believe the women's gossip about the resurrection of Jesus, left Jerusalem and walked toward the village of Emmaus. There, they encountered the risen Jesus but did not recognize him and walked with him, chatting about the hanging of the one they called *"the Prophet intended to deliver Israel."* When they finally arrived at the village and began to eat in the inn, *"Jesus took bread, blessed it, broke it and began to present it to them, while their eyes opened and then they fully recognized him."* Immediately, they got back to Jerusalem to report this meeting to the other disciples, and Jesus appeared again to all the disciples.

    This story is imaginary for many logical reasons. First, the disciples did not recognize Jesus. Did they not know him? Or maybe this incarnation of God is not special and looks like any other person. These disciples did not notice his pierced hands. John used the pierced hands to serve as evidence to Thomas the skeptic. From Jerusalem, Jesus would walk to Emmaus, only to return immediately to Jerusalem. If the disciples had not urged him to eat with them, they would not have recognized him. Jesus had risen during the Passover period, which lasts seven days, during which it is forbidden to eat bread and only unleavened bread is allowed. However, Jesus and the disciples eat bread, which was impossible to find during those seven days. It is written *"then their eyes were opened fully,"* which suggests that they were sleepy and dreaming, and that when they woke up Jesus had already disappeared.

    Luke (24.34) says that the two disciples of Emmaus returned to Jerusalem to tell the other disciples that *"the Lord has . . . really appeared to Simon Peter."* But this is not true. You just have to read chapter 24 to find that Peter discovered an empty tomb and the linen cloths but not a risen Jesus.

11. In Jerusalem or in Galilee? For Luke, the disciples did not return to Galilee. Instead, Jesus met them in Jerusalem and took them to Bethany, and then he went to heaven. So no appearance of Jesus in Galilee, contrary to the Gospel of John and the promise of Jesus

in Matthew (26.32), which says: *"But after I am raised up, I will go before you into Galilee."*

In John (20.19), the disciples had seen and even touched the risen Jesus in Jerusalem, and yet chapter 21 describes them back at the Sea of Galilee continuing their work as fishermen as if nothing extraordinary had occurred. In Matthew (28.16), the disciples saw Jesus resurrected for the first time in Galilee. In Mark (16.14), it would be in Jerusalem while the eleven were eating. For Luke, it would be in Jerusalem after Jesus was resurrected and had returned from the village of Emmaus inexplicably. Why then, according to the Synoptic Gospels, did Jesus tell his disciples to go to Galilee and not stay in Jerusalem? Illogical!

John ignores the episode at Emmaus and only shows Jesus at night in Jerusalem. So what did the resurrected Jesus do throughout the day on Sunday? Finally, according to Acts, Jesus appears in Jerusalem without ever visiting Galilee.

12. Many apparitions: To show that the disciples did not have hallucinations, Jesus appeared several times in several places to many followers, and even to doubting Thomas, who did not believe the stories of his co-disciples (why?) and asked to see the marks in the hands of Jesus and put his finger to feel them, as written in John (20.25). Eight days later, seeing with his own eyes and having touched with his own fingers, Thomas is finally convinced. It is bizarre that the wounds of Jesus, the Son of God, after his ascent to heaven and descent would still persist!

    Paul is the only one in 1 Corinthians (15.3–8) to mention that Jesus reappears to 500 followers. The four Gospels ignore this apparition. However, the argument of the 500 people to whom Jesus appeared is false evidence and the scribe could have written 5,000 and it would not have changed anything. Besides, if the resurrection is so important to Christianity, why is it so secretive? Why appear only to a few and not to thousands of residents of Jerusalem or to the world? The multiplication of appearances is part of the strategy of Paul, who understood that by monopolizing the appearances of Jesus to him alone, he will raise the opposition of the apostles. So he turns them into accomplices in the lie.

13. When does Jesus ascend to heaven to his Father and when does he end his earthly visit? John (20. 17) mentions that Jesus, after

his resurrection, tells Mary: *"Do not touch me, for I have not yet ascended to the Father."* This excuse is unacceptable, because the same Gospel (20.24 to 27) described later that to Thomas, the incredulous disciple, Jesus says*: "Put your finger here and see my hands, and bring your hand, put it into my side."* These divergent stories request an explanation, either Mary Magdalene cannot touch the risen Jesus because she is impure, (but she will be made a saint), or according to Jesus himself *"he has not yet ascended to the Father."* When does he ascend to the Father? Would this be before meeting with doubting Thomas, since he is allowed him to touch him? And so Jesus would have ascended to the Father but then came down to be touched by Thomas. All this is illogical and is of course the result of various compilations of irresponsible copyists.

For Matthew (28.9), *"The women approached, touched his feet, and worshipped him."* And in Luke (24.39), Jesus asks his disciples to touch him: *"A spirit has not flesh and bones."* But this one does and his wounds do persist. So how can one explain these contradictions? Is Jesus resurrected as human, flesh, and bones? Can we touch him? Exactly when does he cease to be human to ascend to the Father? In Luke (24.51), Jesus ascends to heaven on the day of Resurrection, and still according to Luke, the author of Acts (1.3), *"he had been seen by them for forty days."* The NIV has the honesty to recognize that in some versions of Luke the ascension is not mentioned. Where did the addition occur? Was it in the Gospel of Luke or in Acts according to Luke?

14. From where did Jesus ascend to heaven? Jesus's ascension takes place in different places in the New Testament. For John, it would be at the lake of Galilee. For Luke, it would be at Bethany. For Matthew, it would be on the mountain in Galilee. For Mark, it would be in Jerusalem. In Acts, it would be at the Mount of Olives, near Jerusalem.

15. The Resurrection transformed the lives of the disciples. Christians justify the truth of the Resurrection by the following argument: they say that it is impossible that the apostles would give up their lives for him if Jesus was not the Messiah. However, there is virtually no evidence that they sacrificed their lives. Still according to the defenders of the Resurrection, the apostles could not have managed to convince the masses if the Resurrection was a

fabrication. One could answer that except for the small group of interested disciples, the Resurrection convinced neither the Jews nor the Nazarenes-notsrim. This is why Paul had to go to the Gentiles, who were thirsty for miracles and were easy to convince.

Between the time of the Crucifixion and Resurrection of Jesus and the first steps of the apostles reported in Acts, about fifteen years had gone by. During that time, the disciples continued to attend the temple and synagogues. So it seems that this Resurrection created no great shock in their lives! On the contrary, what do the disciples do after the Resurrection of Jesus? Nothing special, they return to their former occupation as fishermen in Galilee and then return to pray in the synagogues and in the temple and practice Shabbat and *kashrut*. It is impossible that the Resurrection of Jesus had not changed their habits.

Let's suppose for a moment that it did not happen and it was all invented later by Paul. Indeed, without this resurrection, without his encounter with the risen Lord on the road to Damascus, Paul would have continued his dull life. The disciples would have continued their activities on the lake as miserable fishermen, and all the epic of Jesus would have been forgotten. This *resurrection* gives them a boost and the courage to pursue the second part of the epic, to go out to preach and establish the foundations of Christianity. By inventing the resurrection, Paul convinced some followers that it is the only way to revive and continue the flame that animated them during the lifetime of Jesus.

Important evidence of Jesus's resurrection is lacking

According to the four Gospels and all Christian writings, no one has seen and no one can describe the act of Resurrection and the coming out of the tomb. All the testimony of the disciples comes after the Resurrection. Much credible evidence would have been the reappearance of Jesus to Caiaphas, Pilate, to the historian Josephus, or to disinterested witnesses. But Jesus did not appear to them.

The resurrection is also useless because Jesus does nothing aside from visit his disciples and eat grilled fish with them. True, he used his time on earth to give them the Holy Spirit, the knowledge of foreign languages, the power to heal, and to work miracles. But he could have done this before his crucifixion. So this is not the reason for his resurrection. This resurrection makes of him a God, able to face the gods of the pagans and even to manage to convince them to abandon their gods and to follow him.

The resurrection contradicts Jesus's sacrifice. Jesus, knowing that he was going to be resurrected on the third day, shows no merit of sacrifice by dying for the sins of mankind, especially since he knows that he will be resurrected soon after. Does the actor of a film show sacrifice when he pretends to die in front of the cameras when he knows that he will get up right after? No!

Some contradictions: according to John (14.30 and 16.10), Jesus said to his disciples before his crucifixion: *"I will talk no more with you because the Prince of this world come . . . You will not see me . . ."* Yet Jesus, after his resurrection, speaks to his disciples who see him. Unless the story of the resurrection was added much later! Another contradiction is in Acts (1.3), *"Jesus appeared during forty days"* and no one in the Roman or Jewish administration saw or noticed?

The resurrection of Jesus is actually a plagiarism of pagan cults of the time that mentioned a "suffering God" who dies and rises during the spring equinox. Each year, Tammuz or Adonis, Osiris, and others would die and resurrect. The early Christians knew these mythologies.

In conclusion, Jesus, God the Son for Christians, was not resurrected. What about the common man? Will he experience life after death?

Man and the immortality of the soul

According to religions, the human being is made of a carnal-physical body and an immaterial, invisible soul that is hard to describe. If every human being has a soul, there would be some 7 billion souls today, so God continually creates human souls and therefore did not rest after the Creation. The religions do not say how or when souls are created. Is the soul contained in the sperm and/or egg? Do the unfertilized eggs lose a fraction of their soul? If yes, where does it go? Does the new soul appear at the birth or at conception? At what moment during conception does the fetus develop a soul? Does the soul get older? When the believer goes to heaven, does he go with his twenty-year-old or seventy-year-old soul? Does the soul ascend to heaven immediately after death?

In Genesis (1.20), God commanded, *"Let the land produce living souls according to their kinds, domestic animal, moving animal and wild beast of the earth after its kind."* And in Leviticus (17.11), God forbids eating the blood of animals because *"the soul is in the blood."* Eating the blood is punishable by death. So therefore the Bible acknowledges that animals have souls. Not just the dog or cat, but the snake and the fly. How is it created? Where does their soul go after the death of the animal? How is it possible to kill an animal? Jellyfish are primitive animals that do not have blood, so therefore do they not have a soul? So during what time of evolution does the soul appear?

To get out of these embarrassing questions, rabbis invented an explanation outside of the Bible. They say that there are five types of souls, and animals, just like the trees and stones, have a soul but it is of a lower level. What about burning in hell? How can the dead suffer from the heat if their soul has left them? The answer of the believers is that they suffer from spiritual pain! They say that at messianic times the resurrection of the dead will begin and the souls in paradise would return to the body in the grave and live on earth in an immaterial body made of light. All this would take place before the year 6000; that is to say, in two centuries. What would be the purpose of this immaterial life and why is it on earth? And why would the soul need a body? Yet in Genesis (3.19), God said to Adam, *"For dust you are and to dust you will return"* without any distinction between the immortal soul and the decaying body.

The Jewish doubt about the Resurrection and paradise

The Jewish Bible is unclear about this matter and the New Testament writes about those Jewish doubts. In Acts (23.8), *"the Sadducees say that there is no Resurrection, and that there is neither angel, nor spirit, but the Pharisees believe in those two things."* So a part of the Jewish religious elite rejected the ideas of angels and resurrection. Is this not proof that these concepts are a human creation? And if the Sadducees had taken over the Pharisees, Judaism would not have believed in the Resurrection or in heaven! And neither would have Christianity!

Ecclesiastes (3.21), probably written in the second century BC, rejects the idea of any difference between the human and the animal: *"Who knows whether the spirit of Adam's son goes upward, while the breath of animals goes down towards the earth?"* But also, according to (8.12), Ecclesiastes writes against the injustices of life on earth *"for such a sinner is 100 times evil and sees his life prolonging . . . It is a disappointing fact that happens on earth. He is just being treated in the way of the wicked and the ungodly are treated as righteous."* Ecclesiastes (9.5) states that life ends with death; however, Hosea (6.2) says the opposite: *"The third day He will make us rise . . ."* Isaiah (26.19) says: *"Your dead shall live . . . They will rise . . ."* and the contrary few verses earlier (26. 14): *"The dead do not live again."* Daniel (12.2 to 13): *"Many of those who sleep in the dust of the ground will rise, some to everlasting life, and some to be an object of shame and everlasting contempt . . ."* This difference of opinion was known to early Jewish-Christian and John (5.28) puts into the mouth of Jesus the words of the Pharisees: *"Those who have done good will resurrect unto life; and those that have done evil will rise for the judgment."* However, it is the Pharisee sect that reigns over Judaism today and has imposed to the Jewish faith its belief in the Resurrection and heaven.

Genesis (8.25) writes: *"Abraham . . . fainted and died in a good old age . . . and he joined his fathers."* But his parents were buried in Haran or in Our Kasdim, thousands of kilometers away. Where does he join them? Is it in heaven? But Abraham's fathers were idolaters? Similarly, Genesis (49. 33) writes: *"Jacob . . . then he died and joined his fathers."* But Jacob died in Egypt while his father was buried in Hebron. Where did he join his fathers? In II Kings (2.11), Elijah went up to heaven, while in John (3.13) no one except Jesus has ascended to heaven.

The Resurrection, a first bad solution to reward the righteous!

Daily life shows us that *rasha ve lo tov, tzadik ve ra lo*, which means *"the evil one enjoys life, while the righteous is suffering."* In fact, we see many ardent believers suffering while the bastards around them are laughing. A just God must punish sinners, thus the need for an afterlife to punish or reward bad or good deeds. Without the appeal of heaven and the fear of hell, humans who witness the beautiful earthly life of sinners and the miserable existence of believers would not be convinced to obey any religion. If the reward and punishment are not visible during life on earth, it is essential that there be a life after death, hence the invention of heaven and hell to correct injustices of life on earth. Life after death is therefore an obligation invented by religions to reward those who respect the laws and to punish those who break them. But God could punish immediately after a bad behavior without waiting for a later life. Rewarding the righteous during his life on earth would be evidence of God's existence.

Christianity gives two contradictory statements: on one side, Matthew (16.27) and II Corinthians (5.10) promise that the Son of Man *"will reward each according to his work"* and *"every man shall receive according to the good or evil he has done while being in his physical body."* On the other side, the New Testament says it is not man's actions that lead to paradise but his faith. Every human is a sinner from birth because of the original sin, and the only way to avoid hell would be to believe in Jesus, who has taken upon himself the sins by dying on the cross. Christians, therefore, are not required to have moral behavior because only faith saves. John (3.36) states: *"Whoever believes in the Son has eternal life. He that believes not the Son shall not see life, but the wrath of God on him."* John (12.47) says: *"For I came not to judge the world, but to save it."* Yet this same John (5.22) had said the opposite: *"The Father judges no one, but has given all judgment to the Son."* So Jesus is a judge, and the works of a person would be important to Christianity, not just his faith.

Christians who believe in Jesus believe that at the end of time (when is that time?) he will be resurrected and his body will be transfigured into an immaterial body. For John (5.28), *"the time is coming when all who are in the graves shall hear his voice and come forth, those who have done good will know the resurrection of life; and those who have done evil will resurrect for the judgment..."* The Sadducees, who did not believe in the resurrection, asked Jesus ironically: if a woman married seven brothers successively, *"in the time of resurrection, who will she be the wife of?"* In Matthew (22.30), Jesus answered: *"At the resurrection they shall take no wife, nor be given in marriage, because they are as the angels of God in heaven."*

This sentence contradicts the Quran where the good believers arrive in paradise with their spouses and/or virgins. Whether the Quran or the Gospels, one of the two is wrong and therefore cannot be divine! For Christians, those who do not believe that Jesus is God and that he died on the cross for their sins, mostly the Jews and Muslims, will go to hell. For Muslims, since Christians idolize Jesus, they must go to hell. In the Quran, those who believe that Jesus is God and generally anyone who does not believe that the Quran is "the truth" and that Muhammad is a true prophet sent by God will go to hell.

Men's attitude, whether atheistic or religious, is irrational. Many atheists who are dying cry out to God in whom they do not believe, while believers in heaven and the Resurrection cry when a loved one dies instead of rejoicing. The rabbis say that the Jews have a special soul. How does a convert to Judaism receive it? According to Jewish mysticism, Abraham had sex with Sarah but she was sterile, yet they would give birth to the souls of future converts. And so every new convert would receive a soul previously created by Abraham and Sarah. Where were all these souls stored? According to the rabbis, it is possible to save the soul of a sick person by giving the exact amount of 160 coins to charity.

Reincarnation: a popular belief nowadays, but impossible

The concept of reincarnation is contradicted by Genesis (3.19), *"For dust you were and to dust you shall return."* There is no possibility of going back into another body! Yet some found in the Bible and especially in the book of Job (33.29) a reference to reincarnation: *"God does it two or three times in favor of man."* Should this verse be interpreted as a confirmation of reincarnation? No, it is God's warning that he will *". . . bring back his soul from the edges of the abyss . . .,"* so before death.

But how did reincarnation appear in modern Judaism? Not being able to explain injustices on earth, such as the death of a baby or the opulent life of sinners, rabbis came up with the idea of the Resurrection and of the Last Judgment in order to reestablish the faith of believers. But with the Resurrection and the Last Judgment not arriving soon enough, the impatient believers require more immediate solutions. Thus comes reincarnation, solving the problem, because believers no longer have to wait to receive the reward or a better life or punishment.

When a baby dies, will he go to heaven or hell? Would it be fair for him to go to heaven without having done any good deed? He can't go to hell either because he has not sinned! Is it unfair that one baby is born rich and healthy while another is born infirm and destitute? Could God be guilty of injustice? Reincarnation is the only answer! Without it, God would be unjust. With it, God is innocent of all injustices, because He wouldn't be responsible for anything. This reincarnation allows God to be blameless for the suffering of infants or the death of a righteous man in an accident. Reincarnation gives the opportunity to improve oneself in another life. Each person has a choice in his actions. So every misfortune is explained, without any evidence, as the punishment for a previous life. This is how Jewish mysticism likes to explain the inexplicable.

This late notion comes from the Zohar and the book *The Doors of Reincarnation*, which appeared in the thirteenth century. First anomaly right here, because the prophecy had disappeared from Israel with Malachi, the last of the prophets. This concept is therefore not from God but from man—and by the way, it already existed with the Greeks. The soul must be perfect before encountering God and it perfects itself with each reincarnation. But what is a perfect soul? Does it have the same meaning for Jews, Christians, Muslims, and Buddhists? After several incarnations, on the day of Resurrection, which person will we have back?

Abel was killed when he wasn't guilty of anything, not even of his parents' sins. Now Abel cannot be the reincarnation of another human, since he is the first human born of a human. Why did God allow his death when he was innocent and without history?

Jewish mystics give detailed descriptions about reincarnation. For example, they say that if after three reincarnations the Jew has not repaired all his sins, he will be completely eliminated and the reincarnation is over for him. Others argue that if any type of progress is made during each life, reincarnation is still possible and can take hundreds of lives to perfect. Some texts contradict reincarnation. In Deuteronomy (24.16), *"Fathers shall not be put to death for their children, nor children put to death for their fathers. Each has to die for his own sin."* So why are we still paying for the sins of Adam and Eve? Similarly, II Kings (14.6) and Ezekiel (18.4) state that *"everyone will suffer death for his own wrongdoing"* and *"only the sinful soul will die."* Jeremiah (31.29): *"In those days, they shall say no more: The fathers have eaten sour grapes and the children's teeth are set on edge but everyone shall die for his sins . . ."*

Why do the three religions forbid suicide or euthanasia if there is a chance of reincarnating into healthier bodies? Why cry when a sick relative dies? On the contrary, one should rejoice because he will suffer no more and he will be reincarnated into another body. Believers who mourn the death of their loved one don't believe in reincarnation? Do women reincarnate? The Jewish answer is not clear. Rabbis say that in general the soul of the woman does not reincarnate and men are sometimes reincarnated into a woman's body, but that body is sterile and cannot procreate. Too many women, including the famous singer Madonna, are followers of Kabbalah but ignore that reincarnation is for males only.

According to the Zohar, the dead must be immediately buried, and if not, his soul cannot enter a second body. This means that the soul leaves the body only if it is buried. What happens to the soul if the dead is not buried?

Rabbis said that Moses was the reincarnation of Abel, that Cain reincarnated into Esau, and Adam reincarnated into Abraham, Isaac into Jacob. However, no evidence has ever been given. Christianity, which preaches the incarnation of God in Jesus, rejects reincarnation. According to the New Testament, the Christian does not need reincarnation for his salvation because only faith in Jesus saves. Hebrews (9.27) states that *"it is appointed for men to die once, after this the judgment"* without any form of reincarnation. So who is right, the modern Judaism or Christianity?

But the idea of reincarnation was floating in the atmosphere at the time of Jesus. The priests asked John the Baptist: *"Are you Elijah?"* And he replied: *"I am not."* That simple question shows that the idea of reincarnation was in the air, and some believed that John the Baptist was the reincarnation of Elijah. According to the Gospel of John (9.2), Jesus was asked about a blind man, *"Rabbi, who sinned? Was it this man or his parents, why was he born blind?"* Jesus answered negatively. However, some Christian sects, such as the Gnostics, accept reincarnation.

Orthodox Islam rejects the notion of reincarnation, but some sects, such as the Sufi or Druze, see proof of reincarnation in the verse (2.28): *"Why are you such unbelievers? God gave you life when you were dead. He will give you death and will give you life and you will be returned to him."* Orthodox Islam rejects this interpretation and asserts that this is resurrection, not reincarnation. Yet Reincarnation is used by some Muslims to explain the confusion of Mary, mother of Jesus, with Miriam, sister of Moses and Aaron. Mary the mother of Jesus would be the reincarnation of Miriam sister of Moses, and so there would be no error in the Qur'an.

In conclusion, the three divine religions have three opposing concepts of reincarnation. Who is wrong?

The Day of Judgment never arrived

Three religions promise life after death, heaven and hell. They're all false promises! They frighten believers by saying that the Last Judgment and Resurrection, definitive proof of the existence of God, are approaching, and yet it's been over two millennia that we have been waiting for this day. The Torah ignores the Last Judgment. Only prophets mention it as being the day of God, but Judaism is not only the Bible. The Talmud, the Halacha, and its code of conduct, have been the main pillars of Judaism for almost two millennia. This post-biblical Judaism responded to questions that the Bible did not. Because Jews were tired of waiting for the Messiah and the day of the resurrection that were not coming, the post-biblical rabbis invented the judgment of Rosh Hashanah or New Year, where *"three books are open one for the good . . . The righteous are immediately written in and recorded for life..."* For post-biblical Judaism, the final judgment will take place after the arrival of the Messiah and the Messiah for the Jews has not yet come. So no resurrection has taken place so far and no Jew has yet gone to heaven or hell.

But the three religions are not clear. Will the believer immediately go to heaven or should he have to wait for the last judgment? Maimonides affirmed that after death the soul of the righteous rise to Eden and wait there for the big day of resurrection. Others also say, without any evidence, that the soul of the dead flies over his house for a week before going to the Garden of Eden. Some Jewish mystics say, without hesitation, that during the time of the resurrection the dead come back with the same look, the same age, and the same disease they had before their death. A blind person will rise blind! Others say that the blind will return in a body of light. But no one has ever come back from the dead to prove it.

If the believer goes to heaven as a reward for his good deeds, why wait until he dies? Why does God not allow him to be in paradise during his life? It would be definite proof of the existence of God! Why is God waiting for this Last Judgment that does not seem likely to take place? Up to now, believers and idolaters have received the same punishment: death and decay of their bodies. If, as some claim, the believer will go to heaven immediately after his death, then what will happen to them during the Last Judgment? Will God remove from paradise the lucky ones to judge them again? And in paradise, if a human sins, will he be expelled from paradise? Which laws of God must the believer respect while in heaven? Some theologians, aware of the problem, think they have found the solution: individual judgment at the time of the death and universal judgment at the end of time.

This solution solves the problem but is not the answer for the three religions. Why retry the lucky ones who have already entered paradise? Where are those billion of souls waiting?

Some Kabbalists propose another solution in two stages. At death, the body remains in the grave and it is the soul that goes to heaven. On the big day of the resurrection of the dead, the body and soul come together again so that the body can enjoy eternal life. This is incomprehensible and illogical, because the body would have decomposed by that time.

Christians await the Second Coming of Jesus, the glorious return at the end of time. Jesus would forgive the good Christians who have faith in him. But Jesus had promised *"eternal life"* to the apostles in Matthew (19.29 and 24.34), and *"this generation shall not pass, till all these things be fulfilled."* But they are all dead! In I Thessalonians (3.13 and 4.14 to 17), Paul announces: *". . . At a given signal, with the voice of an archangel, and with the trumpet of God, the Lord himself shall descend from heaven, and the dead in Christ shall rise first . . . we are alive and remain unto the coming of the Lord."* In I Timothy (6.14), Paul recommends to Timothy to *"live unblemished until the appearing of our Lord Jesus Christ,"* so in the coming years. Similarly, in Hebrews (9.28) and (10.37): *". . . Christ will appear a second time to those who are waiting for their salvation . . . A little time, He who is coming will come and will not delay."* We find the same expectation in the epistles of Jude and John (2.18 and 28): *"It is the last hour . . ."* D-Day approaches and time is short in Romans (13.11): *"It's time to wake up, for now our salvation is nearer to us than when we believed."* The psychological pressure is used to convert new followers and to open their purse because the Savior will arise at any time.

But the converts, seeing no change, in II Peter (3.4 to 8), are impatient: *"Where is the promise of his coming? For since the fathers fell asleep, all things continue as they were from the beginning of creation . . ."*

The Quran repeats dozens of times that the Last Judgment and Resurrection are close: Sura 2 says: *"God will give you death and will give you life and you will be returned to him."* Then Sura (3,162 and 185) says: *"Every impostor comes with his fraud on the Day of Resurrection, and each will have his wages . . . Anyone who will be removed from the fire and enters the garden will have won, for this life was a false joy."* But this is confusing. Has that famous day of resurrection already taken place? Is it unique or does it apply to all mankind already dead? The Hadiths of the "night Journey" of Muhammad described Abraham, Jesus, John the Baptist, Joseph, Moses, and Adam already in heaven.

To convince skeptics, the judgment was said to be during the life of the believer or immediately after the death of every human being. The person did not have to wait for that famous day. However, the Quran says in (2.177), *"Piety is to believe in God and in the Last Judgment."* But (18.47) says, *"the day we will cause the mountains to move . . . We will gather all men without leaving one . . ."* And (59.67), *"on the Day of Resurrection, the entire earth will be a handful for him and the heavens shall be folded in his right hand."* The arrival of this day is described in Sura 82: *"When the sky is cleft asunder, when the stars are scattered, when the seas overflow and when the graves are laid open . . ."* Thus, since the day of judgment has not yet come, it seems that hell and heaven are empty and not in working condition. And what about the suicidal *Shaidims* who blow up their bodies, do they taste the delights of paradise and of the virgins? Verse (2.153) seems to confirm: *"Do not say that those killed in the path of God are dead. No, they live."*

Many theologians have tried to predict the famous D-Day. The latest was May 21, 2011, or December 12, 2012, which proved to be a lie! But before that, the big day had been scheduled for October 22, 1844, and the years 1874, 1875, 1914, 1930, 1994, 1999, 2007, 2012, and 2060.

Christianity, heaven, and hell

The Gospels mention hell over fifteen times, and there begin the errors. Luke (23.43) writes that one of the two thieves crucified with Jesus asked him not to forget him. According to this improbable dialogue between two crucified men, Jesus tells the good thief, *"Today thou shall be with me in Paradise."* This means that Friday, the same day of the crucifixion, Jesus and the good thief will ascend to heaven. However, in John (20.17) Jesus said to Mary Magdalene on the day of his resurrection on Sunday, *"Do not touch me because I have not yet ascended to my Father."*

Just as Islam teaches that the one who does not believe in Muhammad will go to hell, Christianity promises that whoever does not believe in Jesus will be condemned while he who believes has eternal life. Mark (9.43): *"It is better for you to enter maimed into this life than to go away with two hands into hell, into the fire that is never quenched."* The Catechism adds: *"After death, the righteous will live forever with the risen Christ and He will raise them on the last day. Like his, our resurrection will be the work of the Holy Trinity."*

For Christianity, in I Corinthians (15, 42), *"the body is sown in corruption, it is raised imperishable . . . It is sown a natural body, it is raised a spiritual body."* This is contrary to Islam, in which believers eat, drink, and copulate in paradise. So who is right? Nobody has risen to tell us! How can Paul say that the resurrected is a spiritual body and how can Muhammad affirm the opposite? Aren't they both spokespersons of God?

Islam's paradise and hell described in detail

Dozens of times, Muhammad used the argument of life after death to convert the pagans of the Arabian Peninsula, but without any proof. God would have weighed the acts of men, *"those whose scales are heavy (good deeds) will have happiness..."* Another example is Sura (2.82), *"those who believe and whose work is faithful will forever be the hosts of heaven..."* Everyone will be paid according to his deeds, good faith will be rewarded, but sinners will go to hell. For (3.85), *"whoever seeks a religion other than Islam will not be accepted"* in heaven. If only the happy Muslims are allowed in heaven, Jews and Christians are fooling themselves! Hell is therefore only for those who do not believe in Muhammad!

A Hadith of Bukhari (52.297) reports that Muhammad said: *"no one will enter Paradise except Muslims."* Quran (87) warns, *"You who prefer this life, the next life is better and longer."* The Quran (16.22) says that *"those who do not believe in the other life are deniers and proud."* Yet the Quran (45.24) reports that some refuse this second life: *"They say there is only this life. We live and we die. It is the time that makes us die... Their only argument is to say, bring back our fathers if what you say is true."* To convince them, God and Muhammad would have immediately resurrected some dead in front of them. This does not happen, and never has any prophet from Abraham to Jesus and to Muhammad given proof of the resurrection! The Quran (23.82) reports the unbelievers' arguments: *"When we are dead and will only be as bone and powder, will we be remembered? Yes, you had promised that to our fathers as well, but it's just an old fable."*

Unlike the Bible, the Quran describes in detail heaven and hell to convince the skeptics that with conversion to Islam, they will avoid the horrors of hell and enjoy the pleasures of paradise. And this leads to the worst inconsistencies and even ridicule! Muslim (6784), *"in heaven there is a tree whose shade is so immense that a rider can gallop 100 years."* The shade is the dream of every inhabitant living in the torrid desert! For the Muslim, paradise is filled with material and bodily pleasure for the fantasies of the believers. A theoretical and intangible paradise would not have been understood by the illiterate Arabs living in the desert.

Muhammad offered them what they want most:

1. Virgins for male Muslims who are not satisfied with their wives and slaves
2. Young boys for homosexuals—forbidden on earth
3. Shade, water, and rivers—rare in Arabia but present in this green paradise
4. Luxury—jewelry, silk, carpets, and beautiful ornaments
5. Fruits and good food to compensate for the frugal life of the desert
6. Wine—banned in life on earth, but allowed in heaven

The Quran describes in detail an erotic paradise, which is the dream of every male *"immortal youths will circulate among them with cups, jugs and goblets of a clear brew they will not be tired and not drunk, with fruit that they choose, with the flesh of birds as they desire and big-eyed houris . . . among jujube trees without spines . . . The devoted slave of God . . . For them, a white cup filled with pure liquid will circulate, delicious to drink, not intoxicating and inexhaustible. Near them will be chaste virgins with big eyes like a secret pearl . . . We will marry them to houris with big eyes . . . Beautiful and good virgins . . . removed from their houses . . . that will not have been touched by men nor jinn."* Jinn or demons have also sexual needs, but are they attracted by human virgins? Are these sexual acts giving birth to little babies? Who will raise them and whose milk will they drink? According to a Hadith, the virgin deflowered will be virgin again to please the Muslim male.

Some Arabists argue that the word *hur* does not mean virgin but white grapes. That would change everything for suicidal *jihadis* who would receive only grapes in paradise. Yet the Hadith of Muslim (6793) makes it clear that every man will have at least two women in paradise. As for the female believer, almost nothing is said about them. Those who go to heaven, will they be rewarded sexually or will they watch their pious husband copulate with virgin girls and boys? In the Quran (76.19), it is written: *"circulate among them young boys . . . forever."* Why these boys? Are they in paradise for the believing women or for the gay men? Is homosexuality allowed in paradise but punishable by death on earth?

Whoever described the sexual paradise did not anticipate the impossible consequences of these descriptions.

The lucky winners are rewarded with finest clothing and food. According to (18.31), they *"will be adorned with bracelets of gold, dressed in green silk garments and brocade, reclining on thrones."* Why this luxury and these jewels? Is paradise a materialistic reward? (47.15): *"description of the Garden promised to the faithful... the inalterable milk streams, creeks of delicious wine, pure honey streams..."* Verse (83.25): *"They will drink a rare wine sealed, with a musky character and those who will want some will be entitled to it... We will circulate among them gold plates and cups and all that is desirable to them and that pleases their eyes."* In Quran (63.72), the lucky ones will eat a lot of fruits and drink in paradise. This means that the digestive system of the human will continue to operate, and so the microbes and enzymes that help break down food would be present in paradise. What about the excrement of those in heaven? This question was probably asked by a skeptic, to whom Muslim (6798) replied that God has planned everything and the lucky ones will expel feces through their pores by a scented sweat. Where do these foods come from? Who produces them? Are there workers or slaves? A cripple who goes to heaven with a missing leg, does it grow back? Does the blind recover his sight in heaven? Will the toothless enjoy the foods of paradise thanks to new teeth?

In heaven, it is said in Muslim (6805 onward), that there is a huge tent 60 miles long, and that the Euphrates and the Nile are the rivers of paradise. Are there three separate heavens for the three religions, a Jewish, a Christian, and a Muslim paradise? Because a devout Christian who eats pork can go to heaven while the Jewish or Muslim that eats pork would go to hell! Hell for Muslims is reserved for those who do not believe in Islam. See also (3.10), (5.80), and many other verses that say that non-Muslims will go to hell.

For the Muslim, hell *"awaits all who rebel against God and His Apostle and transgress the laws."* It has seven gates, each gate will have a determined group. *"Whenever their skin will be burned, we will give them another skin so they may taste the torment."* Verse (22.19) describes *"fire clothing will be cut for unbelievers, we will put the boiling water over their head, their entrails and skin will be consumed... Never will their death be decreed, never will their torment be lightened."* Verse (37.60) describes *"a tree that grows from the bottom of the furnace. Its fruits are like devils' heads. The guilty shall feed from it, they will fill their stomach and drink a boiling mixture and return to the furnace . . . Chains, handcuffs and fire . . .*" Verse (74.30) says that *"nineteen angels"* ensure the care to the fire of hell. Yet the Quran begins with *"in the name of God the merciful . . ."* The God who created hell and the torments of punishment is not merciful. And of course atheists will go to hell! Some Muslims respond that the description in detail of heaven and hell are just allegories. It would be like explaining the taste of chocolate to one who has never eaten it. So are all these details wrong?

The religions were wrong about shape of the earth and astronomy but still describe in detail heaven, paradise, purgatory, and hell. For the three religions, heaven is the reward for good deeds and hell is the punishment of those who break the rules. The Civil Code meets the same goals immediately without waiting for heaven or hell.

11

The prophets and the prophecies

Are the Jewish prophets inspired by God or by their own interests?

Why Does God not appear to the peoples directly but only through prophets? At this tricky question, Judaism has found the best answer. In Exodus (20.16), God appeared to the Hebrews, but they were afraid because *"if God does speak to us, we could die."* So they asked not to see God directly but through middlemen who bring the word of God. This is exactly the definition of *prophet* or *navi* in Hebrew, which means "bring" the word of God. Judaism used the prophets for a double goal: to explain the silence and absence of God and to say what God wants. Why would the sight of God be fatal? Why does God need intermediaries? Can He appear before the unafraid people, at least give proof of His existence? Why did God obey the frightened Hebrews at Sinai who asked not to see Him?

Jews, Christians, and Muslims claim that God inspired the prophets, with whom He communicated daily, and they transmitted his orders to believers. However, there is no more Jewish prophet since the third century BC and Malachi was the last one. Does God have nothing more to say to the Jews? A rabbi says that the Jewish people misbehave, so God does not reveal Himself in order to give them a mitigating circumstance. This argument is unacceptable, because all prophets operated while the Jewish people behaved badly. Why also has no prophet spoken to Christians since Jesus and to Muslims since Muhammad? Why did the prophets always have visions in secret? These prophets who have not seen God in front of witnesses or crowds but always in secret or in dreams govern the lives of the Jews, Christians, and Muslims!

In biblical times, the prophets abounded. In II Kings (2.7), *"fifty young prophets"* and in I Kings (22.6), Ahab, king of Israel, consulted 400 prophets. The prophets Jeremiah (28.15) and Hanania compete as vulgar merchants. The first said to the second, *"YHWH has not sent you, and you reassured this people with a lie . . ."* Is it possible that these two prophets who claim to be inspired by God give two opposing messages? They are often "politicians" close to power. Ezekiel and Jeremiah are sons of priests, Nathan uses Batsheba to give the kingdom to Solomon. When the people had enough of hearing a prophet, they threw stones at him. These prophets say contradictory things about God.

For some, God is like a man with arms and legs, with the same passions: love, jealousies, sorrow, rage. But they also say that God is pure spirit. Some say that no one can see Him, yet most say they saw Him as a fire or in the form of tongues of fire. Others saw Him sitting, dressed in white, in the form of an old man. For Ezekiel (18.23), God is good, gentle, charitable, loving, patient, and takes no pleasure in the death of the wicked. But Deuteronomy (28.53) says the opposite: God is severe, terrible, takes pleasure in killing the bad guys. Samuel I (15.29) says that God does not retract but Jeremiah (18.8) and Joel (2.13) say that He changed his mind.

Christianity is forced to admit that the Jewish prophets say the truth; otherwise, all the descriptions of Jesus-Messiah would be useless. Yet Jesus himself admits that no prophet is accepted in his own country, or more so, is despised. Why this attitude toward the prophets? Because they claimed to have received revelations from God, while they were only dreams or nightmares. Isaiah (9.4) itself says some *"prophets teach the lie"* and Deuteronomy (18.22) says: *"How to recognize these false prophets? When what the prophet said will not take place. . . ."* And also: *"However, if a prophet had the audacity to announce in my name something I would not have ordered him to report or if he was speaking on behalf of a foreign god, that prophet must die."* Deuteronomy (13.1) forbids adding or subtracting anything to the Torah, and says that someone who encourages people to follow other gods or no longer practice God's laws is a false prophet. So it is understandable that the Jews rejected Jesus and Muhammad.

In Jeremiah (5.31), (6.13), and (14.14), God condemns those prophets who *"prophesy falsely... All are eager to gain... I have not sent them... I have not spoken them. This false vision, vain predictions... these prophets will perish by the sword and by famine..."* Ezekiel (13.1) adds: *"... The unworthy prophets who follow their inspiration and visions... Like foxes among the ruins, so are your prophets, O Israel! They announced false and misleading oracles, visions... saying the Lord's words, while I was not talking... Visions of peace when there is no peace... I stretch out my hand against him, and will destroy him..."*

Isaiah (52.1) prophesies, *"Jerusalem, the holy city! From now no uncircumcised and unclean will enter you!"* But Isaiah is wrong because many uncircumcised occupied Jerusalem. And Zachariah (12.9) is mistaken when he says: *"In that day I will seek to destroy all the nations that come against Jerusalem,"* when in 70 AD then in 135 AD the Romans destroyed Jerusalem.

Jeremiah (33.18) is mistaken when he says: *"The priests the Levites will not stop... to offer burnt offerings, to burn oblations and sacrifices at all times."* They are no more sacrifices in Jerusalem. God requires sacrifices, for example, in Leviticus (23.27): *"you shall offer a sacrifice to YHWH,"* but the prophet Jeremiah (7.22) states that these are lies: *"I have not ordered anything to your ancestors... about burnt offerings and sacrifices."* Who is the liar? The explanation is that Jeremiah's prophecies were written well after the fact and everything becomes logical, and also confirms all the reversals and chronological errors in Jeremiah's book. Chapter 26 repeats Jeremiah's sermon at the temple described in Chapter 7. Chapter 38 repeats Jeremiah's arrest described in chapter 27. According to Jeremiah (36) himself, his prophetic writings were put to fire by the Judean king Jehoiakim, son of Josiah, and Jeremiah dictated again to his scribe Baruch: *"all the words written in the book that Jehoiakim king of Judah has burned. Many other similar words were added to them."* Are they really the same words? It is surprising that chapter 52 is a repeat of Jeremiah chapter 39 and both describe word for word the fall of Jerusalem and the death of King Zedekiah. Chapter 26 describes events twenty years prior to the siege of Jerusalem described in chapter 21. All these are proof that the texts of Jeremiah have been manipulated.

The Bible tells the story of the prophet Balaam and his donkey who speaks with a human voice. I Kings (20.35) describes a prophet who *"told his colleague: hit me . . . The other refused to strike him. He said: since you have not listened to the word of God . . . a lion will attack you . . . He met a lion who killed him."* Another prophet Habakkuk is seized by his hair and an angel carries him from Judea to Babylon to bring a meal to Daniel in the pit, and then sent back by air to Judea. Children mocked the prophet Elisha who was bald, he cursed them and *"a bear broke into pieces forty-two children."* Is this the love of God? In Jeremiah (23.13), the prophets of Jerusalem *"practice adultery, live in a lie, encourage the evil . . ."* The prophet Ezekiel has hallucinations and should have been transferred to a mental asylum. Isaiah (37) is identical word for word to 2 Kings (19). How is this possible? Is Isaiah the author of some of the books of Kings or a scribe had copied verses?

Why the negative description of the prophets? To give more importance to the wise rabbis. Indeed, the Talmud, Baba Batra12a says that a wise man exceeds the prophet and the wise can interpret some writings (see section on oral tradition).

But on the other hand, the prophet is greater than the king. In Chronicles II (36.12): King Zedekiah *"did that which was evil in the sight of YHWH his God and does not humble himself before the prophet Jeremiah, who spoke for YHWH."*

Prophecies as irrefutable evidence that the Torah is divine?

For believers, the Bible has predicted everything, including the destruction of the towers of New York, the assassination of Israeli Prime Minister Rabin. Even the genocide perpetrated by Hitler would be mentioned in Deuteronomy (31.17): *"That day, my wrath will burst against the people . . . I will conceal my face from them . . . because of the evil they did when they turned to other gods."* A rabbi gives as proof the prophetic verses of Deuteronomy (28.64): God said to Moses, *"And YHWH shall scatter you among all peoples, from one end of the earth to the other, and there you shall serve foreign gods . . . And among these nations you will find no rest . . ."* If Deuteronomy was written by Moses, it could have been prophetic, but this passage was written during or after the exile of Babylon, and so it is not prophetic but rather describes a known reality. Moreover, the prophecy of the following verses, *"And YHWH will take you on ships through the roads of Egypt"* did not come true. The rabbis are trying at all costs to confirm this prophecy and take as evidence a German historian who related that the Jews were sold into slavery by the Romans and taken as slaves in Egypt, sometimes by land, sometimes by boat from Gaza.

The prophecies were not written by chance, and the prophecies of Isaiah are perfect examples. According to (44.28), Isaiah prophesies, *"I say to Cyrus: You are my shepherd . . . And he said to Jerusalem: be built . . ."* Isaiah lived when king Uzziah died toward 742 BC, and Cyrus allowed the Judeans to return to Jerusalem toward 538 BC. And so this prophecy took place about two centuries after Isaiah! Or was it simply written after the fact? The prophecies of Isaiah (13.19, 14.22, and 45.1) proclaim that *"Babylon, the pearl of kingdoms, the glory and pride of the Chaldeans . . . will never be inhabited and no longer serve as residence until the end of time . . . of Babylon, I will destroy the name and track . . . to Cyrus."* Indeed, Babylon was destroyed and this once famous city is no longer inhabited. This is a miracle, because the prophecy of Isaiah would have been written 200 years before their realization. All details, including the name of King Cyrus, who destroyed Babylon. Except that in reality the texts of Isaiah were written or completed after the historical facts. The second option reduces to zero the prophecy of Isaiah.

According to Jewish tradition, King David wrote the Psalms, including Psalm 137, which says: *"On the banks of the rivers of Babylon we sat and wept when we remembered Zion."* It describes a later period, several centuries after David. The rabbis explain that David was a great prophet. We are entitled to doubt and prefer to imagine that these Psalms were written much later, and not by David. Daniel would also be a great prophet when he reported his talks with the Babylonian king around 600 BC. Daniel (8.20) predicted that Babylon will be defeated by the Medes and Persians, which will in turn be defeated by the Greeks. The prophecy was fulfilled and Alexander the Great won against the Persians around 330 BC, 300 years after the prophecy of Daniel. This is remarkable, if this prophecy was written around 600 BC. But the specialists state that the book of Daniel was written after the events by an impostor.

Daniel prophesied about the succession of the regional powers so precisely that it is hard for skeptics to deny it. Yet he is wrong about the facts that took place in his own life, especially on the names of the kings of his time. Daniel (9.1) writes for example, *"Darius, son of Ahasuerus, of the seed of the Medes . . ."* But Darius is the father, not the son, of Ahasuerus. In Daniel (5), Balthazar is son of Nebuchadnezzar, when in fact he is the son of Nabonidus. The explanation for these errors is that Daniel lived around 160 BC, long after the fact that he "predicted," so previous historical facts were unclear to him.

Christians give another prophecy of Daniel referring to a later period, posterior to the fixation of the biblical texts. So we can no longer say that it is a prophecy after the fact. Daniel (9.25) prophesies *"from the time when the order was given to rebuild Jerusalem until an anointed prince, there are seven weeks. And during 62 weeks, Jerusalem will be rebuilt . . . And after 62 weeks, an anointed one will be deleted without a successor. The city and the sanctuary will be ruined by the people of a king to come . . ."* This prophecy is used by Christians to prove that Jesus was forecast by the sacred writings. It would apply to the death of the Messiah Jesus and to the destruction of Jerusalem and the temple, which actually happened in + 70 on order of the Roman general Titus. There is no evidence that this prophecy applies to Jesus, who has never been anointed and has always been rejected by the Jews who never considered him as Messiah. One day representing a year, some Christians have calculated that it exactly matches the coming of Jesus. Without entering into the details, all dates are set arbitrarily to match the date of March 30, 33 AD, that fundamentalist Christians consider as the date of Jesus's entrance into Jerusalem on his donkey. Jews never used see this text as a prophecy that was realized.

To prove that the Prophet Muhammad was inspired by God, Muslims give a verse, (30.2), in which he predicted the Roman victory over the Persians: *"The Romans have been defeated in the neighboring country, and few years after their defeat, they will be victorious."* Indeed, after the defeat of the Romans at Antioch in 613, the situation turns around and the Romans won a new battle against the Persians in 622. But the pious Muslims fail to mention that these prophecies were written after the event, since Muhammad died in 632 and his words were written down long after his death; therefore, necessarily after the "prophecy" that took place ten years before his death.

The rabbis explain that any prophecy is conditional, and if the people improve their conduct God will change his decision. By making it conditional, faith of the believer is not shaken if the prophecy is not fulfilled. Moreover, it pushes the believer to improve his behavior to change the future decision of God. This tool explains anything, like Saul becoming king by decision of God and losing his throne in favor of David because he disobeyed to God. If a prophecy is just, it does not prove that it comes from a prophet inspired by God. Because there is always a probability that a prophecy will be fulfilled. All the prophecies of the same prophet have to be realized in order to say that this prophet was inspired by God.

Is there a secret code written in the Jewish Bible?

According to Michael Drosnin's book *The Bible Code*, the Bible contains prophecies hidden between the letters of the Hebrew text. After removing punctuation and spaces, the letters are placed one next to the other, and by skipping the same number of letters, horizontally, vertically, or even diagonally, historical events are discovered, such as the assassination of John F. Kennedy or the Israeli prime minister Yitzhak Rabin, the Second World War, the explosion of the towers of New York. It would not be a coincidence, but evidence that the Bible is divine.

Yet for many scientists, it is possible to find the same results with other texts, like *Moby Dick* or *Harry Potter*. Skeptical scientists discovered nine political killings in Moby Dick using the same system as the famous code of the Bible. This exercise can also be repeated in other languages and other texts, like the New Testament and the Quran, to prove that they too are divine. Moreover, with only consonants, words have different meanings. For example, *bkr* can mean *boker* = morning, or *bakar* = cow, or *biker* = visited. The choice of the starting letter is arbitrary and the computer will choose his starting point even if illogical. To prove the existence of a code, what is important is not the past but what will happen tomorrow. Supporters of the code have not issued any prophecy that we can verify except one big mistake: the end of the world scheduled for 2006 following a nuclear conflict.

For the Talmud, Sanhedrin 21b, the Torah was originally given to Moses in Hebrew letters and the Hebrew language, but later, during the time of Ezra, the Torah was written in the Asshuri (Babylonian) alphabet and in the Aramaic language. And so for the sages of the Talmud, the Torah we know today is not the language of Moses but a double translation in alphabets and languages. These translations and changes of alphabet necessarily necessitated the use of an alphabet and words other than those God gave to Moses. And so the Bible code, if it exists, should only use the divine letters of God in Hebrew and not its translation using Aramaic letters

Jesus is not the suffering servant prophesied by Isaiah (53.2 to 12)

The prophets are of vital importance to Christianity and the doubt on them void Christianity. The saga of Jesus is actually a copy of many prophecies that have nothing to do with Jesus. The text of Isaiah (53) is the best example. It is so perfectly similar to the epic of Jesus that many people are convinced of the truth of Christianity through the shock of this single prophecy: "... *He is despised, rejected by men, a man of sorrows, knowing the disease, he was like an object whose face is diverted, a vile thing ... And yet it is our diseases he was carrying, he bore our sufferings, while we took him for an affected, unhappy, smitten by God, and afflicted. It is because of our sins he was bruised ... That's his injury that brought us healing. We were like sheep going nowhere ... Oppressed, abused, he did not open his mouth, like the lamb to the slaughter. Because of lack of protection and justice, he was removed ... caused by the sins of the people. He was assigned a grave with the ungodly, his tomb with the rich, though he had done no wrong ... But God has determined to break him, to overwhelm diseases, wanting him to offer himself as atonement ... He will bring justice to many and take charge of their iniquities ... Because he himself went to death and was left with criminals, he, which merely bear the sins of many ...*"

For Christians, this text, so similar to the epic of Jesus, proves that the prophecies predicted the coming of Jesus. Matthew (12.18), Luke (24.26), and Acts (3.18), (17.3), (8.26 to 40), (26.23) tell us that Jesus is the suffering servant. Yet the "suffering servant" is the most blatant case of copying, similar to an amateur painter who copies the great masters. From this Isaiah text, the Evangelists have drawn the ideas of rejection, the sins he took upon himself, the injury, the silence of the lamb in death, the grave with the rich. For skeptics, these similarities prove that Jesus's "epic" was built according to previous prophecies, and they bring great doubt on the historical reality of Jesus. Christianity must first prove that the story of Jesus is not a scaffold built from the prophecy of Isaiah and that this prophecy refers to Jesus at a distance of a few hundred years. Nothing is less certain.

For Isaiah, the Jewish people sinned and were exiled. This punishment of exile was the price to pay to be forgiven and become again the people of God. Isaiah does not mention once the word *Messiah*, and speaks of past suffering of the Jewish people, and not of the future. No Jew before

Christianity thought that this passage applied to the coming Messiah, who was a glorious figure and not a hanged criminal. Isaiah says nothing about the break with Judaism and the establishment of a new religion that would cancel the Sabbath, circumcision, and *kashrut*, and above anything, the resurrection of the servant and his divinity.

The prophecies: tools to build the Jesus epic

The Jewish prophets are the backbone of the New Testament. It is in order that the "writings of the prophets get realized" that Jesus sacrificed his life when he could have escaped. For Christians, Jesus was foretold by the Jewish prophets hundreds of years before his arrival. The Church sees in these similarities a miraculous fulfillment of Old Testament prophecies, the divine intervention, and the truth of the facts. For skeptics, Jesus's followers built an epic from the religious material they knew the best, the Jewish Bible, and three conditions are not respected: the epic of Jesus must be real and historic, these prophecies must relate to Jesus, and finally these prophecies must not be modified. Jesus and his disciples were familiar with the texts of the Jewish prophets they read every Sabbath in the synagogue. Paul, in I Thessalonians (I, 5.20) requests: *"Do not despise prophecies. Examine them and keep what is good."* Then, it is easy to build the epic of Jesus by matching the frame with the already known texts.

The following parables explain the technique. A couple walking in a forest discovers hearts with the initials A and B engraved on trees, and decided to name themselves Agnes and Bernard to give the impression that their great love was predestined. In another parable, a visitor in a forest discovers circles drawn on trees and an arrow in the middle of each circle made by a hunter. Astonished, he asks the hunter what is his secret. *"It's simple,"* answered the hunter. *"First I shoot my arrow on a tree, and then I draw a circle around it."* It is what the Evangelists have done with the prophecies.

We can classify this plagiarism into four sections:

1. The copy, word by word, from the biblical text is evident in reading a New Testament annotated with referrals to the Old Testament. It is like an amateur picking details from the works of great masters and then presenting his composition as original. This painter will hide the works of great artists to avoid a comparison that

would reveal the plagiarism, as the Church has prohibited the unaccompanied reading of the Bible.
2. The erroneous copy: Genesis (46.27) says *"All the people from the house of Jacob in Egypt: 70."* This number is repeated in Deuteronomy (10.22) and Exodus (1.5), and yet Acts (7.14) gives a different number: 75. How is it that hundreds of copyists made this error? We do not know.
3. The deliberate falsification of words: for example, the wrong translation of the word *alma* to *virgin*. Or in Romans (11.26): *". . . as it is written: The deliverer will come from Zion, and He will turn away ungodliness from Jacob."* But it is the opposite that is written in Isaiah (59.20): *"The deliverer will come to Zion and to those of Jacob who repent from sin."* Because for the Jews, the role of the Messiah is not to forgive our sins but to appear after the abandonment of sins.
4. The complete fabrication of a nonexistent text, as in Matthew (2.23): *"He came and dwelt in a city called Nazareth: that it might be fulfilled what was announced by the prophets, He shall be called a Nazarene."* The prophets never mentioned Nazareth. This prophecy does not exist, and *Nazarene* is not linked to Nazareth. Paul says in Acts (10.42 to 43): *". . . all the prophets bear him witness that whoever believes in him gets, in his name, the forgiveness of sins."* Contrary to what Paul says, no Jewish prophet has said that anyone who has faith in Jesus will be forgiven of sins. Jewish prophecies have no connection to Jesus and are wrong so often that they cannot be considered as evidence of the future resurrection of Jesus. The prophets would not predict the coming of God the Son, considered the greatest sacrilege for monotheistic Jews.

Christians used the following argument to prove the divinity of Jesus. They say that more than 400 prophecies of the Jewish Bible are fulfilled in Jesus's life and death, and they calculate that the probability that a man fulfilled only ten prophecies is so tiny that for sure Jesus is divine. Unless the life and death of Jesus were built using "the bricks" of the prophecies.

The Gospels could not exist without Jewish sources from which they have drawn more than 80 percent of their information; the historical background is 10 percent and plagiarism of other religions and myths fulfill the remaining 10 percent. In 1986, visiting the synagogue of Rome, Pope John Paul II recognized the Jewish inspiration: *"You are our elder brothers!"* Plagiarized Jewish writings in the Gospels are intended to give to the epic of Jesus more authority and thus convince Jews and pagans that Christianity has deep roots and is the culmination of a long process beginning in the Old Testament. Hebrews (1.1) stresses the importance of the Jewish prophets, *"God, who once spoke to our forefathers, many times and in various ways, through the prophets, spoke to us in recent times by his Son . . ."*

The Epic of Jesus was built from Jewish prophecies carefully selected and edited to show they were realized in Jesus.

- The young pregnant woman - Isaiah (7.14), Matthew (1.23)
- His kingdom will have no end - Isaiah (9.6), Luke (1.33)
- The Magnification of Mary - I Samuel (2.1), Luke (1.46)
- Born in Bethlehem - Micah (5.2), Matthew (2,2)
- A star soars from Jacob - Numbers (24.17), Matthew (2.2)
- Egypt called - Hoseah (11.1), Matthew (2.15)
- Newborns are massacred - Jeremiah (31.15), Matthew (2.16)
- In the desert, before me - Isaiah (40.3), John (1.30)
- John the Baptist as messenger - Malachi (3.1), John (1.29)
- John crying in the wilderness - Isaiah (40.3), Matthew (3.3)
- Disbelief of Jews - Isaiah (53.1), John (12.37)
- Hated by his people - Isaiah (49.7), John (10.20)
- He will heal the blind - Isaiah (35.5), Matthew (9.27)
- He will heal the deaf - Isaiah (29.18), Mark (7.33)
- He will heal the lame - Isaiah (35.6), John (5.9)
- He will heal the dumb - Isaiah (32.4), Matthew (9.33)
- He will speak in parables - Psalms (78.2), Matthew (13.31)
- He will enter Jerusalem on a donkey - Zachariah (9.9), Luke (19.35)
- He will be hated without cause - Psalms (35.19), John (15.24)
- He will be betrayed by a friend - Psalms (41.9), Matthew (26.48)
- He will be sold- thirty pieces of silver - Zechariah (11.12 to 13), Matthew (26.15)
- This award will be thrown to the potter - Zechariah (11.13), Matthew (27.7)
- Silent while facing accusers - Isaiah (53.7), Mark (15.4)
- He will be hit - Micah (5.1), Mark (15.19)
- They spit on him - Micah (50.6), Matthew (26.67)
- He will drink gall and vinegar - Psalms (69.21), Matthew (27.34)

- The darkness in the daytime - Amos (8.9), Matthew (27.45)
- He will be abused - Zechariah (13.6), Mark (15.25)
- He will have his hands and feet tied - Psalms (22.17), John (19.23)
- He will be drilled - Zechariah (12.10), John (19:34)
- His clothes are shared - Psalms (22.19), John (19.24)
- No bones will be broken - Exodus (12.46), John (19.33)
- Why have you forsaken me? - Psalms (22.2), Matthew (27.46)
- He will die and be resurrected - Isaiah (53.5 to 10)
- In a tomb of rich - Isaiah (53.9), Matthew (27.60)
- He will ascend into heaven - Psalms (110.1), Mark (16.19)
- He will be endowed with the Holy Spirit - Joel (12.28–29), Acts (2.33)
- The son of the man in the clouds - Daniel (7.13), Mark (13.26)

Jewish prophecies are divine for Christianity, and therefore anyone who does not believe in the divine inspiration of the prophets must reject all of Christianity. For example, Psalm 22, attributed to King David: *"My God, My God, why have you forsaken me? . . . All who see me turned away from me in derision . . . From the womb you have been my God . . . I have been poured out like water . . . and my tongue sticks to my gums . . . I can count all my bones . . . they divide my garments among them, and upon my clothing they cast lots . . . And all the nations of the earth shall worship before You . . ."* The Passion of Jesus is so similar to what David (?) wrote some 800 years earlier that Christians are forced to admit that the prophets of Israel are true and have a parcel of divinity. It would be more logical to say that from hundreds of prophecies the Evangelists have chosen the appropriated prophecies to build from scratch a story adapted to these prophecies. The Jewish Bible includes over 1,200 dense pages and it's easy to find something to feed the 140 pages of the Gospels.

Christian theologians kept the Jewish Bible, which they called the Old Testament, to find there the prophecies about Jesus. But the Jewish Bible contradicts Christianity because it addresses itself only to the Hebrew people, command of the eternal laws, circumcision, *kashrut*, Shabbat and holidays, canceled by Christians. These contradictions of the Christian attitude toward the Jewish Bible are the result of the staging of the story of Jesus by plagiarizing the Jewish prophecies. No prophet predicted the life of Jesus, but the Gospels use prophecies made by different prophets at different times to establish that the epic of

Jesus was foretold by the prophets. Why not a single coherent prophecy? By not using the same prophecies, the four Evangelists gave different descriptions of Jesus's life.

Conclusions: The Gospels built the epic of Jesus by plagiarizing the Jewish Bible, and this explains errors and contradictions, because it was necessary to adapt the story of Jesus to the Jewish prophecies used.

The prophecies contradict Christianity

Isaiah (31.1): *"Woe to those who go down to Egypt to seek help there,"* yet Jesus and his family descended to Egypt to escape the wrath of Herod.

Isaiah (2.18) speaks against the idols, and yet Christianity allows some idolatry with statues of Jesus and the Virgin.

Isaiah (10.12) said that the descendant of Jesse will assemble the exiles of Judah when the contrary happened at the time of Jesus. Then (11.6), *"the wolf shall dwell with the lamb"* in the time of the Messiah, who therefore had not yet arrived.

Jeremiah (17.27) cursed against violators of the Shabbat, yet Jesus's disciples will cancel it. Jeremiah (33.16) states that at the arrival of the Messiah *"Judah will be freed and Jerusalem will live in safety."* If Jesus was the Messiah, that prophecy is false since he has brought no liberation of Judah and no security for Jerusalem.

In Psalm (89.31) God affirms *"I will not betray my covenant and the statement of my lips, I will not change it."* It is thus difficult to understand how Christianity voided the Jewish laws like Shabbat or circumcision.

Psalm (72.8) and Zechariah (9.9) describe the arrival of the Messiah, copied by Matthew (21): *"Behold, your king comes to you; he is just and victorious, he is humble and rides on a donkey . . . He shall declare peace to the nations, and have dominion from sea to sea, from the river to ends of the earth . . ."* If Jesus is this king, where is the peace of nations?

One will notice another false prophecy of Luke (1.67): *"Zechariah, father of John the Baptist, filled with the Holy Spirit, prophesied by saying: Blessed be the Lord God of Israel . . . who raised us . . . a savior who delivers us from our enemies . . ."* This prophecy is a mistake because neither John the Baptist nor Jesus delivered the Jewish people from their enemies and the occupation and killings continued long after John and Jesus.

The prophet Hosea (13.4) transmits that God stated: *"And I am the Lord your God . . . You know no God but me, and there's no savior besides me."* So how can Christianity see in Jesus the savior?

Another example, Isaiah (60.18): *"You will no longer hear about violence in your country."*

The prophecies say nothing about Nazareth, nothing about a new religion that will void the circumcision, Shabbat, and dietary rules, or that it will be the source of so many massacres of Jews by the pogroms and the inquisition. And especially, there was no prophecy foretold about God the Son, the Holy Trinity, or Islam.

Muhammad, the prophet foretold by the Bible and New Testament?

The arrival of Muhammad and Islam are important events in the history of mankind. Moses and Jesus should have alerted of the future arrival of a messenger or an impostor who will convince more than a billion people that he is the messenger of God. If the Torah and the New Testament do not mention him, it would mean that the Scriptures do not have the gift of prophecy or that Muhammad is a false messenger of God. Similarly, for those who claim that the Torah contains a code, where is the clue about Muhammad and Islam?

Christianity asserts that Jesus was the last prophet and that after him there will be no other prophet. In the parable of the vine grower transmitted by Mark (12.6): *"There was still a beloved son, He will be sent last unto them . . ."* But Muhammad appears six centuries later and asserts that he is the last prophet and that after him there will be no prophet. And twelve centuries later, John Smith appears as the Mormon prophet who claims to be the last prophet. One of those prophets necessarily has to be wrong!

Christianity and Islam need the Jewish Torah for their faith, and say that their messiah or messenger was already announced in the Torah. According to John (5.46), Jesus said to the Jews: *"If you believed in Moses, you would believe in me, for he wrote about me."* This brings us to Deuteronomy (18.18), where God promises to Moses, *"I will raise them up a prophet from among their brothers, like you, and I will put my words in his mouth."*

That prophet would be Jesus for the Christians, and Muhammad for the Muslims. Yet when we read the Hebrew text, it does not concern Jesus or Muhammad but the Hebrew prophets, because God reassures the Hebrews who fear dying upon sight of Him by telling them that a Hebrew prophet will speak to them. This verse of the Jewish Bible was probably inserted to answer skeptics who complained of never having seen God. The answer was that God no longer appears because the Hebrews from the time of Moses had asked not to see Him face to face. This kind of subterfuge is similar to the lack of archaeological and historical evidence of the Exodus. It would be Pharaoh who asked to erase all memory of Moses from the Egyptian tablets. These Hebrews will not see God directly but He will speak to them through the prophets, and it is not a question of Jesus or Muhammad who arrive centuries after these facts.

Jesus was a Jew coming from among his Jewish brothers, but Jesus is divine for Christianity, different from the human Moses. The terms *"their brothers"* and *"raise them"* clearly prove that it is the people of Israel.

Muhammad was not the brother of the Jews. Are Arabs descendants of Ishmael? Is Ishmael a historical figure? And finally, only the sons of Jacob would form the Hebrew people, and therefore Ishmael is not the brother of the Israelites. In fact, the genetic relationship of Muslims with Ishmael and the claim that Arabs and Jews are brothers through the descendants of Ishmael is a fiction necessary to Islam. And Jews have fallen into the trap, repeating erroneously that Arabs are their cousins through Ishmael.

John (15.26 onward) makes Jesus say: *"When will come the Comforter that I will send to you from the Father . . . he shall not speak of himself, he will speak only what he heard . . ."* For Islam, this comforter is Muhammad. Yet Jesus says also in Matthew (7.15): *"Beware of false prophets, they come to you in sheep's clothing, but inwardly they are wolves."* For the Jews, the prophecy was over and they rejected Jesus and Muhammad. Christians rejected Muhammad. Muslims accept all the prophets from Abraham to Muhammad, including Moses and Jesus, as sent by God but affirm that their message was falsified. Yet the Quran rejects the divinity of Jesus, preached by Christianity, but accepts his virgin birth by giving Adam as an example, (3.59): *"Jesus is as Adam that God created from dust."*

Jesus's disciples knew perfectly the Bible they read every day, so it was easy to draw verses with which they built artificially Jesus's biography. This was not the case for Muhammad or his disciples. In the Quran (7.157), they would follow *"the apostle, the unlettered prophet foretold in the Torah and the Gospels."* And (61.6) says that Jesus said, *"Sons of Israel, I am to you an apostle of God and I announce after me an apostle with glorious name."* Some false translations add *"named Muhammad."* We do not find this prophecy in the New Testament.

Muhammad cannot be a true prophet in the Jewish Bible, because it is written in Deuteronomy (13.1) that if a visionary proclaiming himself a prophet requests a change in the laws of Moses, this false prophet is to be killed. Muslims also see in Isaiah references to Muhammad. Isaiah (42.11) prophesied that God's chosen will be hosted by the *"villages where Kedar lives"* and Kedar, according to Genesis (25.13) is the second son of Ishmael. On one hand, Muslims are obliged to say that the Bible was falsified to explain the contradictions and differences with their Quran; on the other hand, they use any Bible verse to ennoble the Quran or Muhammad!

This crazy research into the Jewish Bible for evidence of the authenticity of the Prophet of Islam leads to ridicule. For example, Muslim scholars give as proof that Muhammad was predicted by the Bible verse (5.16) of the Song of Songs, which describes a beloved person: *"his mouth is sweetness, he is altogether charming . . ."* In this verse appears the Hebrew word *mahmadim*, which means *charms*, and these Muslim scholars see the prophetic name *Muhammad*. Another verse in the Bible, Hosea (9.16), uses the common name in singular *mahmad*: *"the best (mahmad) of their money, or their entrails . . . will invade their homes."* So *mahmad* cannot designate the future Muhammad! Similarly, II Chronicles (36.19), *"all the beautiful objects (mahmadim) it contained were prey to destruction."* No connection between the words *mahmad* and *Muhammad*.

How can one explain that no Arab before the time of Prophet Muhammad was called Muhammad? Muhammad was the first to bear this name! Can we conclude that the prophet had a different name and then decided to adopt this name himself by drawing in the verses of the Jewish Bible without understanding?

Sometimes Muslims choose another verse of Isaiah (29.12) to prove that Muhammad was foretold in the Bible, *"and if we present this book to an illiterate man, saying, read this. He replies: I cannot read."* But reading the text, it is clear that on the contrary, the text complains that the literate and the illiterate have their eyes closed to the words of God. These two prophecies of Isaiah, (42 and 29), and Deuteronomy (18.18) are used by Muslims to prove that Muhammad was foretold by the Hebrew prophets yet they reject Isaiah 53, which according to Christians predicts the crucifixion of

Christ. So if the Bible was falsified according to Muslims, which part of the prophecy is true?

The Quran: absent from the Israeli-Palestinian conflict

To counter the Jewish claims to the holy land, some Muslims say that the Arabs were the first inhabitants of this land. But this contradicts the other Arab claim of being descendants of Ishmael, Abraham's son who walked to Arabia and built with his father the first Kaaba in Mecca. The Arabs, who claim to be descendants of Ishmael, would thus have lost any right to the land of Israel, occupied by the descendants of Isaac.

Muhammad was the author of a prophecy that Muslims never boast about as it is the only prophecy that got realized. In (5.21), Muhammad said: *"My people, (the Jewish people) enter the holy land that God destined for you."* And in (17.111), *"After the death of Pharaoh, We said to the son of Israel: Seeing the country and when will be fulfilled the promise of another life? We will come back in droves."* On the Day of Judgment, therefore, all Jews will return to live in Israel!

It is repeated in the verse 104: *"After him, we said to the children of Israel. Dwell on Earth, then when the promise (of life) last, we will come in droves."* What pro-Zionist statement? The Quran qualifies many times the children of Israel as the chosen people, in Al-Baqarah, verse 47: *"O Children of Israel, remember My favor which I bestowed on you (remember) that I have preferred you to all peoples."*

In fact, the Quran is never mentioned in the Israeli-Palestinian conflict, neither by the Israelis, who ignore the Quran, nor the Palestinians, who want to hide the recognition of the land promised to the Jews. If Muhammad authenticates the Jewish people, their history, and their territory, he completely ignores the Palestinian people and the Palestinian Arabs. The prophet did not predict the Israeli-Palestinian conflict. And finally, if Jerusalem is mentioned hundreds of times in the Bible, it is not once in the Quran. Similarly, the word *Palestine* is totally absent from the Quran.

12

Kashrut, dietary laws, and the three religions

Kashrut is a series of rules partly mentioned in the Bible and partly codified in the post-biblical writings as the Talmud or Shoulhan Aruch. In Genesis (9.3), God permits *"anything that moves, everything that lives shall be your food, as well as plants, I give you everything."* But here is a first contradiction, because just before, in Genesis (8.20), after the flood, Noah *"took of every clean quadruped, of every clean bird, and offered the burnt offering . . .,"* which means that there are unclean animals. Therefore, the notion of *kashrut* was known to Noah long before Moses, or this sacrifice was introduced well after Noah and perhaps even long after Moses.

Leviticus (11) gives a list of dietary restrictions ordained by God to the Hebrew people repeated in Deuteronomy (14): *". . . So you will not eat the camel, the hare and the rabbit . . . You will not eat pork that has a split hoof but does not chew the cud . . . You shall not eat of those in the waters that have not fins and scales . . . You will not eat the eagle, the osprey . . . stork . . . It is unclean to you . . ."* Are there logical reasons for these dietary restrictions?

Jewish *kashrut* is not food hygiene!

Pork, forbidden to Jews and Muslims, is mentioned in Leviticus (11.7): *"And the pig, for its hoof is split and completely separated, but it does not chew its cud, it is unclean for you."* Similarly, the Quran (2,173) prohibits pork, but without any explanation. The pig is a filthy animal that wallows in its waste. Its meat is fat and high in cholesterol, and contains larvae dangerous to humans. Predators and scavengers have conveyed diseases of prey, seafood provoke allergies and poisoning, clean animals contain fewer toxins than the impure. These statements, although not verified, are not convincing, because: pork, preserved poorly in warm climates (without refrigeration), needs overcooking to remove bacteria. If this argument is correct, in modern societies with refrigerators and ovens pork should be allowed.

The *kashrut* contains no list of prohibited plants while some are harmful. The Universal God cannot ignore the health of Gentiles. Why did He allow to Christians the consumption of pork if it is unhealthy? Are Christians sicker than Jews and Muslims? Some, including the famous Maimonides, claim that the pig was used for Egyptian or pagan sacrifice and therefore banned to differentiate them from Egyptians. Why did God not prohibit other foods high in cholesterol or fat, such as eggs, whole milk, liver, and heart? In beef, 95 percent of the cholesterol comes from the red meat (permitted) and very little from the fat (prohibited). If these prohibitions were dictated by hygiene requirements, what about the stork? The hare? And why is the horse forbidden? It is a clean animal and its meat even recommended by some doctors. One oddity remains unanswered: Leviticus (11.22) prohibits insects, but Jews can eat grasshoppers. Why? Another curiosity: according to the *kashrut*, the sciatic nerve of edible animals should be removed and not consumed. Why? No hygienic reason but a legend recorded by Genesis (32.26), Jacob's struggle against the messenger of God: *"Jacob's thigh was dislocated . . . that's why the children of Israel still will not eat the sciatic nerve . . ."* This rule is respected until our time by the Jews, who did not raise the question of why.

Does the ban on meat-milk mixture have logical reasons?

Kosher laws have two sets of rules. The first is the list of forbidden foods mentioned above, and the second is the ban on meat-milk mixture. Judaism alone forbids eating meat and milk together. This prohibition is one of the pillars of Judaism and rules the life, hour by hour, of all Jews, including those who do not strictly follow the other rules. Thus a Jew never eats meat and butter, or finishes a meal with a good cheese. He will have two different sets of dishes, one for meat and one for dairy. This is why the Jew will eat in a kosher restaurant or with another Jew but never in the house of his Christian or Muslim neighbor. This terrible rule comes from the strange extrapolation of a verse mentioned the times, in Deuteronomy (14.21), Exodus (23.19), and Exodus (34.26): *"You shall not cook a kid in the milk of his mother."* The word used in the Bible is not *kid* but *gdi*, which is more difficult to translate.

Abraham does not respect the meat and dairy separation and in Genesis (18.7), God sends three messengers to Abraham, who welcomes them, *"And Abraham ran to the herd and fetched a calf tender and good and gave it to a servant who hurried to prepare it. And he took cream and milk and the calf which he had dressed . . . and they ate."* So Abraham and God's messengers do not respect the rule imposed later by the Pharisees and rabbis. To this, a rabbi replied that the Torah had not yet been given and that angels do not have to respect the rules of *kashrut* formulated for Hebrews. So is it possible that Judaism misunderstood this interdiction?

In Deuteronomy (32.14), God fed the people of Israel with the *"cream of cows and milk of sheep with the fat of lambs."* So mixing milk and meat, with no mention of the ban. Similarly, in II Samuel (17.29), David is welcomed with *"honey, butter, and sheep and cow cheeses . . .,"* so dairy and meat together. A Jew does not eat chicken cooked in butter even if it is obvious that eating chicken and butter does not contradict the order given above of not cooking a kid in its mother's milk

To explain the enlargement to all meat and dairy products, the Talmud says that *gdi* does not mean *kid* but all the small cattle or sheep. And so the ban covers all meat, not just the kid. The rabbis extended the prohibition of mixing milk/meat even if they are not cooked together, why? The ban has also been extended to poultry for fear that a pagan or an ignorant Jew seeing an educated Jew eat poultry with cream come to think he can consume a mixture of milk/meat. It would be possible to eat veal in goat's milk (not his mother), but the rabbinate prohibited it. What can we learn from this? That everything is confused and the Bible gives no rational explanation for the ban, and the explanations given by the rabbis are not acceptable.

1. Medical: The ban on meat and milk mixture is not medical, as no scientific study has demonstrated the harmfulness of the mixture.

Also, Judaism permits first drinking milk and then eating meat, which are then mixed in the stomach. In addition, Jews who don't eat meat with butter are not healthier than Gentiles.

2. Avoid cruelty: The Bible contains other prohibitions that are of the same nature.

   Deuteronomy (22.6) says, *"If you meet on your way a bird's nest on a tree or on the ground . . . and the mother sitting on the young or on the eggs do not take the mother with the young, send away the mother and take the young for yourself so that you may be happy and it will prolong your days."* The ban on boiling a kid in its mother's milk could mean not cooking a kid while it is still being breastfed in order to avoid shocking maternal instincts. Besides, Leviticus (22.28) states: *"Big or tiny beast, you may not slaughter its offspring on the same day."* However, this prohibition is not dictated by humanitarian reasons since Judaism allows cooking and eating meat of calf with more mature beef; eating chicken and eggs; killing a newborn lamb or hundreds of chickens to ask for forgiveness of sins.

3. Some followers of Kabbalah explain this prohibition by the fact that the milk symbolizes life for the newborn while meat symbolizes death. Yet according to the rabbis, it is permissible to eat an egg with chicken, which contradicts the symbols of life and death.

Other more acceptable reasons for the ban would be not to imitate the neighboring peoples who prayed for fertility by baking a young animal in its mother's fat. The Jews wanted to disassociate themselves from these customs. Similarly, the Bible forbids drinking the blood of beasts, permitted by neighboring peoples.

Helev or *halav*: According to Leviticus (3.17), God commands *"any fat and any blood, you shall not eat of."* The words *fat* and *milk* are written with the same consonants *hlv*, and the only difference is a vowel. Originally, Hebrew was written without vowels. So is it possible that there was confusion between fat and milk?

So the Bible forbids eating blood and certain fatty parts. Blood contains the life given by God. The brain and heart also represent life, and yet are allowed. The fat was considered the richest part that was to be offered to God (and to the priests) and not eaten by the Hebrews. Leviticus (3.17) makes it clear: *"All the choice parts for God."*

The Karaites, a Jewish sect that applies only written rules, eat meat with milk after checking that the milk did not come from the mother of the beast, and of course eat fish or chicken with milk.

In conclusion, the reason for all the prohibitions mentioned above is not medical because it is illogical that God is only concerned with the health of Jews and do nothing for the health of all other humans. Besides, the rabbis themselves refuse hygiene as a reason for *kashrut* because of the contradictions mentioned above and invoke other more spiritual reasons.

The ban on fishes without fins and scales, a challenge for skeptics

Leviticus (11.9) and Deuteronomy (14.10) prohibit *"between aquatic animals . . . all that is deprived of fins and scales, you shall not eat, it is unclean for you."* Seafood is forbidden to Jews yet allowed to Muslims and Christians for no clear reason. Aquatic animals deprived of fins and scales, which are scavengers, clean the depths of the seas or filter the water in their bronchi, and for that would be prohibited. Yet Jews eat fish that eat banned marine crustaceans, and some permitted fish with scales and fins are also scavengers. Are there sea creatures with fins but without scales? The Talmud says that any marine creature that has scales inevitably has fins. How could the sages of the Talmud risk such an assertion? If one discovers a sea creature with scales but no fins, it would prove that the Talmud makes mistakes and is not divinely inspired. Until today, we have never found a case that contradicts this risky affirmation of the Talmud, and it is a challenge to skeptics.

Are kosher rules spiritual or just racist?

For the rationalist Maimonides and other rabbis, one reason for the prohibition of certain foods is the effect of food on our nature or even on our physical and mental health. Maimonides, who was a doctor, said in his *Guide for the Perplexed* that *"food forbidden by the Torah are unhealthy."* For him and others, the food we eat becomes a part of our flesh and our blood and thus affects our nature. So it is forbidden to eat the beasts and birds of prey, pork, and some other creatures in order for us not to acquire the natural features of the carnivorous animals, birds of prey, or dirty animals. On the contrary, the animals that chew the cud and have split hooves would be peaceful, not cruel and bloodthirsty as beasts of prey. Thus, kosher food stimulates us to act morally and to repel evil. This argument is unacceptable because it is allowed to eat scaly fish like barracuda, which is a dangerous fish. Indeed, almost all fish are carnivorous and yet permitted. The chicken, also permitted, is carnivorous and eats earthworms.

Permitted foods would contain a positive spiritual charge that bring us closer to God, but forbidden foods have a negative charge. This argument seems very elaborate but is actually meaningless. Why is horsemeat negative while cow meat is positive? The tendency to use an obscure philosophical vocabulary can meet the spiritual needs of the modern Jews, but this is an illusion. Just attend a course on Kabala, very popular in modern Judaism, to be convinced that the use of a "psychological and metaphysical" vocabulary is a new need of Judaism.

The episode of Samson

In the Book of Judges, long after the law of Moses, Samson was born to be Nazir devoted to God, to whom alcohol is prohibited. Yet Samson ate and drank with the Philistines without any consideration for *kashrut*. So can it be that the kosher rules are subsequent to the time of Samson? Is the episode of Samson foreign to Judaism? Or both? Finally, God anointed Samson as Nazir while he violated a commandment given by God to Moses, that of not marrying a foreign woman.

Is *kashrut*, in fact, only a tool against assimilation?

Dietary rules would be a late addition, and stories of the Jewish Bible give a shred of evidence. Indeed, dozens of times, God punished the Hebrews for breaking His commandments, mainly the ones that prohibit idolatry, but never for breaking *kashrut* dietary laws. Not once is a Hebrew caught in flagrant consumption of prohibited foods. In I Kings (17.13), Eli the Tishbite eats at a Phoenician woman's, house without any comment on the ban.

The famous Samson lives and eats and feasts with the Philistines, but nothing is said about the forbidden food. Is it possible that for more than a millennium the Hebrew people, described as so unwilling to commit to monotheism, were fully compliant with the dietary laws? Unless these rules were included late! Only in Daniel (1.8), a millennium after Moses, is it noted that Daniel was invited to the court of King Nebuchadnezzar, but *"he resolved not to defile himself with the king's food and with the wine served to drink."*

No text in the Bible, including the texts of the prophets and other stories, expressly forbids the eating of meat and milk. Neither the writings of Flavius Josephus nor those of all other historians and writers mention the ban of meat-milk mixture. In addition, Deuteronomy (4.2) and (13.1) orders *"do not add anything to what I command you and do not subtract anything, to keep the commandments of the Lord your God."* Any addition would be contrary to the commandments of God. So why did the rabbis add dozens of new rules? The Pharisees and rabbis considered contact with non-Jews as a stain, and in order to prevent assimilation, they added new rules to live only among themselves.

Further evidence that the ban on mixing milk and meat is a late invention and not biblical is found precisely in the New Testament. The cancellation of the *kashrut* is operated after the so-called divine appearance to Peter: *"There were all kinds of four-footed beasts and creeping . . . And a voice said to him: Arise Peter, slaughter and eat! But Peter said, no Lord, for I have never eaten anything profane and unclean . . ."* Peter mentions only the prohibition of eating unclean animals, but not the meat and milk mixture, and this is further evidence that this prohibition did not exist and appeared after the destruction of the temple in 70. After the destruction of the second temple, sacrifices were abolished and the differences between Jews and non-Jews diminished. To preserve the Jewish people from assimilation, it was necessary to expand the ban and its new interpretation: *"You shall not eat milk with meat."* Poultry was included to avoid confusion.

The true purpose of the *kashrut* rules is to prevent a meal with non-Jews. The Jew maintains his particularity by separating himself during meals, and therefore the *kashrut* creates an effective defense to stop assimilation. The first Christians voided these interdictions in order to convert the pagans to the new sect, allowing them to have a meal together.

The fear of assimilation is repeated in the Hebrew and Jewish epic, and mixed marriages are considered a sin till today. In Deuteronomy (16.20), *"in the cities of these peoples that God gives you for inheritance, you shall save alive nothing that breathes . . . so they do not teach you to imitate their abominations . . ."* This total destruction only applies to people living in areas assigned by God to the Jewish people. Several verses earlier, it is mentioned that before attacking distant cities the Hebrews will not reside in and cannot assimilate, *"you shall offer him peace . . ."* So only destruction of peoples that may assimilate with the Jewish people. To avoid this assimilation, Deuteronomy (7.3) forbids mixed marriage: *". . . You shall not intermarry with them . . . Because your son will turn away from me, and they worship foreign gods."* Returning from exile, in Ezra (9), *"we have sinned against our God and have married foreign women . . . separate yourselves from the peoples of the country and foreign women . . . send away their wives and offer a ram for a trespass offering . . ."*

All the kosher rules and the prohibition of mixed marriages are the defense of a small nation to preserve itself from assimilation. By creating these dietary rules, a Jew cannot sit at the table of a non-Jew; he will not even enter into the house of a non-Jew, and therefore cannot be assimilated. It is possible that eating apart to preserve their particularity was learned from the Egyptians. In Genesis (43.32), *"Egyptians who ate with him were served separately because the Egyptians could not eat with the Hebrews, because it is in the eyes of the Egyptians an abomination."* This sentence is unclear. It would be an abomination to the Egyptians either because they cannot eat with slaves or because the Egyptians have certain dietary rules not respected by the Hebrews, for example the prohibition of eating birds, which was sacred to the Egyptians. Joseph would have learned in Egypt that eating separately prevents the mixing and assimilation of peoples. According to the historian Herodotus, who traveled in ancient Egypt, the Egyptians hated pigs and thought that its milk gave leprosy. If someone even accidentally touched a pig, he had to dive into the river with his clothes on. Egyptians who were guarding the swine could not enter the temple. Egyptians never sacrificed pigs to their gods except on two occasions, the feast of the full moon and in honor of Bacchus-Osiris, and only on these two occasions were they allowed to eat some.

Unlike the Egyptians, Jews never sacrificed pigs. The Egyptians believed that the flesh of the eel and other fish thickened blood and decreased sweating. This is why the Egyptian priests had forbidden eating these fishes, and to convince the people they declared them sacred. Moreover, Egyptians refrained from physical contact with Greeks and did not use a knife or blade or Greek cooking pots, and did not taste the beef cut by the knife of a Greek.

An additional hint: the northern kingdom of Israel was conquered by the Assyrians in 722 BC and tens of thousands were exiled and disappeared, assimilated into the host country. Why this assimilation? Because at that time Jews had nothing really particular when they were away from the temple. Circumcision (other people practiced it and this sign is hidden and personal), the first rules of kashrut (not exaggerated then, without prohibition of milk-meat mixture), the Shabbat (also without extremism) were not sufficient to preserve the exiles from a total assimilation without their priests and leaders.

Toward 586 BC, the kingdom of Judea was conquered by Babylon and the elite was exiled, but returned later with Ezra and Nehemiah and rebuilt the temple. This exile, unlike the northern kingdom exile, led to a partial and not total assimilation. Why? The fact that this exile was short (two generations) and that these exiles remained supervised by their elite (exiled themselves) would be an explanation for their non-total assimilation. But after the destruction of the temple by the Romans and the new forced exile, religious leaders understood the need to make changes to protect themselves against any assimilation. It would be at this time that the rules of *kashrut*, Shabbat, and others were exaggerated to ensure the particularism.

Minyan and *kippah*

Jews need to gather in a group of at least ten adults to pray. This need, added later by the Mishnah, is also intended to preserve the Jews from assimilation. To find ten other adults, the Jew must live in community with other Jews. Without this community of Jews, he can neither pray nor perform several acts of his religion. Similarly, the yarmulke (dress, accoutrements such as black hat or fur) enables Jews to maintain their distinctiveness and avoid assimilation. These signs are actually additions imposed after the destruction of the temple (see also paragraph on oral tradition).

Jesus respected kosher laws but Christianity canceled it!

Jesus always respected Jewish dietary rules and did not cancel them. Nowhere in the New Testament is Jesus described as eating foods forbidden by Jewish law. The accusation made by the Pharisees, reported by Luke (15. 2): *"This man, Jesus, receives sinners and eats with them"*, concerned the Jewish tax collectors and not the gentiles. If the message of Jesus was that all foods were permitted, he would have given himself as an example and would have eaten pork. *Kashrut* was not canceled by Jesus, and his followers continued to eat kosher after his death. A few years after the death of Jesus, the apostle Peter reminds of the ban in Acts (10.28): *"You know as it is illegal for a Jew to join a man of another race."* But the disciples of Jesus trying to convert not Jews but pagans had to sit at a table with them. The apostle Peter wanted to enter the house of the pagan Cornelius to convert him to the sect, and for that he invented an ecstasy and a voice described in Acts (10.11): *"He fell into a trance and saw heaven opened and a kind of great sheet . . . descending to him . . . There were all kinds of four-footed beasts and creeping . . . And a voice said to him: Arise, Peter, slaughter and eat! But Peter said, no Lord, for I have never eaten anything profane and unclean . . . And the voice spoke to him again; what God has made clean, stop to call it unclean."*

Without any explanation, with an easy but divine vision (?) Christianity canceled the Jewish dietary rules and opened up to the huge pagan market. In fact, it would be the apostle Paul who crushed kosher laws before Peter. In the Epistle to the Romans (2.16), Paul says, *"I know and am persuaded by the Lord Jesus that nothing is unclean in itself."* In his Epistle to the Corinthians I (8.8), Paul says *"this is not a food that brings us closer to God . . ."* Then according to (10.23): *"if a non-believer (a pagan) invites you and you accept to go, eat whatever is offered to you without question for conscience."* And to close the circle, Paul, through his disciples, puts into the mouth of Jesus incomprehensible words: *"Nothing that enters from outside cannot pollute man"* and *"It is not what goes into the mouth that pollutes a man, but what comes out."* These two above sentences are meaningless and wrong, because what comes from outside into the body of a man can harm him! Jesus probably said: *"It's not **only** what goes into the mouth that pollutes a man but what comes out."* This means that not only the dietary laws of what goes into the mouth are important, but also be careful of the words out of your mouth.

In conclusion, Jesus had always respected Jewish dietary laws, but his followers canceled them in order to convert the Gentiles.

If Jewish dietary laws are beneficial, why have they been abolished by Christianity? These dietary laws are part of the 613 laws of the Bible. Why cancel them and retain others, like some of the Ten Commandments?

Leviticus (3.17 and 7.26 and 17.10) prohibits *"all fat and whole blood," "any sort of blood or bird or quadruped," "as the vital principle of the flesh in blood."* Jesus never ate blood, according to the Gospels, and had always respected the law. Also, after his disappearance, in Acts (15.20–29), Jesus's disciples ordered the pagans *"to abstain from meats offered to idols, from blood and from things strangled and from fornication."* It is therefore clear that Christians should continue to refrain from eating blood. Besides, early Christians like Tertullian confirm: *". . . We do not even look at the blood of animals as a food allowed to eat, and for this reason we abstain from things strangled and dead animals, not to be polluted in any manner by blood . . ."* So who abolished the ban? Not Jesus and his apostles. And so the sect of Jehovah's Witnesses, like the Jews, do not eat blood and are in agreement with the Jewish Bible and the New Testament while all other Christians transgress their own religion, especially the Europeans, who love blood sausages.

The Quran and its unexplained dietary restrictions:

The Quran invented nothing and instead copied the Jewish food restrictions with some variations. Sura 5 says, *"You are not allowed dead animals or their blood, or pork meat . . . nor strangled or stunned or dead from a fall . . ."* Why all these dietary restrictions? No explanation is given. It is the sole decision of God. The flesh of pork is described as *"filth"* or *"abomination."* Why? Verse (5.87): *"Do not ban the food that God allows."* Verse (5.1): *"the beasts of the herd you are permitted except those that we will tell you . . ."* But there is no list of banned foods in the Quran.

Muslim sects disagree on what is permitted and on what is banned. Some allow all types of fish and seafood. Shiites, just like Jews, refrain from fish without scales and from horse meat.

Islam is concerned with hygiene, for example, the Hadith of Bukhari (69.534) reports an order from Muhammad: *"when you urinate, do not touch the penis with the right hand, and when you wipe yourself after defecation, do not use the right hand."* Do we really need God to teach us about elementary hygiene? What about the left-handed person? The Quran says nothing about food allowed to Christians. The only mention however is an error in (5.114): *"Jesus, son of Mary said: My God, my Lord, bring us down from heaven a table that is a feast for all of us."* Muhammad is wrong because it is not Jesus but Peter who described this table filled of forbidden food. Jews and Muslims have common dietary restrictions, like pork, blood, and the sacrificial food offered to idols. However, some foods are forbidden to Jews but allowed to Muslims, like the meat of rabbit and camel. Wine is allowed to Jews but forbidden to Muslims. On the other hand, Muslims are unaware of the ban on mixing meat with milk.

Dietary laws of the Quran created to win the sympathy of the Jews

The Koran (3.93) asserts that *"all food was allowed to the sons of Israel, except what Israel had itself banned before the revelation of the Torah. Tell them: Bring the Torah and read it if you speak the truth."* Just look in the Bible and see that Muhammad is mistaken. And how is it that an illiterate asks his listeners to read the Torah. In what language? His Arab followers could not read Hebrew because it had not been translated yet.

The Quran refers in several places to some remarks about Jewish dietary rules but maybe the one who wrote them did not understand them? The Sura (3.50) says: *"I just confirm what you knew by the Torah and declare allowed a part which was not."* Why all these interdictions for the Jews? Why the permissions for the Muslims? The Sura (4.160) says: *"There are good foods we have allowed to you that are forbidden to Jews because of their iniquity, because they deviated too much from the path of God."* But Sura (5.5) is wrong when it states: *"The food of those who have the book (that is to say, the Jews), are allowed to you and yours to them."* This is not true. If a Muslim can eat crabs for example, it is forbidden to the Jew. Similarly, the Sura (6,146) incorrectly states: *"We banned the Jews from eating beasts with claws . . . the fat of cattle and sheep, except that of the back and guts and that which is mixed with the bone. This was the punition for their revolt."* This statement is incorrect because it is different from what is written in the Jewish Bible. Pigeons and chickens have claws and are permitted to the Jews. It would mean also that the *kashrut* is a punishment for the Jews, but to the contrary, it is a sign of purity. Finally, if these dietary rules are a punishment for Jews, are they for Muslims as well?

The disciples of Jesus, Paul and Peter, canceled kosher laws in order to make possible a common meal with the pagans and convert them. Muhammad banned pork to facilitate the conversion of Jews to Islam. The Quran forbids pork without any explanation except that of a divine order. Muslims can eat camel but camel meat is forbidden to Jews. Why does the Quran reject certain Jewish laws and keeps others? It is probably because they did not want to clash with the culinary traditions of Arabs, who were used to eating meat and drinking the milk of camels. The desire to differentiate themselves from the Jews after failing to convert them could also have played a role.

Wine and Islam

The Bible does not prohibit wine or alcohol but condemns drunkenness. Proverbs (23.20 and 31) say, *"Be not among wine drinkers . . . it glides slowly and bites like a snake."* Or in (31.4) it says: *"It is not for kings to drink wine, nor for princes to indulge in strong drink, lest they drink and forget the law and pervert the rights of the poor."* The Quran (2,219), (4.43), (5.90) go further than the Bible and ban alcohol even in small doses. The Hadiths also prohibit alcohol. They say: *"Alcohol is the mother of all vices and is the most shameful vice."* But if alcohol is clearly prohibited during life, it is permissible to paradise where *"rivers of delicious wine streams . . ."* Verse (47.15) says: *"immortal youths will circulate among them, with goblets . . . a clear beverage . . . they will not be drunk."* So God forbids drinking wine on earth but allows it in paradise.

13

Circumcision and the three religions

Female circumcision is condemned by the world, but in silence

The circumcision of girls is widespread in Africa, including Egypt, Yemen, and Nigeria and other Islamic countries. Islam did not invent the practice of female circumcision, which is an African heritage. One possible explanation: the Talmud, Niddah 28a says that during sex: *"If the woman emits her semen first, she bears a boy and if the man emits first, she bears a girl."* But the Hadith 546, narrated by Bukhari, says the contrary. Allah's Apostle said *". . . As for the resemblance of the child to his parents: If a man has sex with his wife and discharges first, the child will look like the father. If the woman discharges first, the child will look like her."* And also in Hadith 469 of Muslim about the erotic dreams of women, Muhammad says: *"Does the woman ejaculate? 'Yes,' replied the Prophet, 'if she didn't, who would the child look like? The liquid emitted by man is thick and white, while the woman's is smooth and yellowish. The resemblance (of the children to their parents) depends on which of the two liquids reaches the uterus first."* It is not the race of the two liquids that determines the similarity between the child and his parents but the genetic information contained in the DNA of each parent. So the Talmud and the Hadith say two opposite things and at least one is wrong.

Can it be that to have baby boy, the Islamic tradition would have to delay or cancel the sexual pleasure of women and so introduced excision? Why does the Hadith say the contrary of the Talmud? Is it because of misinterpretation? The affirmation of the Talmud would lead to reducing the sexual pleasure of men and maybe was the reason for the circumcision while the affirmation of the Hadith would lead to reducing the pleasure of women and maybe was the reason of the excision.

Although excision is prohibited in all Western countries, it is still practiced in Europe by some African emigrants under the nose of social services. How can we condemn circumcision of girls yet accept male circumcision? Both are mutilations without the consent of the circumcised. And while male circumcision is benign, female circumcision is a serious operation. Jews and Muslims fear opposing it because they could be told to stop male circumcision. Christians also are fairly quiet, although they canceled circumcision to facilitate the conversion of pagans. In fact, only atheists openly oppose circumcision of girls, and the debate often drifts on the circumcision of boys. Traditions and customs must be analyzed and then refuted or accepted.

Circumcision of boys ordered by the Bible without any explanation

Circumcision, which is the removal of the foreskin that exceeds the gland of the male penis, is one of the most respected commandments of Judaism. All Jewish male babies are circumcised whether from religious or atheistic families. This rite called *brit milah* is performed on the eighth day after birth. In Genesis (17.9), *"God said to Abraham . . . this is the covenant . . . You will cut off the flesh of your outgrowth and it will be a symbol between me and you. At the age of eight days, every male among you shall be circumcised . . . children born in your house or bought with money from the son of the stranger that is not of your race . . . And the uncircumcised male who has not been circumcised in the flesh . . . was cut off from his people; he has broken my covenant."* Non-Hebrew slaves included! And also in Leviticus (12.3): *"On the eighth day, the child shall be circumcised."* Is it possible that the universal God granted circumcision only to the Hebrew people and their slaves?

In Joshua (5), just before entering the Promised Land, God commanded Joshua: *"arm yourself with sharp knives and undergo circumcision of the new children of Israel . . . For all who were born in the desert after the Exodus from Egypt, were not circumcised."* Why is there no circumcision during the forty years in the wilderness? No logical explanation is given! Especially if it is noted in Genesis (17.14): *"And the uncircumcised male who has not cut the flesh of his excrescence will be deleted off from his people for having broken my covenant."* So all males born during the forty years of wilderness would have been excluded not only by the Jewish people but also put to death for violating the order of God. Circumcision of all males aged under forty years old seems impossible because it endangers the Hebrews, who knew the episode of Shechem as described in Genesis (34). Dinah the daughter of Jacob, was allegedly raped by Shechem, son of Hamor, who wants to marry her and offers: *"Give us your daughters and marry ours; stay with us, the country is open to you . . . exploit it yourself . . . The sons of Jacob were cunning . . ."* and asked that the males of Shechem first be circumcised. But that circumcision was a trap, and while they were resting from their circumcision, *"two of the sons of Jacob, Simon and Levi, killed all the males . . . took their flocks, their herds all their . . . property, their children and their wives . . ."* Is the reaction of Dinah's brothers due to the rape of their sister or their opposition to mixed marriage, which appears often in the Bible? In fact, this episode of Dinah has a triple purpose: to devalue the tribes of Simon and Levi, to strengthen opposition to mixed marriages, and also to explain why the men of Shechem practice circumcision.

Aware of this episode, it seems unlikely that Joshua would endanger all the people by ordering the general circumcision of all Hebrew males. In addition, if the wilderness did not grant the proper conditions for circumcision, how then, in Exodus (4.25), *"Moses stopped at an inn, YHWH approached him and wanted his death."* Then his wife *"Tsipora grabbed a pebble, entrenched outgrowth of her son, and cast it at his feet . . . She said, yes, you are united to me by blood, through circumcision."* Why would God want to kill Moses? Is it because he has not yet circumcised his son? This is not clear! Why did Moses not circumcise his son when since Abraham, all Hebrews circumcised their sons, even their slaves. Moreover, according to Exodus (4.20), Moses has several children, so why only circumcise one? The only possible explanation is that this episode had been added to teach generations of Jews that nothing should stop a circumcision. This circumcision performed by a woman is unique.

According to the Jewish tradition, circumcision should not be postponed, even if the eighth day falls on a Shabbat. So how is it that during the forty years of Exodus thousands of babies were not circumcised and waited till they got to the outskirts of the Promised Land?

All these oddities lead us to the question: is it possible that the circumcision of Abraham is an addition inserted after the Exodus from Egypt? Moreover, many books of the Bible, such as Numbers, Kings, Ruth, Ezra, Nehemiah, Esther, Psalms, Proverbs, and many prophets do not mention circumcision and circumcision was not practiced, in I Kings (19.14), during the reign of King Ahab and Queen Jezebel, who *"repudiated the alliance."*

Are there logical or medical reasons for circumcision?

Two thousand years ago, Philo of Alexandria gave five reasons for circumcision:

1. To fight against an incurable disease of the foreskin called anthrax.
2. For the cleanliness of the body.
3. The analogy with the circumcision of the heart according to Jeremiah.
4. The promotion of fertility.
5. Spiritualization of the act by reducing sexual pleasure.

In fact, there is no rational explanation for this law. If the reason is hygienic, circumcision would have also been practiced among non-Jews and non-Muslims. A study carried out in 1954 of thousands of women from Boston found that Jewish and Muslim women have uterine cancer rate eight times lower than other women. It would also appear that Jews are less often diagnosed with penis cancer than uncircumcised men. A study in Australia shows that circumcision reduces the risk of infection with the AIDS virus. Other studies have shown that circumcised African populations are less affected by the AIDS disease. In 2010, millions of Zulus of South Africa were persuaded to be circumcised. Yet these studies and evidence are not always objective and are rejected by other scientists who argue that the good results are due not to circumcision but to cultural behavior. Opponents of circumcision counter that these diseases are due to sexual relations with multiple partners and poor hygiene. Others point out that the dangers of infection resulting from circumcision are greater than the risks of AIDS, and the use of a condom or proper hygiene is more effective. If male circumcision protects against AIDS, how is it that the percentage of patients in the United States is much higher than in Europe when the circumcision rate in the United States is 10 times higher than in Europe? Opponents of circumcision argue that the foreskin is part of the anatomy of humans and primates and would have a dual role of hygienic protection and sexual pleasure. The foreskin has a very high concentration of nerve endings that would increase sexual pleasure.

Why circumcision on the eighth day?

The normal blood coagulation rate, called prothrombin, is 100 percent. If this rate decreases, blood has trouble clotting. Prothrombin, which is only 30 percent in the first days of the birth, rises above normal at about 110 percent to 115 percent on the eighth day and returns to normal on the ninth day. Therefore, the risk of hemorrhage is lowest and the most auspicious for surgery on a baby would be on the eighth day of his birth. If this pseudo-scientific argument is true, Abraham and Moses would have several millennia ahead of modern science. Or maybe, from experience, it was found that babies had fewer cases of hemorrhage on the eighth day. This kind of statement is not confirmed by the doctors and all cited arguments are contradicted by other medical research and do not receive general approval.

Why did the circumcision of Abraham happen at ninety-nine years and at thirteen for Ishmael, his son? The circumcision of all of his slaves was done at different ages. And the Hebrews after the Exodus were circumcised at different ages. Is there any danger if circumcision is done after eight days? And finally, why don't the Muslims practice circumcision on the eighth day too? Why does God create the male with a foreskin if it needs to be cut off? God opposes tattoos and cuts, how can He be the one who ordered circumcision? Is the foreskin just like the appendix, useless? Why did God request that Jews practice circumcision? And what about other humans like the Chinese or the Indians?

If the medical reasons for circumcision are not convincing, is it possible that this custom was introduced to mark a community with a distinctive sign? Just like the *kashrut* and the *kippah* are used to distinguish the Jews and preserve them from assimilation, was circumcision invented for the same purpose? Probably not, because the sign of circumcision is not visible!

According to the Talmud (Moed Katan 18a), it is forbidden to cut your nails and throw them on the floor because if pregnant women walk over it, they will abort. I'm betting that this is a superstition that has nothing to do with reality. Christianity of the Middle Ages repeats this superstition and says that the devil will take the nail clippings to make a hat. Are circumcision and kosher laws relics of the superstitions of those dark times?

Circumcision: originated in Egypt or divine order?

Abraham went to Egypt and came back to the Promised Land without being circumcised. Then under God's command, he performed circumcision on himself and his family. Baby Moses was hidden because Pharaoh wanted to kill all Hebrew newborns. At three months (already circumcised according to the covenant of Abraham), Moses was abandoned in a basket near the riverbank. Pharaoh's daughter saw the baby circumcised and adopted him. The Egyptians should have noticed it unless, as one rabbi explained, Pharaoh knew that Moses was Hebrew and spared him in order not to hurt his daughter. In this case, Pharaoh's heart was not so hard. Unless the Egyptian boys were circumcised as well. Another possibility is that Moses was not circumcised and circumcision of the Hebrews applied after the Exodus.

Designs on the tomb of an Egyptian noble named Ankhamahor, between 2300 and 2200 BC, show that circumcision was done with a flint on a boy standing up. Egyptian sculptures of the third millennium BC describe circumcision as mandatory for priests. Another circumcision description was found on a tomb at Saqqara in Egypt dating back over 5,000 years. Yet most mummies are not circumcised. Circumcision might have been mandatory for the Egyptian priests, who also shaved hair and bodies as a sign of purity. Herodotus, the famous historian of the fifth century BC, wrote, *"The people of Colchis, Egypt and Ethiopia are the only ones on earth who have practiced circumcision all the while. Phoenicians, and those of Palestine admit that they took circumcision from the Egyptians. The Syrians . . . and neighbors admit that it has not been long since they have complied with the custom of Egypt . . . With regards to Ethiopia and Egypt, the practice is very old in these two nations . . . It is likely that the Ethiopians took it from the Egyptians. Instead, the Phoenicians abolished the use of circumcision since they have more trade with the Greeks . . . ."* He also wrote: *"They, the Egyptians, however, are circumcised . . . principle of cleanliness."* But nothing about the circumcision of the Hebrews or maybe Palestine designed the Hebrews? The testimony of Herodotus is contradicted by Origen, an Egyptian citizen who claimed that circumcision was only for priests and not for all the people. No people claimed to have received the circumcision from the Hebrews, and it would be more likely that the small Hebrew people imitated the custom of their Egyptian masters rather than the masters having copied the custom of their runaway slaves. Philo of Alexandria says that circumcision was established to prevent an evil, dangerous, and difficult disease called coal. This evil would come easily to those who have their foreskin. The book Joshua (5.2), cites, "And . . . Joshua circumcised the Israelites." Then God said: *"I delivered you of the disgrace of Egypt from upon you,"* this disgrace is the foreskin. But it is not yet clear. However, an order from God to Moses, in Leviticus (18.3), contradicts the Egyptian origin: *"Practices of the land of Egypt, where you lived, do not imitate . . ."* A rabbi explained that on the contrary, the Egyptians were uncircumcised, and that's what made the difference with the Hebrews.

Circumcision was canceled not by Jesus but by Paul

1. Just like his twelve disciples and Paul, Jesus was circumcised, and this is clearly stated in Luke (2.21): *"And when eight days were accomplished for his circumcision, he was called by the name of Yeshua, the name given by the angel before he was conceived."* Nowhere does Jesus cancel circumcision and the Nazarene-notsri community preached circumcision to all, Jews and Gentiles.

    In John (7.23), Jesus said that *"Moses gave you circumcision on the Shabbat . . .,"* and therefore circumcision, an act so important, is performed even during the Shabbat. Not a word against the law and Jesus did not cancel the written rule of circumcision.

    Even some twenty years after the death of Jesus, in Acts (15.1): *"Some men (of the sect of Jesus) came down from Judea and began to teach the brothers: If you are not circumcised according to the Law of Moses, you cannot be saved."* The discussion on circumcision for the newcomers to the Christian sect begins well after the death of Jesus. Acts (15.6) proves as well that after the disappearance of Jesus's apostles *"the elders met to consider this matter"*—the circumcision of the pagans. If Jesus had decided on the subject, their meeting would be useless since its decision would be known.

And if Jesus did not say anything about circumcision, it is because he did not want to cancel it.

If Jesus had canceled circumcision for the conversion of the Gentiles, it is impossible that his disciple Paul would have circumcised his disciple Timothy. The apocryphal Gospel of Thomas (53) makes Jesus say, *"If circumcision was useful, their father would already have been circumcised . . ."* This argument must be rejected because one could say the same about the celibacy of priests who would have been born without sexual needs. If God wanted to cancel circumcision, He would not have allowed the circumcision of his *"only begotten Son."* The Gospels use the prophecies only when it serves their purposes. But Isaiah, so often quoted, says in (52.1): *"Awake . . . O Jerusalem, the holy city! For no uncircumcised or unclean will come into you."* What do Paul and the Christians say about this prophecy of Isaiah? Nothing! Is it another false prophecy?

2. The circumcision was not canceled by the Council of Jerusalem after the death of Jesus. The Nazarenes were a sect inside Judaism, and so it was natural for all pagans wanting to enter the sect to be circumcised and observe the laws of Moses. Acts (21, 20) describes the Nazarenes' opposition to Paul, who wanted to cancel circumcision, not only for the converted pagans but also for Jews themselves. Paul, a good tactician, stepped back by purifying four men at the temple. James and the Nazarenes of Jerusalem demanded circumcision and dietary laws for all even after the Council of Jerusalem, forcing Paul in Acts (16.1) to circumcise his disciple Timothy, a half Jew: *"Timothy . . . Paul wanted to take him with him . . . he circumcised him because all knew that his father was a Greek."* So any new member of the sect, non-Jewish, had to be circumcised, just like Timothy. It was clear to Paul that adult circumcision is painful and would push away many new converts. So Paul used the expression of the prophet Ezekiel, (44.9) *"circumcision of the heart."* But Ezekiel was never opposed to circumcision of the flesh. Later, according to Galatians (2, 3), Titus, who was with Paul, was not circumcised. Not because the circumcision of the pagans was canceled by James, Jesus's brother, but because James and the Nazarenes, tired of the attempts of Paul and doubting his sincerity, pushed him away and cast him out of Jerusalem.

3. Paul canceled circumcision as a necessary step toward the conversion of the Gentiles despite the decision of James and the Council of Jerusalem. Paul preached his compromise in which the converted Jews will continue to be circumcised but the Gentiles will be exempted. According to I Corinthians (7.18 to 19): *"Someone called being circumcised? He does not become uncircumcised! Someone called being uncircumcised? Let him not be circumcised! Circumcision means nothing . . . But what means something is keeping the commandments of God. That everyone remains in the state he was when he was called."* But circumcision is one of the 613 commandments.

Paul will take one step closer to the cancellation of circumcision, and in Galatians (5, 2) he states: *"If you become circumcised, Christ will profit you nothing . . . Every man who becomes circumcised must keep the whole law . . . For neither circumcision nor non-circumcision avails anything, but faith working through love."* This would mean that Jesus, Peter, and Paul, all three circumcised, were required to practice the whole law and would have sinned if they had not.

And yet in Romans (2.25): *"Circumcision indeed is only useful if you practice the Law, but if you are a transgressor of the law, your circumcision has become non-circumcision. Therefore, if an uncircumcised man keeps the righteous requirements of the law, his non-circumcision will not be counted as circumcision . . ."* It is necessary to reread this demonstration to understand how it is illogical.

According to Paul, if a man does not comply 100 percent with all the difficult commandments of Jewish law, then it is better that he does not respect any commandment at all, including circumcision. Today, this would mean that if a driver runs a red light, he can continue on his way at a stop sign. Or because the citizens sometimes violate the laws, the Civil Code must be canceled. Without hypocrisy, Paul should have simply said that circumcision is an obstacle to convert the "big market" of these uncircumcised Gentiles.

Paul declares another truth in his letter to the Galatians, which is very questionable for the same purpose of winning the pagan market: *"When I was a child, I was under the Law, now I'm an adult,"* and so he is free to abolish the law, circumcision, and other precepts of Jewish law. Paul definitely separated from Judaism and the Nazarene sect of Jesus and James. He arrived later in Rome to establish his new religion: Christianity.

Paul's position on circumcision is not new. A century before him, two Jewish rabbis, Eliezer and Joshua, did not agree on the terms of conversion to Judaism after the conquest of Edom by Hyrcanus. Eliezer requested circumcision and ritual immersion, Joshua was content with immersion without circumcision.

4. Abolition of the circumcision for all Christians.

Paul and the early Christians canceled circumcision for all pagans who wanted to convert to Christianity. Jesus, himself circumcised, promised in Matthew (5) that *"Not a single sign, not a single iota will pass from the law..."* How then can the link between the "new Christian brothers" and Abraham, the ancestor of Israel, be maintained if circumcision, the sign of this the alliance, is canceled? For the Greeks and Romans, circumcision was a form of mutilation and a pattern of mockery. Antiochus IV Epiphanies forbids it two centuries BC. After the disappearance of Paul in Rome, circumcision was equated with castration and Jews were compared to the eunuchs who had a bad reputation. At that time, it was forbidden for the circumcised to frequent gyms and bathhouses and participate in sports competitions in which athletes were naked. After year + 72, the circumcised had to pay a tax to the worship of Jupiter Capitoline. It is also possible that circumcisions were performed without sanitation, creating infections. That convinced the Romans to ban what they saw as a mutilation. Around 135, Emperor Hadrian banned all mutilation and suspended provisionally the privilege given to the Jews that allowed circumcision. Justin Martyr, in the second century, claimed that God commanded circumcision for Jews to designate them as guilty people. And Jesus, was he also guilty?

While the Nazarenes who were faithful to Jewish laws got smaller in number, the new Christians, eager to find favor in the eyes of Roman power, banned circumcision and opened the doors to the immense pagan market. The Copts of Egypt and Ethiopia continue to practice circumcision. Seven days after the birth of Jesus (on December 24), Christianity celebrated the holy foreskin every January 1, the day when Jesus was circumcised and was given his name. Around 1970, they realized that it was illogical to celebrate the circumcision of Jesus while circumcision was canceled for Christians and changed the meaning of this day to make it instead the feast of the Holy Mary, Mother of God.

The sect of Jehovah's Witnesses gives the answer: *"because the Jews did not accept Jesus, they were rejected by God and their circumcision ceased to have meaning for God."* How do they know? Still, some evangelists like the American pastor Pat Robertson say that *"if God commanded his people to be circumcised, there must be a good reason . . ."* And so millions of Americans circumcise their babies without ever seeing the following contradictions: if what is commanded in the Bible for the Hebrew people is good, why were kosher laws dropped? What about the Shabbat? And also, if circumcision is a positive thing, why did God create Adam with a foreskin? And why did Christians cancel this circumcision?

Muhammad hesitant about circumcision, but tradition dictated it

Although all Muslims are circumcised, the Quran does not mention circumcision for either boys or girls. It is prescribed only by the Sunna (custom). And so it is possible to become a Muslim without being circumcised because it is not included in the "five pillars" of Islam. It seems that Muhammad, repelled by the Jews and influenced by his Christian friends, wanted to cancel circumcision and mentioned it in some verses, like (3.191), *"Lord, You have not created in vain."* Or (30.30): *"There is no change in God's creation."* Or (4.119): *"God cursed . . . change God's creation . . ."* Verse (95.4): *"We created man in his best stature."* Muhammad therefore asserts that the Creation is perfect and there is no reason for circumcision. But later, when Jews repel Muhammad, he took Abraham as his model. According to Genesis (17,23), *"Abraham took Ishmael his son . . . He dug in the flesh of their outgrowth that day even as God had told him . . . Ishmael his son was thirteen years old when the flesh of his outgrowth was cut off."* Then, it became impossible to cancel circumcision of the Muslims.

Was Muhammad circumcised? The Quran never mentions it. To fill this gap, the Muslim tradition, not the Quran, says that Muhammad was born circumcised or would have been circumcised by an angel. Most likely, Muhammad was circumcised like other Arabs who practiced this tradition before Islam. Circumcision is practiced by Muslims on boys aged from seven days to thirteen years, with some differences between sects. Conversion to Islam is possible without the painful circumcision and this facilitates the conversion, unlike Judaism. The mullahs condemn makeup or cosmetic surgery because they claim it corrects God's creation, but they see no contradiction in tolerating male or female circumcision.

Must we cancel circumcision?

Jews and Muslims practice circumcision, a cruel and barbaric act, without further explanation than that it is the divine order given to Abraham 3,000 years ago. Although it is written in the Bible, must we practice this barbaric act? Other biblical commandments were canceled, like the law of retaliation or the killing of an adulterous woman or the killing of one who works on the Shabbat. Christians have abandoned this practice although their Messiah, the Son of God, was circumcised and never ordered cancelling it. Yet some Christians practice it. Muslims practice circumcision even though it was a custom prior to their religion.

Some European countries, including Germany, wanted to ban circumcision despite the opposition of Jews and Muslims but allowed it if performed by a doctor.

Circumcision is an irreversible act and it is a violation of physical integrity and freedom of the individual. But do we ask a baby if he wanted to be born in Africa or America, in a rich or poor family, or be vaccinated, and even later, which education he will receive? Circumcision is a simple operation done without general anesthesia, which affects only the skin without any impact on the urinary and sexual tracts. Still, this circumcision should be followed by an extensive scientific study void of any religious influence. This investigation and not a divine order (?) given to Abraham (?) 3,000 years (?) ago will help to make a decision. Unfortunately, while the UN is preparing texts to abolish female circumcision, nothing is being done about male circumcision.

B. The three religions are not a code of good behavior

Morality does not need religious laws

Religions tried to convince that there is no morality without religion because without the fear of God people would act badly. Quran (107) says that he who does not believe in Islam is immoral: *"See the one who denies the Judgment (or religion) is the one who pushes the orphan and does not encourage the feeding of the poor."* A survey in the USA showed that more than 50 percent of US citizens would disqualify an atheist as president. Yet the patriarchs and great figures of the three religions are far from being examples of good behavior. Adam and Eve listened to the snake rather than to God, Cain killed his brother, Noah walked around naked and drunk, Abraham and Isaac were pimps, Lot offered his daughters to others and then slept with them, Sarah used her slave Hagar to have a son with her husband and then sent them away, Jacob deceived his father and stole the birthright from his brother, the eleven sons of Jacob sold their brother Joseph, Moses killed an Egyptian and caused the death of thousands of babies and animals, Joshua the conqueror destroyed everything, the gang leader David collaborated with enemies and took the wife of his officer, Solomon was a selfish dictator who had a thousand concubines. And then Jesus, the orthodox Jew, rebel to Roman power; Paul the collaborator; and Peter the liar who denied Jesus. And finally, Muhammad, the bloody conqueror with two faces. And these heroes of the three religions should be examples for our behavior?

Believers observe religious commandments to open the doors of paradise and avoid hell. Citizens of the world are also obliged to respect the laws, not because of heaven and hell but to avoid prison. Why then is respect of civil laws less moral than religious observances? Religious laws set by God, prophets, or counterfeiters, are they preferable to civil laws decided by human legislators who can adapt and improve them?

The missing commandments: liberty, equality, fraternity

Three commandments essential in modern society are absent in the three religions, the famous "liberty, equality, fraternity" adopted by the French Revolution. And we can add knowledge and responsibility.

14

Instead of liberty, religions impose death penalty on apostasy

The Universal Declaration of Human Rights guarantees freedom of religion, freedom to convert and freedom to proselytize, freedom to wear the symbols of their religion. But the three religions don't give this liberty of choice. Religions fix the rules for the most important part of our life and our death, yet we are not free to choose.

Your religion is a coincidence and not a choice!

Anyone wanting to buy a refrigerator or a car will make a comparative study of different brands, prices, qualities, and warranties, and then choose, with full knowledge, the best of them. But when it comes to religions (and patriotism), 99 percent of people do not decide. Their religion is granted without their consent. They are Jew, Christian, or Muslim by accident of birth, not by rational choice. Native Americans danced around their totem pole and worshipped it as a god because their ancestors practiced that custom. What if the religion you practice is as unfounded as the totem of the Native Americans? If Emperor Constantine had chosen Mithraism for his empire, there would have been no Christians in Europe. If Muslim troops had not conquered North Africa, the Maghreb would be pagan. Some Christian or Muslim countries were converted solely through military conquests and forced conversion, not by free will. South America is Christian; Pakistan, Bangladesh, and Indonesia became Muslim through conquests and pure hazard. Similarly, some countries became Protestant only because of the pure selfish decisions of their king.

Conversion to Judaism is a challenging course that can last several years. On the other hand, you can convert to Islam in three minutes just by pronouncing the assertion of faith: *"God is great and Muhammad is his messenger."* Religions require from their believers not to have contact with other religions. Jews and Muslims are forbidden to visit a church even for artistic purposes, because the representations of Jesus and Mary are considered idolatry. Some rabbis forbid the teaching of the Bible and Talmud to non-Jews because the Talmud, Sanhedrin 59a, said, *"the unbeliever who studies the Torah deserves death, for it is written that Moses gave us the sacred word as a legacy and not to them..."* And again, Sanhedrin 90a, *"those who say that the resurrection is not a biblical doctrine, those who say that the Torah is not divine, and those who read books foreign to our religion... have no place in the world to come."*

The Talmud, Rosh Hashanah 17a, condemned *"those who reject the Torah, those who abandoned the ways of the community ... those who deny life after death ... will all go to hell..."* Interfaith dialogue always avoids a detailed discussion for one good reason: they know that by attacking one or the other they will all come out losers. No confrontation between the three religions has ever been started and will not be until an atheist confronts them. Instead of defending Salman Rushdie, author of a pamphlet on the Satanic Verses of Muhammad, Jewish and Christian authorities simply described them as provocative.

Apostasy in the three religions

According to the three religions, Abraham, who dared to leave the idolatry of his parents to obey the one true God, is a revered hero. But anyone leaving his monotheist religion is cursed and even put to death. For the Jewish Bible, Deuteronomy (13.6), *"If your brother... or your friend... saying: let us go and worship the gods of others... You shall not accede to him... Rather, you shall surely kill him. Your hand shall be the first to kill him... You shall stone him till he dies..."* And also in II Chronicles (15.13): *"Anyone who would not seek YHWH, God of Israel, would be put to death, child or adult, man or woman."*

The New Testament also forbids leaving Christianity. For example, in the letter to the Hebrews (3.12): *"Beware, brothers, lest there be in any of you an evil heart of unbelief in departing from the living God."* Or in II Peter (3.17): *". . . Beware lest you also fall . . . with the error of the wicked."* Or in I Timothy (4.1): *". . . In latter times, some will depart from the faith, giving heed to deceiving spirits and doctrines of demons . . ."* And in Galatians (1.8): *"But even if we, or an angel from heaven, preach any other gospel to you . . . let him be accursed."*

The Quran, on one hand, promised *"no compulsion in religion."* And few Muslims even dare to say that Islam is very tolerant. But on the other hand, the Quran (3.85) condemns those who dare to leave Islam: *"Whoever seeks a religion other than Islam will not be accepted. And in another life, he will be among the losers."* Whoever leaves his religion to adopt Islam will be blessed, but those who leave Islam will be rejected, will go to hell, and are punishable by death under the Islamic law.

The Hadiths of Bukhari and Abu Dawud confirm the interdiction of leaving Islam: Bukhari (52.260), (83.37), (84.57): *". . . The Prophet said: if a Muslim leaves his religion, kill him . . . Allah's Apostle never killed anyone except in three situations: . . . a man who fought against Allah and his Apostle and deserted Islam and became an apostate . . . Whoever changed his Islamic religion, then kill him."* Against these hadiths, modern Muslims answer that it is only a threat without immediate chastisement. And to prove it, they say that Muhammad would have killed all the Jews and Christians of Medina if apostasy was punished by death. We answer firstly that Muhammad killed hundreds of Jews and Christians, and secondly that the Hadiths are considered as reporting the real words of Muhammad. And one more hadith of Bukhari (89.271) says: *"A man who embraces Islam then reverts to Judaism is to be killed according to the verdict of Allah and his Apostle."* So modern Muslims cannot hide the intolerance of Islam because the Quran and the Hadiths are clear.

Proselytism: Islam recommends convincing non-Muslims to leave their religion and join Islam, but it is a crime to try to convince Muslims to leave Islam. Islam is proselyte and wants to convert the whole world, but Muslims should allow reciprocity in their own country. But we have hope that Internet and satellite communications will bring Muslims to question their own religion.

15

Instead of equality, religions accept slavery and privileges

Equality is also missing in religious texts, which accept poverty, supremacy, and privileges of a hereditary caste, the priests who eat the sacrifices. The three religions are opposed to equality of women, who are second-class humans, or worse, commodities to be bought.

Slavery is described in all chapters of the Bible, beginning from Genesis (9.25). After the flood, Ham saw the nakedness of Noah, his father, who woke up and said, *"Cursed be Canaan, may he be slave of the slaves of his brothers!"* First inconsistency because it is Ham, the son of Noah, who saw his nakedness, but Canaan, his grandson, is punished.

Jews claim that the Torah is not racist by saying that slavery is not related to skin color. Slaves mentioned in the Torah were white and Tsipora, the wife of Moses, was *Kushite*, which means black. But the sons of Moses and Tsipora inherited no power while those of Aaron became the high priests. This lack of status of the sons of Moses, is it because of their black or chocolate skin?

The master of slaves, Abraham, *"took Ishmael his son, all the children of slaves and those he had bought with his money, every male . . . he circumcised."* So slavery is permitted by God, who ordered the circumcision of slaves without their consent. Moses's laws did not condemn slavery but protected this tradition, *"Do not lust after your neighbor's wife, his slave and servant, his ox and his ass."*

Exodus (21) states some rules about slavery. In Exodus (21.16), the Hebrew who abducted his brother and sold him will be punished by death. This prohibition applied only to the Hebrews. Note that Joseph's brothers sold him into slavery and should face the death penalty, but instead, became the leaders of the twelve tribes. The Jewish Bible was more generous and ahead of its times, and in Exodus (21.2), *"If you buy a Hebrew slave, he will serve six years, but in the seventh he shall go out free without paying anything."* What progress! Slavery is therefore only temporary, at least for the Hebrew slave, not for others. Unfortunately, you have to read on: *"If his master gave him a wife, and he had son or daughter, the wife and her children shall belong to her master and he shall go out by himself. If the slave says: I love my master, my wife and my children, I will not go out alone . . . Then his master shall bore through his ear with an awl and he shall serve him forever."* The trap is set, the master will take young male slaves that will mate with his female slaves and the slave does not even want to leave his master because he would lose his wife and children. This verse contradicts all the family values.

This rule, even truncated, was not respected by the Hebrews, as noted by the prophet Jeremiah (34.16): *"Then . . . you have blasphemed the name of the Lord, and each has taken his slave and every man his servant that you had set free to themselves, and you have forced to become your slaves!"*

Back to Exodus (21.20), *"If a man strikes his slave, a man or woman, and he dies under his hand, he shall be avenged. But if he survives one day or two, he shall not be avenged, for he is his property."* The principle of *"eye for eye, tooth for tooth"* is not applicable when it comes to slavery. Also, when the slave does not die immediately, the master does not suffer any punishment.

Leviticus (25.39) specifies the conditions of the Hebrew slave in relation to a foreign slave, *"If your brother with you, reduced to poverty, sells himself to you, do not imposed the work of a slave . . . your slave or your maid . . . must come from the people around you . . . you can donate them to your children . . . and addressing perpetually slaves, but over your brothers the children of Israel . . . you exercise on them strict domination."* So slavery was regulated, soft for Hebrew brothers but hard for other people.

Deuteronomy (15), certainly written much later, repeats this rule but more generously, without mentioning that the Hebrew slave must leave without his wife and children, and also *"do not release the Hebrew slave . . . empty-handed, but give him gifts of your flock, your barn and your wine."* Deuteronomy (15.12) states: *"If your brother, a Hebrew man or a Hebrew woman, is sold to you, they will serve six years and the seventh year you* shall let him go free from you." So in Exodus (21.7) it says: *"If a man sells his daughter as a slave, she will not leave his master in the manner of slaves..."* So what is God's command?

The jubilee year—that is to say, every forty-nine years—is explained by Leviticus (25): *"You shall return each man to his family..."* This rule, very progressive for its time, is again mentioned in (25.39) but more narrowly and only applies to Hebrew slaves: *"If your brother... is sold to you... he will serve you until the year of jubilee, then he depart from you, he and his children."* The text explains that the release at the jubilee does not apply to non-Hebrew slaves. In addition, this beautiful rule was never recalled and seems never to have been applied.

We can mention another contradiction of the divine texts. Leviticus (25.10) calls for the release of Hebrew slaves every forty-nine years, while Deuteronomy (15.12) requested doing it every seven years. This paragraph on the slaves would, however, be a great progress since it limits the powers of the master: *"If a man hurts the eye (or the tooth) of his slave, he shall free him..."* Even after biblical times, the Talmud Sanhedrin (58b) does not condemn slavery.

Rape and the Bible

Rape is a horrible crime, and yet, far from condemning it, the three religions accept it. In Numbers (31), *"Moses became angry against the army officers... What, you have left all these women to live... Now kill all the male children, and kill every woman that has known man. As for those too young, who still have not experienced man, keep them for you."* That is to say, take them as slaves and for their sexual pleasure. It is strange that Moses, who took for wife a Midianite, ordered the kidnapping and rape of the virgins of Midian. Also, why preserve virgins? Are they less dangerous than married women or is it just a matter of pleasure for the male? Deuteronomy (20.13) orders: *"you shall kill by the sword all the male inhabitants... There will be women, children, cattle... that you can capture and you will enjoy the remains..."* So God ordered murder, rape, and slavery.

Further, Deuteronomy (21.11*), "If you see a woman of beautiful figure... and that you want to marry her, take her in your house, she shall shave her head and cut her nails..."* Without her consent! Then right after, (21.15), *"if it happens that you have no more taste for her, you shall let her go free..."*

Deuteronomy (22.28): *"If a man meeting a young virgin who is not engaged surprises and abuses her, and they are caught in the act, the man who had intercourse with her will give to the girl's father 50 shekels of silver...,"* and she became his wife because he raped her. This verse allows any man who wants a girl to rape her. He will not be punished, and the girl becomes his wife for life. In the Book of Samuel (II.13), this rule is again formulated, and Tamar, after being raped by Amnon, became his wife. This rule is still applied in some Muslim countries, and in April 2012, Tunisian women protested in favor of a raped girl who refused to marry her rapist.

Judges (21.10) ordered *"12,000 warriors ... Pass the inhabitants by the sword, even the women and children ... all women who lived with a man ... 400 virgin girls ... the Benjamin men came immediately and took for them the virgins ..."* Isaiah (13.16) delivers a divine oracle against Babylon, *"their infants shall be dashed to pieces before their eyes ... their women raped."*

How old was Rebecca when Isaac took her for wife? Although the written Bible does not mention her age, an oral tradition determined that she was only three years old when she married Isaac. For Sanhedrin (55a), a little girl of three years may be acquired in marriage by a Jew. And the rabbis give a bizarre argument, *"At the time of Isaac, humans were much more developed than today and a three-year-old daughter was like an eighteen-year-old woman of our time."* And the Bible says she was a virgin! And Isaac was forty years old. Was he an old man for this three-year-old child?

Christianity allowed and even encouraged slavery

Like Judaism, Christianity accepted and regulated slavery. Neither Jesus nor Peter or Paul opposed it. The New Testament, with hypocrisy, replaced the term *slave* with *servants*. Jesus, called revolutionary by Christians, is silent on slavery and did not oppose that *"the servant who knew his master's will, has not prepared and did not act according to his will, shall be beaten with many stripes."*

After Jesus's death, I Peter (2.18) demands: *"Servants, be subject in all fear to your masters, not only to those who are good and gentle, but also to those who are of difficult character."* Paul preached for the slaves' obedience to their master and not for their rebellion, and this explains its success with Roman authorities. In Ephesus (6.5), Paul asked, *"Slaves, obey your masters according to the flesh, with fear and trembling ... as servants of Christ, doing the will of*

God from the heart . . . serve them eagerly, as to the Lord and not men." In I Timothy (6.1): *"Let all who are under the yoke of slavery regard their masters worthy of all honor, that the name of God and his doctrine be not blasphemed . . ."* So total acceptance of slavery by Paul.

After being recognized as a state religion, the Christian Church practiced slavery and the triangular slave trade between Europe, Africa, and America. The popes encouraged the conquistadors to Christianize the New World regardless of the death of millions of natives. One slave out of five died inside the boats. They used the verse Genesis (9.24) to justify slavery. After the flood, Ham saw the nakedness of his father Noah, awoken from his drunkenness, who cursed: *"Cursed be Canaan; be slave of the slaves of his brothers!"* They explain that slavery was the punishment provided by the Bible for the sons of Ham, whose hallmark is the black color of their skin. But one oddity: for Genesis (9.22), Ham sinned by seeing the nakedness of his father, but the one who was cursed was not Ham but his fourth son Canaan. This divine judgment is unacceptable and no son should be punished for the sins of his father. And Canaan was not black, and neither he nor his offspring, since the inhabitants of Canaan, were white. The black color of the curse of Canaan and of his descendants seems to come from the Talmud, Sanhedrin (108b): *"Three copulated in the ark, and all were punished: the dog, the raven and Ham. The dog was ordered to be attacked . . . and Ham was punished in his skin."* So Christians drew evidence of this racism in the Talmud! Europeans are proud to be the first to abolish slavery, but this abolition occurred in the late eighteenth century by laic governments.

Islam and Muhammad allowed rape and slavery

The three sacred texts of Islam—the Quran, the Sira (Muhammad's biography), and the Hadiths (traditions of Muhammad)—allowed and encouraged slavery. Muhammad was himself a slave trader. Verse (4.24) forbids having sex with *"women already married, except your slaves"* even if they are married. Verse (4.25): *"Whoever cannot afford to marry believing women, take believing slaves."* Or verses (23.5), (70.29), and (33.50): *"Prophet, we allowed wives to whom you have given a dowry, captives that God made you acquire by war . . . But you are not allowed to change women or to take others, except your slaves . . ."* This command enabled Muslims unlimited sex with their slaves. Verse (24.32), *"Marry your honest singles and slaves, men and women..."* This allows marrying the slaves against their will. In (2.178), *"You who believe, you are prescribed retaliation for murder: the free for the free, the slave for the slave, the woman for woman..."* Other verses justify slavery, (4.92) or (30.28). Muslim (32) states that *"the slave who runs away from his master, his prayer will not be accepted."* To all these verses in favor of slavery, Muslims will answer with verse (90.13), which states that to free a slave is good.

Muhammad himself had slaves. Still single, he had a young female slave, Baraka, but Kadijah, his first wife, got rid of her. Did Muhammad have sexual relations with her and for this reason his wife sent her away? To replace this first female slave, Kadijah acquired a young male slave, Zayd, who was from a noble family and could read and write and preferred to stay with Muhammad even after getting his freedom and was declared his adopted son. Some twenty years after the death of Muhammad, Nubia, located in the south of Egypt, was obliged to provide 300 Christian slaves per year to the Islamic power.

Throughout history, Muslims captured more than a million white slaves for resale to Islamic countries. They castrated thousands of black men to become eunuchs for their harems, and captured some ten million black people to turn into slaves for the rich Muslims or to be sent to America. However, it is fashionable for many black Americans to convert to Islam. Was boxing champion Muhammad Ali aware of the enslavement of his ancestors by Muslims? Africans themselves willingly forget Islamic slavery that persisted into the twentieth century in countries such as Sudan and Mauritania.

16

Instead of universal fraternity, the tribes

Fraternity between all humans is unknown, and instead limited to relatives, tribes, or people of the same religion. Very often religious people will bring the verse of Leviticus (19.18): *"Love your neighbor like yourself."* The Hebrew word *re-eha* is always wrongly translated to *neighbor*, but it means "your similar." And so you can love your similar-brother but hate the other-different, as well as your enemy.

The Talmud contains many hateful remarks toward the Gentiles. In Baba Kama (37b), if a cow, belonging to a Jew, harms the cow of a Canaanite, there is no fee whatsoever to be paid. If, on the other hand, a cow belonging to a Canaanite harms the cow of a Jew, it requires complete compensation. In Baba Batra, (10b), the acts of Israel are virtuous while those of the Gentile are sin. Verse (16b) says joy to those who have a baby boy, but the birth of a baby girl is sad. And (54b) says the property of the Gentile is like a desert: whoever gets there first can claim it. In Sanhedrin (54b), homosexuals should be put to death. In Sanhedrin (58a), whoever slaps a Jew is punishable by death, because slapping him is like attacking God. In Sanhedrin (76), whoever returns a lost item to a non-Jew is similar to someone who marries his daughter to an old man. Sanhedrin (57a) says that if a Gentile steals from a Jew, he has to return whatever he has stolen, But if a Jew steals from a Gentile, nothing has to be given back to the victim. In Kiddushin (49b), the Jewish people received 90 percent of the wisdom and the rest of the world only got 10 percent.

The death sentence for homosexuals and marginalized people

In Leviticus (21), God Himself excludes handicapped people: *"No man who has any defect may come near, no man who is blind . . . disfigured or deformed, no man with a crippled foot or hand, or who is hunchbacked or dwarfed, or who has any eye defect, or who has festering or running sores or damaged testicles."* In 2011, Californian police discovered graffiti demanding *"death to homosexuals."* After doing some investigation, the police erased the evidence. But in Leviticus (20.13): *"If a man lies with a man as one lies with a woman, both of them have done what is abominable. They must be put to death."* Should these lines from the Bible, the New Testament, and the Quran be erased as well? The New Testament says: *". . . Men committed indecent acts with other men, and received . . . the due penalty for their perversion."* The Quran approved the destruction of the people of Sodom who wanted to have homosexual relations with Lot's servants. But the Quran ignored the incestuous relations of Lot with his daughters. Isn't God himself the one who created homosexuality? Believers said that God created this perversion in order for humans to fight it. Such unbelievable sadism! And why isn't anything said about homosexuality of women?

Not love, but hate from Jesus, Paul, and Christianity

According to the New Testament, Jesus required that we not only love our brother/neighbor but our enemies as well. This tactic was very useful for the new religion to appear nonthreatening to the Roman authorities. But some verses of the New Testament show that neither Jesus, especially not Paul, came in the name of peace. This will be developed in the chapter about the Sixth Commandment and the interdiction of killing.

Christianity did not act like Jesus and practiced hate and massacres. Hitler did not invent the yellow star that the Jews were obliged to wear during the Nazi reign. He was inspired by Pope Benoit XIV, who obliged by decree, in 1733, *"the Jews, male or female, of the cities of Avignon and Carpentras, to wear, inside and outside theirs houses, the mark of yellow color which distinguish them from the others . . . The men must wear the hat of yellow color, without a veil or any ribbon on top . . . under the penalty of 50 crowns for each violation."*

Are Palestinians Jews converted to Islam?

How many Muslims today are descendants of Jews and Christians? How many Palestinians have Jewish or Christian ancestry, forced to accept Islam out of fear of being killed or simply to avoid paying the Jizya? Tsvi Misinai, an Israeli historian, states that a great number of Palestinians and Bedouins are in fact Jewish farmers converted to Christianity and then to Islam. In 1012, the caliph Al-Hakim, by a decree, forced Jews and Christians to convert to Islam and destroyed the Saint Sepulcher Church in Jerusalem. The Samaritans, a Hebrew sect that were never exiled out of their country, were killed or converted to Islam. What about the Druzes? What was their story before their conversion to Islam? A genetic study shows that Jews and Palestinians have great similarities. Because of Roman and Islamic invasions, the Jewish people were divided into two enemy groups. One group left the area and returned later to the land, while the second group never left but lived under Christian and Islamic authorities. That second group of people is a part of the Palestinians of today. In fact, the only way for these two groups to ever reconcile and bury the hatchet is to abolish both religions. Said Arikat, a Palestinian leader, said that his people were descendants of the Canaanites, and so they were in the Holy Land before the Jews. But if Palestinians are descendants of Canaanites, they cannot be descendants of Ishmael or be Arabs.

The wars between the different religions

Each religious group always believes that its religion is the chosen one. Charlemagne, the French emperor of the 9th century, is known for instituting schools, but people forget that he was also the one who massacred thousands of pagans under the slogan *"Accept Christianity or die today."*

The Crusades: From the tenth to the thirteenth century, hundreds of thousands of Christians believed that the pilgrimage would wash away their sins and secure them a place in heaven. Assured by the pope and the bishops that killing unbelievers was not a sin, these crusaders massacred Jews they met on their way. When they finally arrived in the Promised Land, they had to fight the Muslims. That conflict caused hundreds of thousands of deaths on all sides.

The Inquisition: In order to stop heresy and skepticism, the Church started a war against Jews, Muslims, witches, homosexuals, and all those who dared to doubt. During the thirteenth century, Spain and the Inquisition burned thousands of innocent people simply because they didn't believe as the Church wanted. The term *auto-da-fé* originally meant "act of faith," became synonymous to *setting on fire*. This Inquisition established an index of forbidden books that was regularly updated until 1966.

The expulsion of Jews from Spain: In 1492, a decree ordered all Jews of Spain to convert to Christianity or leave Spain without their belongings. Tens of thousands of Jews who refused to convert were kicked out of the country. This decree was only abolished in 1967!

The slave trade and the killings of thousands of pagans who refused to convert were carried out by Christian conquistadors and supported by the monks and the priests. The conquest of the Americas is depicted in Hollywood westerns, with courageous cowboys killing bad Indians.

Hitler signed his first international treaty with the Vatican on July 20, 1933. Later, the church declared that it had no idea of Hitler's plans, but at that time Hitler had already threatened Jews, banned syndicates, established the one-party rule, and abolished liberties. In 1943, during the genocide, Pope Pie XII published that the New Testament had replaced the Old Testament but he never said or wrote anything about the evil actions of Hitler. In a radio speech on June 22, 1941, this pope applauded the invasion of the Soviet Union by German troops. It seemed that the church was ready to forgive the Nazis their atrocities as long as they stopped the dangerous Communists.

Hate among sects of the same religion

The Protestant Schism: The church told Christians that if they paid fees, their sins would be forgiven and they will not spend eternity in hell. Luther, a German monk, was outraged by the selling of indulgences and founded Protestantism. From there, the wars between Catholics and Protestants started. This same Luther asked for the burning of Jews and witches, and he inspired Hitler and the Genocide. Luther, like Muhammad before him, forced Jews to convert to Christianity. Facing their refusal, he published in 1543 his famous book *Jews and Their Lies*. Here are some quotes: "*set fire to synagogues . . . tear down their homes, burn their books . . .*

prohibit rabbis from teaching, restrict their travel . . . confiscate their property and money . . . get them to work and sweat . . . expel them like mad dogs . . ."

Shia-Sunna: At the death of Muhammad in 632, his companion Abu Bakr (who was also the father of his young bride Aisha) succeeded him. Abu Bakr had the support of the Sunnites. Another group of Muslims called the Shia wanted Ali to be the successor of Muhammad. Ali was the cousin and also the son-in-law of Muhammad (he married Muhammad's daughter Fatima). And so, at the beginning both groups shared the same faith but disagreed on who should get inheritance. Little by little, a gap was formed between the two groups. The Sunnis based their beliefs on the *Sunna* (teachings of Muhammad). The Shiites, on the other hand, followed the teachings of the Ayatollahs. This growing hate is the cause of several bombings in Iraq. For a westerner, it would be almost impossible to differentiate both groups. They are so small that they often appear to be silly. To avoid religious wars and hate, the only solution is to abolish religions and to show that they are not from God. The twenty-first century will again be the stage of religious wars, but let's hope that important debate will be started between religion and atheism.

17

Instead of knowledge, religions demand submission

The German philosopher Arthur Schopenhauer said, *"Religions are like glow worms; to shine, they need darkness."* In fact, the great enemy of religion is not science but the texts of the sacred books filled with implausible, contradictory, or plagiarized affirmations. The three sacred books contain statements that often contradict each other, and thus, making it convenient for each rabbi, priest, or imam to find a verse that will make their religion seem like a love poem.

Religions ask for your submission, not your understanding

The word *Muslim* means submitted, or rather, "to submit." Abraham, who blindly accepted God's orders, including that of sacrificing his son, is the model of submission in the three religions. Abraham did not hesitate and did not question what God commanded, including lifting a knife to slay his son. Genesis (2.16) says: *"All the trees of the garden thou may eat, but the tree of knowledge of good and evil you shall not eat, for in the day that you eat, you must die."* So God forbids man to acquire knowledge. Yet Adam and Eve ate of the tree and would therefore definitely gain a sense of right and wrong. Then in (3.22), God said, *"Behold the man has become like one of us; he knows good and evil."* How is this knowledge wrong? *"Like one of us"?* Why plural? Are there several gods? Does God not want us to know good and evil?

For 2,500 years, religious Jews have focused on their holy books, the only ones worthy of studying, without wasting time on secular sciences. *"We do not think highly of those of us who learn multiple languages,"* noted Josephus. Religious Jews and Muslims teach only the sacred texts in their schools, and keep their students in ignorance of mathematics, physics, chemistry, and other sciences. In Muslim (28.5612), Muhammad forbids the chess game because *"one who plays chess is like one who dyed his hand with meat and pig's blood."* Poetry is despised because *"the poets are only followed by the misguided,"* and in (26.224), drawing and painting are to be lowered as well. Islamic schools force their students to learn the Quran by heart, and then put them in competition on memorizing texts, focusing on singing and intonation rather than on comprehension. Non-Arab Muslims must read the Quran in Arabic and say their prayers in Arabic without any understanding. Even those who speak Arabic do not quite understand the Quran because it is written in classical Arabic, and are dependent on the imams to explain to them the texts. On the contrary, religions should be taught in schools just like philosophy or chemistry, with questions and answers, and only then can the student accept a religion or reject it.

Judaism answers with *naasse ve nishma*, which means that we must practice the religion first, do the prayers, put on the *tefilim*, go to the synagogue, and then our understanding will come. Yet Deuteronomy (5.24) states the opposite: *"we will hear and then we will obey."* If a reader finds oddities in the Bible, they will respond with the famous *pardes*, consisting of four letters (PRDS), which means there are four levels to understanding the Bible? P for *pshat* or simple meaning, R for *remez* or allusion, D for *drash* or parable, and finally S for *sod*, which is the secret level, also known as Kabbalah. So if some texts seem contradictory or wrong, it's just that we have not yet reached the level of understanding.

A rabbi to whom I was asking embarrassing questions gave me as advice to study the Talmud and Kabbalah and all the writings of the Jewish sages. I replied with a question: *"Have you read the New Testament or the Quran or the Hindu texts to be convinced that Judaism is the right religion?"* His answer was of course no. He did not have enough time, he said. We must ask the same question to believers of all religions. An imam told me to read the Quran in Arabic before making any criticism. I answered him that I was studying the Quran and Hadiths from a good translation. Then I asked him if he read the Bible in Hebrew or the New Testament in Greek.

For 2,000 years, Jesus was a taboo for Jews. The rabbis forbade them from talking about him, and so Jews completely ignored the one who caused them so much misery. Some Jews have of course written pamphlets against Jesus, but they focused on the easy points, like Jesus cannot be the Messiah, he is not God the Son, and he was not resurrected, but nothing about his deep respect for Jewish law and his criticism of the Pharisees' additions. What is the real reason for this taboo? The real Jesus is in fact a Jew who criticized the rabbinate, who preferred to keep the censorship in order to ensure their absolute power over the Jews for 2,000 years. Jesus criticized the Sadducees, who were masters of the temple, and the Pharisees, who were teachers at the synagogues. Both groups added new rules in order to please their needs.

A former chief rabbi has banned the act of blowing your nose on Shabbat lest a hair be cut. Others recommend cutting the toilet paper before Shabbat. The teachings of Jesus against the leaven of the Pharisees was misunderstood by Christians and censured by the Pharisees, who had led the Jews since the destruction of the temple in + 70.

The New Testament also avoids any discussion, and Paul, the first Christian censor, warned: *"Avoid foolish questions . . . Keep away from you after a first and second warning, those causing divisions."* In II Corinthians (6.14): *"Do not go associating with unbelievers: they are not suitable partners . . . What can a believer have in common with an unbeliever? That is why the Lord says: 'you must leave and separate yourself from them. Touch nothing unclean . . .'"*

Christianity requires no good conduct, only faith, the only criterion to go to heaven. Independent thinking is harmful, and an unbeliever or even the skeptic will go to hell. Therefore, the Christian will not seek the truth and will suspect the doing of Satan if any doubt crosses his mind. To these critics, John Paul II said that faith and reason *"are like two wings on which the human spirit rises to the contemplation of truth."* By this reasoning, would man be able to understand his religion or repel it? Is it because of these openings that the Church has lost so many of its faithful congregation? After they were permitted to read the Bible and the New Testament in their language, Christians avoided the church.

According to rabbis, there is irrefutable proof that 3 million Jews have seen God. Indeed, the Bible says that God appeared to the Hebrews during the Exodus. Is it only because it is written in the Bible that it is true? One could have written about another religion saying that 100 million people have seen God. This kind of writing long after the fact proves nothing.

However, to a skeptic who wonders why the decrees of Haman to exterminate the Jews and the episode of Queen Esther aren't reported by any text at the time, a rabbi replies, *"according to the biblical writings, this story is mentioned . . ."* The rabbi also said that since the facts are recorded in the Bible, their historicity is accurate. Strange logic!

For Jews, the authors of the Talmud are wise men who were inspired by God. But let's take for example the Treaty of Gittin 69 ab, where we see primitive medicinal solutions, some of them hilarious. For example, to treat pleurisy, they say one must put feces of a white dog on the eyes, but one must be careful not to eat it. Another says to treat fever, you must use water from a dog bowl. Or according to the Talmud, do not look directly at a rainbow because it would be disrespectful to the Creator. When the lightning rod was invented by Benjamin Franklin, the Church opposed it because they said it was an attempt to *"counter the will of God,"* who created thunder to punish humans.

Science and religions

Religions took a big hit with the discovery that the Earth is not the center of the Universe, but a planet among millions of others that revolve around the sun. The Church fought against this discovery for many centuries, but finally accepted it. The second hit was from the Theory of Evolution that emerged in the nineteenth century. The third hit takes place during our time with the development of biblical criticism and the famous documentary theory (explained in another chapter).

It's easy for atheists to say that religions are for the ignorant, but it's not true, because thousands of educated people, scientists, and doctors are religious. Louis Pasteur, the great French scientist, said: *"if a little science takes you away from God, then a lot of it brings you closer."* But the question of the existence of God should be separated from religion.

Why hasn't anyone heard from God since the time of the prophets? For Jews, the silence dates from the time of Ezra and Nehemiah after the Babylonian exile, for Christians after Jesus, for Muslims after Muhammad. Why is God so silent and hasn't appeared since? Jews have found the reason a long time ago. In Exodus (20.19), the Hebrew people were frightened by the appearance of God asked Moses: *"We would like you to speak to God on our behalf... If we let God speak to us directly, we could die."* So this is why God has disappeared! The Hebrew people were the ones who told Him to stay away! What if a skeptic said that he was not afraid to see God face to face?

Muhammad and God, in (26.4), have threatened to give concrete evidence: *"If we wanted to, we could give them a sign from the sky... which would have their necks bowed."* Why didn't God reveal that sign or any other irrefutable proof? Why didn't God give Muhammad a plane, for example? The skeptics would have converted immediately! Verse (17.90) recalls the request for evidence from skeptics. Muhammad said, *"... Break down pieces of heaven or bring God and his angels to your rescue ... or you went up to heaven."* Muhammad, of course, did not give them any evidence! He answers the idolaters later in (27.64): *"Is there a god besides God? Bring your proof if you speak the truth . . ."* Idolaters also provide no evidence of the power of their idols. Angels do not appear as often now as they had appeared to the Hebrew patriarchs, to the prophets, Jesus, Muhammad, and even to John Smith, the Mormon prophet. Smith received God's commandments written on gold plates, but with orders not to tell anyone of their location.

The sacred books, selection, disappearance, or destruction

Acts (19.19) describes the first destruction of books under the orders of Paul: *"And a number of those who had practiced dark magic brought their books and burned them in front of everyone."* Many other book burnings occurred. The Emperor Constantine, previously a sun worshipper, hesitated between the cult of Mithras and Jesus. Around +320, he chose Jesus because he understood that Christianity was a good way to unify his empire, and adopted the new religion. Constantine ordered that all books that cast a shadow of doubt on Christianity be burned. All non-canonical writings were destroyed, but fortunately, some escaped the fire and were discovered later.

The Talmud, which came into existence after Christianity, also preached the burning of books. According to Shabbat (116a), the books of the Christians should not be saved from the fire. And after cutting out all references to God in these books, they should be thrown into the fire.

Jews themselves have burned the book of Maimonides. After a so-called trial in 1242, Christians burned hundreds of copies of the Talmud in Paris. The Talmud was then included in the first index of books blacklisted by the Church. The list was published in the sixteenth century under the pressure of the Inquisition. This censorship banned pious Catholics from reading these "immoral" works. It silenced all criticism against the Church and forced authors to correct their texts. This index included thousands of books, including the works of Diderot, Rousseau, and Voltaire. The list was only abolished in 1966. Oddly, *Mein Kampf* by Hitler, Stalin, and Darwin's writings were not on the list of banned books.

Censorship also flourished in Islam. Arab historians report that the Caliph Omar gave the order in 642 to destroy the famous Library of Alexandria, while others say that it was the first Christian Emperor Constantine who burned the library.

The holy books of the three religions are the result of a process of censorship. Anything written, not defined as orthodox, was destroyed. Orthodoxy has yet failed to completely destroy these sacred books that survived and are even mentioned in the Jewish Bible. For example, the Book of the Covenant in Exodus (24.7). The Book of the Wars of the Lord in Numbers (21.14). The Book of Yashar according to Joshua (10.13) and 2 Samuel (1.18) that records a poem by David. The Book of the Law of God in Joshua (24.26). The Book of Solomon in I Kings (11.41). Many other books mentioned in the Bible are missing and unidentified. Why were these books selected and others declared sacred, repelled, or destroyed? What is the Book of the Covenant that Moses read to the people in the desert? Who wrote this Book of the Wars of the Lord about wars after Moses's time? One rabbi says that the Book of the Wars of the Lord and that Yashar equate the Torah. But then these books would have been written during the events, because the first is mentioned in the middle of the Torah and not at the end. Numbers (21.14) explains that the Book of the Lord describes the crossing of the sea of Yam Sufa, and later fighting on the banks of the Arnon. But if the Book of the Wars of the Lord is the Torah, where is the passage about Sufa and Arnon? Rashi explains that this book is actually a book about future wars. These answers only convince those who already are convinced that Moses can see the future!

Only four Gospels are included in the New Testament, yet Luke begins his Gospel with *"As many have undertaken to compile a narrative..."*

Among dozens of stories, four were retained and others rejected. Why choose the ones consistent with the late Christian theology and repel others? Why only four out of hundreds? The four Gospels tell the same tale, and comparisons show inconsistencies that create doubts about the whole epic. If four or five witnesses described an event, should we add the facts narrated by each or consider the facts that are in common?

Any movie about Jesus must choose between four conflicting versions. The director would still be unable to be faithful to all the Gospels. The last words of Jesus on the cross are those reported by Matthew: *"My God, why hast thou forsaken me?"* Or by Luke: *"Father, I commend my spirit into your hands."* But John says his last words are *"All is finished."* Until the mid-second century, the Church itself cited dozens of apocryphal writings and various canonical gospels: the Apocryphal Acts of Andrew, James, John, Mark, Paul, Philip, Peter, Thaddeus, Thomas, Timothy . . . Then the Gospel of Barnabas, Mary, Philip, Peter, Thomas, Arabic John, Secret of Mark . . . These apocryphal gospels help to better understand the canonical Gospels, and especially that they are a late construction and a result of religious ideologies in conflict. The Church has tried but failed to remove all writings, including the Gospels, Acts, and Epistles. The Church would have done it willingly in order to avoid contradictions and improbabilities.

Tatian, born around + 120, sought to harmonize the writings in one Gospel, called the Diatessarion (one through four) by composing a synthesis of the Gospels and removing their differences. This Diatessarion, used for more than three centuries in the churches of the province of Edessa, was finally rejected. Then, around +180, hundreds of texts were sorted by Irenaeus, bishop of Lyon. In 367, Athanasius, bishop of Alexandria, drew up a list of seventy gospels, and in 397, the Council of Carthage selected the texts and fixed the New Testament in its present form (except the Apocalypse). However, even in 450, Theodore Cyrrhus admitted that about 200 different gospels circulated in his diocese. These false epistles and gospels are however written in the first person, just like the ones written by Paul, Peter, James, or others, but are the work of counterfeiters. Why accept that the canonical Gospels are free from tampering? Why say that only the four Gospels accepted by the Christian Church are divinely inspired? What about the others? Was it divine inspiration that made the Council of Carthage in +397 ban dozens of apocryphal gospels?

But why are there no more miracles today?

The Jewish Bible, the New Testament, and the Quran tell dozens of miracles. Some believers seek natural or scientific explanations to explain miracles, but it is contrary to religions that see the hand of God. In Numbers (22, 28), Balaam's donkey speaks a human language, never been observed elsewhere than in the Bible. All these miracles occurred at a time when the illiterate constituted 90 percent of the population. The people then were superstitious, believed in magic and witches, and had no scientific notion or astronomical, medical, or meteorological knowledge. The believers said that God was the reason and cause of thunder and lightning. Today science explains it differently.

Miracles were always reported many years later. Moses cut the sea in two and 3 million Hebrews would have seen it, but they were all dead when this "miracle" was published. Similarly, the resurrection of Jesus went completely unnoticed and no Roman or Jew has searched the empty tomb, because again, the resurrection of Jesus was published by Paul and the apostles decades after the miracle was said to have occurred. Nothing remained of all these miracles, no archaeological remains! None of these "miracles" is confirmed by other nations, but only by the followers of the religion. If Moses afflicted Pharaoh with ten plagues, why is Moses never mentioned in all Egyptian writings? If Jesus multiplied the loaves, why didn't the Romans ask him to redo this miracle for their armies? If Muhammad split the moon into two and put it back together, why didn't other people notice?

Most of the miracles are "remakes" of previous miracles. For example, Jesus turns water into wine as Moses turned the Nile water into blood. He multiplied the bread to feed his disciples, like Elisha with 100 bread and Moses with the manna. Jesus walking on water was inspired by Moses separating the waters of the Red Sea. If Jesus had given the secret for a potion that modern medicine discovered to be effective, or if Moses or Muhammad had given the distance from the Earth to the moon and our modern scientists had discovered that their predictions were accurate, that would have been something. But nothing!

God suddenly became silent despite the genocide, the Inquisition, Nazism, tsunamis, and other disasters. Either the God of the three religions operated miracles and then disappeared, or all these miracles were invented. Voltaire, the famous philosopher, said: *"The people to whom*

God has done amazing things will probably be the master of the universe. But no, the fruit of so many wonders is to suffer war and hunger in arid sands..."

The Quran mentions the skepticism of those who listen to Muhammad (11.13), *"if they say he invented..."* Or (17.90), *"We will never believe before you make a spring surge for us..."* Muhammad could have immediately convinced them by creating a source, but instead he responds illogically: *"God suffices as a witness between you and me."* Sura (25.5) says: *"These are old stories that have been transcribed and told to him morning and night... If only a treasure had been given to him, if only he had a garden to feed himself."* This request from skeptics remained unanswered! In (11.12) and (6.8), they asked him to send an angel as evidence, but Muhammad escapes the question and the angel never appeared! Many verses of the Quran—(2.118), (6.37), (10.20), (11.12), (13.7), (13.27), (20.133), (29,50)—report that Jews begged Muhammad to give them a sign to convince them that he is a true prophet. It would have been easy for Muhammad, if he was a true prophet, to convince the skeptical Jews by creating a small fire that consumed the offering. However, Muhammad did not produce any miracles, escaped this challenge, and only gave elusive answers, saying that even if he had produced miracles the Jews would not have believed. See (2.145), (17.59), (28.48). Muhammad admitted that he cannot perform miracles, (13.7) and (17.90), *"your role is only to warn,"* *"I'm only a man, an apostle."*

The Quran attacks the belief in idols. For example, verse (66.4): *"Show me what the gods you pray to have created on Earth... The gods that have done nothing fulfilling, who remain indifferent to prayers..."* Where is the proof that the only God is not indifferent to our suffering and that He answers our prayers?

Millions of hungry, unhappy Jews, Christians, and Muslims pray to God. Some even do it five times per day. Has He ever responded by canceling famine, disease, or natural disasters? Muhammad promised the poor, *"Do not kill your children because of poverty, we will give you enough for you and them to live on."* Has God ceased His miracles while millions are starving and sick in the world?

The Jews refused Muhammad the title of prophet because he didn't perform any miracles. Yet the Quran tells about two miracles performed by Muhammad. A strange Surah (54.1) says: *"The hour is approaching. The moon splits. If they see a sign, they turn away, they say it is witchcraft."* The Hadith (6724) and the Islamic tradition argue that Muhammad pointed his stick at the moon and split it in half to convince skeptics that he is the messenger of God. This "miracle" should be rejected because it never took place. It wasn't even reported by any other source in the world. No, the moon has never been split in two and put back together as suggested by Islamic fables.

According to Hadiths, Muhammad's chest was opened and his heart was removed, washed, filled with faith and wisdom, and put back in place. Then a winged horse called Burak took him to a far mosque. There, after tying his horse, he prayed and the angel Gabriel appeared, guided, and dragged Muhammad through seven heavens in which he met the patriarchs, Adam, Jesus, Joseph, Moses, and Abraham. Then Muhammad finally returned to Mecca. Do you believe in this miracle? This miracle is the last obstacle to the resolution of the Israeli-Palestinian conflict. These so-called miracles are in contradiction with what Muhammad humbly acknowledged himself, that he is a man incapable of miracles.

18

Instead of responsibility, destiny and Original Sin

Destiny and free will are two obligations of religions

For the three religions, God, omniscient, knows in advance the destiny of each individual, because for Him past, present, and future are one. And also, God gave to the man free will because He did not want to create a robot. But if God created man in His image and man is weak and sinful, so therefore man is not in the image of God. If man is imperfect, it is because his Creator created him imperfect. The source of man's imperfection is therefore God himself. If everything is decided in advance, what are the prayers and good deeds for? God prohibited Adam and Eve from eating the fruit of the tree of knowledge. But if God sent the snake to mislead Adam and Eve, God would be guilty! Satan, created by God, can only do what God allows him to. God would be the deliberate creator of Satan, sent to torment us. God is sadistic, because on one hand He wants us to keep His laws, and on the other He pushes us, through Satan, to override them. Believers respond that by creating Satan God brought evil in the universe so that man has free will to choose good or evil. According to II Thessalonians (2.11), *"God sends them a delusion operation, that they should believe a lie."* God would be the author of our evil tendencies.

Why this free will? The world would be better without free will and without sins, wars and destruction of millions of humans. Animals also have free will. What are their sins? Free will is, in fact, a necessity used to explain the absence of divine intervention in our daily life. Believers explain that God *"hides Himself"* voluntarily to allow the free will of man, because if God was too present, man would have no free will and would only be a good robot. Why not? What is wrong with that? The newborn of a rabbi suffered from an incurable disease. This pious rabbi asked why God allowed this innocent child to suffer. After dismissing the possibility that God is wicked, he concluded that God had decided not to intervene. Can God remain neutral? If so, God is evil and immoral! Has God, after Creation, abandoned us to our fate? Jews during pogroms and the Nazi genocide could not understand the divine logic. Some left God. Others explained the unacceptable suffering of a baby or the genocide, saying that it was caused either by the sins of the parents or by sins in another life. In fact, believers have no answer and are obliged to state that *"the Lord's ways are inscrutable"*—that is to say, incomprehensible!

The Talmud, Shabbat 156a, says that the personality of men is set according to the day of their birth; not by any astronomical calculation, but by the day of the week. Thus, one born on a Sunday will be a whole man. Whoever was born on Monday will be an angry person. The one who was born on a Tuesday will be rich and dissolute, and so on. Another rabbi said that it is the hour of birth that sets the character. And this nonsense is said by "wise men" of the Talmud.

For the Quran and Islam, everything is destined, *mektoub*, written in advance. The Quran (33.36) states that *"where God and His Apostle have decided a believer or a believer no longer have to choose."* And (64.11) and (57.22) *"No calamity comes without God's permission"* and *"No calamity comes that was not written in a book before Creation."* So God is responsible for all disasters, earthquakes, and tsunamis, and wants these misfortunes for mankind. Viruses and diseases would be voluntarily created by God. Yet other verses say the contrary. Verse (4.79) states that *"While the good that happens to you is from God, evil comes from you."* Or in (38.41), *"Satan hit me in pain and torment."* Satan would be the author of evil. Without the agreement of God?

The Quran (19.83) recognizes that God created Satan to push us to evil. If God is the master of the universe, how can He allow the existence of unbelievers? Verse (2.5) admits that *"infidels, warn them or not, it's the same, they do not believe"* and *"God has sealed their hearts and their ears . . ."* Why? Verses (6,150), (13.31), and (16.93) confirm that God *"if He willed, He would have guided all." "If God had willed, He would have made you one nation."* And so not all men are believers because God does not want it!

The Original Sin is necessary to religions!

In Genesis (2.16), God gave an order to Adam: *"All the trees of the garden you may eat, but the tree of knowledge of good and evil, you shall not eat of it, because the day you eat of it you shall die."* God mentioned a single tree whose fruits are prohibited, the one of knowledge of good and evil. Adam and Eve eat and therefore definitely got the sense of good and evil against the will of God. There then appears a second tree, the tree of life, which was not previously prohibited. Man was allowed to eat of all the trees, including the tree of life, yet God says: *"And now . . . he could pick the fruit of the tree of life. He would eat and live forever."* God therefore did not want man to live forever, so since Creation He should have banned the fruit of both trees, not just one. Then God punished Adam and Eve. The woman will give birth in pain and man *"in the sweat of his brow shall eat bread until you return to the earth from which you were taken, for dust thou and was dust thou become again!"*

These texts contain contradictions:

1. Why did God put trees in the middle of the Garden of Eden if they were prohibited? Would you display delicious food in front of a hungry man? Is God a sadist?
2. The tree of good and evil was forbidden to Adam and Eve because God did not want them to distinguish right from wrong. Are these "irresponsible minors" guilty if they did not listen to God? Why does God not want Adam and Eve to know good and evil and live forever? Why didn't He impose His will? How can man have free will without knowledge of good and evil?
3. Adam and Eve ate the fruit and thus definitely have a sense of right and wrong. Then (3.22), *"YHWH-God said, Behold the man has become like one of us in knowing good and evil."* So God would have first created man without knowledge of good and evil. And why this plural in *"like one of us,"* are there many gods?

4. God says that if Adam ate the forbidden fruit he would die. The snake says otherwise: *"No, you will not die, but God knows that the day you eat... you will be like God, knowing good and evil."* However, after eating, Adam did not die and lives up to the age of 130 years; therefore, the snake was right and God was wrong!
5. The woman, created from a rib of Adam, should not return to the dust from which she did not come.
6. Why would God want man to be physically mortal yet his soul would be immortal, as claimed by religions?
7. Why are animals that have not sinned also to be punished and condemned to give birth in pain? To find their food by sweating? And die?
8. God punishes Eve and their descendants *"to give birth in pain,"* followed immediately by *"your husband will rule over you."* Why would Adam the sinner receive that benefit? Is it to retrospectively explain gender inequality?
9. Why did God *"made for man and his wife garments of skin"* to replace the fig leaves they were covered with? For these skins, did God kill beasts? Species would have disappeared?
10. According to Christianity, God sacrificed his son Jesus to cancel the Original Sin. But Adam was punished to *"eat his bread by the sweat of his brow"* and Eve *"to give birth in pain."* The sacrifice of Jesus seems to have been unnecessary as the man continues to sweat for his food and women to suffer during childbirth.
11. According to the Bible, God forbids the tree of good and evil, while for the Quran (20.120) Satan tempted Adam with the tree of immortality, *"they ate. Their nakedness appeared to them ... But God pardoned him..."* This story is inconsistent, because if they eat of the tree of immortality, they should be immortal yet they are not! Furthermore, if God forgave them, Adam should not have to earn his bread by the sweat of his brow and Eve should not have to give birth in pain! What is the relationship between immortality and nudity? Muhammad confused the tree of knowledge with the one of immortality.
12. The two countries mentioned in Genesis (2.13), Kush and Asshur, did not exist at the time of Adam and Eve. Rashi, the famous commentator, explains that their name was intended. Is it simply an anachronism of the author of Genesis? How is it possible that

of the four rivers in the Garden of Eden, two would be in Africa and two others in Asia?

The Original Sin is an addition

Christianity is based on the original sin of Adam and Eve, which gave to all humans the feeling of eternal culpability. The original sin, so important in Genesis, no longer appears throughout the Bible. On the contrary, the texts contradict it. In Deuteronomy (24.16), *"Fathers shall not be put to death for their children, nor children put to death for their fathers. Each has to die for his own sin."* So why are we, descendants of Adam and Eve, still paying for the sins of our ancestors? Similarly, II Kings (14.6) and Ezekiel (18.4) state that *"everyone will suffer death for his own wrongdoing"* and *"only the sinful soul will die."* Jeremiah (31.29):*"In those days they shall say no more: The fathers have eaten sour grapes and the children's teeth are set on edge, but everyone shall die for his sins . . ."* So unlike Genesis, the men should not be punished for the original sin of Adam and Eve. These verses contradict also the reincarnation and the punition of the man in a previous life.

Jesus had no free will because everything was expected by the prophecies. Jesus, in fact, knows his destiny and repeats (see chapter on prophets) that he runs to his fate and that his crucifixion and resurrection are inevitable. If humans possess free will, how is it possible that Jesus, God's son, did not have this free will and acted like a robot?

Judas the traitor, free will or innocent instrument of the fate?

Jesus cursed Judas in Mark (14.21): *"Woe to that man by whom the Son of Man is betrayed! It would have been good to this man that he was not born."* This curse is wrong because everything is planned and Jesus fulfills his destiny without trying to escape. He does everything to meet the Jewish prophecies. Similarly, the betrayal was planned, even its price, so why curse Judas, who is a tool that allows Jesus to realize what he claims to be? How could Jesus hope that Judas had not been born? In this case, the predictions would not perform. Jesus knew that Judas would betray him since he told his disciples that *"he who dipped his hand with me in the bowl, it is he who will betray me."* Despite this knowledge of betrayal coming,

Jesus does not flee and awaits his predestined arrest. Luke (13.31) states that *"as he advanced, some Pharisees said to him, go away from here, Herod wants to kill you."* But Jesus refuses to flee and expects his arrest because the prophecies must be fulfilled. Judas seems to ignore his future role and acts, driven by prophecy, in Matthew (26.25): *"Judas who betrayed him said, Master, is it I?"* Jesus did not ask Judas not to betray him, but the contrary. In John (13.27):*"What you have to do, do it quickly."* In John (15.6), Jesus chose his disciples, including Judas, and so Jesus should take all the responsibility. Jesus, God the Son, could have changed the course of history by running away or responding differently to Pilate and the Sanhedrin, or *"pray to my Father, who at once will send me more than twelve legions of angels,"* but he does not. The prophecies must be fulfilled and he does not stop their realization. Matthew (26.54): *"How can the Scriptures be fulfilled . . . ?"*

Similarly, in John (19.10 to 11), Pilate asks Jesus: *"Do not you know that I have power to crucify you and the power to release you? Jesus answered: You would have no power over me if it was not given from above."* So Pilate, like Judas, would be only the instrument of God, neither innocent nor guilty, since everything is in the hands of God. In Matthew (16.21) and (20.17), Jesus anticipated treachery, trial, death, and crucifixion, but also resurrection. If it was not Judas, it would be another one to do the dirty work. Jesus could have denounced himself and prevented the sad fate of Judas. Judas, no longer free to act, is unjustly condemned. Judas would not be the traitor that Christians love to hate but a pure dove sacrificed by Jesus to be consistent with the Jewish Scriptures.

If the crucifixion of Jesus saved humanity and the betrayal of Judas is the cause, Judas is also the instrument of this saving. With a touch of humor, using the affirmation of Jesus, according to Matthew (12.50): *"Whoever does the will of my Father who is in heaven, is my brother, and my sister and my mother."* So Judas, who would realize the prophecy of betrayal, should not be cursed, but rather become the spiritual brother of Jesus. The merit of Judas is even higher than the one of Jesus, because Jesus died, was resurrected, and ascended to heaven while Judas dies and goes to hell, sacrificed without reward.

Conclusion: Judas would be an innocent instrument in the hands of God and Jesus, and he should be blessed and not cursed.

The betrayal of Judas is a very late addition

The apocryphal Acts of Pilate from the second century show Pilate in a very favorable light, and make him a Christian convert, but there is no question of the betrayal of Judas and it is never mentioned. Pilate sends a "courier" to bring Jesus. The apocryphal Gospel of Thomas reports 118 words of Jesus, but nothing about Judas and his betrayal. Paul, in his Epistles, never mentions that Jesus was betrayed, only delivered. Jesus, who knows his destiny, ignores the future betrayal by Judas when he gave, in Matthew (10.1): *"the power to drive out evil spirits and to heal every disease and sickness"* to the twelve, including Judas. Then again, in Matthew (19.28): *"You who have followed me will also sit on twelve thrones, judging the twelve tribes of Israel."* This promise, which includes Judas, is incompatible with his betrayal and murder-suicide.

Because of the Gospels, the name Judas has become synonymous with *traitor*. It is also the name of one of the tribes, the name of an area in Jerusalem, and a common Hebrew name. The place of Jesus's birth is Bethlehem, capital of the tribe of Yehuda-Judah, who did not accept Jesus as the Messiah. Is it the reason why the traitor is called Judas, similar to Judean? Another hypothesis for the name of the traitor: Yehuda-Judah, one of the twelve sons of Jacob, sold his brother Joseph to an Egyptian caravan, as Jesus was sold by his Judah. So everything would be symbolic and virtual. Calling the traitor Judas would attack and delegitimize Judah, head of ancient Israel.

If we need a traitor, Judas Iscariot would be the best choice because it allowed the ban of this extremist who opposed the Roman occupation, while the nascent Christianity, opportunistic, had to show its acceptance of the occupying power. The betrayal of Judas adds nothing to Jesus's teaching because it is a late addition and revenge against those who have did not accept the new religion.

Are these five commandments of liberty, equality, fraternity, knowledge, and responsibility preferable to the Ten Commandments?

19

The Ten Commandments. Which ones? For whom?

The Ten Commandments, those known to all, are they the real ones? In Exodus (34), the Ten Commandments were given to Moses by God, then were recovered by Christianity and Islam and became a universal moral code. But in pure logic, if Adam and Eve ate the fruit of knowledge of good and evil, the Ten Commandments and other laws would be unnecessary.

In Exodus (14.12), God said to Moses, *"I will give the tablets of stone, doctrine and precepts that I have written for their instruction."* So God gave not only the Ten Commandments but also all the rules of the Torah. The Bible has 613 orders, but ten of them, a concentrate of biblical morality, are respected by the three religions. The Bible lists them in Exodus (20.3 to 17) and Deuteronomy (5.6 to 18). Despite some differences that will be discussed later, here's the generally accepted list:

1. I am YHWH your God who brought you out of Egypt.
2. You shall have no other gods before me. You shall not make an idol . . .
3. You shall not invoke the name of YHWH your God in support of the lie.
4. Remember the Shabbat day to sanctify it.
5. Honor your father and your mother.

6. Do not murder.
7. Do not commit adultery.
8. Do not steal.
9. Do not give false testimony.
10. Do not lust after your neighbor's wife. Do not lust after your neighbor's house, his field . . .

Exodus 19 ends with: *"Moses went down to the people and spoke to them."* Exodus 20 begins not with Moses's words but with *"Then God spoke all these words . . ."* and follows the list of Ten Commandments. So it is weird and Exodus 24 seems to be a continuation of Exodus chapter 19. Chapters 20 to 23 inclusive, containing the Ten Commandments and all the precepts, seemed to have been inserted into the narrative. In Exodus (19.24), Aaron seems to have a special status because God commands Moses: *"Come down, and then you will return with Aaron."* But in Exodus (24.9), *"Moses and Aaron went up accompanied by Nadav, Avihu and the seventy elders of Israel."* So no privilege for Aaron because it will be Joshua who will accompany Moses to climb the mountain. Then, Exodus (31.18) surprises us because God again speaks to Moses and gives him new commands about the tent of meeting and about the Shabbat, then very suddenly and without explanation or transition, *"God gave Moses . . . the two tablets of the statute, tablets of stone, inscribed by the finger of God."* Moses comes down from Mount Sinai, *"the two tablets of the Statute in his hand . . . He saw the calf and the dancing . . . He threw the tablets and broke them at the foot of the mountain."*

Exodus (34) indicates that God did not give Moses the known Ten Commandments but others. Exodus (34) begins with *"The Lord said to Moses: carve for yourself two stone tablets like the previous ones, and I will write on these tablets the words that were on the first tablets which you broke."* Then follows a list of commands that ends with verse 27 and following, *"The Lord said to Moses, write these words . . . And Moses wrote upon the tablets the words of the covenant, the Ten Commandments."* There is thus a contradiction: God promises to carve the words Himself, but further it is Moses who wrote them.

Here are these Ten Commandments mentioned in verses 12 to 27 of Exodus (34):

1. The Lord is a jealous God who demands exclusivity.
2. You shall not make gods of metal.

3. Observe the feast of enzymes.
4. All the first fruits of the womb are mine.
5. Six days you shall labor and in the seventh you will not work.
6. You will have a feast of weeks.
7. Three times a year all your males will appear in the presence of YHWH.
8. You shall not shed the blood of my sacrifice with leavened bread.
9. New first fruits bring to God.
10. You shall not cook a kid in its mother's milk.

It is therefore not the Ten Commandments universally known but others that Moses wrote in the famous tablets of the law. Moreover, Exodus 35 begins with *"here are the things that YHWH has commanded to observe..."* then follows the Shabbat, offerings... but not the known Ten Commandments.

In conclusion, the different and confused lists show that these ten commandments would be a late decision, not fixed during the Exodus by Moses.

Is it possible that these first ten commandments date from the time of King Josiah while the temple existed and sacrifices were performed there? Is it also possible that the other ten commandments, those used by Jews and Christians, are from the time of Ezra when the temple was destroyed and not yet rebuilt?

These commandments do not apply to Christians and Muslims!

The Ten Commandments are not a universal moral, but a set of rules whose sole purpose is to preserve the cohesion of the Hebrew people at one period. Some commandments concern relations, not with "your neighbor," which is a bad translation of almost all Bibles, but "your brother from the same tribe" or "your similar." This is very important, because it allows causing harm on another human being if he is not similar or from the same tribe. The Ten Commandments apply only to Hebrews and not to other peoples who do not have an alliance with YHWH, the God of the Hebrews. For example, Exodus (20) mentions *"I took you out of Egypt... The land that YHWH your God will give you,"* only the Hebrew and not the European or American. Or in Exodus (31), *"the children of Israel will be so faithful to the Shabbat... immutable covenant between Me and the children of Israel."* Christians or Muslims cannot say that their ancestors were slaves in Egypt.

In Christian countries, the Ten Commandments are never mentioned in their totality. Christians should read the punishments, death, ordered for those who violate these Ten Commandments before writing them on their churches and courts. In Colossians (2.16 to 17), Paul says, *"that no man therefore judge you in meat, or in drink... or Shabbats, which are a shadow of things to come, but the substance is of Christ."* And further, Colossians (2.22): *"... precepts are based only on the commandments and doctrines of men."* Paul therefore asserts that the Ten Commandments and the Jewish laws are not from God but from men! This is a revolution, and the words of a universalist and not a Jew or a Nazarene. If the Old Testament is not divine but founded by men, as Paul said, so also the prophecies on which are based the epic of Jesus. Yet, unlike Paul, in Acts (7.53), Etienne, a fanatic disciple of Jesus, accepts death without denying Jesus, and admits: *"You (Jews) who have received the Law by the disposition of angels...",* These divine commands are only for Jews, according to Etienne. For these two contradictory reasons, Christians should have nothing to do with these Ten Commandments.

Let us note that the Ten Commandments are formulated only for males.

When were these commandments given?

In Exodus (20), Moses gave the Ten Commandments three months after leaving Egypt, on Mount Sinai. But in Deuteronomy (5), it is only forty years later, near Mount Horev, just before entering the Promised Land. Moreover, some commandments are mentioned in the Bible long before Moses, and Joseph knew that adultery was prohibited when he refused the flirting of the wife of Potiphar in Genesis (39). On the other hand, Jacob married two sisters, and Joseph married a non-Jewish woman, which will be prohibited. But is it possible that other commandments were given long after Moses's time? Indeed, some commandments seem anachronistic. How can he prohibit lusting after a neighbor's house while the Hebrew people were living in tents in the desert? The commandment against bearing false witness supposes the existence of courts, judges, and legal trial, unlikely in the wilderness. And when he imposed the Shabbat, it is stated: *"You will do no work, you, your son, and your slave, male or female."* But how could these people have slaves while they themselves were all slaves recently out of Egypt? Unless these rules were ordained long after arriving in the Promised Land, for sedentary people.

The book of Deuteronomy (probably written much later after the establishment in the Promised Land, as explained in the chapter entitled "Who wrote the sacred texts?") gives a list of laws, and among them the ones punishable by death, which became the Ten Commandments:

> Deuteronomy (13.2 . . .) *"It is YHWH your God to be followed, it is Him you shall fear . . . He will be put to death . . ."*
> This is equivalent to the First Commandment about the One God.
>
> Deuteronomy (17.2 . . .) *"If . . . a man or a woman . . . served other gods, and worshiped them, or in front of the sun or the moon . . . you will stone them till they die under the rocks."*
> This is equivalent to the Second Commandment against idolatry.
>
> Deuteronomy (8.13): *"If someone does not comply with what is asked, following a judgment in which it is compromised by taking the name of the Lord in vain, that man must die . . ."*
> This is equivalent to the Third Commandment against blasphemy.
>
> Deuteronomy (21.18 . . .): *"If a man has his libertine and rebellious son, deaf to the voice of his father and his mother . . . all the inhabitants of the city will kill him with stones."* This is equivalent to the Fifth Commandment on respecting your parents.
>
> Deuteronomy (19.11): *"But if anyone hates his brethren . . . strike him as to kill him . . . the elders of the city will deliver him to the avengers for him to die."* This is equivalent to the Sixth Commandment, which forbids murder.

Deuteronomy (22, 20 . . .): *"If the girl was not found a virgin, she will be led to the entrance of the house of her father and the men of the city shall stone her until death . . ."* This is equivalent to the Seventh Commandment against adultery.

Deuteronomy (24.7): *"If a man takes away one of his brothers, one of the children of Israel, and treats him as a slave or sells him, the thief shall die."* This is equivalent to the Eighth Commandment against theft.

Deuteronomy (19.16 to 19): *"If an unjust witness rises up against a man and bears false witness, thou shall put him to death. I order to purge the evil from among you."* This is equivalent to the Ninth Commandment against bearing false witness.

Deuteronomy (22.22): *"If you catch a sleeping man with a married woman, both of them die . . ."* This is equivalent to the Tenth Commandment, later split by Christianity.

The Ten Commandments are a summary of the most important laws, a list of "deadly sins." The only commandment that does not appear in Deuteronomy is the one about resting on the Shabbat. Maybe the offense about keeping the Shabbat was not considered a "mortal sin," but later, during the exile, the observance of the Shabbat became a sign of fidelity to YHWH and was added to the list attributed to Moses, the great legislator. All this would explain the sudden and mysterious interruption that falls in the story of the Exodus about the Ten Commandments. *"Moses came down from the mountain and said . . .,"* verse (19.25). Immediately after, instead of the voice of Moses, it is God that is heard and ordains the Ten Commandments: *"And God spoke all these words,"* (20.1). This would mean that the Ten Commandments given by God to Moses did not form part of the original story and were added later in this part of the text.

Jesus scrupulously respected the Ten Commandments

Jesus, as all Jews, scrupulously respected all the written laws of Moses, and promised in Matthew (5.18): *"Not the slightest sign, not a single iota will pass from the law . . ."* Jesus never violated the written rules of Moses. And Luke (2.22 to 23) mentions that his mother Mary, impure after giving birth, bought, from the merchants of the temple pigeons for sacrifice *"according to the law of Moses."* Jesus is not only circumcised, but he also undergoes the rule of the redemption of the newborn elder, in Luke (2.23 and 39), *"written in the law of the Lord . . . All things according to the law of the Lord."* Like the Jews of his time and today, Jesus wore a fringed garment as required by Numbers (15.38 to 39) and Deuteronomy (22.12): *"The sons of Israel will have to make fringed edges with parts of their clothes . . . And you must see it and remember the commandments God."*

In Mark (6.56) and Matthew (14.36) and (9.20), Jesus, respectful of the Torah, wears this garment with fringes, *"And they begged Jesus to let them touch just the fringe of his garment . . . And a woman approached . . . and touched his garment . . ."* Matthew (23.5) mentions that Jesus accused the Pharisees of lengthening the borders of their garments, but nowhere is it mentioned that he removed his fringed tunic, and we can imagine that he always wore this tunic with fringe that will remind him that he is Jewish, subject to Jewish law. In Mark (10.17) and Luke (18.18): *"What must I do to have eternal life . . . keep the Commandments . . ."* of the Jewish law, of course. Similarly, in Matthew (19.19), a man approached Jesus and asked what he must do to inherit eternal life. Jesus replied that he must respect a list of commandments that he quotes. But this list is truncated because counterfeiters, Paul's disciples, have erased the disturbing second and fourth commandments about idolatry and Shabbat.

In Matthew (7.23), Jesus said, *"Depart from me, you who act like men who despise the Law,"* transformed in certain versions to *"live in iniquity."* Jesus asks the full practice of the written law, Matthew (5.17 to 19): *". . . He who shall break one of these least commandments . . . will be called least, but whosoever shall respect them and teach to observe them shall be called great in the kingdom of heaven."* In Mark (7.8), Jesus criticizes the Pharisees: *"You leave the commandment of God and observe the tradition of men."* In Luke (16.17), Jesus said, *"It is easier for heaven and earth to pass away than one feature of the law to fall."* Jesus therefore had no intention to change the Ten Commandments and the written rules. In John (15.10), Jesus recommends keeping his commandments *"just as I have kept my Father's commandments,"* those reported in the Jewish Torah. The Gospels report no transgression by Jesus, and it is difficult to understand why Christians do not follow the commandments of Shabbat and idolatry clearly mentioned in the Bible.

After the death of Jesus, his followers continued to respect the Ten Commandments. In I Corinthians (7.19): *"The keeping of the commandments of God is everything."* And again in I John (5.3), *"for the love of God is to keep his commandments."* And of course, the followers of James, brother of Jesus and head of the Nazarene sect of Jerusalem, declare in his epistle (2.10): *"For whoever keeps the whole law and yet stumbles against one point, is guilty of all."* It means that James, like Jesus, asked to respect all the laws. And further (4.11), James criticizes those who question about the Law: *"Now if you judge the law, you are not a doer of the law but you are judge."* In Matthew (23.5), Jesus criticizes the Pharisees who wear *"broad phylacteries,"* boxes containing extracts of the law attached to the arm and forehead during prayers. His criticism relates only to the width of the phylacteries and not to written rules, and surely, Jesus and his disciples had phylacteries. Moreover, during his trial, the four Gospels are unanimous on this point. The Sanhedrin do not accuse Jesus of opposition to Jewish laws because he never opposed the Ten Commandments or the written Jewish law.

Long after the disappearance of Jesus, John wrote in his first Epistle (3.4): *"Sin is the transgression of the law,"* and therefore we understand that Jesus's disciples respected the written Jewish laws.

All these quotations show that Jesus was respectful of the commandments of the Jewish law despite the counterfeiters who transformed his words. Jesus respected all written rules of the Jewish Bible; Paul and Christianity have canceled them!

Christianity against Jesus and the Ten Commandments!

Paul, twenty years after the death of Jesus, understood that the Jewish law will be rejected by the pagans he wanted to convert. In Romans (13.9), he lists some commandments, forgetting the second and fourth, just like the three Synoptic Evangelists mentioned above, proving once more that Paul, author of the Epistle to the Romans, is the source of the three Synoptic Gospels. The second and fourth commandments were naturally erased by counterfeiters to enable the Christian church to adapt to the pagan environment of worshipping idols and Sunday, the day of the sun.

Paul preached that by becoming Christian, the convert dies on its original condition and his obligation to respect Jewish law is canceled. In Romans (7.4 to 6): *"But now we have been released from the Law, having died to what we were held from, for us to be slaves in a new sense because of the spirit, and not in the old sense of the written code."* Paul cancels Jewish law by saying that it is impossible to comply to it. Yet in Deuteronomy (30.11), God Himself asserts that *"this law which I command you today is not in heaven..."* Paul's argument must therefore be rejected, because the real reason for his abandonment of Jewish law is to facilitate the conversion of the pagans by removing difficult rules, such as circumcision or kosher laws. Paul also had to cancel the prohibition of idols because the pagans liked their statues. Then he had to modify the sanctification of the Shabbat as the Romans celebrated the day of the Sun, which became Sunday.

Does the church have the right to change the Ten Commandments respected by Jesus? If Paul, the founder of Christianity, said that Jesus abolished the law and the commandments and the Christian will be saved not by works of the Law, but by faith, then why continue to keep the commandments? Paul also said the opposite in I Corinthians (7.19): *"Circumcision is nothing and un-circumcision is nothing, but keeping the commandments of God is everything."* So yes or no, should the Ten Commandments be respected by Christians?

The Catholic Catechism lists the Ten Commandments, copied almost word for word on the Old Testament, except: *"You shall have no other gods before me"* was erased and the first and second commandments were combined into one. But to keep the number of commandments ten, the tenth commandment was divided into two, one forbidding coveting a neighbor's wife and the other forbidding coveting his property. *"Observe the Sabbath..."* became *"Remember to keep holy the Lord's Day."*

Do the 613 rules or the Ten Commandments apply to Christians?

Christianity proclaims its respect of the Ten Commandments but this is illogical, because the Ten Commandments are only a few of the 613 commandments that God ordered to the Hebrew people. It would be absurd to cancel 603 commandments and keep only ten. Remember what the apostle James, brother of Jesus, said in his Epistle (2.10). James remained Jewish, and like Jesus, he will not change an iota of the Jewish law as written in Deuteronomy (4.2): *"add nothing to what I command you and do not subtract anything."* So why was the ban on eating blood canceled while Christianity continues to respect other commandments?

The Ten Commandments must be respected, according to the Epistle to the Romans (7.12) and *"Everyone who sins breaks the law: for sin is the transgression of the law"* according to I John (3.4). Christianity found support for abandoning some Jewish laws too difficult for the pagans in the prophet Jeremiah (31.31) who lived 900 years after Moses and 600 years before Jesus: *"Behold, the days come, said YHWH, that I will make with the house of Israel and the house Judah a new covenant which will not be like the covenant I made with their ancestors when I took them by the hand out of Egypt, My covenant which they broke . . . I will enter my law in their heart . . ."* The Epistle to the Hebrews (8.6) takes the prophecy of Jeremiah but changes the words, and for example, says, *"they continued not in my covenant, and I also did not care of them, said the Lord."* Nowhere does Jeremiah say that the laws will be changed! And it is not Jesus, but Paul who makes all the decisions to cancel the Jewish law, and that, twenty years after the death of Jesus. Besides, if Jesus or his sacrifice had canceled the Jewish law, why do the Christians respect the commandments of the Old Testament? If Paul cancels some laws as Shabbat or *kashrut*, why respect others?

The Quran and the Ten Commandments

The Ten Commandments are scattered and often repeated in the Quran:

1. *"Your God is one God"* (16.22) or *"No God but God"* (47.19).
2. *"Say: I am forbidden to worship the gods you pray to besides God"* (6.55).
3. *"In your oaths, do not take God as a pretext to avoid being good . . ."* (2.224).
4. *"Believers, when you are called to Friday prayer, run . . . and let aside your affairs"* (62.9).

5. *"Your Lord has commanded you to worship him and be kind to your father and mother"* (17.23).
6. *"Do not kill anyone. God forbids except for just cause"* (17.32).
7. *"Do not come to debauchery, it is a disgrace and a bad path"* (17.32).
8. *"Cut the hand of the thief, man and woman . . . punishment of God"* (5.38).
9. *". . . Calling God's curse on them if they lie"* (24.7).
10. *"Be good to your parents . . . orphans, the nearest neighbor . . ."* (4.36).

Verses (6.151) and (17.23) and elsewhere in the Quran repeat these commands. Why did Muhammad change some Jewish laws, such as the Shabbat or *kashrut*? No logical reason is given in the Quran or Hadith, as we shall see.

In conclusion, the Ten Commandments, with their variances, were probably written long after Moses and not by Moses. These Ten Commandments are related to the Hebrew people and their history, and it is ironic that Christianity and Islam, who want to be universal, claim these commandments. Inevitably, this leads to impossible adaptations.

Hypocrisy and the Ten Commandments

The punishment for those who violate these Ten Commandments is ignored because it is death. Whoever violates the Shabbat or curses his parents is punishable by death. Christianity affirms that all the laws of Moses were canceled by the sacrifice of Jesus Christ. Yet some Christians understand that this position is not possible because Jesus has always respected the Jewish laws without changing an iota, and they come back to the Shabbat and some other Jewish laws. Why not all? Why do they not act like Jesus himself? In fact, as we shall see later, no country enforces these Ten Commandments and their punishment. Even in Muslim countries that require the application of Sharia law, punishments prescribed by the Ten Commandments will not be executed. So why not just cancel the Ten Commandments and simply respect the civil law?

20

First Commandment: one God, totalitarian and immoral!

One God, yet why is He different for each religion?

Deuteronomy (5.7) and Exodus (20.3) say: *"You shall have no other God but me!"* It is clear, but the preceding verse says: *"I am YHWH your God, who brought you out of Egypt, a house of slavery."* This YHWH is the God of the Hebrews and not of the Christians and Muslims, whom He did not take out of Egypt. Why would there be a special god for Jews and other gods for other religions? How can Christians display this command in their schools and public institutions when this God is not theirs? Is it acceptable that God gives different laws to believers of the three religions? Why would he impose 613 laws for Jews and cancel some for Christians, and finally brought some laws back to Muslims? A different God for each people is called monolatry. Monotheism is the belief that there is only one universal god for all peoples, one truth for all, and not antagonistic and hateful different religions!

The transition from polytheism to monotheism is considered a great progress for humanity, but faith in one God is in no way superior to belief in many gods, and contains as much superstition, more hatred and violence without providing more morality. Monotheism has not improved the conduct of men among themselves, toward women, toward their neighbors, animals, or nature. Polytheistic religions were tolerant, pluralistic and allowed all to worship the gods they wanted. Instead, the monotheistic religions are fundamentally intolerant. Their One God is jealous and vengeful.

Abraham is not monotheistic but monolatric!

The first episodes of the Creation, Adam and Eve, the flood and Noah, and the Tower of Babel are universal monotheistic stories. A sudden and unexplained change appears within Abraham. God said to him that he will become a great nation, promised him a country, and concluded with him the pact of circumcision.

Abraham is of Babylonian origins, precisely from Ur-Kasdim. But it is odd that the prophets like Hosea, Amos, Tsefania, and Micah never mention Abraham while they relate about Sodom and Egypt for example. Is it because these prophets lived in the eighth and seventh century BC and Abraham was invented later, during the Babylonian exile? Abraham would have been introduced during this period of exile to give to the Judean people noble origins, Babel. Is the character of Abraham an addition or was only his Babylonian origins added? How is it possible that God ordered him to go to the Promised Land and created immediately a famine that forced him to leave the Promised Land for Egypt?

Another oddity: Abraham had a brother named Haran, which is also the name of the place where Terah, Abraham's father, settled with his family on the way to Canaan, and is also the place where he died. The Quran says that Abraham left his homeland after an argument with his father Azar, who believed in idols. The Bible says that both Abraham and his father (here called Nahor) were on good terms together when they left their city of origin. Now if Abraham had left his family in bad terms, he would not have sent his servant to find a wife for his son Isaac, and Rebecca, niece of Nahor, would have been refused to him. Then later, Jacob returns to his home country to work for Laban. Muhammad did not know all these details.

Not once in all of Genesis does Abraham say he believes in just one God. Abraham even seems to accept the other gods' service. In Genesis (14.18), *"Malchitsedek king of Salem, priest . . . he was god Elyon (Supreme) . . . And Abraham gave him a tenth of the spoils."* And *"Abraham said to the king of Sodom, I raise my hand in front of YHWH, which is El Elyon, the Supreme God, creator of heaven and earth."* This El Elyon, *"author of the sky and the earth,"* was the leader of Canaanite gods, while the god of Abraham, YHWH, is his particular god and the god of his tribe. In Genesis (24, 42), Abraham's servant said, *"YHWH, God of my master Abraham!"* as if Abraham had a particular god. Yet Abraham, called *Hanif* in Islam, would become the first Muslim, the first who submitted to God, and the first monotheist, when in fact he was a monolatrist who accepted the existence of other gods.

Moses himself also was not a monotheist, but monolatric!

The Assyrians had a national god, *Asshur*; the Moabites had *Chumash*; the Babylonians had *Marduk*; the Greeks had *Zeus*; the Midianites also, including Jethro, Moses's father, had their own god. These lost gods protected their clan. YHWH is the god of the Hebrews only and there were other gods to other people, so it is not a universal monotheism! YHWH is certainly not the god of the Egyptians, the Babylonians, or the Greeks. Every people attributed their military successes to their particular god, who would be greater than the other gods. The first commandment demands exclusive worship for the national god of the Hebrews without denying the existence of other gods. The Hebrews believed in the existence of a multiplicity of gods but loved only YHWH, who protected them and gave them victory against other peoples and their national deities. This is exactly what monolatry is, each people believing that their national god is the strongest one.

Similarly, if Moses believed in one universal God, he would have said *"unique"* and not *"a"* in the famous verse Deuteronomy (6.4), *"Listen Israel, YHWH our God YHWH is one."* A (*ehad*) and not *unique* (*yahid*)! Why is the word *Elohim*, meaning God, in the plural if there is only one God? What is this *"Elohim"* in Exodus (4.16): Aaron *"speaks for you to the people, so he will be for you a spokesman, and for him, you will be Elohim."* It is often translated as *"inspiration"* but it is not the right translation. And again in Exodus (7.1), *"God said to Moses, look, I will make you Elohim toward Pharaoh . . ."* So is there one or many gods? Besides, why the plural *Elohim* and not the singular *El*? The Jewish sage Rashi explains that God is humble and takes advice from his heavenly court, and so He uses the plural. Other rabbis explain that the word *"Elohim"* means *"powerful."* This is not convincing, and these explanations create more questions.

This God speaks often with the Hebrew ancestors Abraham, Isaac, Jacob, and others, but destroys other peoples. After crossing the Red Sea through the miraculous intervention of their god, Moses and the people sing a song of thanks, reported by Exodus (15.11): *"Who is like you among the gods?"* This simple formulation is deliberately mistranslated in some Bibles to hide the monolatry of Moses. Jethro, father of Moses, in (Exodus 18.11) says: *"I know that YHWH is greater than all gods . . ."* Without any delay, Moses should have retorted that there is only one God. Deuteronomy (4.7): *"Who is the great nation who has close gods as YHWH is to us whenever we call upon him?"* Deuteronomy (10.17): *"For YHWH your god is god of gods and lord of lords."* So the god of the Jews is preferable because he is strong and easy to contact.

In II Kings (18.34) it is mentioned a few centuries after Moses: *"Did the gods of other nations save any person from the hand of the king of Assyria? Where are the gods of Hamath and Arpad . . . Of all the gods of these lands . . ."* Micah (4, 5), a prophet who lived in Jerusalem in the eighth century BCE says, *"Other nations walk each in the name of his god, but we will walk in the name of YHWH our god, always and forever."* Ahaz, king of Judah in the eighth century BC, defeated by the king of Syria, is ready to change gods, according to II Chronicles (28.23): *"Because the gods of the kings of Aram are helping them, I will sacrifice to them and they will help me."* In Psalms (86.8), David prays to his god because *"no divinity equal to you, Lord, no one can equal your works."* And according to the Psalm (135.5): *". . . Great is the Lord, our great Master, more than all the gods."* So long after Moses, long after King David, the Hebrew people recognized the multiplicity of gods, but their particular god, YHWH, was the greatest. Yet even monolatric texts of Moses contain monotheistic assertions inserted later: Deuteronomy (4.39), for example, says that *"YHWH is God in heaven and on earth, and there is none else."*

Some claim that Moses dug his monotheism from the Pharaoh Akhenaton. Now this Akhenaton, who reigned a century before the time of Moses, wanted to impose Aton, the sun god, not a universal God but a personal and powerful god, in order to fight the powerful clergy. Yet in Egypt, the monotheistic idea floated in the air. *The Book of the Dead* found in a tomb of the pharaohs declared a universal monotheism and said, *"You're the One, the God of the earliest beginnings of the time . . . You created the earth and made man."* But this notion of a universal god was ignored by Moses and King Josiah, who preferred the idea of a special god, protector of Israel, with whom they had an alliance. These two religions differ radically, because unlike the god of Moses, the sun god of Akhenaton does not give legislation and does not have a chosen people.

And so, if monotheism was not instituted by Moses, when did he appear? How did this god so tied to the Hebrew people become the one God of the three religions?

Did Judaism create monotheism but remained monolatric?

According to Jean Soler and others, the death of King Josiah would have served as a catalyst to the monotheistic faith. In fact, Josiah destroyed the idols and purified his kingdom, repaired the temple, and restored the commandments of God. Why is this perfect king killed in a battle against Pharaoh Nekho? Monolatry, where god rewards the righteous kings and punishes the idolatrous kings, is unable to explain the death of this exemplary king. Faced with this failure, there would be three possible explanations: either the god of the Jews was not powerful and was beaten by the most powerful god of the Persians, (too hard to accept); or it was a punishment for past sins (Bible stories explain that God does not forgive the sins of his ancestors, Menashe and Amon, an explanation which contradicts all the stories about kings); or finally, that God is universal. The Bible gives the second possibility as an answer, but from this time the doubt about monolatrism is born in the minds of the Jews.

The belief in one God, Creator of the universe, and the absolute rejection of any other gods would arise after the Babylonian exile (587–538 BC) and not at the time of Moses, not even in the time of King Josiah. The Judeans, back from exile, facing their misery despite their patron god who took them out of Egypt by inflicting ten plagues upon Pharaoh, were obliged to admit that their god was lower than the almighty god of the Persians, Ahura Mazda. This god had brought so many victories to Persians that many Judeans converted to the cult of the winner god. But for the majority of the exiles, conversion to another deity was too hard to swallow, and preferred to adopt the concept of a universal god whose *"ways are inscrutable,"* sometimes giving its preference to the Persians, sometimes to the Greeks, and sometimes to the Jews. It would be the unfortunate history of the Jews that is the origin of Monotheism, according to Jean Soler.

We do not accept this argument and say that until today the Jewish religion is not monotheistic but monolatric. Nowhere in the Bible and also in later texts do we find the necessary break that would have explained this revolutionary passage from monolatry to monotheism. No Jewish text reports the existence of one universal God, identical and unique for all humanity except the first chapters of Creation, which prove the non-Jewish influence on these texts. The prophet Isaiah (43.10–11) is not clear on this matter. On one hand he says, *"Before Me no God existed and after me, nothing,"* but also says: *"I am YHWH your liberator, the holy of Israel."* Isaiah (44, 6.8), (45.5 . . .) progresses to monotheism, *"I am YHWH, I am the first, I am the last, besides me, no God!"* This duality of Isaiah has led some commentators to say, rightly, that there were two Isaiahs.

Jeremiah prophesying just before the Babylonian exile describes the god of Israel who protects or punishes his chosen people, talking daily to the prophet. *"At that time . . . I will be the god of all the families of Israel, and they, they will form my people."* It is still monolatry.

Ezekiel and Micah, during the exile, remain completely monolatric. Micah exclaims: *"What god equal you, you who forgive iniquity."* In fact, all the prophets are not monotheists but monolatric. Even after the return from Babylon, Ezra continues to be monolatric. He says *"YHWH, the god who resides in Jerusalem,"* and continues to call the old national god of the Hebrews (3.2) *"god of Israel"* or (8.30) *"our god,"* and (1.1) *"YHWH awoke the good will of Cyrus."*

Nehemiah is on the same line: *"the protection of my god."* If then, after returning from exile the Jews remained monolatric, when did they become monotheistic? Our answer is never! Jews remain monolatric till today and the arguments are: the notions of alliance and chosen people were never abandoned; the Promised Land and the Law of Return are still only for Jews; food rules remain exclusively for one people as if the universal god does not care about the rest of humanity. The 613 laws also concern solely the Jewish people.

Even at the time of Jesus, the temple was reserved only for Jews and sacrifices could only be submitted by Jews, which contradicts the idea of monotheism and a universal god who accepts all, Jews and non-Jews. The Jewish people have been strangely granted the copyright of the first monotheistic religion. Yet even today, if the Jews claim that there is only one universal god, he would have privileged relations with one people. This is no longer the usual monolatry but a special form of monotheism adapted to the history of the Jewish people.

So how can we explain the illogical order of biblical stories? Indeed, the stories of Creation, the Flood, and the Tower of Babel are deeply monotheistic. But the stories of Abraham, Moses, and the centuries of monarchy and exile are those of a national god fighting for its nation, protecting it against other gods, even after the return from the Babylonian exile. The Jewish Bible, to which all attribute monotheism, includes some monotheistic pages, but everything else is monolatric. This means that the stories of Creation, these monotheistic and universalist texts, are foreign to Judaism inspiration and are the latest.

Jesus made God to change the Jewish law!

For Christianity, Jesus is God's son, but in the texts, Jesus says the contrary. In Mark (12.28) and Matthew (22.36), Jesus is asked: *"Master, which is the great commandment in the law? Jesus replied: 'Love the Lord your God with all your heart . . . It is the first and greatest commandment . . ."* Jesus confirmed Deuteronomy (6.5). Mark continues, *"the scribe said to him: Well, Master, you have said the truth that God is one and there is none other than himself."* If Jesus was God himself, he would have corrected the scribe and said that God is three. In Matthew (4.10) and Luke (4.8), Jesus rejected the devil by asserting his monotheism: *"Go away Satan, for it is written, you shall worship the Lord your God, and you serve Him only."* So if Jesus is monotheistic, how was he transformed into one of the Trinity?

After those monotheistic statements, the Evangelist John, (3.6), some seventy years after the death of Jesus, says: *"God so loved the world that he gave his only son, that whoever believes in him shall not perish and be saved."* This sentence is illogical, because if God loves the world, why does He allow so much suffering? Are there no other ways to save the world? How does believing in the Son bring salvation?

For the Jews, not men, but God alone legislated. The Ten Commandments and other written laws are not from man but an order from God. So Peter, who had the habit of eating in secret with the Gentiles is justified in Acts (10.10): *"Peter was hungry . . . A voice said to him: Arise, kill and eat . . . and for the second time, the voice was heard: what God has cleansed, do not call unclean."* Peter had needed the great lawgiver God to change the Jewish law, not God the Son, because at that time, 50 AD, Peter and the other disciples did not yet know that Jesus would be transformed into God the Son. If Jesus was God, Peter would have asked him to change the law. It is Paul, born Jew, and the early Christians who separated God from His Jewish roots. Paul said that since there is a God, he must be the god of all peoples and of all individuals, and therefore there is no reason to make distinctions between Jews and non-Jews. This universalist Paul was at the origin of Christianity.

To say that the Old Testament is true, that the Jewish laws are divine and wanting to modify them is contradictory, there are two possible solutions: to deify Jesus or to affirm that Jewish law is human in origin. Both solutions are used by Paul and his disciples, who invented the Incarnation to give to Jesus the legitimacy to modify or cancel retroactively the divine laws, and he also affirmed that Jewish law is not divine but human. The Incarnation was necessary for Christianized Jews to justify the abandonment of Jewish laws. But if Jesus is the incarnation of God, he did not need to imitate the robot portrait of the Messiah, nor be born in Bethlehem or be a descendant of the house of David. Therefore, the entire messianic portrait is unnecessary because God does not need to claim to be the Messiah.

We cannot accept the double qualification of Jesus, Messiah and God. You have to choose! The Church should explain this unnecessary resemblance, but cancelling this would lead to cancelling half of the Gospels, and would prove that they are manmade. Similarly, Jesus is described like Moses at Mount Sinai, and this is unacceptable if Jesus is the incarnation of God. After the imaginary return from Egypt, his Sermon on the Mount creates an additional symmetry between Moses and Jesus, both transfigured on the mountain. But Moses is not the Messiah, nor the incarnation of God, a blasphemous idea for Jews. Moses is a human leader who took the Hebrews out of Egypt and transmitted the commandments of God. Why does the Son of God need to look like a disappeared Jewish leader?

If Jesus is God, he is not subject to the laws of the Torah that apply to humans. If Jesus is God, the notion of destiny would not apply to him. He could and should change the Jewish prophecies concerning his death, for example. God is above the prophets, and one may wonder why Jesus did not change the prophecies. Anything is fixed by fate, men can do nothing, only God and Jesus, the incarnation, can change this fate. Moreover, Jesus said to Pilate at his trial, according to John (19.10): *"You would have no power over me if it had not been given you from above."* This last remark shows that Jesus did not claim to divinity, it will be the disciples of Paul that will make him God the Son.

The Incarnation to match the pagan gods

After their failure and the death of Jesus, the disciples, shocked, not knowing what to do, go back to fish on the lake, then returned to Jerusalem, to the temple, to pray Jewish prayers and behave like Jews. It is one more proof that Jesus has not changed the Jewish law. And this was so until the brilliant idea of the resurrection developed by Paul, who turned to the Gentiles because for them Jesus as a dissident Jewish leader was not attractive.

The Roman emperor was claiming to be divine, and marked all coins with "the divine Augustus." Therefore, these emperors, themselves divine, could worship only a deity, the only Son of God. What was needed was a more convincing conception: God takes flesh in the person of Jesus, who does not die but rises again. And for this, the Jewish Bible is again the best source. Luke (3.22), by copying Psalm (2.7), transforms a *"son of God"* into *"God's son."* After the deification of Jesus, the early Christians are ripe to create their own religion and convert the world. Without the Incarnation, the story would have ended miserably.

The Christian goal of Incarnation to forgive sins is unacceptable!

For the Catechism (1441), Jesus, the Son of God, like his Father, has the power to forgive sins and exercises this power several times in the Gospels. God the Son forgave sins by sacrificing himself, without any verification of the attitude of the sinner, because only faith is important. This Christian purpose of the Incarnation is unacceptable because Jesus is presented as the savior who forgives sins. But in Isaiah (43.11), God says, *"It is I, I, the Lord, and besides me there is no savior."* So Jesus cannot be the savior. The priests yell to the usurper, because for them, only God forgives sins and He has no son.

The baptism of Yohanan, for Mark (1.4), would be enough to forgive sins and makes Jesus's sacrifice unnecessary. The resurrection of Jesus completely cancels his sacrifice. Moreover, his resurrection is unnecessary since the sins have already been forgiven by his sacrifice, and Jesus would have nothing to do on earth.

The New Testament is hesitant about the Incarnation

In Mark (8.27), the disciples ask Jesus about his identity, and give him all the titles except *God*. Then (12.29), Jesus says: *"The first commandment, the Lord our God is the only Lord."* Also, in Mark (10.17) and Luke (18.18), when a man threw himself at Jesus's knees and asked him, *"Good Teacher, what must we do to have eternal life? Jesus replied: Why do you call me good? No one is good but God alone."* And so Jesus the Nazarene/Notsri recognized that he is not God and rejected the Trinity.

Mark (16.19) is a great step toward the Incarnation: *"Finally, the Lord, after having spoken to them, was taken up into heaven and sat down at the right hand of God."* However, according to Eusebius, this verse was missing in the first versions and was added later to build the dogma of the Incarnation. Moses, in Exodus 36, was afraid to see God's face, but the apostles saw Jesus continuously and his family was treated without respect and therefore not as God. But after the death of their master, the disciples, noting the total and definitive failure of the political liberation that did not happen, got persuaded of the resurrection of Jesus.

The confusing use of the terms *Lord* or *Son of God*, rather than the simple word *God* suggest that in the Synoptic Gospels Jesus was not yet God. In Acts (2.14), Peter refers to Jesus, not as God the Son, but as *"this man"*: *". . . This man . . . God raised him . . . Therefore being exalted to the right of God . . . Let all the house of Israel know assuredly that God has made him both Lord and Messiah, this Jesus whom you have attached to the pole."* Also in Acts (4.24), Peter and John pray to God and not to God's son. Thus, after the resurrection of Jesus, Peter the chief apostle does not know that Jesus is God. He oddly refers to him as Lord and Messiah, not God or God the Son. Peter, a few years after Jesus, in Acts (2.22), keeps asking the Jews: *"Listen . . . Jesus the Nazarene-notsri, this man to whom God has attested to you by miracles . . . This man . . ."* These phrases from Peter demonstrate that Jesus is not yet made God.

For Paul in I Timothy (1.1) and also in the introductions to most of the Epistles, God is called *"God the Father or God our savior"* while Jesus is referred to as *"our hope"* or *"the Lord,"* but not by God the Son. In Philippians (2.6–11) Paul is obscure: *"Although he was always in the form of God, Jesus did not think of usurpation, to be equal to God."* In Romans (1.4), the same Paul says, *"God... about his Son, born of the seed of David according to the flesh, but that was designated Son of God with power..."* Let's try to analyze this statement. Jesus would be born of the flesh of David, so *human*, according to our understanding, but declared to be the son of God, not symbolically as the Jews understand, but really, with power. Why this *but*? Because the seed of David would not be naturally divine. These phrases of Paul are additional proof that the apostles did not know that Jesus was the Incarnation of God. Some twenty years after his death, they reaffirmed what was important: the Davidic descent.

Paul clearly states that Jesus was the Son of God with the power of holiness, which is not divine but like all men; he was called by the Jews Son of God, and this long after the death of Jesus. The Gospel of John will later set the Incarnation. Although in John (14.28), Jesus said, *"The Father is greater than I,"* in John (10.30), he would say the opposite: *"I and my Father are one."* Jews want to stone Jesus and accused him: *"You who are a man, make yourself God."* Yet Jesus does not clearly state *"I, Jesus, I am God the Son,"* instead he backtracked by saying that Jewish writings give the name of the son of God to Jews *"to whom the word of God came."* But in John (1.18) and (3.6): *"... God so loved the world that he gave his only Son..."* This term *"only begotten Son"* would make Jesus a divine being different from other men. He is presented as the only Son of God, but not quite as God's son. And yet in John (14.8 to 10), the apostle Philip asked Jesus at the Last Supper: *"Lord, show us the Father and that is enough. And Jesus answered, Who has seen me has seen the Father and the Father is in me."*

In John (20.31), after his resurrection Jesus says, *"the signs have been written that you may believe that Jesus is the Christ, the son of God."* Thus, John proclaims the divinity of Jesus but does not assert his divinity in this Gospel written around 100 AD, so long after the disappearance of Jesus and of Peter and Paul. An exception is the verse (20.28), in which Thomas saw the wounds of the resurrected Jesus and exclaims: *"My Lord, my God,"* which would be an addition. Thus, the New Testament is not clear and there is no clear statement that Jesus is God the Son. This lack of clarity would come from the struggle between the Nostri-Nazarene current of James, brother of Jesus, and the Christian sect of Paul's disciples, imitated by Peter, who would have introduced so-called original sayings of Jesus to confirm their theories. Therefore, we find contradictions, like in I Timothy (2.5): *"For there is one God, and one mediator between God and men, Jesus Christ man..."*

Incarnation is the result of a late process

After the death of Jesus, several councils and a few centuries will be needed to declare his divinity. Supporters of the divinity of Jesus oriented their focus toward the conversion of the Gentiles and will have the upper hand. Jesus is made God the Son through a long, unstable process. Christians have not always been convinced of the divinity of Jesus and the history of Christianity is full of that doubt. The doctrine of the divinity of Jesus, developed over several centuries, is the result of councils and compromises. The Roman emperors, considered God's representatives on earth, called for councils and took an active part in theological discussions, often without the participation of the pope. Jesus would be made God through these corrupt Roman emperors. These debates on the divinity of Jesus continued for centuries, with several crises on the divinity of Jesus and his double identity, divine and human. Through centuries, the Church fought against heretics who wanted to delete the divine side or the human side of Jesus. Some commentators argued that it was after the second century that the Church developed the earthly biography of Jesus. We reject this argument, because after the destruction of the temple in 70 AD and especially after 135 AD, the new Church would not need any reference to the Jewish people, who had been destroyed and driven out.

In 325, the Council of Nicaea organized by Emperor Constantine proclaimed Jesus *"son of God, consubstantial with the Father"* and the Church reaffirmed that Jesus is the Son of God by nature and not by adoption. The sect of the Evionites (*poor* in Hebrew), closer to the real Jesus, denied the divinity of Jesus. They asked to keep the commandments of Jewish law and believed in the human Messiah, not the divine. This sect was excommunicated.

In 451, despite the opposition of Pope Leo the Great, Emperor Mercian called 350 bishops at the Council of Chalcedon, near Constantinople, and set the doctrine: *"... The same truly God and truly man composed of a rational soul and body, consubstantial with the Father according to the Divinity, consubstantial with us according to the humanity, like us in all except sin... Begotten of the Father before all ages as to his divinity and in these last days, for us and for our salvation, born of the Virgin Mary, Mother of God, according to the humanity... Jesus is true God and true man."* And so the councils, several centuries after his death and without any additional evidence, concluded that Jesus was the incarnation of God, and he has two natures, human and divine.

The Catholic Church established the Incarnation and in fact its central doctrine, clearly stated in paragraphs 464 of the Catechism: *"The unique event... of the Incarnation of the Son of God does not mean that Jesus Christ is partly God and partly man... He became truly man while remaining truly God. Jesus Christ is true God and true man."* But this decision was not unanimous, and even today some churches in Asia and Africa and the majority of the Anglican Church, and the Jehovah's Witnesses unanimously refuse to believe that Jesus is God.

Jesus was transformed into God the Son, first to change the Jewish laws legislated by God the Father, and then to impress and convert the pagans. It took over 400 years for human bishops and emperors to decide of the dual nature, divine and human, of Jesus. Can we believe them? This Incarnation contradicts the story of Jesus, which became insignificant.

The Incarnation is illogical!

God the Son does not have to be anointed by a Jewish prophet! God should not go down to Earth, He who knows everything! Why must God take human form to save mankind? Has he no other means, He who can do everything? If God the Father wants to glorify his Son, why must he die, be buried, and rise again? Is it not more dignified and convincing to rise to the sky in front of the crowd directly from the cross? If Jesus is God, how can he complain on the cross and say, *"My God, why have You forsaken me?"* Has Jesus forgotten that he is God? Would it not have been more effective to preserve this infamous death? The Catechism says that Jesus was God from birth and even before. So why was the conception in the womb of Mary invented? The developing fetus, the baby crying, and especially the circumcision? A Jewish rabbi would cut the foreskin of God, a piece of God's flesh was cut down and thrown, and nothing happened! Why didn't Jesus appear directly at the age of thirty as requested by Marcion? Why did the divine child fear Herod and flee to Egypt? God the Son does not have the strength to lift his own stone from the tomb and needs the help of angels? Why can't he pass through the tomb, he who can walk through the doors, according to John (20.19)?

The time of the Incarnation

Jesus would have witnessed the misfortunes, sins, and injustices of the world, but remained near his Father without doing anything. Jesus appeared and died in due time for Romans (5.6): *"Christ, in due time, died for the ungodly."* The Incarnation of God is an exceptional event that needs an exceptional situation. Why would God send his only son to this very particular time and why not forty years later, for example, when the situation became more dramatic and the temple of God was destroyed by the Roman occupiers? Jesus appears at a certain period of distress of the Jewish people but does nothing special, and in fact achieves nothing as God so that his presence on earth goes unnoticed by historians and authorities. Jesus appears at a particular time of conflict between the Pharisees and the Sadducees, interested in cooperating with the Roman occupiers. Jesus is in fact an episode among Jews turned into a religion by Paul.

The place of the Incarnation

Why would God appear in Israel and not in Europe or Asia or the North Pole? Why did God, who wanted to be the God of all people and not that of the Jews only, choose to give birth to a son in the womb of a young Jewish virgin, illiterate and very common? Why did He not choose a pagan woman? Why does God need to embody a Jew, son of a circumcised Jewish man and respecting the Jewish Torah, to make him the God of the Gentiles? Didn't God the Father know that the Jews would reject His Son? If Jesus is God, does he need to be announced a few centuries before his appearance only by Jewish prophets?

The Incarnation is useless

The world and mankind were not improved by the brief appearance of God the Son, quite the contrary. Jesus, the God of love, would not have allowed the suffering of the sick, wounded, hungry, and martyred babies. Jesus has brought neither love nor brotherhood and morality. His disciples and believers, the Christians, are they better than the rest of mankind? Jesus did not bring the sinners to the right path. He could cure the sick people near him but did nothing to those who were far away, and he has repaired no injustice. If Jesus is the incarnation of God sent to earth to share the human condition and abolish the original sin, did he abolish it? Furthermore, Christians who had faith in him for 2,000 years, did they have eternal life as promised, or did they die like everyone else? In I Thessalonians (4.14 to 17): *". . . By Jesus, God will bring with him those who have died . . . For the Lord himself shall descend from heaven . . . and the dead in Christ shall rise first . . . Then we who are alive . . . will be caught up together with them in the clouds to meet the Lord . . ."* For 2,000 years, Paul and the others expected the resurrection, but they died and were not sent to heaven by Jesus.

It is unlikely that God the Son would appear at a specific point on the earth, be incarnated in a human being belonging to a certain religion, be crucified all to achieve so little. We shall dismiss the possibility that God the Son came to earth only to create a new religion, sister to Judaism. We cannot accept the coming of God on earth as useless as that of Jesus.

The One God of Islam

The Quran forgets the long monolatric phase of the Judaism and sees only two phases: idolatry or strict monotheism. The Quran repeats hundreds of times that Allah is one and universal. But this Allah existed before Muhammad. His father's name was Abd'allah, *servant of Allah*. The Quran (9.30) attacks many times the Christian belief in the Trinity: *"Christians say: The Messiah is the son of God . . . Serious is their error . . ."* Verses (4,177) and (5.17) accuse the Christians: *"unbelievers who say: God is the Messiah, son of Mary,"* or *"The Messiah, Jesus son of Mary, is the apostle of God . . . Do not say three . . . God is one God . . . What child would there be?"* And also: *"Infidels who say: God is the third of three. There is no God but one God."* And again: *"When God asked Jesus, son of Mary, did you say to men, take me and my mother as gods beside God? Jesus said: Glory to you, I do not have to say that I should not say."* Also, God *"has no adopted son, he has associated nobody to his reign."* So either Christianity is true and Jesus is God's son or the Quran is right, and Jesus is not God's son.

Two religions, Judaism and Islam, claim that the Trinity of Christianity is a mistake. Either they are right and the Trinity is false, or they are wrong while Muhammad and Jewish rabbis are under divine inspiration. How is it that Islam and Muhammad can attack Christianity without any violent reaction from Christians, but when a movie or a cartoon is made in criticism of Islam Muslims ignite the world? Despite its clear monotheism, the Quran twice, (23.14) and (37.125), states that Allah is *"the best of creators."* What other creators?

21

Second Commandment against idolatry, King Solomon, the Trinity, Kaaba

This commandment is the logical continuation of the first one and forbids idolatry, considered an offense to the only God and punishable by death. Exodus (20) and (22.19) say: *"He who sacrifices to the gods (except to YWHW only) will be condemned to death."* Deuteronomy (13.7) says, *"If your brother . . . or friend of your heart comes secretly to seduce you, saying, we will serve other gods . . . You'll have to kill him . . ."* Deuteronomy (17.2) says, *"If . . . a man or a woman . . . served other gods and worshipped them in front of the sun or the moon . . . You shall stone them with stones that they may die under the rocks."* Deuteronomy (13.13): *"If you hear . . . Come on, serve other gods . . . You will pass over the sword the inhabitants of this city . . ."* The prohibition against idols is clear and punishable by death. But this second commandment continues with another immoral assertion forgotten by all believers: Exodus (20.5), *"I am a jealous God who prosecutes the crime of fathers upon the son to the third and fourth generation. . ."* Thus, the innocent son pays for the sins of his grandparents!

The occident was shocked when the Talibans broke the statues carved in the rock. But no one mentions that they did what the Bible (23.24) and the Quran command: *"You will not imitate these peoples in their conduct, but you will destroy them and break down their statues."* Repeated in Deuteronomy (7.5) and (12.2): *"You shall destroy all the places where the nations . . . served their gods . . . you shall destroy their pillars, and burn their groves with fire, cut down the graven images of their gods, and you will remove the names of those places."* The Bible thus justifies the destruction of statues and of those who do not have the same faith as us. How can the West condemn the Islamic fanatics without condemning religions themselves?

Talmud, Avodah Zarah 54b, explains that God prohibited idolatry but did not abolish it because the idolatrous worship the sun, moon, and stars, and God would not destroy the universe because of the idolaters. This argument is false, because God could have prevented idolatry without destroying the sun and the moon! Jews kiss the Wailing Wall built by Herod, the half-Jewish ally of the Romans. Christians kiss the wooden cross Jesus was crucified on. Muslims during their pilgrimage to Mecca kiss the Kaaba, a former pagan temple. Are they all not just idolaters, and why do they accuse each other of idolatry?

Idolatry continues in the Bible despite the Second Commandment

Genesis (11) says *". . . Terah took Abram his son . . . they went out of Ur of the Chaldeans, to go to the land of Canaan . . ."* Joshua (24.2), a millennium later, said: *"Your ancestors . . .Terah, father of Abraham and Nahor, and served other gods."* Abraham abandoned the idolatry of his parents to go to the land of Canaan, so it would be Abraham, not Moses, who would first reject the idols. Later, Abraham sent his servant to Ur to find a wife for his son Isaac in order that he does not take a Canaanite woman. But if the Canaanites were idolaters, the inhabitants of Ur, place of origin of Abraham, were too. Also, if Abraham had left idolatry, his example was not followed by the family of his son Isaac and grandson Jacob, since in Genesis (35.2) Jacob *"told his family and all his people: make disappear the foreign gods that are among you . . ."*

Yet even after the prohibition of idolatry by Moses, punishable by death, the Hebrews continue throughout the Bible stories to worship idols. Some examples: the golden calf in Exodus (32), *"Moses delayed to come down from the mountain . . . Aaron answered them, take the gold pendants from the ears of your wives, of your son and daughters, and bring them to me . . . He threw the mold and made a metal calf, and they said: Here are your gods, O Israel, who brought you out of Egypt . . ."* Moses came down from the mountain carrying the first tablets of the Law. Furious, he broke the tablets, burnt this golden calf, *"and reduced it to small dust"* and *"3,000 men perished . . . You have committed a great sin . . . So YHWH punished the people who built the calf that Aaron had made."* Aaron himself was not punished and became the great priest of Israel, one of the few to enter the holy of holies. Why this injustice?

For the Talmud, Sanhedrin (7a), Aaron built the golden calf because he was afraid of being put to death by the Hebrew idolaters, and to gain time until the return of Moses. But the law doesn't mention any circumstances to allow idolatry, and anyone who built an idol must be put to death. Furthermore, God, who prohibits idols, allowed and even ordered the Hebrews to take or steal gold and silver from the Egyptians to make later the golden calf. God knew that this gold would be used to make a golden calf. Who and why did they insert the active role of Aaron in the construction of the golden calf without any punishment while 3,000 Hebrews were put to death by God?

King Jeroboam, in I Kings (12.27), opposed the centralism of the Temple of Jerusalem by building two other temples, *"the king made two golden calves . . . He set the one in Bethel and placed the other in Dan . . . the people went to Dan to pay tribute to one of the calves."* How is it possible that King Jeroboam built two golden calves knowing that God put to death 3,000 men? Unless the first episode of the golden calf was an addition to harm Aaron and the Levis, active accomplices in the construction of the golden calf.

In Exodus (25.18), God commands Moses, *"You shall make two cherubim of gold . . . With outstretched wings . . . their faces turned toward each other on the ark . . ."* These cherubim contradict the ban on statues. In I Kings (7.29) is described King Solomon, who built the first temple, *"these moldings separating levels were depicting lions, oxen, and cherubim . . ."* The response of a rabbi to these contradictions is that even if God forbade the idols, He also ordered to make two cherubim. What about the lions and oxen?

At the time of King Ahab and Queen Jezebel, idolatry prospered and I Kings (18.19) reports: *"450 prophets of Baal and 400 prophets of Asherah eat at Jezebel's table."* In Numbers (21.7), Moses made a snake of brass, which has magical powers. This snake is also a kind of idol built by Moses under God's command. Bizarre! Later, this snake became an object of worship, and that is why King Hezekiah destroyed it in II Kings (18. 4). What is the connection between the snake who induced Eve to sin and the snake of Moses, idolized and then destroyed? Psalm (115.4) attacks the idols: *"Their idols are silver and gold, they are the work of men's hands. They have mouth but cannot speak, they have eyes and see not. They have ears, but hear not . . . feet and do not walk, they do not produce sound through their throat."* And the God of the three religions, does He speak? Does He see the misfortunes of humans?

Inside the Temple was an operation of sacred prostitution, for both male and female, to ensure the fertility of the land, women, and cattle. Often mistranslated, Deuteronomy (23.18) prohibited sacred prostitution, not the common prostitution. In I Kings (14.24) the sacred prostitutes are mentioned, and II Kings (23.7) refers to *"prostitutes . . . for Asherah."* This sacred prostitution continued until the prophet Hosea (4.14), a few centuries after Moses. So the Hebrew idolatry continued despite the divine prohibition and punishment. They violated this so often but never seem to have violated the Shabbat or the *kashrut*. Why? Is it possible that the idolaters' offenses caused a loss for the Hebrew priests while offenses to the Shabbat or *kashrut* didn't hurt them? Is it possible that the building the golden calf in the wilderness and its destruction and punishment were invented at the time of King Josiah to confirm retroactively the prohibition of idolatry? And that, by using the same process used in the story of Isaac's sacrifice, in order to cancel human sacrifices that continued until the time of King Josiah?

King Solomon, chosen by God to build the temple, was actually a selfish dictator responsible for the division of the Hebrew people

Solomon symbolizes, for the three religions, a wise king who builds the first temple. King David was dying, and Adonya, the eldest son, his natural successor, had the support of his father and the priest Aviathar. But the prophet Nathan and the priest Zaddok planned to give the power to the young Solomon. Helped by his mother, the famous Bathsheba, formerly raped by King David, they plotted and convinced the dying king to give the succession to Solomon.

When he became king, Solomon quickly exiled Aviathar and all his opponents, and killed his own elder brother, Adonya. *"Yes, Adonya die today.*

King Solomon gave Benaiah mission . . . who struck him dead." Yet the wise Solomon, just like his father David, should know the order of Deuteronomy (21.15), *"If a man has two women, and he likes one and does not like the other, if he has a son whose firstborn is from the woman he does not love, he cannot share his property between his sons . . . The right of the firstborn is his."* King David chose Solomon his youngest son from his beloved Bathsheba instead of Adonya, and by this choice sinned against God. Is it possible that the two kings ignored this rule of Deuteronomy? If so, does it mean that this rule came after and not from Moses?

Solomon built the first temple 30 by 10 meters, small in size, and made with wood. At the same time, he built his palace 50 by 25 meters, so four times greater. To build his palace and the temple, in I Kings (9.10), *"Hiram, king of Tyra, furnished Solomon with cedar and cypresses trees, and gold, all his desire. King Solomon gave to Hiram twenty cities in the land of Galilee."* Thus, against wood and gold to build his palace and the temple, Solomon gave towns with Hebrew inhabitants to a pagan king who will submit them to idolatry.

But in II Chronicles (8.1), the story is different and Solomon fortifies cities that Hiram, king of Tyra, sold him and brings sons of Israel to these cities. It is obvious that Solomon would have given towns against materials for the temple and his palace, rather than the contrary, which would make no sense. In I Kings (5.27): *"King Solomon raised a quota on the whole of Israel . . . He sent them to Lebanon . . . to bear burdens . . . and extract stones from the mountain."* Further, in chapter (12), the Hebrews from the north complain of the hard yoke that Solomon placed upon them and ask his son Rehoboam to lighten it. His answer is terrible: *"If my father chastised you with whips, I will chastise you with scorpions . . . my father has placed the yoke on you, I'll make it even heavier."* This response is the beginning of the revolt of the Northern Kingdom and the catastrophic separation of the two states.

It is said in I Kings (11.1): *"King Solomon loved many foreign women . . . He had 700 wives, princesses, and three hundred concubines"* and built temples for idols of these foreign women, all this is prohibited by the law. To exonerate King Solomon, the loved one, the oral tradition said that he had no sexual contact with them although he *"loved them"* and his love was platonic and his purpose was actually to convert them. Bizarre! Solomon built *"a high place for Khamos, idol of Moab . . . and another to Moloch, the idol of the Ammonites. And so he did for all his foreign wives who could burn incense unto their gods and offer sacrifices."* Despite these clear verses, rabbis are twisting words to conceal Solomon's sins and claim that, in fact, he did not build these temples of idolatry.

The Quran (38.36) and (21.81) glorifies Solomon: *"We subjected to Solomon the wind, on his order, the storm blows towards the blessed country."* What is this blessed country in the Quran? Is it Israel? And further, in (27.16), Solomon speaks to birds and ants and they answer back! Why the does the Quran glorify the Hebrew King Solomon, who was corrupt and built the first Jewish temple in Jerusalem?

The Quran contains, probably unintentionally, a legend of the third century AD reported by Otsar ha Midrashim of an ant afraid of being crushed by Solomon's armies. Supernatural beings, the *jinns*, helped him to build the first temple in Jerusalem. On the ruins of this temple, Muslims much later built their mosque, El Aqsa, an important element to the Israeli-Arab conflict. Some Muslims who deny the historicity of the Temple of Solomon thus deny their own Quran.

This King Solomon, so revered by three religions, nevertheless:

- Was a murderer who killed his own brother Adonya and stole his birthright - Had thousands of wives and concubines, conduct condemned by the Torah - Had thousands of horses, also condemned by the Torah - Sold Hebrew cities for wood
- Imposed intolerable taxes and work to his subjects
- Built temples and idols for his foreign wives
- Was the cause of the breakup of the once united kingdom
- Was no better than David, to whom God refused the right to build the temple

And it is this detestable king, whose name was changed to *Yedidia* = friend of God!

King Josiah and the priest Ezra are the ones who fought idolatry!

So despite the death penalty, idolatry flourished in Jerusalem. Some kings, such as Hezekiah, destroyed Asherah and other idols, but without success. The young King Josiah, many generations after Moses and after the discovery of the strange book of the law, *"ordered . . . to remove from the temple of YHWH, all objects for worship of Baal and Asherah . . . he burned them outside of Jerusalem...*" The whole chapter of II Kings 23 describes the destruction of idols, which proves that the Hebrew people practiced idolatry until the time of Josiah, openly in the Temple of Jerusalem and without being put to death. Is it possible that Josiah fought idolatry and granted to Moses and to God the authorship of this prohibition by inventing the episode of the golden calf?

Why did the idolatrous King Menashe, cursed by God, live quietly and reign for fifty-five years in Jerusalem and die of old age while the pious King Josiah, who respected the will of God by destroying the idols, was killed by Pharaoh Nekho? How is it that God promised to the pious King Josiah, in II Kings (22.20), *"you will join your ancestors in peace"* when in fact he was put to death? The wise Rashi and Radak justify this contradiction by stating that *"die in peace"* means that the temple was not destroyed during his lifetime—an illogical explanation!

Ezra, a descendant of Aaron, ordered all the privileges of his caste. In Ezra (7.24): "... *To all the priests, Levites ... of this temple of God ... no taxes or tolls.*" And this rule is imposed not by Ezra but by the Persian king Artachasta during exile.

Jesus was against the idols but Christianity permitted them

There were no statues in the synagogues where Jesus preached because it was forbidden. In Mark (8.27), Jesus asked his disciples about his identity, and they answered by giving him all sorts of titles except that of God. Then in (12.29), Jesus repeated *"The First Commandment: The Lord our God is the one and only Lord."* In Luke (18.18 to 23), Jesus said, *"Why do you call me good? No one is good but God alone."* And so Jesus recognized that he is not God, he professed monotheism and rejected idolatry. Then in Luke (4.8), the devil asked Jesus to bow down to him, but Jesus refused and answered: *"You shall worship the Lord your God and serve only him."* Even John, the later Evangelist, rejected idolatry and reported the words of Jesus, (4.24), *"God is spirit, and they who worship him must worship in spirit and truth"*—that is to say, without statue or image. To the Christians of Corinth, Paul gave this advice (I Corinthians 8.4 and 10.7 and 14): "... *An idol is nothing in the world and there is no other God except one ... Therefore, my beloved, flee from idolatry ... Do not be idolaters ...*" This same Paul, in Galatians (5.20), included idolatry in a list of sins. And in I John (5.21), *"Little children, keep yourselves from idols."* So there is unanimity in the New Testament. Jesus, Paul, Peter, and James, all condemn idolatry. Images and statues were rejected by the early Christians still close to Judaism. How did they get into churches?

During his visit to Ephesus, Paul opposed the sellers of statuettes of Artemis in Acts (19.24). This episode ended with a hearing in a legal meeting, whose decision is not reported. After this first experience, the Church allowed icons and statues to avoid losing these pagans who requested statues of gods.

Around 740, the Byzantine Emperor Leo III ordered the destruction of the statues but met revolt that led to a backlash. In the Sixth Council of Nicaea in 787, the Church recognized that Jesus's body and face can be depicted. Later, the popes authorized pictures and statues, highlighting their *"educational"* quality (?). This Catholic response is unacceptable because it contradicts the Bible. Many Protestants condemn the statues of Christ or the Virgin Mary as prohibited idols. To hide the problem, Christianity, thanks to Augustine, merged the first two commandments in one. Then to keep the number ten, the last commandment was divided into two: *"Do not lust after the wife of your similar"* is separated from "do not lust after his house."

The Christian Trinity, a concept unknown to Jesus

The best way to understand the concept of Trinity is to use the example of water, which comes in three different states, solid, liquid, or gaseous. Likewise, God is in three states: Father, Son, and Holy Spirit, integrated in an egalitarian way in the Trinity; not three gods but one, with several characters in Him. Some saw in the Son and the Holy Spirit successive emanations of the Father. Others saw only one deity in three modes. Still for others, only the Father is God and Jesus and the Holy Spirit are His first creatures. For others, three gods coexisted. This concept, incomprehensible for most Christians, has led to theories that "cut the hair into three" and to heresies that have divided Christianity.

No prophet of the Jewish Bible mentions the Trinity, which would be the opposite of Judaism. The concepts of God the Father, the Son of God, and the Holy Spirit existed before the Gospels but always in unity with God and especially without any incarnation of God in man.

After anointing oil is poured by Samuel I (10.10) on the new King Saul, *"immediately the Spirit of God began to act on him . . .,"* but the Spirit of God is not a second character. The concept of father and son existed long before Jesus. In Chronicles I (17.13) and (22.10), God speaks to King David by talking about his descendant, the future King Solomon: *"I will be his father, he will become my son . . ."* Psalm (2.7) and Samuel (II, 7.14) reported: *"God said to me, you are my son! I today have become your father."* But these words, the *son* and the *father*, are used metaphorically.

Long after the death of Jesus, contrary to Exodus (33.20) that states: *"No one can see God without dying,"* John (14.6 and 9) makes Jesus say: *"No one comes to the Father except through me . . . He who has seen me has seen the Father."* Isaiah (61.1): *"The Spirit of the Lord is on me,"* which means that Isaiah was inspired by God. But the Holy Spirit of the Jewish Bible, *Ruach ha Kodesh*, is not another person of the Trinity. There is only God and Him alone. The pagans who converted to Christianity knew the plurality of gods, and so for them the Trinity is a step toward the one God, while for Jews it is a return to idolatry.

The Trinity is a concept that came well after Jesus

The word *Trinity* does not appear anywhere in the New Testament. Jesus himself, the Evangelists, and the early Christians did not use this term that they would also not have understood. This concept is a late addition inserted by copyists of Mark (16.15) and Matthew (28.19): *"Go therefore and make disciples of people of all nations, baptizing them in the name of the Father and of the Son and the Holy Spirit."* This Trinitarian formula was missing in the quotations from Eusebius before the Council of Nicaea, and only appears after + 325.

The Holy Spirit is a very convenient tool, and is used to announce what the logic cannot explain. For Matthew (1.18): *"Mary was pregnant by the virtue of the Holy Ghost."* What does it mean? How does it work? The disciples needed the Holy Spirit to legislate. Jesus must be divine to change the Jewish law given by God and also to impress the pagan public. But if Jesus is divine, there would not be one God, but two. Why do we go to three?

After the death of Jesus, his disciples changed the laws of God on circumcision, *kashrut*, Shabbat or holidays. If these disciples were only human, they could not change the laws of God. But if they were divine, it would lead to polytheism. The solution is that they acted under the influence of the Holy Spirit, which would allow them to change the laws of God and grant them, and later the papacy, the necessary infallibility. The Holy Spirit is a necessity that gives the disciples the dimension they do not have. In Matthew (10, 20), Jesus gives confidence to his disciples, who were not educated or talented, and said: *"It is not you who speak, but the Spirit of your Father speaking through you."* If it is the Spirit of the Father, new converts must respect their words as they would those from God. Through this, the Church later established its sprawling power without discussion because it would have received the infallibility of the Holy Spirit.

The Holy Spirit is developed in the Gospel of John (14, 17) and (20, 22). Hours after his resurrection, Jesus *"breathed on his disciples and said to them, receive the Holy Spirit. Whose sins you forgive are forgiven; whose sins you retain, are retained."* But if the disciples have received the Holy Spirit through Jesus, why did Jesus send it again in Acts (1.8): *"You will receive power when the Holy Spirit has come upon you."* And in Acts (2.2 to 4): *"Then there appeared to them as tongues of fire that shared, and came to rest on each of them. They were all filled with the Holy Spirit."* They had already received the Holy Spirit! Peter uses the Holy Spirit to confirm his words in Acts (10.47): "As Peter spoke these words, the Holy Ghost fell . . . And all the circumcised believers . . . were astonished that the gift of the Holy Spirit had been poured out on the Gentiles, because they heard about different languages . . . And he commanded them to be baptized in the name of the Lord."

The Holy Spirit appears when the apostles need it. In Acts (11.1 to 10), Peter used the apparition of the Holy Spirit to cancel the rules of Jewish hygiene and to eat forbidden reptiles. In Acts (8.17), *"And the apostles imposed their hands, and they received the Holy Spirit."* The apostles now are also able to transmit the Holy Spirit. Then Acts (19.2–5), Paul arrived in Ephesus and asked, *"Did you receive the Holy Spirit . . . They answered him, we have not even heard whether there be any Holy Ghost. And Paul laid hands on them and the Holy Spirit came on them, and they spoke in tongues and prophesied."* Assume for a moment that this power did not exist, the transmission of the Holy Spirit would be interrupted and the second or third generation would be powerless. This transmission of the Holy Spirit allowed generations of popes to declare themselves infallible even if infallibility is contrary to Romans (3, 10 and 23): *"There is none righteous, not even one . . . for all have sinned and come short of the glory of God."* By acknowledging its mistakes, the Church would recognize that it lost a parcel of the Holy Spirit.

The Trinity has led Christians to a new idolatry

The Catholic Catechism says that the distinction between the Father, Son, and Holy Spirit *"does not introduce any division in the one God."* Similarly, the Council of Nicaea in 325 stated that the Father and the Son are of the same substance, so the Son of God is not less than the Father. This thesis is contradicted by the Gospels, especially John (14.28) in which Jesus says, *"For the Father is greater than I."* And also the demand of Jesus recorded by Luke (22.42): *"Father, if you are willing, remove this cup from me! However not by my will, but Yours."* How can there be two wills if the Father and the Son are the same person? If he is identical to His Father, why would God the Son pray to his Father? How can God the Father abandon God the Son?

In Philippians (2.6), Paul declares that Jesus is divine: *". . . Although he was in the form of God, Jesus did not think of usurpation (i.e., be equal with God)."* And in I Corinthians (11.3): *"Christ is the head of every man . . . and God is the head of Christ."* These quotes show that God the Father and God the Son are different, are not on the same level or have the same powers, and this is exactly the definition of polytheism. By trying to change the "divine" Jewish law, without refusing the Jewish Bible, Christianity has entered a dangerous labyrinth that leads to polytheism, with the Trinity, the Virgin Mary (Mother of God), and all the saints. Saint Vincent, for example, the saint of winemakers whose statue is paraded to bless the harvest, is he not a return to the gods of the vine venerated by Romans and Greeks? Some Protestant sects and the Jehovah's Witnesses reject the Trinity and the divinity of Jesus. So who is right? For Mormons, God the Father, Jesus the son, and the Holy Spirit are three distinct persons, distinct but united in their goals.

Idolatry was controlled and then prohibited by Islam:

Islam converted the idolatrous tribes of Arabia to monotheism. The prohibition of idolatry is repeated on every page of the Quran: *"Do not add* gods to God." "Say: I am forbidden to worship the gods you pray to next to God." To add gods is the greatest of sins. The Quran (6.74): *"When Abraham said to his father Azar: will you take idols for gods? I see you, you and your people in manifest error."* Muhammad confused Terah (Abraham's father) with Eli-Azar, who was Abraham's adopted son.

The Quran gives evidence of the superiority of God over the idols. For example, (37.83) says: *"...Abraham crept close to their idols and said... Why do they not speak to you?"* The verses (21.51 and later) describe Abraham breaking the idols of his father except the biggest one. Abraham accuses the large statue and asks questions, but the idolaters recognize that the statue cannot speak. Abraham then replied: *"Why do you worship a god which can in no way serve you or hurt you?"* Similarly, (13.16) says: *"The idols cannot protect you and can do nothing for themselves . . ."* And verse (29.17*),* *"Those whom you worship apart from God cannot feed you."* And what about God, does He speak? Is He not as dumb as the idols? Does He respond to the prayers? Did He provide food for those who died from starvation? Muhammad was inspired by the Psalm (115.4): *". . . Their idols are the work of men's hands. They have mouths but cannot speak, they have eyes and see not; they have ears, and hear not . . . feet and do not walk, they do not produce sound through their throat."*

The Quran rejects the divinity of Jesus and condemns the Trinity:

(112) *"God . . . He did not create; he is not generated."*

(6,100) *"The creator of heaven and earth, how could He have a son without a companion . . ."*

(19.88) *"They say the Merciful has children. You profess a monstrosity."*

(13.81) *"If the Merciful had children, I would be the first to worship them."*

Jesus proclaims that neither he nor his mother is divine. And Muhammad confirms the rejection of the Trinity in (4.171): *"do not say three . . ."* But Orthodox Christianity never said that Mary was the third deity of the Trinity. Muhammad heard it from a Christian sect and not the Gospels. The divinity of Jesus is condemned by Islam, and either Christianity or Islam is right. It is impossible that both are right.

(9.30): *"The Jews say: Ezra is the son of God. Christians say: The Messiah is the son of God... God condemns that. Grave is their error."* This is true for Christians but wrong for Jews. Nowhere in the Jewish Bible is it written that Ezra is divine. Maybe Muhammad takes the story from a Jewish tribe of Arabia?

Christianity adopted the day of the Sun and Sol Invectus, and allowed pagans to make Sunday the day of resurrection, and Christmas the birthday of Jesus. Islam has also recovered some idolatrous traditions, such as Ramadan, practiced by Arab tribes before Islam, and the Kaaba, which existed before Muhammad.

The Kaaba and the clever fight of Muhammad against idolatry:

The Kaaba is an empty black cube 15 meters high located in Mecca, in the Kingdom of Saudi Arabia, and is the holiest place for Muslims. Around this Kaaba, pilgrims turn seven times during their pilgrimage. Ishmael and the Kaaba are two crucial elements of Islam and yet have nothing to do with this religion. According to Muslim tradition, Adam built the Kaaba, which was destroyed during the flood. Then God asked Abraham and his son Ishmael to rebuild it and the angel Gabriel brought the black stone that is in one of the corners of the Kaaba. Quran (2.127) and (14.37): *"When Abraham and Ishmael established the foundation of the temple..."* Or in (3.96), *"Yes, the first temple for men was named Bakka... There stood Abraham..."* But later, the Bedouin tribes defiled the temple by introducing dozens of idols.

These claims of Islam are wrong because:

1. The Almighty God could have saved the original Kaaba from the flood.
2. It is unlikely that the mythical Adam left paradise to build this temple, and that Abraham gave up women, children, and cattle to ride on a donkey for 2,400-kilometer trip to build this temple with his son Ishmael. In all logic, he would have first built a temple close to Hebron, for example, but did not. None of this is mentioned in the Bible and there is no report of Abraham's journey to Arabia. Muslims argue that the Bible was falsified and the journey of Abraham and Ishmael to Arabia was erased. But why would Jews

and Christians erase this passage from the Bible and from all other manuscripts many centuries before the arrival of Islam? And why are no Arabs named Ishmael or Abraham before Islam? Genesis (21.21) mentions that *"Ishmael lived in the wilderness of Pharan and his mother chose for him a wife from Egypt."* Muslims claim that Pharan is the Mecca of Saudi Arabia, but Pharan is mentioned as a step in the exodus from Egypt in Numbers (12, 16): *"the people departed from Hatserot and pitched their tent in the wilderness of Pharan."* This proves that Pharan is not found in Arabia.

Moreover, in Genesis (28.9*), "Esau went to Ishmael and took as wife Mahalath the daughter of Ishmael..." A*nd again Genesis (36.2), *"Esau chooses his wives from the women of Canaan . . . Basemath, daughter of Ishmael . . ."* This would mean that the daughters of Ishmael remained in Canaan (and would Mahalath be Basemath?).

3. Verse (16.36) of the Quran contradicts the possibility that Abraham built the Kaaba. Indeed, *"We sent an apostle to every nation"* would mean that Abraham was sent only to the Hebrews while Muhammad was sent to the Arabs.
4. Verse (2.125) says: *"We, God, have commanded Abraham and Ishmael: cleanse my temple..."* Why should Abraham purify the Kaaba that was built pure by Abraham? And how could God have allowed the pollution of the temple?
5. If the Kaaba dates from Abraham's time, a test of the materials would prove the antiquity of its construction. So if the Saudi authorities permitted it, it would be quite easy to date its construction.
6. The final argument against the building of the Kaaba by Abraham is presented by Muhammad himself in (11.49), where he states that *"neither you nor your people"* knew monotheism while Arabs had to know the one God from Abraham.
7. A Hadith of Bukhari (3.128) says that Aisha, one of the wives of the prophet, reported that Muhammad said, *"if the people were not so close to the pre-Islamic pagan period, I would have dismantled the Kaaba, opened two doors, one to get the other out . . ."* Because this Kaaba was a residue of the pagan period and had nothing divine.
8. According to tradition, by repairing the Kaaba before Islam, they found a text written in Syriac language, a Jewish translation, which said that God had built the Kaaba in the early days of Creation.

Unfortunately, this precious writing has disappeared. Or did it ever exist?

In reality, many Kaaba were built by Arab pagans long after Abraham. But after his victory over the Meccans, Muhammad destroyed the idols and cleverly kept the black cube of the Kaaba, an ancient pagan temple, so as not to irritate the idolaters. The Kaaba is a compromise managed by Muhammad to repel the opposition of pagans of Mecca to monotheism. So instead of destroying the pagan temples all over Arabia, he retained only one, took out its idols, and ennobled it by inventing that it was built by Abraham and Ishmael. Abraham, the monotheist who destroyed idols, could not build a temple for idolatry. Muhammad destroyed the statues that were in the Kaaba but retained the black stone that Muslim pilgrims touch and kiss. This would be a stone meteorite from heaven per Muslims. The Kaaba and the stone are so revered, is it not idolatry?

The strategy of Muhammad and the satanic verses

The Satanic Verses (22,52): *"We never sent apostles or prophets before you without Satan intervening . . . But God abrogates what Satan launches and confirms his verses . . . What Satan launches, God made a temptation."* These verses require explanation. Muhammad, returning to Mecca, faced opposition from the Meccan merchants who feared that his monotheism might ruin their trade based on pilgrimages of pagans to the Kaaba. Muhammad, a great tactician, admitted the existence of pagan deities the Lat and Ozza and the third Manat. The Tabari Hadith confirms that Muhammad recognizes *"these eminent goddesses and their intercession is accepted."* Muhammad would also prostrate before them to please the Meccans, but his disciples, astonished, did not understand the opportunism of Muhammad against idolaters. Later reinforced by his victories, Muhammad asserted that these pro-idolatrous verses were not dictated to him by God but by Satan, and Muhammad negated these Satanic Verses. He replaced them with verses condemning idols, and with the famous verse (22.52) saying that Satan had already managed to fool the other prophets. Then Muhammad announced the verse (53.19), which does not recognize these goddesses, *"God has not allowed them."* In fact, these verses were certainly neither of God nor Satan, but were a clever attempt to convert the Meccans. So where is the truth? Did, for tactical reasons, Muhammad recognize these goddesses, or is it a mistake as claimed by the Muslims? But in this case, why abrogate the verses related by (22.52)?

Safa and Marwa: On these two hills next to Mecca, the pagan Arabs built two idols for Isaf and Na'ila. Instead of fighting idolatry, Muhammad included them in his teaching, (2.158): *"Safa and Marwa are among the symbols set up by God, and there is nothing wrong in running between them."* And Muslims continue to run between these two ex-idols during their pilgrimage to Mecca.

Yet the three religions still believe in angels and in demons!

The three religions describe angels and demons, who spoke so often in the past but became silent and invisible. According to the rabbis, there would be ten kinds of angels. They don't have free will, unlike in the Quran where Iblis is mentioned refusing to obey God. In Genesis (6.2), *"The sons of God saw that the daughters of men were beautiful, and they took them for wives . . . and they gave them children . . ."* Who are these sons of God? And mating is possible? And the son of God would be attracted by the physical and sexual beauty of women? Rashi, the great commentator of the Bible, finds explanations for all the contradictions. These *"sons of Elohim"* would not be gods but powerful men, who like the barons of the Middle Ages had the power to make children with their maids. This explanation is not convincing. Why this specific mentions of *"sons of Elohim"* if they are human too? And who are these Nefilim? From where did they fall? Another explanation would be that these *"sons of Elohim"* are fallen angels who have made human children with these beautiful women. Were they human or angelic children?

The *Nefilim* are another enigma probably from ancient idolatrous beliefs. They appear as a product of the sexual relationship of these *"sons of Elohim"* with women. It is because of the behavior of these *"sons of God"* that in Genesis (6.5) God *"saw that human misdeeds multiplied on the earth . . ."* and destroyed humanity by the flood. Bizarre that the sons of God copulated with women and God would punishing humanity and not his own sons! In addition, the *"Nephilim"* reappear centuries later, long after the flood, when Moses sends scouts to visit the promised land and they come back and report in (Numbers 13.33): *"there, we saw the Nephilim . . ."*

God destroyed mankind through the flood because of the result of his sons copulating with humans and yet they survive the flood. Is this weird or childish?

According to Jewish beliefs, the angels were jealous and told God not create man. After the original sin, the angels were angry at God, saying he was wrong to have created man. In I Kings (22.19), the Mikhayou prophet who reported *"the word of YHWH,"* King Zedekiah, said: *"I saw YHWH sitting on his throne, while the heavenly host was standing near him, right and left."* Does God need assistants? In I Chronicles (21.1), it is Satan who incited David to order a census, but in II Samuel (24.1) it is God who ordered David to do so and then, strangely, punishes not King David, but the 70,000 people who died of the plague.

Angels and demons are part of the New Testament. Jesus is tempted by Satan but angels helped him. In Acts (5.19), *"an angel of the Lord opened, during the night, the doors of the jail and brought them out."* Then (12.7) says: *"an angel of the Lord woke Peter ... and said, put your belt and your sandals on ... and follow me."* According to the Evangelist Luke, an angel appeared to Zacchary, and then another appeared to the Virgin Mary. Satan would prevent Paul from going to the Thessalonians, and finally the Apocalypse is an epic worthy of Hollywood with dozens of angels.

Despite its total monotheism, the Quran contains many descriptions of angels and demons of all categories. The Quran was dictated to Muhammad by the archangel Gabriel and God is helped by angels who watched and counted the actions of men. These angels are all male and have two, three, or four wings. On the day of Resurrection, *"eight angels will carry the throne of your Lord on their shoulders."* Are they human, with shoulders? The Quran (2, 30) describes the Creation of Adam by God, who presents him to the angels, who prostrate before Adam, *"except Iblis who refused proudly..."* Why should the angels prostrate themselves before Adam? Is he superior to them? Why should Iblis, created from fire, bow before Adam, created from clay? Why did God not destroy Iblis? Anyone who does not believe in angels is condemned by God, in Quran (2.98). These angels are called by their Hebrew names, Gabriel, Michael... The Quran (25.21) reported that the skeptics wanted to see angels or God to be convinced. But this evidence has not yet come to convince us once and for all of their existence. Why? These angels are more than 5,000 sent by God to help the believers.

The Quran also describes Satan and *jinns*, who were created from fire and who are the enemies of the prophets. In paradise, *"there will be women who look down and have not yet been touched by man nor jinn."* The *jinn*, therefore, have sexual needs! In Quran (34.13), King Solomon is blessed by God: *"jinns/angels worked for him with God's permission. They did what he wanted: shrines, statues ."* Yet statues are prohibited by the monotheistic Jews and Muslims. If God is the creator of Satan, who drives people to sin and to disobedience, God would be responsible for the sins! If God is not the creator of Satan or Satan is a rebel angel, God would not be almighty! While the Suras (2.107 and 29.22) argue that there is no protector except Allah, other *suras*, (41.31) and (82.10), say that angels are *"friends in this life and the next,"* *"guardians over you."*

22

Third Commandment against blasphemy, Quran and the falsified Bible

Westerners were shocked when in 1989 Ayatollah Khomeini launched his *fatwa* calling for the killing of Salman Rushdie after he published the pamphlet of *Satanic Verses*. Yet it is the punishment commanded in the Bible and the Quran against those who blaspheme.

Religions condemn blasphemy, but each one attacks the other

For the three religions, asserting that the sacred texts include mistakes is a blasphemy punishable by death. For Exodus (20.7) and Deuteronomy (5.11): *"You shall not take in vain the name of YHWH your God because YHWH does not leave unpunished the one who pronounces his name in vain."* Some say that this commandment prohibits disrespectful or frivolous use of the name of God, while for others it prohibits the use of God's name for magical practices. And for others it prohibits breaking an oath given in the name of God. Leviticus (24) says that *"the son of the Israelite woman pronounced the holy name and blasphemed."* God condemned her to be stoned and orders: *"Whoever blasphemes the name of the Lord must be put to death."*

The adultery of David with Bathsheba led others to blasphemy and II Samuel (12) reported the punishment: *"As you by your sin, you led to blasphemy. . . the child who is born to you must die."* Why does David's sin fall back on this innocent baby and not on David? In II Kings (2.23), the prophet Elisha went up to Bethel *"when young boys, out of town, insulted him in these words: go up, baldy, go up baldy! He cursed them in the name of YHWH. Immediately two bears came out of the woods and broke in pieces forty-two of these children,"* all because they had mocked Elisha. A rabbi justifies the massacre and says that by mocking the prophet the children have blasphemed God and therefore deserve death. And finally: *"One of the disciples of the prophet said to his colleague, by order of YHWH strike me. The other refused to strike him . . . Since you have not listened to the word of YHWH . . . a lion will attack you. Having left, he met a lion that killed him."* Therefore, you will meet death for refusing to obey a prophet, even when he asks you to strike him!

Christianity condemns blasphemy, and Paul in his Epistle to Timothy I (1.20) sends two people to Satan because they have blasphemed. This Paul, trying to please the pagan Roman power, expands blasphemy and demands in I Timothy (6.1): *"all those who are under the yoke of slavery regard their masters as worthy of all honor, that the name of God and his doctrine be not blasphemed."* So we must respect slavery. But is a slave revolt blasphemy? The Epistle to Titus (2.4) asks young women to *"love their husbands and children, to be discreet, chaste . . . submissive to their husbands, that the word of God be not blasphemed."* Not submitting to husbands would be a blasphemy according to the New Testament.

The Quran forbids blasphemy and especially the criticism of Muhammad's words. Verse (2.99) says, *"Yes, we have revealed to you these verses and only perverse men reject them."* The punishment of those who blaspheme against God and Muhammad is clear in verse (5.33): *"Their payment will be to be killed or crucified or have a hand and the opposite foot cut, or be banished from the country."*

Salman Rushdie was condemned by Ayatollah Khomeini, who put a price on his head, and also by the pope. In 2005, Danish cartoons enflamed the Muslim world, followed by those in 2011 by the satirical newspaper *Charlie Hebdo*, which was destroyed for daring to criticize Islam. In September 2012, a B-movie attacked Muhammad and set fire to the Muslim world and later the US ambassador to Libya was killed. And again struck *Charlie Hebdo* in 2015. Westerners are always surprised by the violent reactions of Muslims but they are commanded by the Quran (5.33), cited above. Khomeini's *fatwa* for killing Salman Rushdie is consistent with the Quran. Why can we criticize any politician, any writer, Mao, Stalin, the president of the USA or France but it is forbidden to criticize *"the prophets or messengers of God"*? Why do you criticize a literary writer like Shakespeare or Victor Hugo but we must stay silent on the Bible or the Quran?

The three religions blaspheme toward each other. The Talmud rejects the divinity of Jesus and his messianism. Christianity states that the Old Covenant with the Jewish people is canceled, attacks Judaism in words and in barbaric acts, such as the Inquisition or pogroms. Islam is the most offensive and declares that the sacred texts of the two other religions have been falsified. Muhammad denies the Christian Trinity: *"Do not say three, God has no son. Jesus is not the son of God."* The Quran (4.157) also rejects the crucifixion of Jesus, *"they have neither killed nor crucified, but someone looked like it before them."* This criticism is actually blasphemy since the Bible condemns to death those who blaspheme against God.

For Muslims, any statement contrary to the Quran is blasphemous, but Islam allows itself to criticize the faith of the two religions it calls "falsified." The blasphemy ban is unidirectional. If Islam can say that Christianity and Judaism are erroneous and based on falsified texts, can other religions criticize Islam without being punished by death?

Islam is a proselytizing religion, demanding freedom to build mosques in Christian or Jewish lands but refusing the same right in Muslim countries. Proselytizing and conversion to Islam are allowed in the world, but it is forbidden for a Muslim to convert to Christianity or Judaism. The United Nations, under pressure from Muslim countries, prepared texts condemning any denigrating of religions. Western countries oppose it in the name of freedom of expression, but this opposition is weakening, and in 2014, a judge in Belfort ordered a woman who had the audacity to say that *"Islam is crap"* to pay a 2,000-euro fine. Why can Muslims claim very freely that other sacred texts are falsified when it would be forbidden to say the same thing about the Quran?

And finally, why do religions, especially Islam, try to convince the unbelievers while atheists, under fear of death, have no right to preach their doubts? The Universal Declaration of Human Rights Article 18 and 19 declared that: *"everyone has the freedom of thought, conscience and religion. This right includes freedom to change his religion or belief and freedom to manifest his religion . . ."* The three religions also attack atheists, who are called "infidels." So can atheists defend themselves and also attack religions?

The blasphemy ban is in fact the ban on free speech, a right protected by all Western countries. Why can't Islam answer point by point to criticism and always prefers violence as a response?

Dozens of verses of the Quran say that the Bible is from God and recognize the truth of the Bible

(2.91): *"The next revelation (Quran), which is true and which confirms what they knew."*

(3.3.): *"He revealed the Book with the truth confirming previous revelations, the Torah and the Gospel . . ."*

(3.50): *"I just confirm what you knew from the Torah . . ."*

(4.47): *"You who have the book, believe in what we reveal and confirm what you have . . ."*

(4.162): *"The believers who believe in what is revealed to you and to what was revealed before you . . ."*

(5.48): *"We have revealed the Book of Truth to confirm the earlier book."*

(5.68): *"You who have the book, you will not be in the true without practicing the Torah, the Gospel . . . Jews, Christians, whose works are faithful, will have no sadness."*

(6.154): *"Then we gave Moses the Book that explains everything . . ."*

(10.94): *"If you have any doubt about what we reveal to you, ask those who have the Book before you."*

(12.111): *"the stories of the Quran are not inventions, but confirmation of earlier texts."* And also says in (16.43), *". . . If you do not know, ask those who have the warning, the evidence and records...,"* which means that the Bible is true because God will not give the order to question the Jews if their book had been falsified.

(28.49, (35. 31), and (10.35): *"... the Quran confirms earlier messages..."* (45, 16): *"Yes, the son of Israel, we gave them the book, illumination and prophecy..."*

(46.12): *"The Book of Moses is a guide and a mercy. This book confirms the Arabic..."*

All these verses of the Quran, of both Meccan and Medina periods, state clearly that the Torah and the Gospel are genuine and divine, and that the Quran was revealed to confirm the preceding texts. Dozens of other verses say that the Quran confirms in Arabic the Bible of Moses, and explains it in Arabic so the idolaters of Arabia can understand. If the Bible is false, how could Muhammad have said, in (2.85): *"do you believe in part of the book without believing in the other?"*

Around 610, Muhammad received his first revelations, at the age of forty, and he died in 632. His companions put in writing his teachings from their memory. But according to the Muslims, under the reign of his successor Othman in 645 to 656, the Quran was written down and fixed permanently. During those years, was the teaching changed? The Quran (1.79) accuses Jews and Christians of having altered the sacred texts, *"woe to those who write the book themselves and say it comes from God."* Does this charge also apply to the Quran?

But Muslims are forced to say that the Bible was falsified

Because non-Muslims found errors in the Quran (some listed in the chapter about contradictions), the Muslims, and not Muhammad, were obliged to say that the Bible was falsified. Without this affirmation of falsification, the Quran, which differs from the Bible in several points, would be wrong and not divine.

Here are more examples of errors. For Muhammad, David and Solomon are free from sin, but anyone who read the Bible must know the adulterous attitude of David, or the 1,000 women of Solomon. If

Muhammad describes David as sinless, he should have said that despite what is written in the Bible David is innocent of adultery. But he does not do so, simply because he did not know about this adultery, not having been transmitted to him by Jews living in Arabia. Muhammad recounts the episode of Lot but forgets to mention that he offered his two daughters to visitors, got drunk, and committed incest. The story of Jacob, who lies to Esau and deceives his father, is unknown to the Quran. Sura (12) is entirely devoted to Joseph, yet a small mistake proves that Muhammad did not have before him the written text but a popular story: Joseph brings to Egypt his father and mother, (12.99), impossible because his mother Rachel died long ago and was buried in Efrath on the way to Bethlehem. The Quran confuses the meetings of Moses and Jacob with Rachel and Tsipora.

According to (28.27), Jethro promised Moses, *"I desire for you to marry one of my daughters if you work eight years for me."* But according to the Bible, the stepfather of Moses did not ask him to work eight years in order to marry Tsipora. It was Jacob who received a similar offer from Laban. Aaron built the golden calf in the Bible, but the Quran describes him as opposing the golden calf. In Sura (5.116), Jesus demanded, *"Take me and my mother as gods besides God."* But nowhere in the New Testament is Mary deified. It is only a few centuries later that a Christian sect deifies Mary.

All the unflattering descriptions of the prophets are ignored by the Quran, which sees these prophets as pure beings elected by God. For Muslims, Muhammad cannot be wrong because he speaks the Word of God. And so instead of apologizing for the mistakes of the Quran, the Muslims attack and claim that the Bible has been falsified. There are two possibilities: either the Torah was falsified before Muhammad, or the Jews who explained their religion to Muhammad misinformed him by telling him about the oral tradition, the Talmud, and other tales.

The first solution is inconsistent, while the second is the only logical explanation possible. In fact, only four verses are used to assert that the Bible is falsified: (2.75), *"Some of them hear the word of God and adulterate after having understood"*; (4.46), *"There are Jews who are changing the meaning of words; they say: we hear and disobey"*; (5.13) repeated in (5.41), *"They change the meaning of words."*

This criticism concerns only the interpretation of texts by only some of the Jews, not by all, and also what the Jews did not want to reveal or explain to Muhammad. A Hadith of Bukhari mentions that Muhammad came to explain what some Jews wanted to hide. Other Muslims understand these verses as Jews wanting to hide that the Jewish Bible foretold the coming of the Prophet Muhammad. Muhammad never had on hand a Bible written in Arabic, not yet translated in his time. And even if he had, he would not have been able to dissect it. The Jews did not explain to him the differences between the written Bible and the Talmud. In fact, the Quran affirms that some Jews, and not all, have added rules not included in the Bible, and everyone agrees the Pharisees added additional barriers to preserve the biblical laws. Just like Isaiah and Jeremiah, Jesus accused them of these additions, long before Muhammad. According to Matthew (15.6), *"you cancel the word of God by your tradition."*

If Muhammad thought the Bible was falsified, he would have proclaimed it. But he did not, because for Muhammad there was no falsification of the Bible. Muhammad himself recognizes the divinity of the Bible that he came to confirm, and God and Muhammad would not designate a falsified Bible as a reference and guide. This idea of falsification was made necessary after his death! Muslims, after the death of Muhammad, used the verse (2.42) to claim that Muhammad had accused the Jews and Christians of forgery: *"Do not hide the truth, you who know."* This verse concerns two Jews who were accused of adultery and hid the punishment written in the Bible.

The present Jewish Bible or Old Testament, the one we have before our eyes, is the same or almost the same as the Septuagint, the Greek translation of the Jewish Bible from the second century BCE. The same or almost the same as the oldest copy of the Hebrew Bible, which dates from the ninth or tenth century AD. Finally, the discovery in 1947 of the Dead Sea scrolls dating from the first century BC confirms the almost complete similarity between the Bibles of the first and second centuries, the eleventh century, and the present Jewish Bible. Minor differences between the Jewish Bibles have no doctrinal consequences.

Another proof of the preservation of the Jewish Bible can be found is the New Testament. According to the Gospel of Luke (4.16), written in the first century, Jesus reads a text from Isaiah identical to the one in any Bible and also the Dead Sea Scrolls. The Jewish Bible has not changed since its fixation, and the texts have not been altered in more than 2,000 years (which does not mean that the Jewish Bible or the New Testament was not modified several times before they were fixed).

What about the New Testament? First, no verse of the Quran states that Christians have falsified the Gospels. Moreover, wrongly, Muhammad mentions only one Gospel as if he ignored that there were four. He never mentions Paul, Peter, and the other apostles, and seems to ignore the Acts and the Epistles. The best proof of forgery was to present an authentic New Testament. The discovery of a lost Gospel of Barnabas was a bonus for Muslims who supported the theory of falsification. They presented this Gospel of Barnabas as the true Gospel. This text from Barnabas said that Jesus was not divine but only a prophet, that another was crucified in his place, and he predicted the coming of Muhammad as a Messiah. In fact, this text of Barnabas is a crude forgery written in Spain in the Middle Ages, well after Muhammad, and serious Muslims repel it.

In fact, Muhammad couldn't read any text because they were written in Hebrew or Greek. He was only told about easy episodes, like those found in the illustrated Bibles for children and stories transmitted by dissident sects. Muhammad did not read the Torah and the New Testament but listened to oral traditions that often twisted the texts. Muslims use a verse of the Quran and only one, (2.79): "Woe to those who write the book themselves and say it comes from God," to assert that Muhammad denounced the falsification of the sacred texts. This single verse is insufficient because it can be applied to other books, like the Talmud, not the Bible.

23

Fourth Commandment: Shabbat, Jesus respected it, did not rise on Sunday

Shabbat is a revolutionary idea and the weekly rest is a great progress of mankind. This weekly rest restores dignity to human beings, slave or foreigner, and also to the beast. The Romans did not understand the Shabbat and saw it as a waste of time, especially for their slaves. The Shabbat is a pillar of Judaism mentioned clearly in Exodus (20.8) and (31.15): *"Remember the Shabbat to sanctify it. During six days you shall labor . . . but the seventh day . . . You shall not do any work, you, your son or your daughter, your male or female slave, your livestock, or the sojourner who is within your walls. For in six days YHWH made heaven and earth, the sea and all that is therein, and did nothing on the seventh day, that's why YHW H blessed the Shabbat . . . but the seventh day is a Shabbat of complete rest . . . whoever does any work will be put to death for sure . . ."* So death for any Hebrew who contravened to this law, which was not only a threat.

Numbers (15.32) says that *"while in the wilderness, the children of Israel found a man gathering sticks during the Shabbat . . . took him to Moses and Aaron . . . put him in a safe place because it was not explained how Moses had to act against him. And YHWH said to Moses: This man must be put to death . . . and the whole community . . . killed him with stones as YHWH had commanded Moses."* So even if Moses himself did not know so much about the Shabbat rule, the poor man who violated the Shabbat was put to death! Although the written law is clear and the punishment is death, the rabbis are claiming that the death penalty was almost never imposed.

How does one respect the Shabbat? Jeremiah (17.21): *"Do not carry a burden... on the Shabbat and do not work..."* How do you define *work*? Is it cooking, driving a car, turning on the television, or just doing any work? The Pharisees 2,000 years ago and rabbis of all time added prohibitions, and Jesus was against all these additions. The Pharisees compiled a list of thirty-nine prohibited jobs on the Shabbat. This list leads to ridiculous exaggerations. For example, it is forbidden to sow during the Shabbat, and as a result, when eating watermelon you have to prevent any seed from falling in your garden. Or it is forbidden to plow, and as a result, children cannot play marbles on earthy ground for fear of digging. And more, it is forbidden to tear anything, and as a result, toilet paper has to be precut before Shabbat and not on a roll. It is also forbidden to comb hair on the Shabbat, to make a lasting node, to open one's umbrella if it rains. The rabbis try to outdo each other, and this leads to new ridiculous interdictions. Former Chief Rabbi of Israel, Ovadiah Yosef asked not blow the nose on Shabbat to avoid cutting a hair!

The *Iruv*: It is forbidden on Shabbat to transport an item from the public to the private sector and vice versa. The rabbis found a solution by turning the whole city into one area by surrounding it by poles connected by cables. So all the cities in Israel are surrounded by useless poles with cables, whose sole purpose is transforming the city into a single domain in order to avoid the prohibition of Shabbat.

The origins of the Shabbat

Before the episode of the Ten Commandments, in Exodus (16), the Hebrews received the manna and *"the sixth day they gathered a double provision... Tomorrow is a solemn Shabbat... And the people rested on the seventh day."* This episode proves that the Shabbat was given before the Ten Commandments at Mount Sinai, or a scribe was confused. Is it the same for other commandments?

The Bible gives two different reasons to the Shabbat:

1. In Genesis (2.2), "... *God rested on the seventh day from all the work he had done.*" Is the Almighty God tired that He must rest? God does not get tired during the Creation, and the translation of the word *Shabbat* is not easy. Isaiah (40.28), probably written during or after the Babylonian exile, says that *"the Creator of the utmost limits of the world feel neither fatigue nor weariness."* Isaiah will be repeated in the Quran, which states that God does not need to rest. The correct translation would be *to stop doing*. It is clear that God has no need to rest. For Jews, this means that the Shabbat is made to stop the usual activities and refresh the soul by moving closer to God.
2. In Deuteronomy (5.15): *"You shall remember that you were a slave in Egypt ... that's why the Lord your God has prescribed to observe the Shabbat."* This second explanation is related to slavery in Egypt, and therefore Abraham, Isaac, Jacob, living before slavery in Egypt, ignored the Shabbat.

Which of the two reasons is the right one?

Many clues prove that the Shabbat was imposed after Moses. Indeed, the following rule is strange: *"You do not will work, you, your son, nor your slave, male or female, nor the stranger that is within thy walls."* How could they have slaves, while they themselves were slaves recently out of Egypt? How could they have walls, they who lived in tents?

It is strange that the prophets, judges, and dozens of generations of kings did not do or say anything concerning the Shabbat. Not a single violation of this rule. Why this secular silence? Either the Hebrew people totally respected the Shabbat and there was nothing to say (but they violated other rules), or that the Shabbat was forgotten or even invented much later, after the Babylonian exile and the return to the Promised Land, and inserted later in the early books of the Bible.

In Jeremiah (17.27), God threatens that *"if you do not obey me by sanctifying the Shabbat and refrain you to carry burdens and enter the gates of Jerusalem on the Shabbat, I would set fire to its gates."* But we know that Jeremiah was rewritten several times and even after the exile. After returning from exile, around 500 BC, Nehemiah (13.15) condemned: *"I saw people who were treading on winepresses on the Shabbat and transporting loads on the back of the donkey...*" This Shabbat, now established or restored, will be part of the tradition and Jewish law.

A small omission

In Joshua (6), the Hebrews walked around Jericho for six days and on the seventh day attacked and destroyed this city. There is necessarily a Shabbat in these seven days. However, after a thousand years of silence on the Shabbat, the historian Flavius Josephus, under his Hebrew name Yosef Ben Mathetiaou, said that the Romans took advantage of the truce of the Shabbat for their offensive against the Hebrews, *"because during the Shabbat, Jews were not fighting but defending only."* It was necessary to change the rule and allow violating the Shabbat to save lives. Yet we find in the Talmud, Sanhedrin 58b, a rule completely in opposition to what the Hebrews, freed former slaves, should have preached:*" A sage, Rash Lachish said that a non-Jewish who takes a day to rest deserves death ... Even if it is a Monday..."* The rest day is therefore only for the Jews? Where do they get this? From the weird interpretation of Genesis verse (8.32) on Noah after the flood.

Jesus always respected the Shabbat, why did Christianity cancel it?

Some seventy years after the death of Jesus, John (5.16) said that: *"...The Jews persecute Jesus because he did these things (healing the sick) on Shabbat."* This is wrong. Jesus fully respected the Shabbat and was never pursued by the Jews on this question. Indeed, even in the New Testament and its additions, Jesus never worked on Shabbat or lit a fire, nor did his disciples. Instead, Jesus prayed on the Shabbat in the synagogues and even predicted that the Shabbat will continue to be respected when he asked in Matthew (24.20) that at the arrival of the kingdom of God *"Pray without ceasing that your flight may not be in winter or on the Shabbat."*

Jesus certainly did not cancel the Shabbat but admitted that the Shabbat ends when a life is threatened, or to perform a good deed, like the healing of a paralytic. Jesus did not cancel the Shabbat but wanted a more positive interpretation. In Numbers (15.32), Moses hesitated, then, after consulting with God, punished with death *"a man gathering wood on the Shabbat."* If Jesus had wanted to change this command, he would have gathered wood on the Shabbat and said, *"The written law says . . . but I say this . . ."* But he did not. It is not wood that the disciples gather but heads of grains, and that changes everything and makes it possible to affirm that Jesus had not wanted to change the Shabbat commandment.

Indeed, the details in the three Synoptic Gospels are revealing. In Mark (2.23 to 28), Jesus's disciples *"on the way, began to pluck the heads of grains"* without specifying the reason for their actions. Matthew (12.1) specifies *"who were hungry and ate . . ."* And Luke (6.1), the non-Jewish (?) doctor in the New Testament, understood the delicacy of the issue, and noted *"and ate, after having rubbing them in their hands,"* so immediately to satisfy their hunger. Such questions were current at this time, and the Pharisees, contrary to the opinion of Jesus, will impose more rigid barriers to prevent Shabbat violations.

Like the Jews of his time, Jesus made it possible to save a life even during Shabbat. The famous words of Jesus on the Shabbat reported by Mark (2.27) is significant: *"The Shabbat was made for man, not man for the Sabbath, so that the Son of Man is Lord even of the Shabbat."* The Son of Man is Lord of the Shabbat and not man! If Jesus had wanted to downgrade the Shabbat, he would have said that man is the master of the Shabbat and can cancel it. The accuracy of words, even after the falsifications, is revealing.

In Mark (1.21), Jesus preached in the synagogue during the Shabbat and hunted the unclean spirit. In Luke (13.14), Jesus healed a cripple on Shabbat while *"there are six days for work, so come and be healed on those days, not on the Shabbat."* Jesus answered: *"On Shabbat, you detach your ox or your donkey to give him a drink."* This response is inadequate, because drinking is a matter of life or death for the donkey or the ox while healing a chronic infirmity can wait a day. But further, Luke (14.5) used a better argument. Despite the Shabbat, it is possible to save a son or an ox fallen into a well because his life is in danger, as it is established that *"saving a life pushes the Shabbat."* These examples prove that Jesus, before falsifications, understood and respected the commandment of the Shabbat, as accepted then, before the victory of the Pharisees, who settled the most finicky rules.

The Gospels use the so-called Pharisees' silence to give the impression that the Pharisees are opposed to healings on Shabbat. But the Pharisees never said that it is forbidden to save the life of a man or an animal during Shabbat. The Talmud and Jesus say that survival comes before Shabbat.

The question for Jews is deeper and depends on the severity of the disease. If a Jew has only a headache on Shabbat, he will not go to the doctor because it is not an emergency, nor a matter of life or death. Long discussions took place on the interpretation of the Shabbat and what to do in extreme cases. For example, should one milk a cow on Shabbat? All these questions, and more complicated ones, received answers. After Jesus and the destruction of the temple, the Pharisees set thirty-nine principles to describe what it is forbidden during the Shabbat. For example, circumcision must be performed on the eighth day after birth, even if it is Shabbat. Also, a broken arm may be treated and a midwife is allowed to help a birth on Shabbat and even to cut the umbilical cord. To avoid opening the debate again, the Pharisees and rabbis erased the discussion with Jesus.

In conclusion, Jesus always respected the Shabbat commandment but had some differences of interpretation with the too fussy Pharisees. Who canceled the Shabbat for Christians? Certainly not Jesus!

The cancellation of the Shabbat by Paul's disciples

After the death of Jesus, his disciples and Mary Magdalene went to the tomb after the end of the Shabbat, because there would be no urgency, no matter of life or death. Luke (23.56), *"and rested on the Shabbat according to the law."* So after the death of Jesus, the disciples continued to observe the Shabbat, and so the early Christians, and to this day Adventists and some Baptists, continue to respect it. Paul (?) said in Hebrews (4.8 to 11): *". . . It remains a rest for the people of God . . . Let us do our utmost to enter into that rest, lest any man fall into disobedience . . ."* Therefore, Paul wanted to keep the Shabbat, though it contradicts his later teachings when he tried to make the Shabbat more accessible to pagans. This proves once again that the Epistle to the Hebrews is not by Paul but from a Nazarean-Notsri disciple and not from a Christian one. It is also possible that Paul modified his tactic and decided later in pagan land to cancel the Shabbat.

This is clear when in Colossians (2.13 to 17) Paul says, *"therefore that no man judge you about food or drink, or . . . Shabbats . . ."* And further, Colossians (2.22): *". . . precepts are based only on the commandments and doctrines of men."* Paul therefore asserts that the Ten Commandments and the Jewish laws are not of God but of men! This is a revolution, and the words of a universalist, not a Jew or a Notsri. Yet according to Acts (7.53),

Etienne, a fanatical follower of Jesus who accepted death without denying Jesus, said the opposite of Paul and recognized *"You (Jews) who received the law by the commandments of angels and have not kept them."* But if the Old Testament is not divine but founded by men, as Paul wished, so are the prophecies on which the epic of Jesus is based.

So Jesus and his disciples always respected the Shabbat, predicted to continue after the arrival of the Kingdom of God, but Paul's disciples canceled it.

The Christian Shabbat reported by Article 582 of the Catechism

"Jesus often reminded with rabbinical arguments that the Shabbat rest is not troubled by the service of God or by the cure of men." This is right, but why cancel the Shabbat? The law about Shabbat is clear and cannot be transgressed except in urgent cases of patient care and feeding animals, but no argument can be found to allow work during Shabbat. We cannot ask for belief in the divinity of the Old Testament and the Ten Commandments and at the same time not to respect them because of fallacious arguments.

According to the Catechism, the Christian is delivered from the curse of the law and is not required to respect the Shabbat. By becoming a Christian, the obligation to respect to Jewish law is forever canceled. Romans (7.4 to 6): *"But now we have been released from the Law . . . for us to be slaves in a new sense because of the spirit, and not in the old sense of the written code."* If the Christians were released from the Jewish Law, why do they still use it? If Christianity has canceled the Shabbat, why keep the other commandments? Jesus never asked for the Shabbat to be replaced by Sunday.

Jesus was not resurrected on a Sunday!

Sunday is the day of Resurrection unanimously mentioned by the four Gospels: *"The first day of the week Mary Magdalene came to the tomb . . . ."* In the Catholic Catechism (2174), *"Jesus rose from the dead on the first day of the week,"* as in Matthew (28.1), Mark (16.2), Luke (24.1), and finally John (20.1). The Jewish week numbers the days, with Sunday as the first day.

But neither the Old Testament nor the New, or Jesus asked to celebrate Sunday.

The early Christians, according to Acts (20.7), became accustomed to gathering on the first day of the week to *"break bread."* That day was called the "Lord's day" in Latin and Sunday in English. It was crucial that Jesus was resurrected on a Sunday, which was already a day of celebration for Roman pagans. In 37 AD, Caligula became emperor and called himself "Sun King." In 321 AD, Emperor Constantine ordered that the day of the resurrection of Jesus on Sunday will be a day of rest. Is it not the opposite? Christians made Jesus's day of resurrection on Sunday to fit with the day of the sun already celebrated by the Romans.

The third day: According to old beliefs, the dead is really dead only after three days. At the resurrection of Lazarus, to show that Jesus performed a miracle, John (11.17) stated that Jesus waited deliberately so that *"when he arrived, he found that Lazarus had already been four days in the tomb."* In Matthew (12. 40), Jesus proclaims *"as Jonah . . . the Son of Man (Jesus therefore) be three days and three nights in the heart of the earth."* Jesus is wrong, because he is in the tomb only about thirty-six hours, from Friday afternoon to Sunday morning, so only two nights, contrary to what he said. What happened to Jesus during these thirty-six hours playing the dead?

The Gospels have chosen to crucify Jesus on a Passover Friday to symbolize the sacrifice of the paschal lamb and resurrected him on a Sunday to accommodate the day of the sun, which was a tradition already celebrated in Rome. And so too did Christianity adopt the twenty-fourth of December, Sol Invectus, as the artificial birth date of Jesus to make it identical with the preexisting pagan festival. The day of resurrection was also set to fit the Roman Sunday. The Shabbat was not canceled by Jesus, who always respected it, but by Paul much later, to avoid the opposition of the pagan slave owners and to adapt to the Roman custom of the day of the sun on Sunday. Resurrection on Sunday was invented to provide a basis for the passage from Shabbat to Sunday!

The Quran imposed Friday without any reason!

Islam, wanting to do like the two older religions, chose a special day, Friday, not for rest but for assembling. The Jewish Shabbat is based on the story of creation, and the Christian Sunday is based on the story of resurrection. The Muslim Friday is based on nothing, and is mentioned once without explanation in Sura (62): *"Believers, when you call to prayer on Friday, run forth, remember God and leave your affairs."* Nothing, no explanation! Why did Muhammad choose Friday? The Hadiths mention that Friday is a day of prayer but without any explanation other than copying Jews and Christians: Bukhari (13.1), *"Other people are after us to respect God, Jews next day and Christians the day after the next day . . ."* Is it only to distinguish himself from Judaism? Muhammad's followers invented a justification for this Friday by saying it is the day of the creation of Adam.

The Quran mentions the Jewish Shabbat dozens of times, and Sura (16.124) states: *"The Shabbat was appointed only for those who are fighting over."* And if devout Muslims do not quarrel, they should respect the Shabbat!

24

Fifth Commandment: honor your parents

Exodus (20.12) and Deuteronomy (5.16) say: *"Honor your father and your mother, that your days may be long . . ."* Exodus (21.15) and Leviticus (20.9) punish those who do not respect this commandment: *"Whoever strikes his father or his mother shall be put to death . . ."* Leviticus (19.32) demands: *"You shall rise up before the white hair, and honor the face of the old man, and fear your God. . ."*

This commandment seems very moral, but Abraham himself did not respect his parents when he left his father's house and idols. The three monotheistic religions harshly condemn anyone who leaves for another religion or adopts atheism. The Quran (21.51) described Abraham breaking the idols worshipped by his father except the biggest one. This story appears only in the Quran. From where did Muhammad receive it? Several recommendations of Proverbs, as (1.8) demand: *"Son, listen to your father's admonitions, do not forsake your mother's instructions."* It's beautiful, but why ignore the daughter?

The New Testament demands respect for parents. Ephesians (6.1) asks: *"Children, obey your parents . . . Honor your father and your mother . . ."* And also in 1 Timothy (5.8): *"If anyone does not provide for his relatives, and in particular, members of his household, he has denied the faith and is worse than a man without faith."* The Pharisees accused the disciples of Jesus in Mark (7.10) and Matthew (15.4): *"Why do your disciples transgress the tradition of the elders? For they do not wash their hands when they eat bread.' Jesus answered, 'And you, why do you transgress the commandment of God by your tradition? For God said, Honor thy father and thy mother. And the one who curses his father or his mother shall surely be put to death.'"* Jesus's answer, deliberately ignored by Christians and Jews, is that of an extremist, a Karaite before Karaism, who respects only the written law.

Yet Jesus the guru said the opposite in Luke (14.26): *"If anyone comes to Me and does not hate his father and mother, his wife, his children, his brothers and sisters and his own life also, he cannot be my disciple."* While in I John (4.20), Jesus says the opposite: *"If anyone says, I love God but hates his brother, he is a liar . . ."*

Jesus has not a single kind word for his mother, and in Mark (3.33): *"Who is my mother, and who are my brothers?"* Or when his mother tells him that there is no more wine at Cana (John 2.4), Jesus answered insolently, *"Woman, what is between me and you?"*

The struggle of his disciples for power explains the harshness of Jesus to his mother. The allusions to the beloved disciple and the appointment of Simon-Peter as the Church's stone would block the dynasty of Jesus's family. In Romans (13.1), Paul recommends respecting the authorities because *"there is no authority except from God, and the authorities that exist have been instituted by God."* This sentence is a key to being accepted by Roman authorities. But what would Paul have said about Hitler or Stalin? Have they been instituted by God?

Muslims often report a Hadith of Bukhari (52.248): *"A man came to the Prophet asking his permission to participate in jihad; The Prophet asked him: Are your parents alive? He replied by the affirmative and the Prophet said: Go to serve them."* The Quran (29) demands *"We ordered the man to be good to his parents,"* but under certain conditions: *"But if they force you to add what you do not know, do not obey them."* The Quran (9.23) asks the faithful: *"Do not be friends with your fathers and brothers if they disbelief in your faith. Those of you who take them for friends are guilty."* The Quran (1.169) rejects the respect of the parents when they are not Muslims, *"When they are told, 'Follow what God reveals,' they say, 'We follow the custom of our fathers.' And if their fathers had not understood, had not been properly guided . . ."* And in (58.22), *"Those who believe in God and the Last Day, you will not find them with the opponents of God and his apostle, even if they are their father, son, brother, or someone from their clan."* So honor your father and your mother, but only if they respect Islam!

An imam ordered a Christian freshly converted not to attend the funeral of his grandfather because, according to the Quran (9.84), *"Never will you pray over their dead, nor stand on their graves, because they did not believe in God and his Apostle, and their dead are wicked."*

In conclusion, the three religions preach respect for the father and the mother, but only on condition that they respect their religion. Do atheists or believers of other religions not have to honor their parents? Are there more atheists who abandon their elderly parents? No! The Fifth Commandment is not, therefore, a moral progress credited to the three religions.

25

Sixth Commandment: you shall not kill, Jesus not a pacific, jihad

The pope said on September 21, 2014, in response to the terrorist massacres of the Islamist State in Syria and Iraq: *"God cannot be an excuse to kill."* Even though one of His commandments is *"You shall not kill,"* the God of the Bible killed newborn Egyptian babies and innocent animals. Couldn't He have found another way to convince Pharaoh to let the Hebrews go? Why does He harden the heart of Pharaoh instead of softening it?

In Exodus (22.17), God orders the death of the witches. This same verse was used by the Inquisition between the sixteenth and seventeenth centuries to burn more than 100,000 witches in Germany and tens of thousands more in France.

God also caused the death of 3,000 Hebrews because of the golden calf. And then He ordered the extermination of thousands of men, women, and children during the Hebrew conquest of the Promised Land. In short, most of the verses in the Bible describe a god that is thirsty for blood, sacrifices, and punishment. This god is not a god of love but of hate and destruction! To all this criticism, rabbis explain that God is absolute good and that if He decided to kill newborns, we're too small to judge Him. They also say that God destroyed the people who stopped his light from shining on earth. By destroying the source of evil and a few thousand humans, He saved hundreds of thousands of others. But God did not have to use destruction!

Despite the Sixth Commandment, the Bible demands carnage

"You shall not kill" seems to be a great moral progress. This simple commandment is stated in Exodus (20) and repeated in Deuteronomy (5). These verses are used to justify the fight against abortion and euthanasia. However, in Hebrew it is written, *"You shall not assassinate,"* poorly translated to *"you shall not kill."* Yet the two verbs are different, and *"You shall not kill"* would mean the absolute prohibition of taking a life, whatever the reason may be. *"You shall not assassinate,"* on the other hand, means that it is forbidden to take the life of an innocent. So for the Bible, self-defense is permitted, while the killing of a thief or murderer or homosexual or witch is also permitted because they are not innocent. Note also that the prohibition does not concern animals and it is permitted to kill animals.

In Genesis (9.5): *"Whoever sheds man's blood, his blood be shed, for man was made in the image of God."* Even an animal that kills one person must be put to death. However, the first murderer, Cain, killed his brother Abel, yet was not put to death. Why? Was it just to keep the offspring of Adam and Eve or because this story is an addition aimed to insult the tribe of the Canaanim, who were enemies of Israel?

The law of retaliation, *"an eye for an eye, a tooth for a tooth,"* means that a murderer must pay through his blood and cannot avoid punishment by paying a fine. For Genesis (9.6) and Numbers (35.31): *"You will not accept ransom for the life of a murderer. If he is guilty and worthy of death, he must die."* The Babylonian law (and the Quran) allows the payment of a ransom instead of the life of the murderer. While the Torah regards human life as of divine essence, the Babylonian law considers the economic value.

As an adult, in Exodus (2.12), Moses sees an Egyptian striking a Hebrew, and he kills the Egyptian. Moses would be a killer who forbids killing. Is it possible then that the mighty Pharaoh accepts the ten plagues and remains unresponsive when he could easily have killed Moses and Aaron, or at least tried to kill them?

God Himself, who prohibits murder, ordered individual or collective assassination on every page of the Bible:

In Exodus (12.29), God *"slew all the firstborn of Egypt . . . and all the firstborn of the animals."* Why this collective punishment and why also on animals?

In Exodus (22.17), the witch, the one who had intercourse with an animal, and the one who sacrifices to other gods, must be put to death.

In Exodus (23.23), God sent his angel to exterminate the ancient inhabitants of the Promised Land, Amorreans, Hittites, Pherezeans, and Canaanites. Why and in what way have they sinned?

In Exodus (32.27), Moses came down and discovered a golden calf was made. He ordered all those who love God to kill the idolaters, *"that each of you use his sword and go in each tent camp to slay his brother, his friend, his parents . . . About 3,000 men died."* Moses, who prohibits murder, orders the mass murder of his own people but spares his brother Aaron, who was the manufacturer of this golden calf!

In Leviticus (20), homosexuals should be put to death, and those who use evocations and those who curse their parents and those who committed adultery and incest: *"If a man lives with a male in sexual cohabitation . . . Let them be put to death . . ."*

In Leviticus (24.16), *"He who blasphemes the name of God must be put to death, the whole community must stone him."*

In Numbers (1.51), *"Who would approach the tabernacle shall be put to death."*

In Numbers (14.9), *"Fear not the people of this country because they will be your food . . ."* And further, in (25.16): *"YHWH said to Moses: attack the Midianites and kill them because they attacked you first . . . They . . . slew all the males . . . And the Israelites took captive the Midianite women and their children . . . And Moses said: let all the women live . . . And now kill every male child and every woman who has cohabited with a man . . . And all the little girls that have not lived with a man, let them live for you."* So killing and raping ordered by God.

In Numbers (15.36), a man was gathering sticks during Shabbat, and Moses, hesitant, asked God, who orders him: *"This man should be put to death, the whole community will stone him outside the camp."* This was done. *"Whoever does any work on the Shabbat will be punished by death,"* according to Exodus (31.15).

In Numbers (25.1), God commands Moses to kill any Hebrew practicing idolatry, a massacre of 24,000 persons.

In Deuteronomy (2.34), *"We took then all cities . . . even women and children, we left them not a single survivor. We took livestock and plundered and conquered cities."*

In Deuteronomy (17.12), he who does not obey the priest or judge must be put to death.

In Deuteronomy (22.21), a girl who lost her virginity before marriage will be stoned to death, not the man she slept with!

In Deuteronomy (18.20), a prophet speaking on behalf of a foreign god, must die.

In Deuteronomy (13.17), *"If your brother . . . your son or daughter say to you I will serve other gods . . . Do not listen . . . instead, you'll have to destroy him. . ."*

In Deuteronomy (17.2), *". . . If a man or a woman . . . served other gods, and worshipped . . . the sun or the moon . . . you shall order an inquiry . . . that they die under stones."*

The book of Joshua is a long list of the genocide of all the peoples living in the Promised Land.

In Joshua (6): *"Jericho, the wall fell down . . . Men and women, young and old, all perished by the sword."*

In Joshua (8.1), God orders to burn the city of Ai and kill all the inhabitants.

In Joshua (19.47), the tribe of Dan passes the sword on all the inhabitants of Lechem.

In Judges (15.14), Samson kills a thousand Philistines with a donkey's jaw.

In Judges (20 and 21), the tribe of Benjamin was almost exterminated, and there were left only 600 men without females. In order for that the tribe to not disappear, it was necessary to find women for these males. The solution: kill all the inhabitants of a town, men, women, and children, except the virgins that will be given to Benjamin's males. The Israelites *". . . at Jabesh-Gilead, and killed the inhabitants by the sword, even the women and children,"* except *"400 girl virgins . . . and they were taken to the camp at Shiloh . . ."* Why was it necessary to kill all the inhabitants, including children, but leave the virgins alive? How are they less guilty than the children? Is it just to satisfy the sexual needs of the conquerors?

In I Samuel (6.19), *"God struck seventy men of Beth-Shemesh for looking into the ark,"* so punished by death for their curiosity.

Then in to I Samuel (6.6), he killed the poor Uzzah who *"rushed to the ark of the Lord, and held it for the oxen had slipped,"* killed for daring to prevent the ark from falling.

In Samuel (15.8), Saul *"took Agag, the king of Amalec, and killed all his people with the sword."*

In I Chronicles, King David ordered a census of his people *"displeasing to God... Getting angry against David, God did crack the plague and in Israel 70,000 men fell."* David made a mistake and 70,000 innocent men died?

All those who refuse to listen to the priests must be killed. In II Chronicles (15.12), Azariaou and the people of Judah and Benjamin *"promised by a solemn pact... that anyone who will not seek for the God of their fathers, would be punished by death,"* which led to the killing of all non-practicing Jews.

Isaiah (13, 15) and (14, 21) prophesied: *"their infants shall be dashed to pieces before their eyes... Their wives raped... Prepare the field for the carnage of the sons, because of the inequities of their fathers... From Babylon, I will destroy the name and track..."*

We can find other incentives to murder and hatred in Jeremiah (15.3), Ezekiel (9.6), and Hosea (9.11), not the love of a universal god for all his creatures but the hatred of a partial god for the enemies of his chosen people.

False prophets will be put to death according to Zechariah (13.3).

But in any discussion, Jewish sages will answer that according to the Talmud, *"He who destroys the life of a single human being, it is as if he had destroyed all mankind, and whoever saves a soul, it is as if he had saved the world."* It is beautiful, but the uncensored text specifies *"save a Jewish soul,"* limited and therefore immoral! In the Talmud, Sanhedrin (57a), if there is murder, whether the killing of a non-Jew by a non-Jew or that of a Jew by a non-Jew, there is a death penalty. But the killing of a non-Jew by a Jew is not punishable.

Jesus was not a pacifist despite the verses of the New Testament!

According to Christianity, the originality of Jesus is that he demands absolute love. But the true Jesus was different. Some verses paint Jesus as a pacifist. In Mark (12. 28), a scribe asked Jesus which is the most important commandment, Jesus answered: *"The most important one is this: 'Hear, O Israel, the Lord our God, the Lord is one . . .' The second is 'Love your neighbor as yourself.' There is no commandment greater than these."* The correct translation would be *brother-similar* and not *neighbor*. So Jesus preached love among the disciples, and like the Jews, limited love to members of the clan only.

However, in Mark (12.33 to 34), a scribe, so a Jewish scholar, says: *". . . and love your neighbor as yourself is worth more than all burnt offerings and sacrifices."* Love of neighbor has therefore not been invented by Jesus, but existed before him. Leviticus (19.17) orders: *"You will not hate your brother in your heart . . . And you must love your neighbor as yourself."* Deuteronomy (10.19) expands this love even to the foreigner because the Hebrews were foreigners in Egypt.

Jesus answered the question of Simon Peter, *"How often shall my brother sin against me and I forgive him? Is it seven times? Jesus answered: Not up to seven times, but seventy-seven times."* And further, in Matthew (5.38): *"You have heard that it was said, an eye for an eye, a tooth for a tooth; But I tell you . . . whoever strikes you on the right cheek, turn to him the other cheek. You have heard that it was said, 'Love your neighbor and hate your enemy.' But I say to you: Continue to love your enemies and pray for those who persecute you."*

These enemies are of course the Roman occupiers. So Jesus expands the command not only to the foreigners but also to enemies. This would be a real revolution, and for that phrase Jesus deserves the Nobel Prize for love.

But Jesus did not respect what he preached. He did not turn the other cheek to the servant of the high priest who slapped him, described by John (13.24), who plagiarized Plato, who wrote, long before the Gospels, to turn the other cheek to the enemy. Jesus declared in Matthew (5.22) that anyone who is angry against his brother shall be liable for it in hell. In Matthew (10.33), Jesus says: *"Whoever denies me before men, I will also deny him before my Father who is in heaven."* Where are mercy and forgiveness?

In Matthew (10.34), Jesus did not come by way of peace, but with a sword: *"Think not that I have come to send peace on earth: I came not to send peace, but a sword . . . I came to cause division . . ."* Then he cursed, in Matthew (11.20 to 22): *"And he began to rebuke . . . Woe to you, Bethsaida!"* Jesus therefore blesses cities that welcome him and curses those who don't. In Matthew (13.41 and 25.41), Jesus threatens to throw the sinners into the fires of hell.

Jesus is not entirely love! In Matthew (18.6), again he threatens, *"Whoever causes one of these little ones who believe in me to sin, it would be better for him if a millstone was hung around his neck, and he drowned at the bottom of the sea."* And in Matthew (21.19), Jesus does not contain his anger on a fig tree without fruits, when it is not even the season for figs, as noted in Mark (11,13). In Matthew (23.13 to 33) and (25.41): *"Woe to you, scribes and Pharisees... Serpents, offspring of vipers... Then he will say to those on his left, 'Depart from me, cursed! Into everlasting fire...'"* In Mark (16.16), *"He who does not believe will be condemned."* Where is the mercy of Jesus?

In Luke (7.7), what did Jesus say to the Roman officer whose role is to kill? Did he tell to him to disarm himself? No, he said that he has more faith than some Jews. And then in Luke (12.49), Jesus says: *"I came to cast fire upon the earth... Do you suppose that I came to give peace on earth? I tell you, not at all, but rather division..."* In Luke (22.36), Jesus said to his disciples: *"And he who has no sword sell his outer garment and buy one... then they said: Lord, here are two swords. He said to them, it is enough."* Why these swords if Jesus is peaceful?

In Luke (19.27), Jesus explains with a parable what to do to his enemies: *"But those mine enemies who did not want me to reign over them, bring them here and kill them before me."* This sentence is not from Jesus but from Paul, the true master of Luke, who said, according to I Corinthians (15.25): *"For he must reign until he has put all enemies under his feet."* Inspired by Psalm (110.1).

In John (18.36), Jesus, questioned by Pilate, answered: *"If my kingdom were part of this world, my servants would fight, so that I should not be delivered to the Jews."* So if Jesus was human like us, he and his followers would have used force just like other humans. Only the Evangelist John (18.10) described Peter, who during the arrest of Jesus, hits a Jew named Malchus with a sword.

Why all these contradictions? It is therefore evident that Jesus and his disciples were not pacifists. Romans would not have crucified a hippy who professed love and forgiveness, but have instead killed a rebel threatening the power of Rome and of the priests. His pacifism was added by the disciples in order to be accepted by the Roman authorities.

Paul, Peter, and hatred

The Essenians, long before Jesus and Paul preached nonviolence and promised: *"I will not pay evil with evil..."* and this until the day of vengeance which will make them masters of the world, and then, they will put to death the wicked. Paul, like them, talks peaceful tunes and demands in Romans (12.9) to move away from evil and do only good. Through the Evangelists, he also dressed Jesus as a pacifist, hoping that the time for vengeance will come. And in fact, it comes when the Church will be recognized as a state religion. But in the meantime, neither Paul nor the other disciples act as pacifists and do not tend the other cheek, do not love, but hate their enemy. In Acts (23.3), Paul, who received a blow on the mouth, cursed, *"God will strike you, you whitewashed wall."* And the description of Paul in Acts (8.3): *"Saul-Paul was ravaging the church, entering into every house; he dragged off men and women and put them in prison."*

Paul, violent before his conversion to Christianity, will remain violent, according to I Timothy (1.20) and Acts (13.11): *"Of whom are Hymenaeus and Alexander whom I sent to Satan that they may learn not to blaspheme ... A certain man, a sorcerer, a false prophet, a Jew named Bar-Jesus cursed ... Paul: Well, the hand of God is upon you, and you will be blind ..."* This is certainly not the teaching of love of the enemy!

Romans (1.27) condemns homosexuality: *". . . The men leaving the natural use of their women ... men with men ... and receiving the deserved payment for their error."* So death as punishment for homosexuals!

Peter-Simon the Rock is violent. In John (18.10): *"Then Peter-Simon, having a sword, drew it and stuck the high priest's servant named Malchus."* Also in Acts (5.1 to 35), the new Christians sold their goods and brought their money to the community. But *"A certain man named Ananias, with Sapphira his wife, sold his property, and in secret kept something of the price. His wife also knew, and he brought in a part, he laid it at the apostles' feet."* Peter got angry and rebuked them, then suddenly: *"Hearing this, Ananias fell down and died, and great fear came upon all who heard of it."* How did Ananias die? Naturally, Peter, the man with the knife, stabbed him in the belly to make an example and scared those who would try to cheat and would not bring all their goods. Then Peter called the wife of Ananias and asked for money. She hesitated a bit and *"at once, she fell at his feet and expired."* A second stab from Peter. Acts disguises the killings. Is it possible that Jesus, the God of Love, punished with death the couple who cheated and gave only 80 percent of their assets to the community and not 100 percent? These additional killings show that the words of Jesus, *"Love your enemy,"* is an addition by the disciples to be accepted by the Romans.

In conclusion, Jesus would have preached violence and hatred against the Roman and Jewish authorities. Paul realized that he may hate the Jews and be violent against those who refused conversion, but facing the Roman power he was obliged to use the temporary nonviolence copied from the Essenes. The Church, once in power, severely persecuted heretics and Jews. Inquisitions, crusades, pogroms, neutrality toward Nazism, acceptance of the death penalty are evidence that the Church has betrayed or ignored what it pretended to worship.

Hitler: For believers, it is not religion but atheism that kills, and without religion, we have Hitler, Stalin, and Mao. What about Hitler? Despite the subterfuge of the Church, Hitler was not an atheist or pagan but a Christian, baptized and raised as a good Catholic in Austria. He said about himself that he was *"Catholic and will always remain one."* Hitler drew his hatred against the Jews from Christianity, and this is clearly expressed in his famous book *Mein Kempf.* He stated that he acted according to the will of God the Creator and that *"in defending against the Jew, I am fighting for God."* According to *Mein Kempf* and Hitler's speeches *". . . The man . . . recognized these Jews for what they were and summoned men to fight against them . . . In boundless love as a Christian and as a man, I read through the passage which tells us how the Lord at last rose in His might and seized the scourge to drive out of the Temple 'brood of vipers and calculators.' As it was terrible, his fight for the world against the Jewish poison! . . . As a Christian . . . I have the duty to be a fighter for truth and justice . . . For as a Christian I have also a duty to my people."* Hitler was never condemned by the Christian Church. On the contrary, his birthdays were celebrated with great pomp.

And Stalin? He studied to be a priest but left after several years. What were the influences of these religious studies?

The Quran is against and for murder

As expected, the Quran is against killing at the beginning of the adventure of Muhammad but in favor of murder when victory is near. The Quran (5.32) says that life is sacred, *"We ordained for the children of Israel that whoever kills someone who has neither killed nor created disorder, it is as if he killed all men."* And (2.84): *"We made a covenant with you: do not pour the blood . . . And you are among those Jews who kill you . . . The payment of this conduct will only disgrace in this life . . ."* These verses are used to prove that Islam is opposed to murder.

Like the other two religions, the Quran (17.32) seems to prohibit killing: *"Do not kill anyone, God forbid . . ."* But unfortunately adds, *"Unless there is just cause. Whoever is killed unjustly, we give the right to revenge . . ."* This verse allowing revenge and murder for a just cause is usually hidden by the Muslims. This is the famous *kitman* or lie by omission. Just like the other two religions, the Quran also has verses that deal with love. Verses (41, 34) and (13. 22) say: *"prevent evil with good."* These verses will often be quoted by Muslims to convert westerners. They will also bring out the verse (2.256), which says: *"no compulsion in religion."* But these few gentle verses are contradicted by a long list of other verses and by history.

Islam and the massacres of unbelievers

Contrary to what President Obama thinks, the word *Islam* does not mean *Salam* or peace but *to submit or be submitted to the one and only God.* Muslim terrorists who blow themselves up are in fact believers following the texts of the Quran. Sura (2.190) exhorts the believer to *jihad*: *"Fight in the cause of Allah . . . Kill them wherever you find them . . . Kill them . . . is the wage of the believers . . ."* Verses (3.158 to 163): *". . . Those who were killed in the path of God, do not believe them dead, they live close to their Lord and do not lack anything. The grace that God gives them fills them with joy . . ."*

Verses (4.74): *"And those who fight to the path of God, if they are killed or if they are victorious, we will give a boundless wage."*

Verses (4.89): *"Do not take friends home before they flee in the way of God. If they turn renegades, seize them and kill them wherever you find them . . ."*

The Quran describes the attacks and killings of caravans by Muhammad and his men during the month of Ramadan, which shocks his neighbors. A sudden revelation in (2.217) comes to his rescue: *"They ask you about the sacred month: can we fight? Answer: fight . . ."* In (3.12), the unbelievers *". . . will be defeated and gathered into hell."* Verse (8.68), *"a prophet has not to take prisoners before he prevailed on the ground,"* or *"massacring"* according to another translation.

Sura 9 spreads hate: *"And when the sacred months have passed, then kill the polytheists wherever you find them and capture them and besiege them and wait for them at every place of ambush. But if they should repent, establish prayer, and give zakah, let them go on their way. Indeed, Allah is Forgiving and Merciful."*

(47.4): *"So when you meet those who disbelieve in battle, strike their necks till you have inflicted slaughter upon them, then secure their bonds, and either confer favor afterwards or ransom them until the war lays down its burdens."*

The Quran preaches hate toward the infidels, Jews, Christians, polytheists, and nonbelievers and encourages good Muslims to kill them. Islam is not a religion of peace; it's a religion of war, and Muhammad is its chief warrior. Unlike Judaism that wants to be the religion of an elite, Islam, on the other hand, wants to convert all of humanity. The following verses prove that fact: (21.107) and (34. 28) *"And We have not sent you, except comprehensively to mankind..."*

In order to spread Islam throughout the world, dozens of verses call Muslims to *jihad* and the beheading of infidels.

(2.191): *"Indeed. Allah does not like transgressors. And kill them..."* (2.216): *"Fighting has been enjoined upon you."* (2.244): *"And fight in the cause of Allah."* (3.56): *"And as for those who disbelieved, I will punish them..."* (3.151): "*We will cast terror into the hearts of those who disbelieve."*

(4. 74): *"And he who fights in the cause of Allah and is killed or achieves victory, We will bestow upon him a great reward."* (4. 89): *"But if they turn away, then seize them and kill them..."*

We could also quote the following verses: (4. 95 and 105), (5. 33), (8.12), (15.39 and 57), (9.5, 14, 20, 29, 38, 41, 73, 88, 111, and 123), (17.16), (18.65), (21.44), (25.52), (33. 61), (47.3 and 35), (48.17 and 29), and more. And the Hadith of Bukhari (52.177): *"Allah's Apostle said, time will not be established until you fight the Jews, and the stone behind which a Jew is hiding will say: O Muslim! There is a Jew behind me..."*

(52.220): *"Allah's Apostle said, I was made victorious with terror."*

(52.258): To the question of whether it is permissible to attack the pagans at night at the risk of accidentally killing women and children, Muhammad answered yes.

And so it is permitted to kill women and children while attacking your enemies and that is exactly what the terrorists are practicing with their bombs. However, Muslims will quote Bukhari (52.258): *"a woman was killed, and Allah's Apostle forbade the killing of women and children."* Which unveils the two faces of the Prophet Muhammad. Tabari (9.69) explains that killing was a common thing for Muhammad. Several Hadiths clearly state that killing non-believers was recommended by Muhammad himself. In fact, Muhammad was a military chief who led expeditions, seized cities, massacred, raped, and enslaved many people like the ones of Quresh.

Hadith Muslim (37.6666) reports Muhammad's words: *"No Muslim will die without Allah admitting in his place a Jew or a Christian in the fire of hell."*

Bukhari (84.57), *"He who leaves the religion of Islam, kill him."*

Muslim (1.33): *"The Messenger of Allah said: I have been ordered to fight all unbelievers until they recognize that there is only one God, Allah, and Muhammad is his prophet."*

And (19.4294) *"When you're running into your enemies who are pagans . . . invite them to accept Islam . . . if they refuse to adhere to Islam, demand from them the jizya (tax) . . . If they refuse to pay the tax . . . fight them."*

For Muslims, the world is divided into two: *Dar-al-Salam* (where Islamic or Sharia law reigns) and *Dar-al-Harb* or House of War (where peace will only come once everyone there has converted to Islam).

Muslims say that Judaism and Christianity have also engaged in horrific wars of conquest. It is true, but for those two religions, this belongs to the past and there should be no fear that Christianity or Judaism will go on the war path. Islam, on the other hand, is another different story and Muslims still think of conquering non-Muslim countries.

After the attacks on the Twin Towers in New York City, ex-president Bush and the West explained that they weren't at war with moderate Islam, which they said is a religion of peace. It is still "politically correct" to say that terrorism is the work of "fundamentalists" or of those who have not "fully understood" the Quran. That is pure fantasy, or worse, a cowardly approach of a hopeless western society.

Some Muslims wrongly believe that Islam is capable of being modern, laic, and moderate. The Quran has too many passages of hate and violence and is clear about the fate of all those who don't accept Islam as their true and unique religion. People weren't converted to Islam through dialogue but by the sword and the tax of the *jizyah* imposed on non-Muslims. There isn't and will never be a moderate Islam because there is only one Quran.

Islam has done such a great job at converting people that some of them have forgotten that they weren't Arab or Muslim, and became the most extremist Muslims. Nobody mentions the conquest of North Africa, the Berber massacres and enslavement of their women, the conquest of Persia and of India and the massacre of the Buddhists, the forced conversion of children of east Europe and their recruitment as janissaries. From 2012 to 2015, Christians in Iraq were forced to either convert to Islam or be exterminated.

When a non-Muslim converts to Islam out of fear or under pressure from the *jizyah*, he cannot leave Islam or he will be put to death. This explains why Islam has managed to spread so successfully in the conquered populations. Entire peoples, Muslims today should investigate how and why their ancestors embraced the faith. Was it with conviction or by force or to avoid paying the *jizyah*?

The status of the Dhimmitude and the *jizyah*

Certain Muslims want to make us believe that the Jews have always been treated fairly by Islam. They forget that Muhammad had a history of killing Jews. (just look it up in the Quran). Muhammad sought the support of the Jews, but when they refused to accept him as a prophet, he massacred and enslaved Jewish tribes: (13, 26), *"And He brought down those who supported them among the People of the Scripture from their fortresses and cast terror into their hearts [so that] a part you killed and you took captive a part. And He caused you to inherit their land and their homes and their properties."* In other words, murder, looting, theft, and rape. The status of *dhimmi* was ordered by the Sura (9.29): *"Fight those who do not believe in Allah or in the Last Day and . . . who do not adopt the religion of truth from those who were given the Scripture - [fight] until they give the jizyah willingly while they are humbled."*

Bukhari (53.392): *". . . The Prophet said, 'Let's go see the Jews,' and then we went to Bait-ul-Midras. He told them, 'If you embrace Islam, you will be out of danger. . . This land belongs to Allah and His Apostle, and I want to drive you from the land . . . The world belongs to Allah and his prophet.'"*

In Bukhari (53.386): *"Our Prophet, the Messenger of God gave us the command to fight you until you adore Allah and only Allah or you give the jizyah."*

In 628, Muhammad established the *dhimmi* status to non-Muslim monotheists (Jews, Christians, Sabeans, and Zoroastrians) when he conquered the city of Khaybar and obliged the inhabitants to pay a tax. (He also took two beautiful Jewish women as captives.) The *dhimmis* were forced to stand in the presence of a Muslim. They were forbidden to build new churches and synagogues, to bear arms, to ride horses, only donkeys. They were also forbidden to drink alcohol or eat pork. Sometimes, they were forced to wear distinctive clothing such as a large belt around their waist or a yellow, red, or black hat, or to wear little bells while at bathhouses.

For many Muslims, Khaybar represents a great victory over Jews, and some dream of a similar victory during our century. That is why Hezbollah named *Khaybar* one of its missiles and Iran used this name for one of its guns. In 2011, during the Gaza blockade, one of the flotillas named *Pacifica* was singing, *"Khaybar, Khaybar,"* proving that their intentions were not peaceful.

In the territories conquered by Muslims, Jews and Christians had to pay a special tax, the *jizyah*. This tax guaranteed their protection. With the expansion of the Muslim empire, a new code was established by Omar, Muhammad's son-in-law and second caliph. The code varied according to the mood of the ruling government.

Later, many *dhimmis* converted to Islam to avoid paying these high taxes. Muhammad used the *jizyah* to finance his wars. Today, Muslims such as the Taliban and Hamas, would like to reinstate the *jizyah* and the status of *dhimmi* for non-Muslims as part of the Sharia law.

The Quran, like the Bible, makes the difference between who is allowed to be killed and who it is forbidden to kill. (4.92): *"A believer should not kill a believer . . . who kills a believer willingly, his reward will be hell forever."* But in fact, a Muslim can kill another Muslim for adultery or if he wants to quit Islam.

Muhammad and his troops killed all the 700 Jews from the tribe of Bani Qurayza, including teens having pubic hair. All the women were taken as slaves or sold as slaves to provide weapons to Muhammad.

The Quran allows revenge and even killing the one who killed or who sowed disorder and justifies all possible murders. Verse (2.178) recalls the famous law of retaliation, *"eye for an eye, tooth for tooth,"* and adds, *"But the one to whom his brother forgives a little, one who pursues the custom and pays willingly,*" and so retaliation can be avoided towards a believer of Islam.

Many other verses of the Quran incite hatred and murder:

(2.191), "*. . . God does not like transgressors. Kill them wherever you find them . . .*"

(4.89 and 91), The infidels "*. . . if they turn back . . . kill them . . .*"

(5.33), "*Those who make war against God and His Messenger . . . Their salary will be killed or crucified or have a hand and the opposite foot cut . . .*"

(8.17), "*It is not you but God who killed them (the unbelievers).*"
(9.5), "*When the sacred months have passed, slay the unbelievers wherever you find them.*"

(33.61), "*The hypocrites . . . cursed wherever they are, they will be . . . killed.*"

(47.4): "*When you meet the unbelievers, smite their necks and slaughter them . . .*"

A Hadith confirms that murder is permitted by the Quran: "*When Allah's Apostle had cut off the feet and hands of those who had stolen his camels . . . Allah scolded him and told him: punishment of those who wage war against . . . Allah is the execution.*" Or narrated by Muslim, "*Allah's Apostle stoned to death a person of the tribe of Banu Aslam . . . .*" Another hadith narrated by Bukhari (84.57): "*He who leaves the religion of Islam, kill him.*"

In January 2012, the Mufti of Jerusalem preached by citing the Quran: "*killing the Jews is a blessing.*" Do we have to prosecute the Mufti for encouragement to murder or to prohibit the source, which is the Quran? For if a writer or journalist wrote that we should kill this category of persons, his book would be banned in all western countries.

Jihad or holy war is idealized by the Quran

The West separates the acceptable moderate Islam from these fundamentalist fanatics who are terrorists and jihadis. Now it is not some crazy extremists but the text founder of Islam, the Quran, which preaches hatred and *jihad*. In Quran (9.33), *"God sent His Apostle as a guide to the true religion..."* So no tolerance, Islam is superior to other religions and must dominate and delete them. In a Hadith of Bukhari (3.63), Muhammad said that he is Allah's apostle sent for all mankind. Muslims deceive Westerners, stating that suicide is condemned by Islam and giving a Hadith as evidence. Indeed, if suicide is a sin, suicide attacks would be too. However, the aim of the attack is the death of infidels, which is permitted and encouraged by the Quran, and by Muhammad, who promised paradise to those who die in the path of God and fighting the infidels. So it is obvious that believers seek the reward of paradise.

When Muhammad's followers attacked a caravan, seized the booty, and gave a fifth to the prophet, they hesitated because this murder and looting took place during the Holy Month. Fortunately, a divine revelation, (2.217) provided the answer: *"Fighting in this month is serious, but being unfaithful to God... is more serious."* And so Muhammad allowed the holy war, the *jihad*, even during the holy month.

The martyrdom of one who dies for his faith is idealized in (2.169) and (47.4) and (4.74): *"Those who were killed in the path of God, do not believe they are dead. They live close to God, they lack nothing... God will admit them to the garden... Those who fight to the path of God, if they are killed or if they are victorious, we give them a boundless wage."* A jihadist will not die when he blows himself up in the middle of the infidels, he will to go to heaven!

In (9.111), *"God buys the believers their souls and their properties so that they have the garden. They fight in the way of God. They kill or are killed. Promise of God in the Torah, the Gospel and the Koran."* Also, (61.10): *"You believe in God and his apostle, you fight all hands in the path of God... God will make you into gardens..."*

The jihad is ordained by the Qur'an. It is necessary to kill unbelievers. These fighters for God, these *shaidims*, according to (3.168 and 195), will go to heaven. The promise of paradise is repeated in (4.75), (4.95), and (61.10). Also read (2,186). Verse (8.67): *"A prophet is not required to take prisoners before they prevailed on the ground,"* as the prophet kills the infidels unless they convert to Islam. And according to (9.123), *"Fight the unbelievers who are in your neighborhood and they find you hard."*

The strategy of Muhammad, acting under the instructions of God, is this, (47.35): *"Do not ask peace when you are stronger."* This means that we must continue the war and massacres if you have it. If the Arab states had been stronger than Israel in the last five wars, would they have ordered a ceasefire or a truce? No, Israel cannot afford one defeat!

Other verses allow murder:

> (2.191): *"God does not love transgressors. Kill them wherever you find them . . . their death is the wage of the unbelievers."*

> Or (4.89): *"Do not take friends among the infidels until they flee in the way of God. If they turn renegades, seize them and slay them wherever you find them."* And also (4.91) and (5, 33): *"Those who wage war against God and His Messenger . . . Their wage is to be killed or crucified or have a hand and the opposite foot cut . . ."*

> (8.12 to17): *". . . the unbelievers, strike them in the neck . . . You did not kill them, it is God who killed them."* (33.61): *"The hypocrites will stay longer . . . your neighbors . . . cursed wherever they are, they will be caught and killed."*

Jihad, suicidal terrorists stuffed with explosives, and holy war are not, as some politicians assert cautiously, the product of fundamentalist or extremist Islam, but rather are the natural result of the texts of the Qur'an as the verses quoted above and many others prove. Some Muslims will tell you that conversion by force is forbidden by Islam and will quote the verse (2.256*): "no compulsion in religion."* They forget to quote the later verses (9.5 and 11 and 29) that preach: *"Once past the sacred months, kill the unbelievers . . . if they repent, make prayer and pay the alms, let them free rein . . . Fight them until they pay the tribute . . ."* These verses and many Hadiths written after the victories of Muhammad confirm that it is the duty of the Muslim to convert "unbelievers" by force or kill them.

But there is a third way of survival: the *jizya* or tax paid by Jews and Christians. See also verses (48.28): *"the true religion, for the triumph of any religion.*" Or (4.95): "*God puts fighters over those who remain at home.*" Or (9.39), "*If you are not going to fight, God will strike you with a horrible torment.*" Therefore, in great disorder, the Quran allows and even encourages murder and genocide of those who do not believe in Islam.

Paradise is described as an orgy of sex and food, and the young Muslim, frustrated in his earthly life, will blow himself up to receive his reward in heaven. Jihad, hatred, and incitement to murder are not external to Islam, but instead are the heart of Islam. When a French Muslim indoctrinated in Afghanistan massacred French Muslim soldiers and Jewish children, an imam replied that the killer had acted contrary to the Muslim faith and gave as proof that he had also killed Muslims. But the verse (2,217) condemns those who left their religion, as probably the soldiers of Muslim origin had done, "*those who turn away from their religion (Islam) will forever . . . Fire hosts.*" Many Hadiths confirmed the death penalty for apostasy or quitting Islam. Bukhari (9.83.17) and (9.84.57): "*The blood of a Muslim may not be paid for that . . . One that moves away from Islam*" and "*one who changes his religion (Islam) kill him.*" So the killer acted in accordance with Islam by killing not only Jewish children, but also the ex-Muslim soldiers suspected of having quit Islamic behavior! Besides, several Islamic countries punish apostasy by imposing death.

Jihad aims to transform the Dar al Harb into Dar el Islam, and every Muslim is obliged to participate in the jihad until the whole world becomes Muslim. Muslims explain that jihad has a philosophical side, yet Hadiths about jihad only describe the war, looting, and the distribution of the spoils, such as Bukhari (1.2.24): "*The Apostle said: I have been ordered to fight the people until they say, no one should be worshiped except Allah. If he says that, if he prays our prayers . . . then his blood and his property will be sacred to us . . .*" Or (52.46): "*Allah guarantees that the mujahidin enter Paradise if he is killed . . . You will fight the Jews until they hide behind stones . . . Kill him.*"

In Muslim (4320), where a woman was killed in a fight, Muhammad "*forbidden to kill women and children.*" This Hadith is always reported to present the moderate and progressive face of Islam, but is contrary to the following Hadith (4321), which says: "*when questioned on polytheistic women and children killed during the night raid, Muhammad said, they are of them,*" and allows the death of women children and idolaters.

26

Seventh Commandment: adultery, King David, Quran, and adultery

In July 2012, Westerners were "outraged" by the video of an adulterous Afghan woman executed by the Taliban. Yet the Taliban acted in full compliance of the laws of the Bible and the Quran! In Exodus (20.14), *"do not commit adultery!"* In Leviticus (20.10): *"If a man commits adultery with the wife of another man, with his neighbor's wife, the adulterer and the adulteress must be put to death . . ."* And no forgiveness is possible. The application of the Seventh Commandment would lead to millions of deaths. Are believers of the three religions aware of this? Is the Seventh Commandment an obligation of loyalty in marriage?

Abraham offered his wife to Pharaoh, so did his son Isaac

Abraham, the founding father of the three religions, would be a liar and a pimp. In Genesis (12.11) and (20.1), he said to his wife Sarah, already sixty-five years old: *"You're a beautiful woman, when the Egyptians will see you, they will say she is his wife, and they will kill me . . . Say that you are my sister so that I will be treated well because of you."* When they arrived in Egypt, in fact, Abraham said that Sarah is his sister, and he was well treated and even received *"sheep, oxen, donkeys, servants . . ."* while Sarah was brought to the house of Pharaoh, who took her for his wife, which means he slept with Sarah. Pharaoh then let go of Sarah and Abraham, now *"very rich in cattle."*

Abraham repeated the same lie to King Abimelech, who also took Sarah, now about ninety years old but still very attractive (?). Fortunately, God appeared before the king slept with Sarah. Abraham said to the king that Sarah is his half-sister and received livestock and slaves he could not refuse.

To avoid making Abraham a liar, a solution had to be found. Abraham explains to King Abimelech (Genesis 20.12): *"In fact, she is my sister, the daughter of my father, but not the daughter of my mother, and she belongs to me as a wife."* This marriage is forbidden by Deuteronomy (27.22): *"Cursed be he who lives with his sister, daughter of his father or the daughter of his mother."* But this curse doesn't apply to Abraham because this rule was given only much later by Moses. If Sarah was Abraham's half-sister, why the verse (11.31) of Genesis:

"Terah took Abram his son, Lot the son of Haran, his grandson, and Sarai his daughter-in-law, wife of Abram"? Terah should have mentioned that Sarai was his daughter.

Isaac, described by the Quran (37.112) as an *"honest prophet,"* like his father, said that his wife Rebecca is his sister and *"she was almost taken as a wife by one of the people of the Philistine king Abimelech."* Here, unlike the story of Abraham, Isaac necessarily lied because Rebecca is not his sister or half-sister and Isaac cannot be justified by saying that he was *"afraid to die because of her."* These three stories, two about Abraham and one about Isaac, seem to be a repetition of the same legend.

Abraham, under pressure from the jealous Sarah, sent away Hagar and Ishmael, his first son. A second son, Isaac, was now born, and Hagar and Ishmael are pushed into the desert. Like all of us, the rabbis felt that the attitude of Abraham and Sarah was not very moral, and to appease the guilt, they invented two fictions: that Ishmael was an idolater, and that a few years later Abraham took back Hagar and renamed her Keturah, and had other children with her. Genesis (25.1) gives the names of the children of Abraham and Keturah as Zimrane and Yokchan. This fiction, invented to soften the cruelty of Abraham and Sarah, fails because the text states that Abraham took another wife without any mention of Hagar or of Ishmael, and Keturah is not Hagar renamed.

Lot, the last righteous man of Sodom, is also a pimp and a liar

In Genesis (19.8), Lot welcomes two messengers of God and gives them shelter, but the inhabitants of Sodom gather around his house and ask to *"know"* these foreigners, which means having sex with them. Lot, placing hospitality above all, tells the crowd, *"Look, I have two daughters who have not known man . . . make of them what you wish . . ."* Now a little further, *"Lot went out to speak to his sons-in-law, husbands of his daughters."* These "in-laws" contradict previous affirmation of the virginity of his two daughters, unless Lot has other girls who are married. But later, it is confirmed that Lot has only two daughters. *"Stand up, take your wife and your two daughters . . . And his wife and two daughters . . ."* So Lot, the last fair man of Sodom, is a liar willing to sacrifice his two daughters to the crowd hungry for sex.

God destroyed Sodom and saved Lot, his wife, and two daughters. Where are the in-laws? The famous commentator Rashi explains that Lot had four girls, two who were married and two who are virgins. But there is no indication that Lot had four daughters, only two. This explanation of Rashi aims to save the contradiction, but is not convincing, because the biblical text is clear. Other wise men gave a better explanation. They said these sons-in-law would be future husbands of Lot's daughters, hence their virginity remained intact. But if they were promised, why does Lot offer his daughters? Other details that show the inconsistency of the stories: Where did Lot obtain his flock? What happens to this flock? The Sodom region is unsuitable for farming. Why does Lot, the shepherd, end up in the city of Sodom? Lot asks the angels to not send him to the mountain (19.19), but the nearby town is in the mountain (19.30).

Then the daughters of Lot got him drunk night after night, slept with him, and gave birth to the ancestors of the Moabites and Ammonites. Lot was spared by God because he was the last of the righteous and he was in fact only a bare drunkard who had incestuous relations with his two daughters. Where does the wine come from? How can a drunkard who could not recognize his daughters have sexual relations with them? Lot's daughters were wrong when they said that there is no man on earth because the city of Zohar is nearby.

In the Quran (21.74) and (27.56), Lot *"was among the righteous,"* and nothing is said about his drunkenness and incest with his two daughters.

Faced with this distortion between Lot in the Bible and in the Quran, Muslims are obliged to say that the Bible has been falsified.

Adultery during the time of the Bible is not the same as in our time

Our understanding of adultery (fidelity in marriage, exclusive romantic and sexual relations) is not that of the Bible, where polygamy is widespread and the men had sex with their wives and also with concubines, slaves, and prostitutes. Abraham, who had a child, Ishmael, with his slave Hagar, is not an isolated case.

Having sex with the wife of a man of the same clan would lead to hatred and violence. It is the same as stealing the donkey of his neighbor. Proverbs (6.23) compares the thief of a loaf of bread to a man who steals the wife of his neighbor. This commandment against adultery is a repetition of the Tenth Commandment, which forbids coveting someone else's property or wife. It actually means: *"you shall not take a woman who already belongs to your neighbor,"* as you will not take his ass, his robe, and his property.

Adultery in the Bible is a violation of the exclusive right of the husband to his wife. The woman, being the property of the man, has no rights and there is no reciprocity. The man who commits adultery with a married woman should be punished only because he has violated the property of another male.

Leviticus (18.20) is another affirmation of the Seventh Commandment: *"Do not sleep with the wife of your similar!"* Many translations use the term "neighbor," but this is incorrect, because the correct term would be "from the same clan or people," allowing sleeping with a married woman if she belongs to the enemy or to another country or if she is a slave. So contrary to what believers think, rape is permitted if it is done on a foreign woman.

In Leviticus (20.11), *"If a man commits adultery with the wife of another man, with his neighbor's wife, both the man and the adulteress must be put to death."* No details if the woman was consenting or forced, and this neighbor's wife, even if she was raped, must be put to death for adultery. Leviticus (19.20) says: *"If a man lies with a slave, engaged to another man . . . they will not be put to death because she was not free. And he will bring up for his fault . . . a ram . . . and the sin he has committed will be forgiven."* The problem is only a question of male ownership. So if a married man sleeps with an unmarried woman there is no adultery and no punishment. There is adultery only if a man, married or not, sleeps with a woman married to a man of the same clan. A married man can have extramarital sex with a single woman or widow, a divorced woman, or a married foreign woman or a slave. All these cases are not considered adultery!

Thus the attitude of Abraham, Isaac and Lot can be explained as follows: these men have let their property for a short time to Pharaoh, the Philistines, or the people of Sodom, who are not from the clan of Abraham. All three take back their possessions without being punished. Joseph's story is a bit awkward. He refused to commit adultery with Potiphar, the wife of his master, saying in Genesis (39.9): *"How can I commit a great trouble and sin against God?"* But adultery with a woman who is not part of the clan would not be a sin against God in the Torah. The Talmud, Sanhedrin 52b confirms that adultery with the wife of a Gentile is not subject to death because Moses prohibited adultery with "the wife of your similar," and a Gentile is not Hebrew's similar.

The adulterous Jewish married woman must be put to death without any possible forgiveness, for her adultery is not only an affront to her husband but also to God, and so the husband cannot forgive his wife. Faced with this moral inequality, rabbis answer that at the wedding, part of the soul of the husband goes into the soul of the woman, but not the other way around. Thus, if a woman cheats on her husband and has a relationship with another man, there would be different fractions of souls in her that would cause a problem. Is it through the sexual act that the husband sends a fraction of his soul or is it by legal marriage? It is said that it is when the bridegroom puts the ring on the finger of his wife that a fraction of his soul goes to the wife and would return to the husband in a divorce, this explanation must be rejected, because putting a ring on a finger cannot transfer soul. In addition, if the fraction of the soul of the husband goes into the woman when he puts the ring on her finger, there should be no problem since the wife committing adultery would not be getting a new ring from her lover. So does this transfer of soul happen during sex? Does it happen during each act? These explanations from rabbis do not hold water, but allow a man to have relationships with several women!

Yet the Bible contains two cases of adultery that have gone unpunished: The first is the one of Reuven, who committed adultery with Bilhah, his father's concubine. They had to be put to death, but the law was set much later by Moses.

The second case is King David, who should have known about the ban on adultery.

King David committed adultery in the biblical sense and murder

He is the second king after Saul and would have ruled the united kingdom of Judah and Israel between 1010 and 970 BC for nearly forty years, the golden age of the Hebrew monarchy. In the New Testament, King David is the ancestor of Jesus. The Quran reveres his wisdom by mentioning garbled extracts from the Jewish Bible, but there is no word about the rape of Bathsheba and other crimes of David.

In II Samuel (11), David *"was walking on the roof of the royal house, he saw a woman bathing who was very beautiful..."* He was informed that she is the wife of Uriah the Hittite, an officer of his army. And despite this, David *"sent people to look for her... and he lay with her... the woman conceived, and she told David: I am pregnant."* So David brought back from the battlefield Uriah the officer, not to confess his sin and ask for forgiveness, but to deceive him again by pushing him to go to bed with his wife, who was already pregnant, in order to make him believe that he, Uriah, was the father of the future baby. But Uriah is a humble officer and did not allow himself the luxury of sleeping in his house while his soldiers fought.

Plan A did not work, so David wrote a letter to the chief of his army. He sent the note through Uriah himself (who will not read the letter). In the letter, David ordered to send this loyal and exemplary officer to death. Uriah was killed, along with several men whose lives did not matter to David. Bathsheba became David's wife and bore him a son. All these reprehensible actions are perpetrated by this king glorified by Jews, Christians, and Muslims. On the contrary, he would have been sentenced to death by the biblical laws or to life imprisonment by any civil court. How do religious explain this distortion?

Some rabbis say that Uriah was not even Jew, but Hittite, and therefore there is no adultery since the ban exists only towards "your brother." But this is false, and Uriah was certainly a convert because he was one of David's officers, he was the husband of Bathsheba, and has a Hebrew name, which translates to *God is my light*.

So the Talmud found another answer and said in Shabbat (56a) and Ketubot (9b) that at the time of David the soldiers going to war gave to their wives an act of preventive divorce in order not to leave them as widows indefinitely if they die in combat without witnesses. Therefore, the marriage of Bathsheba would have been cancelled before she even had sex with David, who would have had an affair with a divorced woman, which was allowed. This answer is wrong, because when David asked about Bathsheba, *"they replied, Bathsheba is the daughter of Eliam, the wife of Uriah the Hittite,"* and the text contains the words *spouse* and *her house*, leaving no doubt that Uriah is married to Bathsheba.

If Uriah was divorced, could he go to his ex-wife and sleep with her whenever he wanted? If Uriah was divorced, King David would not have said to him, *"Enter your house . . ."* and Uriah would not have replied with *"lie with my wife,"* and all this without mentioning that she is divorced. On the second night, the king got Uriah drunk to bring him to his house and sleep with his wife. Why? And also, why would David ask Uriah why he has not slept in his house, the one he owned with Bathsheba, if they were divorced? Finally, if Bathsheba was divorced, why does David wait for the announcement of the death of Uriah before taking her home?

This rule on preventive divorce is also impractical. Let's suppose that Uriah gets divorced before going to war, like David's defenders claim. So the beautiful Bathsheba would be free. Sex with another man would bring up the issue of a baby, so what will happen when the husband returns alive from the battle? It is therefore mandatory that the wife has not had sex with another man. In addition, a sexual relationship with a woman, even divorced, must ensure that the paternity of the future baby is clear. Yet it is not the case, because David has wasted no time. If with this sexual relationship with the ex-wife of a soldier a baby was born, we would not know who the father is. Was it David or Uriah? David wanted Uriah to sleep with his wife to cover up the pregnancy.

All these problems show that the preventive divorce is impossible and invented to exonerate David! This rule is not found in the Bible; otherwise, thousands of cases should have been noted. Deuteronomy (20.7) defines certain rules for the soldiers, *"If someone promised marriage to a woman and has not yet married, he will leave and return to his home, because he could die in battle and another man would marry her."* But not a word about preventive divorce, which is an invention to exonerate David. If this rule existed, why is it never mentioned throughout the Bible? Also, why is this law no longer applied? And if that preventive divorce rule was canceled, when, by whom, why, and who had the right to cancel it? The rabbis confirm that they know nothing about it.

In II Samuel (12), the prophet Nathan tells David the story of *"two men, one rich and the other poor... who only had a little lamb... and the rich man... took the sheep of the poor man and served it to the guest who had come to visit him...."* Furious at what he heard, David exclaimed that this rich man deserves death. Nathan explains to him that he, David, is the rich man who took the wife of Uriah the Hittite, and explains to David, *"You have slain by the sword Uriah the Hittite and taken his wife for yourself...YHWH... will raise up evil against you, your own home, will take your wives and give them to others who will lie with them in the sight of the sun."* David is illogically forgiven, but still someone has to pay, *"the child who is born to you shall die."* If David is innocent as proclaimed by the Talmud, why cause the death of this baby? An innocent baby is put to death while the cheating David continues to live! God's justice is detestable. Adultery is punishable by death, except when it comes to King David!

Instead of punishing David with death, *"the Lord then brought a plague to Israel... 70,000 men died."* The culprit was not injured but 70,000 innocent people lost their lives. Where is the justice of God? Oddly enough, the Book of Chronicles tells in detail the life of David but is silent on his cheating. Jewish sages and also Christian pastors wanted to exonerate David, ancestor of the Messiah, and claimed that Bathsheba, missing her husband who was in the war, baited David by taking her bath naked and encouraging the king's advances.

In the Quran, all the prophets, including David, must be pure, and Islam cannot accept David's adultery and the episode with Bathsheba. Yet Sura (38.22) did not understand the story or wanted to hide the misdeeds of David, and transformed the metaphor of the prophet Nathan, which was poorly digested by Muhammad! Two litigants came to ask David for his arbitration because one had ninety-nine sheep, and the other only one. *"And David knew that we wanted to judge him. He asked forgiveness from his Lord, he fell to his knees and repented."* What did he want to repent from if not from adultery, which Muhammad wanted to ignore? The Muslims' answer that the little sin of David was that he watched Bathsheba bathing, and having learned that she was married, he called Uriah and asked him to divorce her so he could marry her. All this contrary to the biblical writings. Muhammad has not read any of the books himself, but the stories were orally transmitted to him by his Jewish and Christian friends. They obviously have hidden from him the fact that their great king and ancestor of the Messiah had committed adultery. The three religions, therefore, agree to erase the sin of adultery committed by David, though it is clearly mentioned in the Bible.

The first book of Kings gives two slightly different judgments about King David. In I (14.8), *"David, who kept my commandments, which he obeyed with all his heart, doing only what is right in my eyes."* So without sin! But a little further, it is written (15.5), David *"did which was right in the sight of the Lord . . . Except the case of Uriah the Hittite."* Is this further indication that different scribes wrote the Bible?

David is not only an adulterer, but also a gang leader and a traitor

The prophet Samuel, the last judge in Israel, was obliged to appoint a king because his corrupt sons could not succeed him. He chose a weak character who did not threaten him, someone from *"Benjamin, one of the smallest tribes of Israel, and from the smallest family among all those in the tribe of Benjamin."* Against his will, Samuel anointed Saul but tried to retain power by making bitter the life of the new king. This King Saul ceased to be docile and dared to exceed his authority by providing a sacrifice, in I Samuel (13.9), a role exclusively reserved for Samuel. Then he discovered David, a young ambitious man, and anointed him before that Saul ceased to be king.

David didn't kill Goliath:

Jews, Christians, and Muslims celebrate David killing Goliath with his sling. The Quran also embellished the tradition, *"David slew Goliath and God gave him the kingdom and wisdom . . ."* The following details show that the texts have been altered. See I Samuel (16 and following). After being anointed, David was asked by King Saul to play the harp and bear his arms. During the war against the Philistines, *"David went home from Saul and returned to Bethlehem to graze the herds of his father,"* while David should have been bearing Saul's armor. Further, after David killed Goliath, Saul asked his army chief: *"Who is this young man the son of?"* as if he did not know his armor bearer and harp player.

But strangely after David slew Goliath, in Samuel II (21.19): *"In a new war against the Philistines . . . Elhanan, son of Yaare-Oreghim, from Bethlehem defeated Goliath from Gath."* So it would not be David, but Elhanan who killed Goliath. Faced with this contradiction, some rabbis explain that this Goliath is actually a brother of Goliath. How do they explain that? Maybe that in I Chronicles (20.5), which states: *"Elhanan son of Yair, defeated Lahmi, brother of Goliath."* This unconvincing explanation of Chronicles is made up, written centuries after the facts to justify the contradiction.

Four indices show that Goliath was not killed by David's sling. The two accounts used the same detail, *"the spear was like a weaver's beam,"* to describe the weapon of Goliath and that of his brother. Judges (20.16) point out that the men of the tribe of Benjamin, like Saul, who *"with their stone sling, aimed at a hair without missing,"* while David belongs to the tribe of Judah, not known for the use of the sling. (Elhanan, a Judean too, is not described using a sling). Moreover, according to Samuel I (17.54), after cutting off the head of Goliath, *"David took the head of the Philistine Goliath and brought it to Jerusalem."* Have they forgotten that Jerusalem was a Jebusite town at that time and that David conquered it long after his victory over Goliath?

One last clue: if David killed the Philistine Goliath, he would not later ask refuge in a Philistine country and would not have been accepted into the ranks of Akhish, king of Gath, as described in I Samuel (27).

David was a mafia leader:

According to I Samuel, King Saul appointed David as his regimental commander. David is successful in his new role and is loved by all. Saul, jealous of the success of David, would try to kill him. David fled and told Samuel. From then on, or maybe even before, Samuel and David conspired against King Saul. *"All those who were in distress, who were in debt or were discontented, gathered around David, and he became their leader."*

David, as a mafia leader, was also paid for *"protection."* I Samuel (25) describes *"David sent ten servants . . ."* to Nabal, a rich owner of sheep and goats, *"we have not molested your shepherds . . . please give what you can to your servants and your son David."* Nabal refused to pay the mafia fees, and David, furious, rode at the head of 400 of his men and Nabal died of a heart attack and David took his wife Avigail. Then *"David smote the land. He left alive no man or woman, and took away the sheep, oxen . . . clothes . . ."*

David was a traitor:

Then he took refuge in the land of the Philistines and became the faithful guard of the enemy of Israel and walked with the Philistines against Saul and his army. Saul is killed, and the texts state that David had nothing to do with it, perhaps not to tarnish his image. David fights against the successor of Saul, emerges victorious and is anointed king over Israel. Can we be proud of David and his rise to power?

Divine interventions have been invented to embellish betrayals and alliances of the gang leader David and his greed for power! In I Samuel (16.13), Samuel anointed David and *"the spirit of YHWH came upon David from that day."* I Samuel (27) reports that *". . . David stayed with the philistines one year and four months . . . By incursions, he ravaged the country, killing men and women, captured flocks . . . On the south of Judah . . . Akhish counted on David . . ."* This collaboration of David with the enemies of Israel is confirmed by I Chronicles (12.19): *". . . David when he came with the Philistines to fight Saul . . ."* This David is thus a traitor to his people, and the only thing that interests him is the seizure of power.

After taking power, David began the purge and killed his opponents. It will be Avner, commander of Saul's army, and Ish-bosheth, the son of Saul (2 Samuel 4.7), and Sheba the son of Bikhri, who rebelled against the king. According to II Samuel (21), David asked God the reason for the famine plaguing his kingdom, and God answered that it is because of Saul, who had killed the Gibeonites. To appease them, David gave them the seven sons of Saul to be hanged. And as personal guard, he took foreign mercenaries, *"the Kerethi, the Pelethi and Gittheens"* because he did not trust men of his own tribe.

David didn't respect God's law:

Let's see Deuteronomy (21.15), *"If a man has two women, likes one and does not like the other, and if he has a son firstborn from the woman he does not like . . . he cannot recognize as the firstborn the son of the woman he loves instead of the one he dislikes . . .*" Abraham did not respect this rule and gave his inheritance to his younger son Isaac instead of Ishmael his elder brother. Abraham can be excused because this principle was only introduced later by Moses. But what about King David, who preferred his younger son Solomon from his wife Bathsheba instead of Adonya, his older son. David is inexcusable and has broken the rule. But what is worse is that the Bible never mentions this sin of David, and so we can believe that this rule was made up at a much later date after the time of Moses and David.

Yet this detestable David received all the blessings from God, in II Samuel (7.9): "*. . . I made you a great name, equal to the greatest names of the earth.*"

Sacred prostitution forbidden but not common prostitution:

The Bible condemns the sacred prostitution of women and men employed by the pagan temples to bring believers fertility to their fields and to their family through intercourse with these prostitutes. Deuteronomy (23.18) willfully mistranslated, does not specify that it is sacred prostitution that is prohibited. Similarly, I Kings (14.21), II Kings (23.7), Hosea (4.14), and Leviticus (19.29) concern the sacred prostitution ritual to ensure the fertility of crops and herds. The Hebrews, like the Canaanites, prayed to Baal for a good harvest and had sex with prostitutes operating in the sacred temples. This mimicked the act of union between the gods Baal and Astarte. These prostitutes, male and female, were operating even in the Temple of Jerusalem until King Josiah chased them out. Leviticus (21.7) says that the priest will not marry a prostitute or a divorced woman, and the daughter of a priest, dedicated to prostitution (sacred), will perish by fire.

Common prostitution was not condemned. Genesis (38.15) says that Judah has relations with Tamar, who was disguised as a prostitute, but without any blame against prostitution. Joshua (2) enlists the help of Rahav the prostitute, but again no blame. And King Solomon, who judges the two prostitute mothers of the one child, does not condemn their profession, which was not a crime punishable according to the Bible. Later, Jesus said nothing wrong against prostitution, but rather, in Matthew (21.30), he said that they *"will precede you into the kingdom of God."* Jesus himself was a descendant of two prostitutes, Tamar and Rahav, according to the genealogy of Matthew (1).

The *muta* or the Muslim "temporary marriage":

In order to circumvent the ban on sex with prostitutes, the Shiite community has invented the practice of "temporary marriage" by using a verse of the Quran (4.24): *"Just as you have enjoyed sexual relations, give them their dowries as a thing due. There is no sin against you that you enter into any agreement after the duty of the dowry."* Only the male can stop this relationship when he wants, without the consent of the woman.

This temporary marriage, informal and verbal, does not need to be registered or published, can last one hour or a few days, and can be consummated immediately, allowing men to have sex with prostitutes after giving them a symbolic dowry. This temporary marriage is automatically canceled at the date fixed in advance. A married man can contract this temporary marriage without the consent of his wife and even without her knowing; for example, when traveling in another city.

The New Testament is hesitant about the sin of adultery:

Matthew (5.27) recalled that Jesus is more extreme than the Pharisees when he said: *"You have heard that it has been said: You shall not commit adultery. But I say to you that whoever looks at a woman lustfully has already committed adultery with her in his heart."* Yet the New Testament forgot King David's adultery. In Matthew (19.6*), "Whoever divorces his wife, except for sexual immorality, and who he marries another, commits adultery."* So Christianity forbids divorce (except if adulterous). Note also that it concerns only the man. And yet the divorce rate in Western countries is approaching 50 percent.

Mark (10.11) makes Jesus say: *"Whoever divorces his wife and marries another commits adultery against her, and if a woman divorces her husband and marries another, she commits adultery."* The second part of this verse is an addition, because during Jesus's time, the Jewish woman had no right to divorce. This is further evidence that this episode was written for Rome where a woman could divorce her husband. Furthermore, similar sentences were said by Paul in Romans (7.3), which is another proof that Paul, master of Mark, is the source of the Gospels.

The parable of the adulterous woman is another proof that Jesus always respected the written Jewish law and never changed it. In Deuteronomy

(22.22), adulterers, male and female, should be put to death. But strangely, in John (8.3 to 11), contrary to the written rule in the Torah, Jesus did not condemn the adulterous woman and prevented her killing, and thus would seem to contradict Jewish law. This episode could be explained in two ways. The first explanation is that Jesus managed to avoid the trap set by the Pharisees. Indeed, while the law requires that the man and the woman caught in adultery be punished by death, only the woman was presented to Jesus. If Jesus condemned this convicted woman without the man, he would have violated the law. Similarly, if he let the woman go, he would have violated the law.

Jesus avoided the trap by asking witnesses to throw the stone at the woman. Indeed, for a case that deserves death, the law prescribes that witnesses must be the first to throw the stone. Jesus did not witness the adultery, and so could not be the first to stone the woman. Since the witnesses of adultery did not throw the first stone, Jesus himself could not do so; otherwise, he would have violated the Jewish law. He got out of the situation by telling this woman to not violate the commandments of God.

The second explanation, the most likely one, is that this parable of the adulterous woman is an addition, recognized by all commentators. This story of the adulterous woman is not in the oldest manuscripts, like those in the Vatican or in London, and not in the one discovered in the Santa Catherina monastery in the Sinai. This addition was performed by a Christian very familiar with Jewish rules, and who ignored that Jesus was God, because the rules of the Bible apply only to human Hebrews.

Adultery of a man was common and allowed by Rome and therefore was not to be raised. Condemnation of adultery could have angered the Roman pagans. Paul, as always, is the source of this addition of a woman being forgiven for adultery! In Romans (2.1), Paul asks, *"O man, you who judge . . . you are inexcusable, because by judging others you condemn yourself, because you, the judge, you do the same things . . ."* Paul, a few decades after Jesus, once again, puts in the mouth of Jesus useful words like the story of the adulterous woman in order to win over his pagan audience. This parable is also a bad lesson: no one can punish a drunk driver because even the police and the judge violate traffic rules at least once in their lives.

What about Hebrews (13.4) condemning adultery: *"Marriage is honorable in all . . . but God will judge fornicators and adulterers"?* This Epistle of Paul was not at all destined to Romans and was not written by Paul.

The Quran allows multiple sexual relationships for men:

Muslims will quote the verse (30.11) to show their progressive side and the verse (17.32), *"do not come to debauchery (or fornication), it is a disgrace."* The definition of adultery in the Quran is not acceptable to the modern Westerners because it allows sex with multiple wives and slaves, married or not. The Quran (4.24), (33.49), and (70.30) allows polygamy with war captives: *"married women are not allowed, but your slaves, yes (even if they are married) . . . The others you are allowed to marry . . ."* This verse allows sex with married slaves.

A Hadith says that during a military expedition, Muhammad's companions asked his opinion about sex with married slaves, and Muhammad received a revelation for them: *"Whoever cannot afford to marry a believing woman can take believing slaves"*—not one, but several—or *"those who have relations with their wives and captives of war are not to blame, but to desire other married women is transgression."* It is not the exclusive relationship with one's wife, but it permits a maximum of four wives, (4.3), and an unlimited number of captive women, even married. No loyalty is requested from the Muslim male! Adultery is for Muslims a ban that applies only to the married woman; the man is not concerned, the slave woman too.

Punishment for the single depraved woman is one hundred lashes (24.2) but for the adulterous wife, the punishment is death, (4.15): *"If your women commit the infamous shame (adultery), call four witnesses. If their stories come together against them, lock them in house until death or until God gives them salvation ."* So for wives who commit adultery the consequence is death.

Muslims have adopted the Jewish law because it suited the men. But while the death sentence for adultery was not practiced by Judaism and Christianity, this punishment is, however, still in force in Muslim countries. Stoning as a punition of adultery is practiced in some Muslim countries, but this punishment is not mentioned in the Quran. The only explanation is that verses, including stoning for adultery, were forgotten in the final compilation. Many Hadiths, especially those of Muslim, confirm stoning of adulterous woman: (17.4206) reports that a pregnant woman confessed her adultery to Muhammad. He allowed her to have her baby and later ordered for her to be stoned. Also, according to 682, Muhammad said that *"the stones should not be too small because death may not follow; not too big, because death may come too soon."*

The Hadith (17.4196) reports that Muhammad ordered the stoning of a man guilty of adultery four times. *"The messenger of Allah said: When an unmarried man commits adultery with an unmarried woman, they will receive a hundred lashes and will be banned a year. In case they are married, he will receive one hundred lashes and be stoned to death."* Finally, Ibn Ishaq (970) reports that during his pilgrimage to Mecca, Muhammad says that "he who commits adultery should be stoned."

In conclusion, the Muslim male can have sex with multiple wives and slaves, so no exclusivity for males. But on the other hand, the woman can only have relations with her husband. Moreover, according to a modern *fatwa*, denying this necessary death sentence for adultery is considered contrary to Islam.

27

Eighth Commandment: you shall not steal from your brother, and the other?

This commandment has two parts: do not kidnap a relative to make him a slave and do not steal the property of others. But this double interdiction is not respected by the sacred texts.

Abduction of your similar-brother is forbidden:

In Deuteronomy (24.7): *"If a man takes his brother, one of the children of Israel, and treats him as a slave or sells him, that thief shall die."* Repeated in Exodus (21.16). What about Joseph's brothers who sold him into slavery? Yet the eleven brothers of Joseph will become the leaders of the twelve tribes. This *"You shall not steal"* concerns only the kidnapping of another person of your clan, but does not prohibit the abduction of a foreigner. In Numbers (31.9), *"the Israelites took captive the women of Midian and their children. They took all their animals . . . all their property."* The Talmud prohibits the abduction of a freed slave or a resident who practices the commandments of the Bible, but he who steals a man who is *"half slave and half free"* will not be punished.

The Bible forbids theft from your brother but allows it from others:

Exodus (20.15) and Deuteronomy (5.17) clearly state: *"You shall not steal!"* And in Leviticus (19.11 . . .): *"You shall not steal or deny falsely, and you shall not lie to your brother . . ."* Here again, we prefer to use the word "brother or similar" and not "neighbor," because, indeed, to steal is prohibited from a brother or a similar but not from others. Exodus chapter 22 is devoted to punishment of the thief, but only for theft inside the tribe. Similarly, all the rules on weights and measures and those about the lost donkey or ox apply only to members of the tribe.

In Numbers (5.6), the thief should *"fully restore the object of the offense, adding to it a fifth."* Do we prefer the punition of the Bible or the Quran, which cuts the hand of the thief, or that of the secular justice system, which judges case by case? Exodus (3.22) describes the Hebrews leaving Egypt: *"every woman shall ask of her neighbor who lives in her house jewels of silver and gold and ornaments . . . and you shall spoil Egypt."*

Why would the Hebrews, who had no time to raise their bread, need jewels and ornaments? In addition, gold was reserved for the monarchy, not the slaves. The scribe who invented the episode of the golden calf had to explain where this gold came from. This paragraph is an addition to explain, incorrectly, from where the gold came that allowed the construction of the golden calf.

Exodus (12.35) specifies the source of the jewelry: they belong to the Egyptians. The oral law explains that this gold belongs to the Egyptians who were pursuing the Hebrews and were engulfed in the waves, and this gold was recovered by the Hebrews on the shore. This explanation must be rejected, because Exodus (32) describes the gold as jewelry and not from Egyptian soldiers: *"Aaron asked them to take off the golden earrings off the ears of their wives . . . Having received this gold, he threw them into the mold and made a metal calf."* In fact, according to the Eighth Commandment, the Hebrews did not steal from the Egyptians, who were not "of their tribe," so stealing was permitted. In addition to this amount of gold that was used for this golden calf, the Hebrews possessed thousands of coins. Numbers (7) describes the gold and the coins offered by tribes' leaders, whose weight exceeds all understanding. Were these slaves rich? In Numbers (11.5), the Hebrews regret the meat and fish *"they ate in Egypt for nothing, cucumbers and melons, leeks, onions and garlic."* For slaves, their situation was not so bad! Unless it was all invented!

Joshua (7.24) describes the punishment of one Hebrew who had stolen and hidden a part of the booty, *"All Israel killed him with stones,"* and his son and daughters were killed as well. In the Talmud, Baba Kama 113a and b, there is discussion to see if it is allowed to rob a nonbeliever or take advantage of his mistake. Some permit it while others condemn it. Rabbi Simon, a pious man, forbids theft but says it is allowed to grab an object that has been forgotten by a Gentile. Some rabbis say they have better technique than the police to apprehend thieves. They use scissors to support an open book on the verse of Exodus (1.22). If the book falls, it means that the thief is right in front of you. This is not a joke, but a superstition still used by the naive.

Should lost property be returned?

According to Deuteronomy (22.1), *"you must not see the ox or sheep astray from your brother and steal them, you are required to bring them back to your brother."* It's very moral, but what is obvious is the term "brother." In fact, this rule is valid, like many others, to your brother and not to others. Similarly, the Talmud asks the return of lost items, but only to "brothers."

According to Sanh (76), who returns a lost object to a non-Jew is like one who marries his daughter to an old man. According to Baba Metzia 24a, if someone finds a lost object, if the majority of residents are Jewish the discovery is to be announced, but if the majority is Gentile, it is not required.

Christianity condemns theft but forgives the thief:

Christians like to say that theft is prohibited by the Ten Commandments and the New Testament, and cite the words of Jesus reported by Mark (10.19), Matthew (19.18), and Luke (18.20): *"You shall not steal."* Roman (13.9) includes also *"You shall not steal."* Yet unlike the Jewish Bible, the thief can be forgiven if he repents, since according to Matthew (18.14) *"it is not the will of your Father who is in heaven that one of his cubs is lost."* Or in Ephesians (4.28): *"Let him that stole steal no longer, but must work."* Christianity seems to be more in line with modern secular law, and more universalist than Judaism and does not limit the prohibition to one's "brothers" only. So why do Christians keep the Jewish Eighth Commandment?

Islam and theft:

The Quran, very similar to the Jewish Bible, forbids theft from Muslims, but permits it from infidels. The Quran (5.38) states: *"Cut the hand of the thief as a punishment for what they have acquired..."* This verse is clear and compulsory for all Islamic jurists. In Bukhari (81.780), Muhammad said: *"the hand of a thief must be cut when the stolen property is worth a quarter of a dinar or more."* Or in (81.792), Aisha, one of Muhammad's wives: *"the prophet had cut off the hand of a lady..."* And in Muslim (17.4185), *"The Messenger of Allah said: The curse of Allah is on the thief who stole an egg and his hand will be cut off, as well as one who steals a rope and his hand will be cut off."*

Yet the Quran (33.27), (48.20) allows theft of property of the infidels: *"He gave for you to inherit their land, their homes and their property...,"* *"God promises you to take much booty."* The Hadiths confirm that stealing from infidels is authorized and confirmed by Bukhari (44.668): *"We were with the Prophet at Dhul-Hulaifa. People were hungry and laid hands on camels and sheep..."* Muslim (4328) reports that a fighter took as booty the sword of an infidel who was killed, but he was forbidden to do so by Muhammad, who had a divine revelation about what to do *"about the spoils of war, say the spoils of war belongs to Allah and His Apostle."* So this booty is for Muhammad.

Yet another Hadith (4330) describes Muhammad sharing the spoils between his looters: *"The Prophet sent an expedition to Najd and each fighter received as booty eleven or twelve camels and one camel more."* And (4337) states: *"a fifth of the booty is for Allah and His Prophet in all cases."*

28

Ninth Commandment: you shall not lie, Machiavellian lies, and Islam

This commandment is often simplified as *"You will not lie!"* We have more details in Deuteronomy (19.16): *"If a malicious witness comes . . . If this witness is a false witness . . . You must purge the evil from among you . . ."* The false witness is put to death because lying is punishable by death! Is it what the world wants today? Furthermore, again it is stated "against his brother." What about the foreigners or the enemy? Why not a positive statement, "Tell the truth"? Abraham lied when he said that his wife Sarah was his sister. Similarly, Isaac lied to King Avimelech when he presented his wife Rebecca as his sister! But both lied to a stranger and not to their brother, and that is not forbidden by the Bible! Similarly, Jacob's sons Simon and Levi lied when they promised Shechem not to take revenge if he and his brothers get circumcised, but then took advantage of their suffering and killed them all. These liars will become tribal leaders.

Jacob is an immoral liar and the story about Esau would be an addition:

Isaac had twin sons Esau and Jacob, *"the first, Esau, came out red, then came his brother, Jacob, whose hand was holding the heel of Esau . . ."* Later, Esau asked his brother for some lentil stew, and Jacob sold this soup against his birthright. Yet Jacob kept secret this agreement and did not reveal it to his dying father, Isaac. *"He called Esau his eldest son . . . and said . . .make me a dish that my soul may be blessed by you before I die."* Rebecca, his wife, who was spying, asked Jacob to replace Esau and deceive his old blind father by dressing in a sheepskin to impersonate Esau. Jacob deceived his old father and receives the blessing instead of his brother. Jacob lied to his father Isaac and therefore deserved death, according to the Ninth Commandment.

To this, a rabbi replied that Jacob disguised himself as Esau to recover what he had legally bought from his brother. But if the contract of sale of the birthright was honest, Jacob should have unveiled this to his old father. Why deceive his father Isaac? The rabbi says that if Jacob had told the truth to his father, the latter would not have believed him and would have called Esau, who would have denied everything. And then Isaac would have decided in favor of Esau. Thus, it is permissible to lie under certain conditions.

Another rabbi said that Jacob did not actually lie, because when he answered the question of Isaac: *"I hear the voice of Jacob, but the hands are the hands of Esau. Are you my son Esau?"* Jacob did not answer *"yes"* but simply said: *"I am."* The hypocrisy is boundless, and rabbis often allow themselves to change the meaning of the words of the Bible. A little further in (27.33), the same question is repeated: *"Isaac, his father, asked him: Who are you? Jacob answered: I am your son Esau, your firstborn."* There can be no dispute, and even by twisting the words, Jacob deceived and lied to his old, dying father. He deserved death, according to the Bible. Yet it is he who will be the one of three patriarchs and the father of the twelve tribes. Isaac is a poor patriarch if his son can deceive him so easily.

Rebecca, the mother, who preferred a son over another and lied to her dying husband, is immoral. What wrong did Esau do to lose his birthright? Nothing! Decades later, Jacob and Esau met again, and Esau, instead of acting in revenge for the deception of his brother, is generous and fraternal. Esau should be a good example while Jacob and his mother Rebecca should be designated as reprehensible and not become emblems of Judaism. The rabbis explain that there are lies allowed when they are for the good of the world. Without this lie, Isaac would have blessed Esau. These rabbis say it is permissible to lie in order not to get robbed or to not get killed. So this commandment is very relative and personal, unlike the biblical text!

Why doesn't Isaac, having discovered the deception, cancel his blessing? It would be right to do so since he was mistaken. Not only should

Isaac have canceled his blessing, but he should have cursed Jacob the liar. So why this curse on Esau? In (22.37), Esau and his brothers will be the servants of Jacob. Isaac has other sons? Nowhere are sons other than Jacob and Esau mentioned!

Conflicting details indicate that the story was introduced later. Jacob covets this birthright, because in Deuteronomy (21.17) this gives him a double portion of the inheritance. But this law is stated several generations after Jacob. So is it possible that this episode was added much later? In Genesis (25.32), Esau said that he will die soon and that his birthright is useless, yet no danger was upon him and he lived many years after this episode. Similarly, Isaac wanted to bless his son just before he dies. However, the years passed and he did not die. Esau, described by Judaism as the bad son, respects the will of his father and does not take a Canaanite girl as wife, according to Genesis (28.9). When Isaac finally dies, Genesis (25.29) states that *"Esau and Jacob, his sons, buried him."* Esau is mentioned first as if he was always the elder and there was no question about the distribution of the inheritance in proportion of one-third for Esau and two-thirds for Jacob.

In addition, the rabbis exonerate Jacob, giving as an argument that he *"was simple and lived in tents,"* studying, opposed to Esau, who was a skillful hunter and a shepherd living in the fields. But strangely, Jacob became the owner of a large herd of cattle. Another contradiction indicates that the story about Esau is artificially introduced into the Bible. According to Deuteronomy (23.7), God commands: *"Do not abhor an Edomite, for he is your brother,"* the Edomites or inhabitants of Edom were descendants of Esau, called *Edom* = red. But this commandment has been forgotten several times. II Kings (14.7) describes a massacre, *"The King Amaziah killed 10,000 men in Edom . . ."* The prophet Ezekiel also ignored the ban on killing the descendants of Esau (25.13*)*: *". . . God, I stretch out my hand upon Edom, and I will cut off man and beast . . . my revenge against Edom will be entrusted to the hand of my people Israel . . ."* And for the prophet Malachi (1.2), God said, *"Jacob I have loved, but Esau I have hated, so I gave its mountains to the devastation and heritage to the jackals of the wilderness . . ."* Also see Jeremiah (49.7) and Isaiah (34.5).

Jeremiah and Ezekiel mention Edom without specifying that Esau was the brother of Jacob. The late prophet Ovadiah, after 587 BC, promised the massacre of the descendants of Esau. It seems that throughout history, the inhabitants of Edom were sometimes friends of the Judeans and thus

Esau was described positively, but sometimes they were the enemy. The people of Edom would have helped Nebuchadnezzar II in the destruction of Jerusalem and the massacre of the Judeans. And so we understand the hatred of Judeans against their neighbors from Edom.

All these lead to the conclusion that the story of the sale of the birthright was inserted later, during a period of fighting between Judah and Edom. It is another case of etiology, as explained in chapter 5. Edom, the area in the south of Judah, means *red*, and one of its hills is named *Seir*, meaning *hairy*. The character of Esau was invented to be the ancestor of the people of Edom. He was described as red and hairy to match the friend/enemy country of Edom. It is not a coincidence!

Joseph's brothers were liars:

Jealous of Jacob's love for his favorite son Joseph, his brothers decided to get rid of Joseph. They sold him to a caravan, which took him to Egypt. Jacob's sons lied when they told their father that *"a wild beast has devoured him."* These lying brothers, jealous and potential killers, will be the heads of the tribes. Joseph became the right hand of Pharaoh but he did not announce his new status to his father, suffering from famine. When his brothers arrived in Egypt, he used an interpreter rather than reveal his identity, and wrongfully put a silver cup in Benjamin's sack in order to accuse him of stealing.

Christianity allowed lying:

The New Testament condemns lying. Colossians (3.9) says: *"Do not lie to each other."* Yet Paul, in Romans (3.7), would allow the white lie: *"And if through my lie, the truth of God abounded to his glory, why am I myself judged as a sinner?"* To convince the Jews that his statements are true, Jesus presents "evidence" in John (8:17): *"It is written in your law, that if two people bring the same testimony, this testimony is valid. I bear witness to myself and the Father who sent me bears witness to me."* Completely illogical! Everyone can tell the worst lies and take as witnesses himself and God! Yet Jesus himself said in John (5.31): *"If I bear witness of myself, my witness is not true."* The apostle Peter is a liar described in the New Testament. He who was the companion of Jesus and later became, according to Christianity, the first pope, said in the house of the high priest: *"I do not know him"* and repeats three times that he did not know Jesus. Although the Gospels differ in their accounts, all confirm that Peter is a liar.

The Machiavellian lie and Islam:

First, the Quran does not mention the episode where Abraham and Isaac gave their wives to Pharaoh or to King Avimelech, or the episode where Jacob lies to his father to steal the birthright from Esau. Why these omissions? The Quran considers the patriarchs as saints without any sins.

The Quran (40.28) prohibits deceiving other Muslims because *"God does not guide the frantic and the liar."* Yet lies and deceits are allowed against non-Muslims. It is the principles of *kitman* or lie by omission and *taqiyya* or simple lie. Muslims use this *kitman* when bringing the peaceful and tolerant verses, the ones Muhammad preached at Mecca. But they will not say that these verses have been abrogated by those intolerant and hateful after the travel to Medina. For example, a Muslim will quote the verse (5.32), very humanistic, condemning murder, and will omit the rest of the verse that allows *"those who fight against God and His Messenger and seek corruption in the earth, their wage will be to be killed or be crucified or have their hand cut off..."*

God himself lies and authorizes the lie in the Quran (2.225), *"God does not ask you of your vain oaths"* Or (66.2), *"God requires you to untie yourself from your vain oaths."* Verses (3, 34) and (8.30): *"The others began to plot, but God also plotted and it is God who frames the better."* Or (10.21): *"They plotted against our signs. Say: God is a faster framer and our angels see your tricks."* Verse (9.3) allows Muhammad not to respect the oath he made with the pagans of Mecca, *"God and His Messenger do not have to uphold any agreement with the polytheists..."*

Deceit was used by Muhammad, who signed a ten-year agreement with the inhabitants of Mecca. This agreement gave him access to the city, but at the same time he prepared his men for an attack. Two years later, Muhammad broke the agreement and conquered Mecca. Lying and deception are permitted towards non-Muslims and the goal justifies the lie.

Taqiyya is permitted, according to a Hadith, in three cases: a Muslim can lie to his wife for peace in the household, to settle a dispute between two Muslims, and finally, for the purposes of war. The Quran (3.28) allows lying to non-Muslims if your interests are at stake. So it is okay to bow down to idols when a Muslim fears persecution because of his faith. Verse (16.106) allows a Muslim to deny God in front of non-Muslims to save his life. A companion of Mohamad said: *"smile to the face of some people while your heart curses them."*

Like Machiavelli, Islam justifies telling lies during war, but this war is perpetual until all infidels submit to the new religion, for the Quran (8.39), until *"there is worship to God."* According to Islamic law, *"it is permissible to lie if the goal is allowed . . . and it is obligatory to lie if the goal is obligatory . . ."*

29

Tenth Commandment: you shall not lust, Jerusalem, woman, Mohammed's wives

This remarkable command does not condemn the act but the intention or the desire. This command also applies only to "your neighbor" or someone close to you, and so it is possible to covet the house or wife or donkey of someone not of your religion or an enemy. The Tenth Commandment is also anachronistic, because how can the Hebrews who were living in tents in the desert covet the "house" of their relatives, unless this commandment was written much later, after living in the Promised Land.

If lust is forbidden, how is it possible that the sons of Jacob, jealous of their brother Joseph, became the leaders of the tribes of Israel? What about King David, who sent Uriah the Hittite off to die because he wanted Bathsheba, his wife? This murderous, covetous king of Israel became the symbol and the ancestor of the Jewish and Christian Messiah also highly revered by Islam.

We would expect the Torah to preach equality and solidarity among the members of the clan, but this commandment protects the established power and the rich. Proverbs (23.1) commands: *"When you sit down at the table with a powerful . . . You shall not covet his food and he, the bread of illusions."* And Ecclesiastes (5.9): *"He who loves money can never have enough money... Sweet is the sleep of a laborer, whether he eats little or much."*

The New Testament also forbids lust. The apostle James writes in (1.15): *"Lust brings sin, and sin, when it is consumed, brings death."* The whole chapter of 1 Timothy (6) requires respecting the established power: *"if we have food and clothing, we will be content"* and so Christianity became the great protector of the rich Romans and of the European lords against any claim of the people.

The three religions accept social inequality. Is that why rich classes have always been in favor of religion? And that Karl Marx and Communism have opposed religion, named the opium of the people?

The conquest of the Promised Land, was it a genocide or a fable?

For Jews, this land was given by God to Abraham and his descendants, and then again to Moses and the Hebrews. God appeared to Abraham and ordered him to *"go to the land that I will show... They left to go to the land of Canaan... there, he built an altar to YHWH who appeared to him..."* Yet at the first famine, Abraham left the Promised Land for Egypt. No trust in God? And God, why after sending Abraham to the Promised Land, did he bring famine?

In Genesis (13.9), Abraham and Lot returned from Egypt with considerable herds. Abraham received *"flocks and herds"* "and *"was well treated by Pharaoh for love of Sarah,"* the wife Abraham. But how did Lot acquire his considerable flocks? Then because of disputes between their shepherds, Abraham decided to separate from Lot and offered him a choice: *"If you go left, I'll go right; if you go right, I will go left.' Lot looked up and... chose all the plain of Jordan and walked the eastern side, and they separated."* So Abraham seems to have forgotten the promise of God and walked toward his promised land, the one that Lot had not chosen. The Promised Land could well have been Jordan if Lot had decided otherwise. But Genesis (14, 18) said the opposite: *"That day, the Lord made a covenant with Abraham, saying, I have granted your race this territory from the river of Egypt till the great River Euphrates."*

So who chose the Promised Land, Lot or God? And what are the correct borders of the Promised Land? Do they include Jordan? But this territory belonged to Lot. The considerable herds of Lot are completely forgotten in the episode of Sodom. Why would Lot, a shepherd who lives under a tent, go to a house in the city of Sodom? Was this episode invented to explain retroactively the cursed relationship of the Moabite and Ammonite with their neighbors of Judah? Did God ignore that other people already lived in the Promised Land? Could He not find a more divine solution than the massacres of human beings? The response of a rabbi is God wanted to destroy these evil people, like Amalec, who wanted to harm the Jewish people. But these people have also been created by God. Another rabbi retorted that these people were like the Nazis who wanted to destroy the Jewish people, and so God has done well to precede their evil deeds. But then, why didn't God do anything against Hitler, who wanted to destroy the Jewish people?

Some justify the killings by the following arguments: No they say, the land already belonged to the Hebrews because God, the owner, had given it to them. In addition, the natives living in the Promised Land were depraved and immoral, and sacrificed children and had sex with animals. So this conquest is different from the expansionist religious wars of Islam and Christianity. Are you convinced?

The borders of the Promised Land are unclear and contradictory. In Deuteronomy (32), Moses approached the Promised Land and God himself promised: *"And when you come beyond the Jordan . . ."* followed by Deuteronomy (34) *"This is the land I promised on oath to Abraham . . . I have caused you to see it with your eyes, but you shall not enter. It is here where Moses died, the servant of YHWH in the land of Moab . . . facing Beith-Peor."* So Moses did not enter the Promised Land. But Moses was already in the Promised Land when he stood on the eastern bank of the Jordan River, since this land is devoted to one of the twelve tribes and included in the Promised Land according to Deuteronomy (11): *"The whole area where the soles of your feet will be, belongs to you, from the south desert to Lebanon, from the river Euphrates to the western sea, will be your land."* In Joshua (1), *"the land which I give to the children of Israel . . . from the desert here to Lebanon, from the great river, the river Euphrates, all the land of the Hittites, to the great sea in the west, will be your territory."* So what are the boundaries of the Promised Land? Did Moses die inside or outside the Promised Land?

In Joshua (22), the tribes of Gad, Reuven, and the half tribe of Menashe, after having helped the others tribes take possession of the Promised Land, are returning on the eastern side of the Jordan to occupy their own territories. So it confirms that the Promised Land includes territories located east of Jordan. Yet these territories appear to be second class, according to Joshua (22.19): *"If the land of your possession is unclean, go back to the country that is the territory of YHWH, where the residence of YHWH stands, and take possession among us."* So eastern Jordan was occupied by two and a half tribes but is not the territory of YHWH. What happened to these territories and tribes left on the other side of the Jordan, for example, during the kingdom of David and Solomon? The silence is total! Why? How could God have promised this land to the Hebrews? Either God does not follow the commandment He himself gave about not lusting or this commandment is only valid among Hebrews.

The land promised to the Jews was already inhabited by many other peoples mentioned in Joshua (3): *"The living God is among you and you will drive out the Canaanite, the Hittite, the Hivite, the Pherizean, the Ghirgachean, the Amorrean and the Jebusite."* Between the two options, cohabitation with the pagan peoples or the destruction of these peoples to make place for the Hebrews, God chooses the multi-genocide. Can't He solve the problem of the Promised Land without these killings and battles? Some quotes from the book of Joshua: *"... The booty and livestock, you will loot for your profit ... when you will be masters of the city, you shall set fire according to the word of YHWH ... the inhabitants of the town were cut to pieces without sparing one ... when the massacre was over ... 12,000, both men and women ..."* Joshua (11) ends with a false statement: *"Joshua, who conquered the whole country, as God had promised to Moses ... rested from war."*

Yet the historical truth would be less cruel, and the genocide of the people already living in the Promised Land probably did not take place. Judges (1.27) described, not the conquest and genocide, but the cohabitation with the indigenous peoples: *"Ephraim also did not drive out the Canaanites. Zebulon did not expel the inhabitants of Kitron, nor those ... Asher ... Naphtali not expelled ..."* Judges (1.28 ...) says that *"becoming more powerful, Israel submitted the Canaanites to a heavy price but they were not expelled. Ephraim, either ..."* Later, the episode of Gideon, Judges (7) describes the hostile presence of other peoples, including the Midianites. God had promised these territories to the Hebrews but failed to deliver them, because, in Judges (1.34), the tribe of Dan was pushed back, and several decades after the entry into the Promised Land will continue to wander, according to Judges (18).

Moreover, Jerusalem was not yet conquered, because in Judges (19.11): *"Let us go to the city of the Jebusites to spend the night. His master said to him, we will not go into a foreign city where there are no children of Israel..."* And this other contradiction, in Joshua (10.23 and 42), he killed the king of Jerusalem and captured the city, while later (15.63), *"As for the Jebusites inhabiting Jerusalem, the children of Judah could not dispossess them, so they remained in Jerusalem with the children of Judah to this day."* Also, if there was genocide, why does II Samuel (24.21) say that David *"acquired the area and livestock at the price of 50 shekels"* from Aravna the Jebusite to build an altar to God, several generations after Joshua and his bloody pseudo-conquest?

The city of Jerusalem, worshiped by Jews, was therefore called Jebus and already inhabited by the Jebusites, and David conquered it a few centuries later to make it his capital. Moreover, it would be impossible for the Hebrews to imitate the idolatry of other people if they were completely eliminated.

The episode of Samson describes a co-existence with the Philistines a few generations after Joshua. In Numbers (31.7), the Hebrews *"fought against Midian... and slew all the males... and took captive the women of Midian and the children."* Yet later, the chapter of Judges (6) describes *"the superiority of Midian..."* And even after the return from the Babylonian exile, the mixed marriages prove the presence of non-Hebrew people, as written in Ezra (9.1): *"the Canaanites, Hittites, Perizzites..."*

The explanation for these inconsistencies is that the genocide and cruelty of the conquest was invented and included in the Bible at the time of King Josiah, who wanted to impose monotheism and destroy idols and idolaters. The Hebrews would have lived, in fact, next to other peoples until the decision of Josiah to eradicate idolatry, and for that he rewrote history by inventing Joshua and the conquest. But this rewriting described the Hebrews as a people arriving on this territory because of God's promises to Abraham, to Moses, and to Joshua, when in fact they had been there for an eternity. Is it possible then that the character of Joshua, the successor of Moses, was invented by the pious King Josiah in order to make Joshua a second Moses? Both send spies, both were ordered to remove their shoes because the soil is sacred, both separated the waters to cross on dry land... Is Joshua (Yoshua in Hebrew) a clone of Josiah (Yoshiaou in Hebrew)?

Several other questions arise. Why is the possession of land so important to God? Why specifically this land and not a more fertile one that has no occupants? Some crazy people explain that Jerusalem was the center of the world before the continents moved away from each other. No evidence is given for that statement!

The New Testament confirms the concept of the land promised to the Hebrews. Acts (7.2) repeats God's promise to Abraham and continues: *"after that, they will come out and serve me in this place,"* the Promised Land. The Epistle to the Hebrews (11.9) says that Abraham *"by faith sojourned in the Promised Land..."* The Quran makes mistakes regarding the Promised Land. For example, according to (7.129), Moses said, *"maybe he will perish your enemy and he will make you heir of the earth to see how you act."* Would Egypt thus be the promised land? Then (7.110) and (20.57) say: *"the advisors of Pharaoh told him... He (Moses) wants to drive you from your land."* To seize and stay in Egypt? And yet in (10.87): *"And We asked Moses and his brother to build houses for your people in Egypt..."* Instead of fleeing, the slaves would build houses to accommodate them? Or in (5.20), Moses reminds the Hebrews that God *"has chosen among you prophets, and made from you kings."* This is an anachronism because the kingdom will only happen a few centuries after Moses. Verses (26.57) and following are not clear: *"We have stripped them of gardens and springs, treasures and good home... and we gave it to the sons of Israel."* Muhammad said that the Hebrews received in Egypt gardens, sources, and homes. Where is the slavery? In (28.2), it would be Pharaoh and his wife who collected the baby Moses and not the daughter of Pharaoh. Why the changes? Are they due to errors in Muhammad's memory?

Muhammad, at his first period, surprises us. In the Quran (5.21), it is written: *"My people, enter the holy land that God destined for you."* Then (7.137), *"We gave the oppressed (Hebrew) the east and west of the blessed land."* And in (17.111), *"After the death of Pharaoh, We said to the sons of Israel: when the promise of the next life will be fulfilled, we will make you come back in crowds."* On the Day of Judgment, therefore, all Jews will return to live in Israel! What a surprising pro-Zionist statement. Why are Muslims opposed to Israel if the Quran recognized that it was promised to the Jewish people? Forced to find an answer to this Zionist statement of the Quran, the imams explain that the promise only holds if the people of Israel obey the orders of God; however, this temporal promise was canceled because they disobeyed.

The Arabs of today claim that the Holy Land belongs to them because they are the descendants of Ishmael, Abraham's heir, and therefore the recipients of God's promise of the Promised Land. But this is not true, because according to Muslims themselves, Abraham and Ishmael descended to Arabia to build the Kaaba of Mecca, and the Quran does not mention the return to the promised land of Ishmael, nor his claims to the land.

Genesis (37, 25) and Judges (8.22) seem to mix Ishmaelite and Midianites. In fact, there is no contradiction, and the descendants of Ishmael would have lived in Midian, got assimilated, and disappeared.

After the death of Muhammad, the entire world is a promised land to the Muslims; his disciples divide the world into two, Dar al-Islam, or House of Peace, and Dar al-Harb, or House of War. All Muslims must fight until the people of Dar al-Harb recognize the sovereignty of Islam. Yasser Arafat, the former Palestinian leader, had declared that the Palestinian people were descendants of the Canaanites and of the Jebusites of Jerusalem, and therefore had rights to the Holy Land older than those of the Jews. The Quran contains no reference to the Palestinian people, past or future. Some Muslims have found a new argument to cancel the rights of Jews to the Promised Land. According to the Bible, Jacob, who is also named Israel, is the ancestor of all the prophets. But according to some Muslim "experts," the ancestor of the Jews would not be Jacob but Israel, a descendant of Cain, the nasty murderer. These experts have not yet realized that Jacob is Israel, and so one person.

Is Jerusalem also promised to Muslims?

Jerusalem is sacred to Jews, yet it was a Jebusite city conquered by David. It is also sacred to Christians because Jesus was crucified and then resurrected there. It is sacred to Muslims who built the Al Aqsa Mosque there, the third monument of Islam after the Kaaba in Mecca and the Mosque of Medina. This Al Aqsa Mosque is in fact the heart of the Israeli-Palestinian conflict. Even though Jerusalem is not mentioned once in the Koran, Muslims proclaim the sanctity of the mountain where the Jewish temple was erected then destroyed by the Romans, and later a mosque was built there.

A single verse of the Quran (17.1) refers to a miraculous journey of Muhammad, *"Glory to the one who took his servant by night from the sacred place of worship to the most distant worship place . . . to show him some of our signs."* But Jerusalem is not named, not here and not in the whole Quran, not even in one verse!

Long after the death of Muhammad, a Hadith reports the details of a night journey: under the direction of the archangel Gabriel, a fantastic winged donkey named Buraq, with a head of a woman and a peacock's tail, carried Muhammad from his bed in Mecca to a distant mosque, where he met the prophets of the Bible and from there ascended to heaven to meet Allah. All this in a single night, on the same donkey which was to have carried Abraham two thousand years ago when he visited Mecca with his son Ishmael. Although it is not specified in the Quran, the Hadith states that this *"far away mosque"* is the Temple of Jerusalem. But several questions arise: is this journey from Mecca to Jerusalem only a vision, as claimed by the skeptics, or a miraculous physical journey like Muslims believe? The journey to Jerusalem would be useless for Muhammad, who reports nothing of Jerusalem. In addition, there was no mosque in Jerusalem during the lifetime of Muhammad. And finally, Muhammad, attacking and cursing the Jews, would have no reason to go to Jerusalem, which was in ruins.

Orthodox Muslim historians claim that this night journey and ascension have indeed taken place physically in Jerusalem. A Hadith of Bukhari (5, 58,227) says: *". . . He opened my heart, cleaned and filled it with faith and put it back in its place. Then a white animal smaller than a mule but larger than a donkey was brought to me . . . It was Buraq . . . Gabriel and I went on to the next heaven . . . The door opened and when I entered the first heaven, I saw Adam . . . In the second heaven . . . John the Baptist and Jesus . . . In the third heaven, Joseph, Aaron . . . Then . . . In the sixth heaven, Moses . . . In the seventh heaven, Abraham . . ."* Other Hadiths report that Muhammad was not in his bed that night, according to the testimony given by his companions. Yet his wife Aisha stated that *"the noble body of Muhammad had not disappeared that night,"* weird testimony because she was not yet his wife at the time of this journey, and so her testimony should be rejected.

Honest Muslims and historians claim that this trip was only a dream, because Muhammad himself acknowledges in (18.109) that he is a human being like us, but also that the verse (17.60) *"We have made you see a vision,"* would apply to this nocturnal journey. And again, the decisive verse (17.1) designates *"a temple or distant place of worship,"* while the Hadith uses the Hebrew word *Beit Hamiqdash*, which means the Temple of Jerusalem. A Hadith of Bukhari (52.221) calls Jerusalem by its Roman name *Ilya* without any reminder of the famous night journey. While another Hadith

(69.482) oddly mentions the night journey to Jerusalem and promotes the consumption of milk instead of alcohol. These Hadiths give clues. To the skeptics, Muhammad described the Temple of Jerusalem, including the number of doors, as he saw it. This description is a bad plagiarism of Ezekiel (40–48) which describes the visionary temple and its many doors. For proof of this miracle and the visit of Muhammad to Jerusalem, Muslims cite Abu Bakar, the first caliph, confirming that the description of the temple made by Muhammad via the Hadiths is exactly what he himself saw during his journey to Jerusalem. They have all forgotten that the temple was destroyed by the Romans six centuries ago. It was nothing more than a pile of trash. And after the complete destruction of Jerusalem by the Persians in 614, there was certainly no temple or mosque in 620, and no doors to the ruins during this *"night journey."*

So where did Muhammad pray? Muslims answered that *Al-Masjid Al-Aqsa* means a place of prostration and not necessarily a real building. It can even be a field. But it is not convincing because of the description of the doors and windows, and also because the first *Al-Masjid-Ul-Haram* was a building and not a piece of land. This miracle is neither confirmed by the Jews or by Christians, and this fantastic donkey has never been seen by anyone and has since disappeared. This "miracle" is not actually described in the Quran.

Abraham, the first Muslim according to Muhammad, had nothing to do in Jerusalem, not yet built in his time. If Muhammad had made this extraordinary journey to the mosque of Jerusalem and had climbed to heaven and met the angels, why would God allow the Christian crusaders to seize Jerusalem? How do Muslims explain their dispossession (provisional) of the sacred city? How do they explain how Muhammad, who boasts of being just a human, was able to perform this miraculous journey? Is it possible that this trip was not to Jerusalem, but was actually a real journey of Muhammad from Mecca to Medina?

Some honest Muslims recognize that this *"far away mosque"* was not Jerusalem but Medina, and this trip actually took place but was no miracle. Opponents of the idea argue that the mosque of Medina was not yet built at that time, so this trip to this mosque would make no sense. But all become logical if this verse was written after the emigration from Mecca to Medina, which happened indeed in 622.

This journey to Jerusalem is contrary to the hostile attitude of Muhammad to the Jews in this period, especially after he switched the direction of prayers from Jerusalem to Mecca (2,142) in 623. Muhammad attacked Jews and cursed them and would have no reason to go to Jerusalem, which was in ruins. This change of direction contradicts the assertion of Muslims that Muhammad always prayed to God correctly. These dates show that the night journey is not about Jerusalem but Medina.

And finally, maps show that the three cities of Mecca, Medina, and Jerusalem are aligned, with Medina in the middle. If Muhammad had taken off from Mecca to land in Jerusalem, without mentioning Medina, this would undermine the sanctity of Medina, disdained by Muhammad during his nocturnal journey. In fact, this night journey of Muhammad is drawn from a text of the second century, and is of Egyptian origin. It is a testament of Abraham, which describes the rise of Abraham in heaven guided by an angel. This trip made by Muhammad is also inspired by another text, the second book of Enoch, who rose to the seven heavens and was guided by the angel Gabriel. This trip finally contains Zoroastrian influence. The priest Arta Viraf, many centuries before Muhammad, ascended to the different skies guided by an angel and visited paradise. Muhammad, and especially the authors of the Hadiths, knew these texts and the Persian legend.

Some historians like Dr. Motti Kedar of Bar-Ilan University say that the truth would be that in the beginning, to convince the Jewish tribes, Muhammad decided to imitate some of their rules, such as dietary prohibitions, and established prayer toward Jerusalem, to the north, like the Jews of Medina. Then, seeing his failure to convince the Jews who refused his prophecy, Muhammad change the *kiblah*" or direction of prayer to Mecca in the south (2,144). Jerusalem is then forgotten and not once mentioned in the Qur'an.

Some fifty years after the death of Muhammad, a conflict between the caliphs prevented the Muslims of Damascus from reaching Mecca for pilgrimage, and seeking an alternative, chose Jerusalem. Then, they justified this choice by interpreting an obscure verse (17.1). They built on the ruins of the ancient Jewish temple a new mosque, which received the strange name of *Al-Aqsa*, meaning *distant* in order to identify it with the verse (17.1). Long after Muhammad, Muslims felt the need to capture Jerusalem, the city not mentioned in the Quran but holy for the two other religions. Even after the Muslim conquest of the Holy Land, not Jerusalem but Ramallah, a neighboring town, was chosen as the capital. The interest of the Muslims in Jerusalem declined with the end of the conflict between the caliphs and interest was reborn with the conquest of the Crusaders. It was later off again for a few centuries until the establishment of the Jewish home in the Holy Land and the revival of State of Israel.

This verse (17.1) is central to the Israeli-Palestinian conflict, and some Muslims deny the right of Jews to Jerusalem by stating that there is no evidence that the Jewish temple ever existed. However, the stories of the nocturnal travel of Muhammad and the Hadiths are the best evidence to prove to the contrary. If the temple never existed, the Hadiths describing the journey of Muhammad to the Temple of Jerusalem are not true. Why would Muhammad go to the site of the Jewish temple if no ancient temple had been established at this location? The Israelis must use enough of the Quran and the Hadiths to confirm their rights to Jerusalem. And if the miraculous journey of Muhammad to Jerusalem never took place, this would completely negate Muslim claims to Jerusalem. In fact, Jerusalem is not mentioned once in the Koran and was never the capital of any Arab or Muslim state.

The status of the Jewish woman in the Bible and the rabbis:

One point of agreement between the three religions is that they all treat the woman like a second-class person or a piece of property. The word *Baal* means *husband* and also *owner*. Although the Bible contains examples of women as prophetess, such as Deborah, most of the verses describe the inferiority of women when the heroes are all men. The woman must be virgin when she marries; otherwise, according to Deut (22.20), *"They will lead her to the entrance of the house of her father and the men of the city shall stone her to death until death ensues . . ."* But nothing against non-virgin males at the time of their wedding! The girl had no right to the inheritance, all goes to the son, except only: *"If a man dies without a son, the inheritance will pass over to his daughter,"* according to Numbers (27.8).

The Law on jealousy: Numbers (5.11–29) remind us of the "question" of the terrible time of the Christian Inquisition. *"If the husband is seized with a spirit of jealousy and suspicions about his wife, the man shall bring his wife to the priest and bring offering for her, a tenth of an ephah of barley meal . . . and the woman will drink the bitter water . . . If she is unclean and has been unfaithful to her husband . . . her belly shall swell, and her thigh will dry out and this woman shall be a curse . . ."*

The Hebrew slave woman does not have the same rights as the male slave. According to Exodus 21, *"he will remain a slave six years, and in the seventh he shall be released without ransom."* So the Hebrew male slave is freed after six years but not the woman. Even though he is released after six years, *"if his master gave him a wife, and she he has given birth . . . The woman with the children belong to his master."* This rule is detestable.

The woman is unclean during her period, *"and whoever touches her shall be unclean until evening."* Religious Jews today sleep in separate beds during their wives' menstrual period. After delivery of a male baby, the woman is unclean for only seven days but fourteen days if it's a girl, and cannot touch anything sacred. Christians too often forget that Mary respected this rule when Jesus was born.

Leviticus (27.3) states that the value of a male is 50 shekels but only 30 shekels for a woman.

What do the rabbis say about the status of women? The study of the Torah and religious decisions are man's exclusive domain, while women would practice "modesty, prayer and education of children." And also, the coming Messiah cannot be a woman but only a male. According to the Talmud, Ketubot 110b, if a husband desires his wife and she refuses twice, he may divorce her. According to the Talmud, Avot 1, a man should limit his conversation with the wife or with other women because it is a waste of time that could be used for religious studies.

Despite this second-class status, the woman has duties when it comes to sacrifices. The book of Leviticus lists sacrifices without excluding women, using the term *nefesh*, which refers to the man or woman as a subject who has to perform a particular sacrifice. In addition to the common sacrifices practiced by men and women after childbirth or after her period, according to Leviticus (12.6) and (15.28), the woman must bring a sacrifice by herself to the high priest. Can this sudden rise of women be explained by the interests of the priests who take advantage of these sacrifices?

The Christian woman censored by the New Testament:

Jesus says almost nothing about the woman, according to Mark (10.7): *"This is why a man leaves his father and mother and joined to his wife and the two will become one flesh . . ."* How does he explain polygamy of the patriarchs? Paul, speaking under the inspiration of Jesus, says in I

Corinthians (11.3 and 14, 34): *"The head of the woman is the man . . . Let women keep silence in congregations, for it is not permitted to speak . . . And if they will learn anything, let them ask their husbands at home, for it is a shame for women to speak in the church."* In Ephesians (5.22), Paul asks: *"Wives, be subject to their husbands as to the Lord because the husband is the head of his wife."* Paul also calls in I Timothy (2.9): *". . . Women . . . adorn themselves with modesty and good sense, not with braided hair carefully arranged, or gold, or pearls or expensive clothes . . . That woman learn in silence with all subjection . . . I do not permit a woman to teach or to have authority over a man. She must keep quiet. For Adam was created first, then Eve. And it was not Adam who was seduced, but the woman who seduced, has disobeyed. Nevertheless, she will be saved through motherhood."* The Christian woman became a belly for procreation, cloistered for over a millennium by Christianity, which saw the woman as a means of procreation.

Supporters of Peter-Paul repeat the arguments against women in I Peter (3.1): *"Women, be in subjection to your own husbands . . . Let it not be the outward adorning of plaiting the hair, ornaments gold or clothes he takes, but hidden person in the heart . . ."*

The woman is a good second class for Islam:

As is very often seen in the Quran, there is a verse favorable to women that Muslims emphasize, forgetting to mention the verses that make women an object of second or rather third category after the male and the camel, according to an Arab proverb. The Quran (4.34) proclaims the superiority of the man who was created first (?): *"Men have authority over women because of the preference of God . . . Your wives, if they don't obey, admonish them and relegate them to their room, hit them . . ."* Muhammad would educate a disobedient wife in three steps: admonition, not to invite her to bed when her turn comes, and finally beat her. In the Quran (2.228), *"men come before women,"* sometimes better translated to *"husbands are superior to the wives."* Just like the Jewish Bible, the Quran (4.1) repeats the same story of Creation where the woman is created after the man.

The woman is a possession of the male and he does with her what he wants, she is a commodity used to satisfy the sexual needs of the male. Verse (2.222) says: *"Menstruation . . . is evil. Move away from women in their menstrual period. When they are purified, come to them . . . your wives are your ploughing. Go to your work as you please . . ."* The opinion of the wife is never requested.

Verse (65.4) sets the period of repudiation of wives *"for your women who no longer expect menstruation, if you have doubts, the period shall be three months. The same for those who do not yet expect the menstruation."* So sexual relations are permitted even with girls before puberty, and Muhammad gave the example when he consummated his marriage with Aisha, then aged nine. And in (2.220), *"Do not give your daughters to idolaters until they believe."*

The woman is a good that is given, and can easily be rejected. Verse (2.226) and (65.1): *"if they decide repudiation . . . They can repudiate two times."* The right to divorce belongs only to the male! Polygamy is permitted, (4.3): *"Marry women you like. Take two, three, or four . . . or slaves."* Muhammad himself set the example, but he took not just four, because the verse (33.49) gives him privileges: *"Prophet, We have allowed you your wives, and the captives that God made you acquire in war, the daughters of your uncles . . . those who migrated with you . . . That is your privilege, but not of the believers."* Muhammad therefore could have as many wives, concubines, and slaves, while Jesus, in the New Testament, is described without wife and sexual appetite. Only Turkey and Tunisia banned polygamy.

The woman is not a person responsible, she is judged according to the deeds of her husband in (37.22): *"Gather the culprits, their wives and their idols."* Verse (2.282) explains that the testimony of a woman is worth half that of a man. The same for inheritance (4.12 and 176), *"the boy has two times more than the girl."* And (4.176): *"If he has brothers and sisters, each brother has two times more than each sister."* When a man is tired of his wife, he can get rid of her quickly, because the procedure (2,228 and 65.1) is easy for the Muslim male and for him alone.

The woman in the Quran is the husband's burden just like his livestock. The man can dispose of her as he decides and use force against her. In Bukhari (72.715), a wife complained that her husband beats her, and Muhammad ordered the woman to submit to the blows of the husband. According to Abu Dawud, Muhammad allowed the beating of wives. In Muslim (4.2127), Muhammad hit his wife Aisha. An imam questioned by Western television claimed that it is allowed for him to beat his wife to educate her but not to break a tooth unless she rejects the sexual advances of her husband. In this case, it is permitted! In Bukhari (52.111), Muhammad said: *"If there was an evil sign somewhere, it is in the woman, the horse or the home."* In Muslim (4921), the Prophet said that women are in the minority in paradise and the majority in hell.

The veil and the three religions:

The goal of the veil is to preserve men from lusting after women. The Jewish Bible is almost silent in this area and Genesis (24.65) reported that Rebecca *"took her veil and covered herself."* Later, (29.25), Jacob slept with Leah but thought he was sleeping with her sister Rachel. The mistake came from the veil that covered the two women. But even during sex, this is too much! In Song of Songs (4.3): *". . . through your veil."* Another text, Genesis (38.15 . . .) suggests that the veil covered the face of prostitutes only: *"Judah, having seen her, took her for a prostitute since she had veiled her face."* Then after sex, *"she got up and went; she left her veil and took the garments of her widowhood."* This is not very clear.

Faced with the silence of the Bible, the rabbis use Deuteronomy (23.15): *"God . . .will not see a shameful thing (ourva) among you . . ."* What does this Hebrew word *ourva* mean? Is it nudity? And what about the men? Jewish women must wear a veil to hide their hair, but some have found a tip: they wear a wig, and so they respect the requirement to cover their hair while maintaining their femininity. Deuteronomy (22.5) prohibits women from wearing male clothing. And in our time, in Jerusalem, orthodox rabbis prevent women from singing in front of men and ask them to sit separately in buses in order not to wake the male urges.

The New Testament requires women to wear the veil, and this rule is forgotten by Christians who criticize the obscurantism of Islam without seeing the beam in their own eye. According to I Corinthians (11, 3 . . .) *". . . Every woman who prays or prophesies with her head uncovered dishonors her head . . . If a woman is not covered, let her cut her hair . . . The woman, because of the angels, must have on her head a sign of authority on which she depends . . ."* I Corinthians (11.10): *"That is why the woman must have her head covered as a sign of her dependence on compliance with God's messengers."* Modest dressing is not limited to the veil, but is defined in I Peter (3.3): *"Your dress will not have outer hair ripples, gold jewelry, elegant toilets . . . A gentle soul and peaceful in his secret. That is what is precious in God's eyes . . ."* The veil, previously mandatory, was abandoned in the twentieth century and is no longer in the canonical code since 1983, but persists for the bride or the widow.

Just like the two other religions, the Quran (33.59) orders the veil: *"Prophet, tell your wives and your daughters and the believing women to cover with veil..."* to be recognized as pious women. This led to banning the exposure of the hair, arms, and legs, and women must wear the veil (24.30) to hide their female body: *"... Look down, be chaste, show only the outside of their finery, fold their veils over their throats, not to show their adornment but only to their husband, father..."* The woman must not only be veiled, but also dress in a bag to hide her form and walk by shaving the walls, almost be invisible.

There are several Islamic veils: the *hijab* that covers the hair, the *niqab* that only hides the bottom of the nose and mouth, and the *chador* that covers the entire body and face and leaves only a small grid. Muslim women are so trapped by centuries of indoctrination that they fully accept their slavery, polygamy, and the sexual urges of their husband, and for them, *"the veil is the liberation of women."* They also accept their inferior status for inheritances, testimonies, education, male paradise, and even the prohibition of driving a car, like in Saudi Arabia, where only a few brave ones attempt to defy the ban.

Some Muslims refer to the whole woman's body as *awrah* or shameful area, while for men it is limited to the parts between the navel and the knees. Ali, a cousin of the Prophet, opposed women learning to write, and as a result Muslim countries have the highest illiteracy rates among women in the world, 50 percent is normal. In Pakistan, in 1977, it was forbidden for women to participate in sports competitions.

Muslims claim the right to wear the Islamic veil in western schools and can freely wear it in public places, but if a Westerner visits Muslim countries she must cover her hair with a headscarf, and of course cannot wear a miniskirt under penalty of imprisonment. Another two weights and two measures.

The veil came back strong in Muslim countries. Would the fault lie on the bad example of Western women, called *liberated or emancipated*? The carnal and disrespectful exhibition of *modern* women in advertising and television, the woman as *sex object*, are these an improvement over the veiled woman? Is there not a balance that respects the woman without the veil?

For the three religions, the veil is a protection against the lust of males, but it is only the women who are subjected to it. Former US President

Jimmy Carter met, in 2013, leaders of different religions to fight violence against women and *"to review the misinterpretation of the sacred Scriptures."* In fact, there is no misinterpretation, the sacred writings promote the veil and inequality of women.

Is the marriage of Muhammad an example for Muslims?

The conjugal life of Muhammad is an example for Muslims but irritates any modern person, and this is why the imams interviewed by Western media hide it. Khadija, the first wife of Muhammad, is an enigma that psychoanalysts should investigate because she is the opposite of the future teachings of Muhammad and Islam. She was over forty years old, widowed twice, and had given birth to several children, so not a virgin when Muhammad was only twenty-five years old on their wedding. She inherited her father's wealth and was an active woman, not a woman who stayed locked in her house. She had taken the initiative in their relationship while looking for a manager for her caravan business, so not a marriage in the interest of the tribe but for personal reasons. Muhammad went to live in the house of his rich wife, and he remained monogamous till the death of Khadija after twenty-four years.

The second Muhammad, a more macho leader, broke free of all that his first wife symbolized, but only after the death of Khadija took more than a dozen wives and numerous concubines and slaves. Can psychology explain the reactions of Muhammad, and also the rules of Islam so opposed to the Khadijah period? A first example: According to a Hadith of Bukhari (58.236) and (7.62), three years after the death of Khadija, his first wife, Muhammad married a widow named Saida.

Then, at fifty-one years old, he *"married Aisha, who was a six-year-old girl. She was nine years old when he consummated the marriage."* So Muhammad had sexual relations with Aisha when she was just nine years old, and she became his favorite wife until his death. Of course, this was because the angel Gabriel ordered Muhammad to marry that girl. Hadith, Bukhari (3.47, 755) reports that according to Aisha, Muhammad received his divine inspiration when he was in bed with her, but she never saw the angel Gabriel.

Because of the example given by Muhammad, Islam permits marrying a nine-year-old girl. In our time, he would be accused of pedophilia. The

Quran (65.4) allows marriage with a very young girl but requires a period of three months for repudiation *"of those who do not yet expect their menses."* We must reread this sentence several times to understand how it is shocking. Millions of Muslims follow the example of Muhammad and marry young girls. Hamas organizes each year, including in 2013, collective weddings where dozens of men of twenty to thirty years old marry girls under the age of twelve. Islamic tradition relates that this Aisha was alleged to have cheated on her husband Muhammad with an officer, and harmful rumors persisted until Muhammad received a revelation that cleared her. Then he established the law that requires the testimony of four people in good faith in order to prove adultery.

A second example: Muhammad has many wives, concubines, and slaves. But this was still not enough, and when he visited Zaid, his adopted son, and saw his wife Zainab, he flattered her. But according to (4.23), it was forbidden to take as a wife the women of your son and your daughter-in-law. Muhammad found the solution and the Quran (33.37) enabled the wedding by making a distinction between the wife of his son, forbidden, and the wife of his adopted son, permitted. *"God . . . did not . . . that your adopted son will be like your son . . . when Zaid had no more desire for her, We married her to you so that they would not complain about the women repudiated by their adopted sons."* Allah changes the laws to fit the specific needs of his prophet. The honest solution would have been to help Zainab, the poor wife of Zaid, marry another man. Why was it necessary to cancel the previous law? Why was Muhammad the first to execute this change in law? The only good explanation is that Muhammad wanted the beautiful Zainab. In 2013, Iran voted on a law allowing men to marry their adopted daughters when they reach the age of thirteen.

A third example: the oath broken between Muhammad and one of his wives. Sura 66 begins strangely, *"Why, to satisfy your women, do you forbid what God allows you . . . God requires you to untie you from your oaths . . . When the Prophet confided a secret to one of his wives, she shared it with another . . ."* What is this oath and why cancel it? What does it have to do with Islam? Some explain that Muhammad had eaten honey with Maryam, one of his slaves, and had promised to his other wives that he would not eat more honey. But later, he broke his oath and ate some more honey. This story is of no interest unless the truth is different. Some others say that Muhammad wanted to sleep with his servant Maryam but it was the turn of another wife . . . Caught in the act by the neglected wife, he promised her he would not lie with Maryam, but later he broke his oath. The two versions are without any interest but prove that the Quran is a human book written by a human being who can change the laws.

A fourth example: Muhammad can marry whoever he wants, unlike other believers. Sura (33.49): *"Prophet, to you, We have allowed your wives... the captives, the daughters of your uncles and aunts, and those believers who migrated with you, if you want to marry her. That is your privilege, but not the one of the believers..."* According to a Hadith of Bukhari (52.130), Aisha, one of Muhammad's favorite wives, said that when he had to go on a trip he drew straws among his wives to decide which one will accompany him.

A fifth example: According to the Quran (4.3), the Muslim can have up to four wives without counting sex slaves. But the prophet Muhammad had eleven wives or thirteen, depending on different versions. Some Muslims say that only after receiving this new law did Muhammad want to repudiate some brides and keep only four, but they refused to leave and wanted to stay with him. All this would lead to verse 33.51: *"But it is no more lawful for you to change women, nor to take others, except slaves..." Did the new law curb the sexual appetite of Muhammad?*

Muslims explain that the many wives Muhammad had were for political alliances. If that is the case, he should have started the alliances while Khadija was still alive, when he started his mission. Also, if weddings are political necessities, how do concubines and sex slaves contribute to political alliances? What about the beautiful Jewish Safia? He took her as a wife after killing her family and her husband. How did Muhammad hope for an alliance with her tribe?

Muhammad's wives played a very important role in the establishment of Hadiths and the biography of Muhammad. What does rivalry and jealousy between these women have to do with historical reality? Muhammad married a widow, but he himself banned his wives from remarrying after his death.

Your conclusions

Are the sacred texts of the three religions from God or invented by men?
Do you want to replace the Civil Code with the rules of the religions?
Remarks are welcome at: threefamousimpostors@gmail.com

Selected Bibliography

The Bible. The New Testament. The Quran.
The Talmud. The Catechism. The Hadiths. Can be found on the Internet or published books
Treatise of the Three Imposters, unknown author
101 Myths of the Bible by Gary Greenberg
Who Wrote the Bible? by Richard Elliott Friedman
How to Read the Bible by James L. Kugel
Why I Am Not a Muslim by Ibn Warraq
The Trouble with Islam Today by Irshad Manji
Atheist Manifesto by Michel Onfray
Sacred Kings of the Bible by Israel Kinkelstein and Asher Silbermen
Lifting the Veil" by I. Q. Al Rassoli
Who Is the Chosen People? by Avi Bekar *History of God* by Karen Armstrong
Trial and Death of Jesus by Haim Cohen

About the Author

Two centuries ago, in France, was published a very little book entitled *Treatise of the Three Imposters*. These three imposters were Moses, Jesus and Muhammad. The author's name was kept secret because he feared the reactions of the religious establishments. It is the same today, and the author of this book preferred also to remain anonymous. Tolerance and open discussion are not the qualities of religions, and we see it every day.